The Politics of Immigration in France,
Britain, and the United States

Perspectives in Comparative Politics

Published by Palgrave Macmillan

The Politics of Immigration in France, Britain, and the United States

A Comparative Study

Martin A. Schain

THE POLITICS OF IMMIGRATION IN FRANCE, BRITAIN, AND THE UNITED STATES
Copyright © Martin A. Schain, 2008.

First published in 2008 by
PALGRAVE MACMILLAN®
in the United States—a division of St. Martin's Press LLC,
175 Fifth Avenue, New York, NY 10010.

Where this book is distributed in the UK, Europe and the rest of the
world, this is by Palgrave Macmillan, a division of Macmillan Publishers
Limited, registered in England, company number 785998, of Houndmills,
Basingstoke, Hampshire RG21 6XS.

Palgrave Macmillan is the global academic imprint of the above companies
and has companies and representatives throughout the world.

Palgrave® and Macmillan® are registered trademarks in the United States,
the United Kingdom, Europe and other countries.

ISBN-13: 978–1–4039–6216–4 (paperback)
ISBN-10: 1–4039–6216–2 (paperback)
ISBN-13: 978–1–4039–6215–7 (hardcover)
ISBN-10: 1–4039–6215–4 (hardcover)

Library of Congress Cataloging-in-Publication Data

Schain, Martin, 1940–
    The politics of immigration in France, Britain, and the United States : a
comparative study / Martin Schain.
        p. cm.—(Perspectives in comparative politics)
    Includes bibliographical references and index.
    ISBN 1–4039–6215–4
        1. France—Emigration and immigration—Government policy.
    2. France—Emigration and immigration—Political aspects.
    3. Great Britain—Emigration and immigration—Government policy.
    4. Great Britain—Emigration and immigration—Political aspects.
    5. United States—Emigration and immigration—Government policy.
    6. United States—Emigration and immigration—Political aspects.
    I. Title.

JV7933.S34 2008
325—dc22   2008012345

A catalogue record of the book is available from the British Library.

Design by Newgen Imaging Systems (P) Ltd., Chennai, India.

First edition: October 2008

10 9 8 7 6 5 4 3 2 1

Transferred to digital printing in 2009.

For Wendy

CONTENTS

LIST OF FIGURES
AND TABLES

Figures

Tables

SERIES EDITOR'S FOREWORD

All books in this series, Perspectives in Comparative Politics, are designed to be scholarly, topic-oriented studies of a particular problem, fully accessible to undergraduate students who are approaching the subject for the first time as political scientists, as well as replete with new information and new insights that will intrigue graduate students and professors who have prior knowledge of the subject. Each begins with an introductory chapter, covering the relevant literature and laying out the problem, and ends with a concluding chapter, summarizing what has been learned about the problem at hand in the three or more nations covered, and elucidating the important comparative lessons learned.

Despite adherence to the overall design of the series, every book has its own very special character. The topics, the nations chosen as case studies, and, above all, the author, ensure this rich variety. Professors adopting different books in the series for classroom use will always find not only the comforting familiarity of the expected design, but also the surprise and delight of engaging new ideas presented by authors working from long experience, deep understanding, and passion. The authors in this series care deeply about their topics, and it shows. They maintain impeccable loyalty to the norms of objective scholarship, and at the same time demonstrate how well such scholarship can serve an argument for change. Students learn not only about the topic and the cases, but they also learn, by the example set within the book itself, important lessons about the comparative method and the norms of scholarship.

THE POLITICS OF IMMIGRATION IN FRANCE, BRITAIN, AND THE UNITED STATES: A COMPARATIVE ANALYSIS, by Martin A. Schain of New York University, nicely demonstrates the capacity of its author to provide an absolute wealth of essential information, offer instruction by example in the comparative method, and at the same time make strongly original and insightful comments, well documented, on the topic. This book begins with an overview of the problems of immigration policy and the politics of immigration as they have presented themselves in the world—and in the political science literature—and then offers three chapters on France, three on Britain, and three on the United States, before concluding with a chapter that points out the strongest differences and similarities found among the three as they grapple with this most timely—and sometimes most vexing—problem: how to balance the complex and often contradictory needs that emerge and compete for political and governmental solution when large numbers of others wish to join existing citizenries on territories they consider to be unalienably their own.

The thoroughness of Professor Schain's research, presented in nearly 60 tables and figures as well as in clear and persuasive text, has led to numerous new discoveries and new understandings. He finds, for example, that Muslim immigrants in France "are, by far, the most integrative in their orientation, and the least conflicted between their Muslim and national identities." He brings out the multitudinous ways in which sheer racism has infected the policymaking process at times in the histories of all three nations. He shows that both prongs of the commonly held belief that the British have been strongly in favor of "zero-immigration" and good at enforcing such a policy is not supported by the facts. He has given us, overall, a strikingly well-documented study, one that summarizes, compares, contrasts, and challenges. It is both an important contribution to the literature, and a highly competent text.

I am very pleased indeed to have this book, THE POLITICS OF IMMIGRATION IN FRANCE, BRITAIN, AND THE UNITED STATES: A COMPARATIVE ANALYSIS, join the Palgrave series Perspectives in Comparative Politics.

KAY LAWSON

PREFACE AND
ACKNOWLEDGMENTS

This book began with a few impassioned comments from a group of Communist mayors, whom I was interviewing for a study of Communist local government more than 25 years ago. I was interested in how they were able to develop local policy, but they were far more determined to talk to me about immigrants and immigration. To my surprise, they were neither sympathetic with this new working class, nor were they particularly supportive, and their comments provoked me to investigate the reaction of the left to a growing immigrant population from outside of Europe.

During the years that followed my interest in the emerging politics of immigration brought me to France with some frequency, where I was welcomed by a community of scholars who helped shape my thinking about politics and immigration. I was invited to give presentations, to participate in colloquia, and to exchange ideas with a small, but growing group of scholars, who were beginning their own scholarly work in this area. Over the years this group has increased both in size and in visibility, as the study of immigration has become important among social scientists in Europe and in the United States.

I count myself lucky that some of the most talented and innovative scholars on both sides of the Atlantic decided to work in this area. This community of scholars has been engaged in a continuing conversation that has spanned generations, as well as the Atlantic. We have talked with one another, and been influenced by one another's work.

In France, I am particularly grateful to Jeanne and Daniel Singer, who welcomed me into their home on the Rue de Bièvre where countless numbers of scholars have gathered for many years. Sophie Body-Gendrot and I have written together, and my work on immigration policy has been deeply influenced by our continuing discussions year after year, both in Paris and New York. Catherine de Wenden shared with me both her own work and her perceptions into immigration policy, and Patrick Weil has been an unending source of ideas and insights. To Riva Kastoryano I owe a special debt for her insights and analysis of immigrant integration and Virginie Guiraudon has taught me a great deal about immigration policymaking at the EU level. I am also grateful to Ariane Chebel-d'Appolonia who invited me to be a visiting scholar at the Institut d'Etudes Poliques de Paris, and to Nancy Green, who invited me to share a seminar with her at the ècole des Hautes Etudes in 2003. Thanks to these invitations I was able to present many of the ideas in this book, and test them out with both of these fine scholars, as well as their colleagues.

Sciences-Po (The Institut d'Études Politiques de Paris) has been my university away from home since I was a graduate student, and has welcomed me back many times since. Pascal Perrineau, the director of the Centre d'Etude de la Vie Politique Française (CEVIPOF) has given me friendship, support, and space to work. Martine Papacostas created miracles to help me and my wife Wendy through the immigration bureaucracy during our two extended stays in France, a feat that I continue to admire. Our two stays in Paris were also enhanced by the many friends and colleagues who had little to do with my research and writing, and who helped to make Paris our second city. I am grateful for the friendship of Monica and Francis, Irene and Hugo, Michel and Elisabeth, Pierre and Marie-Hélène, Pascal and Gisèle, Alain and Sophie, Yvonne, and Michèle and Suguru.

In the United States, I was privileged to interact with a growing community of scholars whose work on immigration has been seminal for scholarship in comparative politics and international relations in this area. I was lucky enough to encounter Aristide Zolberg after he arrived at the New School. Soon after, we became co-directors of the New York Consortium for European Studies, and were able to organize a series of workshops that brought a new generation of immigration scholars to New York. Some debts never get paid back, only acknowledged. Ary's work in this area has had an enormous impact on my own thinking, and helped provide a comparative context for understanding the politics of immigration. I am also grateful for the work of other scholars with whom I have shared ideas, papers and dialogues. Jim Hollifield and I have been talking about comparative immigration questions since we first met twenty years ago. Jeannette Money strongly influenced my thinking about the importance of immigration in electoral politics, Miriam Feldblum my thinking on neo-nationalist change, and Gary Freeman my thinking more generally on immigration impact. I am very pleased that Richard Alba and Nancy Foner, two of the most creative scholars working on immigration in the United States, shared their work with me on immigrant political participation. Gallya Lahav has been a very special scholar for me. She was my graduate student, and is now a major scholar in her own right. More to the point, I am appreciative of her scholarly work that has given us original ways of understanding the relationship between public opinion and immigration. Finally, I am grateful to Christopher Mitchell, my friend and colleague in the Department of Politics at New York University, for his comments on the chapters on the United States.

In Britain, this study has been influenced by Randall Hansen's analysis of the shift of British immigration policy in the 1960s. Erik Bleich's groundbreaking work on discrimination has helped define my understanding of the formulation of British policy on immigration; and Tariq Modood's work consistently challenges my ideas about multiculturalism and integration. Anthony Messina's recent book is one of the best books on the politics of migration in Western Europe, but I have relied a great deal on his equally impressive earlier work on race relations and British political parties.

There is relatively little work that deals with comparative immigration politics. Therefore, I am thankful for the pioneering work of Christian Joppke and Andrew Geddes that is cited in this volume. During my years as director of the Center for European Studies (now the Center for European and Mediterranean Studies) at New York University, dozens of visiting scholars working of the politics of immigration spent time in New York. I am particularly indebted for the feedback and interactions over many years to Ted Perlmutter, Leah Haus, Amy Elman, Jonathan Laurence, Marco Martiniello, Damir Skenderovic, Michael Minkenberg, Anand Menon, Willem Maas, and Elise Langan.

Kay Lawson, the editor of this series, has been a perfect editor. She has been patient, prodding, and encouraging. She is a friend and colleague whom I have known for many years, and, at the end of this process, we are still friends. I am grateful for her careful reading or this entire manuscript, and for her perceptive comments. Anthony Wahl, my editor at Palgrave has equally admirable virtues. For most of the past decade, we have worked on numerous projects together, including my own series for Palgrave. I am thankful for his keen sense of the possible, and for his support and encouragement of this book. I also want to thank Leah Ramirez, who has assisted me on many projects, for her careful work on the index of this book.

Finally, I am most grateful for the support of my family and especially my wife Wendy. Wendy has been a part of this project in many important ways. She has traveled with me, has been subjected to my endless discussions of this passionate subject, and has met friends and colleagues—many of whom have become her friends as well—who have been equally passionate. She has been my most challenging critic, and has taken the time to be my best editor as well. She has certainly made this a better book.

Of course, the usual disclaimers apply. Although the scholars and friends I have acknowledged have made this a better book, only I am responsible for what I have written.

CHAPTER ONE

Introduction: The Politics of Immigration

Since the last decades of the twentieth century, new waves of immigration have been transforming both Europe and the United States. In Europe, immigration has produced new multicultural populations that now include large numbers of Muslims who have arrived from Turkey and Africa. In the United States, immigration from the Western Hemisphere and Asia has altered an ethnic mix that had been primarily European in origin. These patterns of immigration, in many ways similar on both sides of the Atlantic, have been related to very different policies on immigration during the past 40 years. Immigration policy in Europe has been relatively restrictive, while policy in the United States has been relatively open.

Using the cases of France, Britain, and the United States, in the chapters that follow, by focusing on comparative analysis, I will examine immigration policy and the dynamics of politics through which that policy has been developed. The advantage of comparison is that we are able to deal more easily with questions of relativity across similar dimensions: relative intensions, strength and effectiveness of policy, for example; relative framing of political issues; and relative processes for the development of policy.

The core question analyzed in this volume is how can we understand the variation of policy among these countries over time? I argue that, with relatively similar levels of immigration on both sides of the Atlantic, the most important differences between Europe and the United States are not those of levels of immigration, but differences in immigration policy and the dynamics that drive this policy. I first describe the ways that each country has developed policies on immigration, and has approached four issues about which both scholars and policy-makers have been concerned. I then explain the variations among countries by the political dynamics that have driven policymaking in this area. I argue that electoral dynamics have been important in driving policy, but that they work very differently in Europe and in United States.

Both Western Europe and the United States are "countries" of immigration. Each year about 1.5 million immigrants legally enter the fifteen member-states that comprise the European Union before enlargement, with considerable variation among countries. In recent years, about 650,000 immigrants per year have been entering Germany, 250,000 enter the United Kingdom, and 140,000 have immigrated into France. They have done so for a variety of reasons. Most come either to join their families (family unification) or to work, but cross-country variations are considerable. In 2003, almost 20 percent of the immigrants into the United Kingdom were labor migrants, and a third came under family unification (including the families of those who came for work); while the same year in France, 60 percent came to join their families, and only 4 percent were admitted directly under labor provisions. (See table 1.1.)

A generation ago, the most important differences within Europe were between countries that had historically needed and received immigrants (France, Germany, Switzerland, and—in a more complicated way—the United Kingdom), and those that had been the providers of immigrants (Italy, Spain, Ireland, and Portugal). Now, however, all of the senders are receivers, and the variation is among the levels of immigration into each country.

Each year about a million immigrants legally enter the United States, more than two-thirds of whom under some form of family unification. Although there has been considerable variation from year to year, this number has been increasing during the past decade. The United States is generally perceived as a country that now welcomes immigration (at least legal immigration) compared to Europe. Nevertheless, the rate of immigration into Europe has been marginally higher than that of the United States. Indeed, Europe now receives between 4.7 immigrants per thousand of the population on the high end (1992) and 3.9 on the low end (2001), compared with about 3.8 per thousand in the United States. (See table 1.1.)

France and Britain are in many ways the most emblematic of both open and closed historic patterns of immigration policy in Europe, as well as the changes in policy that have taken place during the past 40 years. In different ways, both countries have had historically open policies of immigration, and both have integrated successive generations of immigrants through citizenship and naturalization laws that have made citizenship relatively easy to obtain. In both countries, policies changed sharply in the 1960s and 1970s in ways that were quite different from parallel changes in the United States.

The United States, on the other hand, had more or less closed its borders in 1924 to immigrants from outside the Western Hemisphere, and had kept them shut for 40 years. At the very moment that the United States initiated a more open policy that gradually increased levels of immigration, France and Britain, along with the rest of Europe, reversed their immigration policies, with the goal of reducing immigration to the lowest possible levels.

The French decision was, in many ways, the most logical, at least in terms of the labor-market. It was taken at a moment in time when the

Table 1.1 Immigration and immigrant populations in France, Britain, and the United States, 1992–2001

A. Immigration Inflows (th)

	1992 total	per thousand population	2001	per thousand population
UK—Inflow	175	3.0	373.3	6.2
UK—Accepted for Settlement[a]	51	0.87	106.8	1.8
France[b]	116.6	2.0	141	2.4
United States[c]	974	3.8	1064	3.8
EU 15	1727.6	4.7	1465.7	3.9

B. Immigrant Population (th)

	Year	Thousands	% of population
United Kingdom (Foreign)	2001	2587	4.4
France (Foreign)	1999	3263.2	5.6
France (Foreign-born)	1999	5868.2	10
United States (Foreign-born)	2001	31811	11.1
EU 15 (Foreign-born)	2001	39790	8.6

C. Inflows by Entry Category (2003)

	France	Britain	United States
Total	173,097	243,709	705,827
Family (%)	60.7	32.4	76.0
Non-discretionary (%)	54.5	14.5	37.2
Discretionary (%)	6.2	17.9	38.8
Work (%)	4.0	18.3	5.2
Other (%)	35.3	49.3	18.8

Notes:

a This figure is closer to the equivalent of France and the United States in terms of immigration.

b Part of the increase for 2001 can be accounted for by better estimates by the Ministry of the Interior in France.

c Does not include those born of U.S. citizens.

Source: OECD, Trends in International Migration, Annual Report 2003 (Paris: OECD Publications, 2003), pp. 117194, 286, 291, 305–310.

need for immigration seemed to have run its course. The oil crisis marked both the end of the 30-year growth spurt in the European economy, as well as the transformation in the balance of employment between the service sector and smokestack industry. The British decision, however, was made at the height of postwar economic expansion, at a moment when there seemed to be a greater—if diminishing—need for immigrant labor.

Finally, the American decision seemed to have little initial relationship to labor-market needs, since the relatively expansive immigration policy initiated in 1965 was maintained through bad and good economic times.

In general, the differences in policy between Britain and France, on one hand, and the United States on the other, appear to be consistent with the national models that are often referred to in the literature, which compare by focusing on long traditions of immigration and citizenship as a way of understanding strong differences among countries. Thus, the United States has been characterized as a country of immigration, which presumably helps us to understand the explicitly open policy the United States has had since 1965. On the other hand, neither does this formulation help us at all to understand the more restrictive policies legislated between 1921 and 1924, nor does it help us understand the explicit exclusion of Asians after 1882.

Thus the key question in this volume is how can we understand the difference between France and Britain, on one hand, and the United States on the other, with regard to both policy and practice? The rich social science literature that deals with the politics of immigration points to several issues that are essential for understanding policy.

Issues of Immigration

Some of the best recent work that deals with the international political economy of migration focuses on four important issues that are relevant for public policy. The *first* is the question of migration itself—why people choose to leave their home countries, to cross frontiers and settle somewhere else, and how this is related to public policy. The *second* major question, related to the first, is the continued relevance of frontiers, and the ability of the liberal state to maintain control over its frontiers. The *third* issue is concerned with the impact of immigration, on national identity and on bounded notions of citizenship. The *fourth* issue is the way immigrants are integrated and incorporated. Each of these questions has a strong political and policy dimension.

Why People Migrate

Consider the question of why people migrate. The push and pull factors that influence transnational migration are often understood in terms of socioeconomic conditions on either end, rather than policy choices made by either the sending or receiving country.[1] Although there is no agreement on the effectiveness of immigration control policies, it does seem evident that similar socioeconomic conditions—particularly those that would tend to "pull" immigrants into wealthier countries in need of immigration, should be very much influenced by public policy. Public policy is variable, both within countries over time, and among countries over space.

The question of why some people leave their home countries to embark on a journey that is at the very least difficult and uncertain, but that may be dangerous as well, has stimulated considerable commentary, scholarship and debate for many years. Since the work of E.G. Ravenstein in 1885, there has been an abundance of scholarship on the causes of international migration, the push factors in particular, with lesser consideration given to the pull factors of receiving countries in Europe and the United States. These analyses, however, seem to be deeply flawed for explanatory purposes in two ways. Aristide Zolberg has emphasized that theories of immigration are particularly weak in their analysis of the importance of political obstacles: obstacles to the entrance of immigrants, but also obstacles to their exit from home countries as well.[2] To this must be added the importance of comparison. Otherwise, it is difficult to understand why immigrants would choose to go to one country rather than another; and to go to one country in greater numbers during one period than during a different period.

In addition, the process through which obstacles are constructed and removed also needs to be explained. State agency is dynamic and changing, and how it changes is part of understanding the politics of immigration. We need to understand not simply variations in state policy over time and across space, but also the process through which policies change. Thus, both the United Kingdom and France have had exclusionary policies of immigration for many years, but levels of immigration have varied from year to year. Moreover, there has been considerable variation with regard to the kinds of immigrants who have entered and become long-term residents. The ratio of workers to family members, for example, has grown far greater in Britain than in France, and the source of immigrants for both countries has changed somewhat over the years. Are these variations simply changes in labor market forces, or are they related to public policy?

Control over Frontiers

Even when their stated goal appears to be strong and restrictive, immigration control policies may be difficult to enforce. Control over frontiers—that essential aspect of sovereignty—it has been argued, is subject to legal and judicial controls. Thus, what has been referred to as "embedded liberalism" in the legal and political systems—values that protect individual and collective rights—makes it difficult to pass legislation that restricts immigration, and makes it even more difficult to enforce legislation that has actually been passed.[3] Indeed, this is at the root of arguments that policies may be less important that they appear to be when administration and court decisions loom more important.

Attempts to define and establish controls over immigration, over who has a right to cross national frontiers and settle in space within those frontiers, has often evoked impassioned debate and conflicting politics. Such issues raise basic questions about the nation-state: the control over the frontiers of the state and the identity of the nation. The core question is whether and how the capability of the state in liberal democracies to control immigration has been eroded by a combination of international agreements and the increased role of courts in establishing individual and collective rights.

On the other hand, "embedded liberalism" can also be seen more simply as a political and legal resource, among others, that have determined the effectiveness of legislation on immigration control. In this sense, Christian Joppke argues that diagnoses of international constraints on the state's ability to control immigration are highly overrated, either because they are based on erroneous assumptions of strong sovereignty that never was, or because the limits on frontier controls are more obviously domestic than international. Although notions of state sovereignty have been linked to control over frontiers since the sixteenth century, effective control of borders through military and administrative mechanisms goes back only to the late nineteenth century.[4] Ever since state capabilities began to catch up with theories of sovereignty, the struggle to maintain the frontier has been a balance between what the state is capable of doing, and contradictory interests that support a more open or closed border.[5]

In a collection edited by Joppke, Saskia Sassen largely confirms Joppke's critique.[6] On one hand, she convincingly argues that immigration policymaking has been made more complex by international agreements on human rights, by judicial development of human rights and by ethnic lobbies. But has the overall effect been "...to constrain the sovereignty of the state and to undermine old notions about immigration control?" Perhaps not. Sassen also admits that both in Europe and the United States there has been a reaction of "renationalizing" immigration policymaking.

Then there is the question of whether anything substantial has changed, whether liberal-democratic regimes are more constrained in this sense than they were in the past. There may be transnational processes and transnational regimes that influence and constrain the national process, but has this not always been the case with regard to immigration control? Freeman's essay gives strong support to Joppke's argument that only by analyzing domestic politics—and the domestic forces of powerful economic interests, ethnic lobbies and civil libertarians—can we understand the changing political constraints on policy-makers, either for or against immigration controls. Why, for example, is the more or less consistent opposition of host populations to immigration frequently ignored by governments?[7] For domestic political actors, the legal system and international accords are means and resources in the domestic political process.

Therefore, Sassen's point that the conditions within which immigration policy is being made and implemented today are imbedded in pressures of globalization and human rights accords may be important, but not necessarily in the ways that are usually asserted. If there is an ascendance of "...agencies linked to furthering globalization and a decline of those linked to domestic equity questions," the impact on the immigration agenda may not necessarily be effective, in part because the enforcement of immigrant rights supported by transnational human rights regimes is closely tied to agencies that deal with domestic equity questions.[8]

Then there is the question of whether the unification of Europe has diminished the ability of states within the EU to control their frontiers with regard to immigration. Within Europe the issue of sovereignty has become increasingly complex. Especially with the incorporation of the Schengen Convention into the Amsterdam Agreement, member states have made strides in cooperation on transferring sovereignty to the Union for the migration of EU nationals; they have also made lesser strides in the development of common policies with regard to non-EU immigrants (third country nationals—TCNs).

Rey Koslowski argues that such agreements on harmonization effectively cede sovereignty, but this is not entirely clear.[9] For example, it has been argued that the implementation of Schengen has created pressure on Italy and Spain to "do what they would not otherwise do" in terms of controlling immigration through their frontiers, but without an analysis of domestic politics, it is hard to know what this means. As we know from the French experience in 1993, when a right-wing government amended the constitution in order to circumvent a decision by the French Constitutional Council that overturned some elements of Schengen, these agreements have also become factors in a domestic political process that governments use to promote their own agendas. In the end, on high-salience immigration issues, harmonization has tended to reinforce the capacities of states to control and exclude immigrants, leaving more expansive immigration policies to the member-states themselves.[10]

On balance, immigration control has become imbedded in a network of European and global institutions and rules that are as dynamic as they are constraining. They are not fixed in place, and can be used by domestic political actors to alter the domestic *rapports de force*.

One final issue is the changing nature of the frontier itself. As an article in the Washington Post noted a short while ago:

> A country's borders should not be confused with those familiar dotted lines drawn on some musty old map of nation-states. In an era of mass migration, globalization and instant communication, a map reflecting the world's true boundaries would be a crosscutting, high tech and multi-dimensional affair.[11]

Border agents of the United States and Europe check passports and visas in a multitude of foreign countries, not just at their own ports of entry. To determine acceptable from unacceptable migrants, most countries have established procedures abroad that may include far more than processing visa applications by embassy personnel.

As far back as 1924, for example, the United States required all foreign nationals wishing to enter the United States to produce an entry visa before boarding a U.S.-bound vessel (a procedure similar to what takes place at virtually all airports today). As a result, all of the screening that had formerly taken place at Ellis Island now took place abroad, and embassies now included all of the personnel necessary for screening applicants.[12]

Prior to that, the 1902 Passenger Act made carriers responsible for transporting passengers who were not admitted to the United States back to their ports of embarkation. A similar procedure was integrated into the Schengen Agreement in 1990, and fines were added in 1994.[13] Thus, what Aristide Zolberg called "remote control" entry regulation was imposed well before the current period of immigration, and has effectively extended the legal frontier to the points of exit for immigrants.

Nevertheless, remote control processing is only the most time-honored transformation of the frontier. In fact, in Europe there are different frontiers for different kinds of migrants. Citizens of the European Union (independently of Schengen) have an established right to move freely for employment under Article 39 of the European Community Treaty, a right confirmed by the European Court of Justice in 1991.[14] For the 13 EU countries (the United Kingdom and Ireland have thus-far opted out) that are party to the Schengen Agreement, their citizens also have the right to cross the "internal" borders (for all practical purposes so do the citizens of any country, who have already penetrated the external frontier), but Schengenland also includes Iceland and Norway, not members of the EU. Finally, even after the accession of ten new member-states to the EU, the free movement for labor principle was not universally applied by each of the original EU 15. Therefore, within the EU, there are different frontiers for those who are tourists, those who wish to work, those who wish to settle, as well as those who wish to exercise fuller rights of citizenship.[15]

In recent years, the fluidity of state sovereignty and the frontier has been growing, and not just within the EU. Thus, the most important trade decisions are no longer made by states alone, but by collaboration and negotiation in the World Trade Organization. Collaboration on issues of crime and security takes place cross-nationally, often through bilateral agreements that permit police from one country to operate within the borders of another. In the early part of the twentieth century, states discovered that it was often easier to control the frontier within the boundaries of someone else's country. The updated version of this is that less sovereignty over the frontier may result in greater security for all participants.

Nevertheless, in the United States and in most countries in Europe, there have been efforts to reorganize and better coordinate the frontier police and customs forces, primarily for reasons of security. The staffing of the U.S. Bureau of Customs and Border Protection is now projected to grow by 25 percent to about 51,000. The comparable agencies in France and Britain are far smaller, approximately 7,500, but the ports of entry are also far less numerous.[16] For the United States the long land borders (over 7,000 miles) with Canada and especially Mexico have received a great deal of attention, and the Border Patrol has been greatly augmented to a force of about 10,000 officers. Britain's only significant land border is the frontier with Ireland (just over 200 miles), and the land borders of France are now within the Schengen area. This means that the most import frontier points are no longer land borders, but airports that receive international flights.

Impact

If there has been a serious questioning of the effectiveness of policy for immigration control, there seems to be less doubt that immigration has an impact on public opinion, on accepted notions of national identity, as well as on accepted definitions of citizenship.

Public Opinion

Cross-nationally there have been certain elements of consistency in mass opinion. In the three countries on which we are focusing, only small minorities of mass publics have ever supported policies that would increase levels of immigration. Indeed, since surveys have been taken, through good times and bad, even as public policies on immigration have varied considerably, only small percentages of publics in France, the United States, and Britain have favored increased immigration. Not surprisingly, when governments have promulgated restrictionist immigration policies, these policies have been widely supported in mass opinion.[17]

These attitudes are consistent with mass attitudes toward immigrants and immigration in other countries in Europe. As immigration and the number of immigrants increase, negative public opinion generally increases as well, but not uniformly, and not uniformly against all immigration and all immigrants. For example, the intensity of support in favor of immigration restriction among mass publics in the United States and Western Europe is consistently weaker among younger age cohorts, and strongest among older cohorts; and among younger age cohorts, opposition is stronger in the United States than in Britain or France. (See table 1.2.)

The relationship between the size of the immigrant (or "foreign" population) and negative public opinion may be mediated by media attention;

Table 1.2 Extent of support for restricting immigration, percentage by age cohort, 2004

Country	Age:18–29	Age: 30–49	Age: 50–64	Age: 65+
France	24%	33%	54%	53%
Britain	37%	47%	49%	52%
United States	40%	45%	49%	50%

Source: Pew Research Center, *A Global Generation Gap* (Washington, DC, February, 2004), p. 2.

a finding in a 1989 Eurobarometer study, for example, shows that public debates increase as the immigrant population grows larger[18] Both the size of the immigrant population and economic conditions appear to explain a great deal of the variation of prejudice in Europe.[19] More recent immigrants are generally more opposed than those that preceded them,[20] and opposition to immigration may be related to perceptions based on interactions with different immigrant groups.[21] Finally, there is evidence that it is useful to differentiate between long-term and short-term influences. The former (patterns of political tolerance of outsiders, for example) are difficult to change, while the latter (economic cycles, for example) change over time.[22]

However, the question that most interests us here is how the impact of public opinion, always negative, becomes politically salient. In other words, if public opinion needs to be explained as a dependent variable, it also needs to be analyzed as an independent variable that has (or does not have) an impact on politics. If public opinion always dominated policymaking on immigration, there would never be a more open policy on immigration control, and—indeed—there would be very little variation in immigration policy either cross-nationally, or over time. Although, there has been considerable research on immigration and public opinion in general, there has been relatively little work that attempts to link public opinion to the political process. Three exceptions are Gary Freeman, who links attitudes to the costs and benefits of immigration policy,[23] Jeannette Money, who relates attitudes on immigration to electoral mobilization,[24] and Gallya Lahav, who notes the country by country gap between mass opinion and less negative elite opinion (with the exceptions of Denmark, Greece, and Ireland).[25]

Immigration, by its very nature, tends to challenge established ideas of national identity, which in turn tempts leaders and parties to mobilize voters around such questions. Two dimensions seem to be particularly important for understanding the relationship between immigrants and the national community. The first, "sympathy/antipathy," can be understood as an inclusive or exclusive attitude. This dimension is reinforced by attitudes with regard to "integration/separation," that projects into the future or the past an estimation of the possibilities of including the group in question into the national community. Both dimensions approximate those through which respondents draw what Michèle Lamont has call "standards of worth" or moral boundaries.[26] These boundaries imply two challenges. The first is the challenge of difference, which implies that immigrant groups are or are not like "us" in essential ways; the second is the challenge of acceptance and rejections, which implies that immigrant groups can or cannot become like "us" over time. Identity, however, is not fixed, and one aspect of the challenge is the degree to which there is political resistance to an evolving identity within the host society. In this sense, the challenge is not just from immigrant groups, but within the host society as well.[27]

Citizenship

Questions of immigration often become politicized around the issues of citizenship and naturalization. Immigration has always posed a challenge to citizenship in the sense that, while states have "transformed" immigrants into citizens, the very nature of citizenship has been influenced by the process of integration, and by the way that the state has conceptualized the nature of citizenship and naturalization. In the politics of identity, immigrants have often been the objects of politics for purposes of political mobilization. In the politics of citizenship, however, the literature argues that the presence and behavior of immigrant communities has had an active impact on citizenship. Indeed, scholars have argued that policies on citizenship and naturalization have always been related the needs of state construction and development.[28]

More recently, however the domination of national models has been challenged by analyses that focus on pressures created by transnational migrant communities and what is frequently referred to as "postmodern" citizenship.[29] Citizenship, in the more traditional sense, this literature argues, may matter far less than it used to in determining rights and obligations, as well as protections in law. In addition, as recent experiences in the United States have indicated, the legal protections afforded by acquired citizenship may be overestimated.

On the other hand, the criticism of the postnational literature has noted that transnational communities in Europe are neither new,[30] nor are they well protected by international regimes. Alhtough some scholars have made a convincing case for the emergence of a postnational citizenship—at least in the case of Europe—others have argued that the advantages of national citizenship may be underestimated. As Peter Schuck states so eloquently, postnational citizenship rights possess only a limited institutional status, protected mostly by judicial institutions, and can be easily swept away by tides of tribalism and nationalism.[31] Since rights and claims—even if they are judged by international courts—are still enforced within bounded national systems, advantages of national citizenship may very well remain. Moreover, similar multiple memberships and patterns of transnational loyalties were evident in Europe before WWII, and were not seriously undermined except during periods of extreme nationalism and war. In the more recent case of Europe, Miriam Feldblum has demonstrated that postnational citizenship has run up against what she calls "neo-nationalist" tendencies to reassert bounded national citizenship requirements.[32]

Citizenship represents a formal recognition as a member of the national community, and easy or automatic attribution of citizenship to immigrants has often reflected assumptions of what constitutes the national community. Thus, a "right to return" (and claim citizenship) for people historically linked to the national community exists in some form in at least ten countries now in the EU, and numerous other countries as well.[33] The history of empire in Britain and France also was important for understanding claims to citizenship. Until 1962, all British Commonwealth citizens and citizens of the Republic of Ireland, had a right to abode in the United Kingdom, and to exercise citizenship rights. Even after this system came to an end, after 1962 (see ch. 5), Commonwealth citizens, citizens of the colonies, and citizens of the Irish Republic resident in the United Kingdom were (and remain) eligible to run for office, and to vote in all UK elections, as well as for deputies for the European Parliament. Also, all immigrants who came to France from Algeria, who were born in Algeria before independence in 1962, have a right to claim French citizenship, although this claim is based on changes in French citizenship policy in Algeria that did not take place until after WWII.

Claims to automatic citizenship are also based on laws and common-law traditions that are generally known as *jus solis* or *jus sanguinis*. The former recognizes citizenship for those born on the soil of the country, while the latter recognizes claims based on birth or familial heritage from parents who are ethnic nationals. The application of *jus solis* automatically transforms immigrant-aliens into citizens after one (sometimes two) generations, while the impact of *jus sanguinis* has been to maintain the alien status of generations of immigrant families born in the host-country, unless they choose to go through a process of naturalization. The three countries analyzed in this volume all have *jus solis* traditions and laws, which in practice have meant that integration through citizenship has been the normal process. In addition, naturalization for immigrants has also been relatively easy in comparison with countries with *jus sanguinis* traditions.

One benefit of relatively easy access to citizenship in Britain and France has been that immigrant families in these countries have gained access to free movement within the European Union, since all European citizens—defined as citizens of the member states—have rights to free movement across the internal boundaries of the EU. However, since citizenship and naturalization laws vary considerably within the EU, immigrants and their descendants—even those from the same family who settled in different countries—may have very different rights, depending on where they reside. Moreover, scholars have emphasized that enhanced rights of EU citizens during the past two decades have been accompanied by increased restrictions on noncitizens (or TCNs). For example, the portability of labor and welfare state rights for citizens, generally does not apply to TCNs.[34]

In this sense, access to citizenship can have serious consequences in everyday life for immigrants and their families. On the other hand, the extension of economic, social, and even some political rights to noncitizen residents—augmented by a stronger judiciary—has certainly meant that citizenship as such may be less important than before in gaining rights and benefits. Moreover, the widespread acceptance of dual citizenship and protected rights have encouraged maintenance of "multiple memberships" and transnational loyalties.[35]

Integration and Incorporation of Immigrant Populations

Integration and incorporation of immigrant populations has been the subject of widespread debate in recent years. Scholars have frequently compared various "models" of incorporation as if most countries have well thought-out policies based on either national traditions or reasoned strategies for "making" foreigners into Frenchmen, Britons, or Americans. The three countries that are the subjects of this volume appear to be committed to very different ways of integrating immigrant populations, which vary by the use of state institutions, the kinds of policies pursued and the assumptions behind these policies. They also vary in terms of what they expect integration to mean, what *should* emerge at the end of the process. Finally, they appear to vary in terms of what *has* emerged through the process of integration.

The most explicit process seems to be the French Jacobin model, which has often been misunderstood as a coherent government program for integration. In fact it has been more of an orientation—what one scholar has called a "public philosophy"—of how public policy should be used. The details of this orientation have become more explicit as its assumptions have been challenged by the most recent waves of immigration. In principle, collective ethnic and religious identities are recognized by the French State only for very limited purposes (the official religious council, for example). The French State does not officially engage in "positive discrimination" in order to advance the fortunes of groups to remedy past discrimination, and French law does not permit the census to count those who are defined as "minorities."

French scholars have sometimes compared this model with the more anarchic American multicultural approach.[36] The American multicultural model has been frequently defined as the public recognition of collective identities as a basis for public policy, strongly linked to widespread ethnic lobbying. Indeed, as it emerged from the civil rights movement of the 1960s, public protection and financial support for a variety of ethnic, religious, and even language expressions has been widespread. This pattern is in marked contrast with the orientations of French policy, but also with the more Jacobin "Americanization" approach of the early part of the twentieth century, which left far less room for expressions of diversity.

The ideal of the United States as a "nation of nations" is a recent phenomenon, dating more or less from the period around WWII. During most of the nineteenth century there seemed to be a sense among social and political leaders of something increasingly American. Basically, this reflected a more widespread attitude about the nature of American homogeneity and the basis of American citizenship that endured until the last decade of the nineteenth century.

Although this ideal lacked the power of the French Jacobin model, it supported intermarriage, the hegemony of English cultural and political values together with English as a common language. The ideal gained increased institutional support at the local level, as education spread after the Civil War, even if ethnicity did in fact form a basis for initial settlements and political organization for collective advancement.[37] During the decade before WWI numerous states, and then the Federal government, established structures to aid immigrants and (eventually) to encourage "Americanization". By 1920, the combined public/private effort was impressive.[38]

The change emerged through a process that began with ethnic organization before WWII, by the recognition of a diverse population portrayed in government propaganda during the war, and reinforced by the emergence of what Martin Kilson has called "Black neo-ethnicity" in the 1960s.[39] Very rapidly, this new model of how America was portrayed challenged the dominant melting-pot model, with consequences for policymaking elites at all levels.

Similarly, the French orientation is frequently compared with a different kind of British multicultural approach to integration, based on race. As Ira Katznelson observed 30 years ago, while British integration policy was still in formation:

> I would suggest that the central dynamic of British elite reaction to Third World migration has been an attempt to structure the politics of race to take race out of conventional politics. Seen in these terms, the attempt to produce a coherent politics (or non-politics) of race has passed through three...distinct stages: (i) pre-political consensus (1948–61)....(ii) Fundamental debate (1958–63)....(iii) political consensus (1965 to the present), when the front benches of the two major parties developed a new consensus, politically arrived at, to depoliticize race once again.[40]

As we shall see, this policy consensus was partly based on a race-relations approach to immigrant integration that was sharply different from the French approach, but different from the American approach as well. The Race Relations Act of 1965 provided an institutional base for integration, based on anti-discrimination policy that was agreed to by both major political parties.[41] By 1968, anti-discrimination policy had been combined with a multicultural approach to education, and was disconnected from considerations of immigration control, influenced by a parallel movement in the United States.[42] All New Commonwealth immigrants were regarded as racially different from those who arrived from the Old Commonwealth of Canada, Australia, and New Zealand, but, in contrast to France, their treatment was embedded in a policy framework that focused on instruments to combat discrimination, and on support for pluralism and multiculturalism.[43]

These understandings of how immigrants are incorporated into the host societies are based on what Theodore Lowi has called a "public philosophy," a model that colors, shapes and justifies state formation of public policy, and well as by public policy in the form of legislation and administration.[44] Each of the countries in this volume provides us with a very different public philosophy of what the objectives of integration should be. In the French Republican ideal—or Jacobin model—these objectives are both cultural and political. A familiarity of French history and cultural references is certainly considered important. Perhaps most important, the expectation of public institutions is that immigrants will conform to French cultural and legal norms, and that there is an acceptance of a common public space that is separate from religious faith and expression.[45] Although the British model accepts, protects, and even promotes cultural and racial diversity and religious diversity, as a necessary dimension of participation in society, we shall see that the limits of such diversity have been probed and explored during the past few years. In the United States, however, multiculturalism and diversity have not only been seen as acceptable, but as desirable. Indeed, as we shall see, the Immigration Act of 1990 seeks to promote diversity.

Although public philosophies are often clear on objectives, their link with public policy is highly variable. In each of the countries in this volume, the active role of the state is limited, and often contradictory. There is often a wide gap between stated public philosophies and policy on the ground. Marco Martiniello notes that deviation from any public philosophy is inevitable, and that both integrationist and multiculturalist policies can and have been applied in ways that are quite different from their intended goals.[46] Nevertheless, for many scholars, and for much of the political class, "...principles [the public philosophy] continue to inspire government policy towards immigrants." To alter this approach, moreover, "...would break with a long tradition of national integration...and weaken (and perhaps even dissolve) the social fabric."[47]

These understandings of integration models, moreover, often ignore the evolution over time of both public philosophy and policy. In all three countries, both have changed substantially since the end of WWII. I would argue that public philosophies are ultimately altered when they are challenged by evolving empirical reality and the very public policies they are supposed to describe. Finally, such models often fail to consider how the process of integration itself has altered what it means to be French, British, or American.[48]

In practice, there appears to be a tendency toward convergence in Europe, with the state playing a far greater role than it had before. Christian Joppke has argued that "...distinct national models of dealing with immigrants are giving way to convergent policies of civic integration and anti-discrimination."[49] On one hand, understood models are increasingly giving way to legislated policies, particularly those that define criteria of civic integration, which create an obligation for immigrants who wish to attain the rights of citizens to individually demonstrate that they have earned those rights. The first of these programs was the year-long obligatory integration course, inaugurated in 1998 in the Netherlands, which emphasized language instruction, civics and preparation for the labor market. The key was the set of examinations at the end. The integration policy was then linked to immigration control, through a requirement that applicants for family unification first take the course and pass the examination before they arrive. Similar programs have now been initiated in France, are being debated in Britain, and have become a model for the rest of Europe. At the same time, anti-discrimination programs in all European countries have grown in importance, and have increasingly benefited those immigrants who have made it past the door. First initiated in Britain in 1965, the anti-discrimination approach was given a major push by two directives of the European Council in 2000.[50] The directives obligated all EU countries to constitute commissions that would both monitor and act against patterns of racial discrimination. Since immigrant communities have been racialized in Europe, the emerging institutions have begun to offer them a measure of recognition and protection.

Both of these evolutions in policy have created overlapping similarities in the approach of all European countries to questions of immigrant integration. Nevertheless, differences remain within Europe, and are likely to remain for some time. Perhaps the biggest difference, however, is between state-oriented processes of integration in Europe, and the relatively more laissez-faire approach of the United States.

Comparing Integration

If models and processes of integration have varied considerably from country to country, and over time, what can we say about the results of integration policy? Although each strategy is somewhat different in emphasis, they EU countries share a number of common goals, most of which have been formalized in a list of "Common Basic Principles for Immigrant Integration Policy in the European Union," agreed to in the Hague Program in 2004 as part of a common program for integration. Among the 11 agreed-upon principles, the following are the most important:

- Employment is a key part of the integration process and is central to the participation of immigrants, to the contributions immigrants make to the host society, and to making such contributions visible.
- Efforts in education are critical to preparing immigrants, and particularly their descendants, to be more successful and more active participants in society.
- Access for immigrants to institutions, as well as to public and private goods and services, on a basis equal to national citizens and in a non-discriminatory way, is a critical foundation for better integration.
- The participation of immigrants in the democratic process and in the formulation of integration policies and measures, especially at the local level, supports their integration.
- Integration is a dynamic, two-way process of mutual accommodation by all immigrants and residents of Member States.[51]

From these principles we can derive several measures of integration that can give us some indication of relative success and failure. The first is that immigrants should be integrated into the economy, should be employed, and indeed should provide a crucial element of support within the economy. The second is that, over time, the educational system should be an effective instrument of integration. The third is that the political system should provide effective representation of immigrant populations. Finally, the end result should be both acceptance of immigrant populations by the host countries, and an acceptance of the host countries by the immigrant populations.

The tables that follow illustrate some aspects of these criteria for integration. Unemployment rates among immigrant populations have been generally higher than those of the native population. Compared to the United States and Britain, unemployment is higher by far among French immigrants. Moreover, youth unemployment is also highest among the French, almost three times the level of immigrant youth unemployment in the United States. (See table 1.3.)

Educational attainment is more complicated. On one hand, educational attainment among immigrant populations at the university level is as great or greater (in Britain) than that of the native population. On the other hand, the proportion of immigrants who drop out, or who never get to upper secondary education (a prerequisite for good jobs in most Western societies), is disastrously high in France, and very high in Britain and the United States (and Germany). (See table 1.4.) It is also important to note that the proportion of native born French who fail to attain upper secondary education is also very high, and even higher among native born British, but that the failure rate ("no qualifications") among French immigrants is 50 percent, compared with 10 percent among British immigrants.

This is important because educational attainment has a strong impact on unemployment rates for immigrants (for natives as well). However, the impact is far greater in Britain and the United States than in France.

Table 1.3 Unemployment rates for immigrants and natives in 2003–2004

Country	Immigrants (Youth unemployment)	Non-immigrants
France	13.8% (29%)[a]	8.0%
Britain	7.3%	4.7%
United States[b]	7.2%9.3%)	5.6%

Notes:
a For France, ages 25–35; for United States, ages 20–24.
b From CBO, ages 20–64.

Sources: Data from OECD, *International Migration Outlook* (Washington DC, OECD, 2006), p. 73; European Community Labour Force Survey; U.S. Bureau of the Census; U.S. Congress, Congressional Budget Office (CBO), *A Description of the Immigrant Population*, November 2004.

Table 1.4   Educational attainment of immigrants populations, 2004

Country	Less than upper-secondary education		University degree or greater	
	Native-born	Foreign-born	Native-born	Foreign-born
France	35%	56%	13%	12%
Britain	49%	45%	20%	28%
United States	12.5%	32.8%	27%	27%

Sources: (France and Britain): OECD in Figures, 2005, p. 65; European Community Labour Force Survey; INSEE, Enquête emploi de 2005; University College London, CreAm, Christian Dustmann, and Nikolous Theordoropoulos, "Ethnic Minority Immigrants and their Children in Britain," CDP 10/06, p. 20; (United States): U.S. Bureau of the Census; U.S. Congress, CBO, *A Description of The Immigrant Population, November 2004.*

Table 1.5   Unemployment rates of foreign-born populations, by level of education attainment, 2003–2004

Country	Lo education	Med. Education	Hi Education	Diff lo/hi
France	18.4%	14.4%	11.8%	-36%
Britain	12.2%	7.9%	4.2%	-66%
United States	9.1%	5.7%	4.3%	-53%

Source: Data from OECD, *International Migration Outlook* (Washington, DC: OECD, 2006), p. 53.

The reduction of unemployment rates is brought down only 36 percent in France by higher education, compared with 66 percent for Britain and 53 percent for the United States. (See table 1.5.)

Therefore, in terms of employment and education, the outcomes for British immigrants have been quite good, especially compared with the outcomes in France. Political representation is roughly similar for all three countries at the local/state levels, but sharply different at the national level, where the more porous American system has generally succeeded in providing better access than either Britain or France. We will examine these questions in greater detail in the following chapters, but it appears clear that France has consistently had the worst record by far in political representation, as well as all of the other areas of comparison. (See table 1.6.)

On the other hand, the results of attitudinal surveys are quite different. Throughout Europe, the core problem of integration in recent years has been understood by governments and mass publics as the problem of integrating immigrants from Muslim countries. Therefore attitudes about and of Muslim immigrants tend to probe the sharp edges of problem of integration.

Surveys indicate that by several measures, France has been at least as accepting of these immigrants as Britain and the United States, and by others, even more accepting. Indeed the idea that "immigration is having a good influence" is (perhaps surprisingly) accepted in both Europe and

Table 1.6   Political integration of immigrant populations

Country	% Population	% Electorate	% State/local reps	% National representation
France	5	2.7	3.3	0 NA 0.6 Senate
Britain	7.9	6.6	2.6	2.3
United States[a]	12.5	7.4	3.2 (state only)	5.3 HR 3.0 Senate

Notes:
a Hispanics only.
NA: National Assemble; HR: House of Representatives.

Source: Richard Alba and Nancy Foner, "Entering the Precincts of Power: Do National Differences Matter for Immigrant-Minority Political Representation?" Unpublished manuscript.

Table 1.7   Attitudes toward immigrants and Muslims

	A good thing people from Middle East and North Africa coming to your country	Immigration having good influence on your country	Muslims in your country mostly want to adapt to national customs	No conflict between being a devout Muslim and living in modern society	Growing Islamic identity—good
French responses	58	46	45	74	11
British responses	57	43	22	35	27
Spanish responses	62	45	21	36	13
German responses	34	47	17	26	11
U.S. responses	—	52	33	42	37

Sources: Pew Research Center, *The Great Divide: How Westerners and Muslims View Each Other* (Washington, DC: Pew Global Attitude Project, June 2006), pp. 3, 6, 8, 10; Global Attitudes Project, July 22, 2006; IPSOS Public Affairs, Associated Press International Affairs Poll, May 2006.

in the United States, but the confidence that Muslim immigrants seek to adapt to customs in their country, and that there is no conflict between devout Muslim practice and living in modern society, is far more strongly held in France than in other countries. (See table 1.7)

These societal attitudes are reflected in attitudinal patterns among the immigrant population who identify as Muslim. French Muslims are, by far, the most integrative in their orientation, and the least conflicted between their Muslim and national identities. They are the most positively oriented toward "national customs," as well as the most accepting of Christians and Jews in their societies. On the other hand, among the countries cited in table 1.8, the idea of national "customs" and citizenship is certainly the strongest in France.

These conclusions are supported by a recent study of Muslim elites in Europe. Jytte Klausen has developed a typology of four preferences as modes of integration for Muslim populations:

Table 1.8 Muslims in Europe: Attitudes toward identity, fellow citizens, and modernity

	Positive views of Christians	Positive views of Jews	No conflict between being a devout Muslim and living in modern society	Consider yourself first: a citizen of **your country**/ Muslim	Muslims in your country want to adopt national customs
French Muslims	91%	71%	72%	42% /46%	78%
British Muslims	71%	32%	49%	7% /81%	41%
Spanish Muslims	82%	28%	71%	3% /89%	53%
German Muslims	69%	38%	57%	13% /66%	38%

Sources: Pew Research Center, *The Great Divide: How Westerners and Muslims View Each Other*, pp. 3, 11–12; Global Attitudes Project, July 6, 2006.

Secular Integrationist: respondents believe that Islam is compatible with Western value and that the organization of Islamic practice should be integrated into existing frame works of church-state relations.[52]

Neo-orthodox respondents believe that Islam is not compatible and should not be integrated into existing frameworks

Voluntarist respondents believe that Islam is compatible in terms of values, but should not be integrated into existing frameworks

Anticlerical respondents believe that Islam is not compatible in terms of values, but should be integrated into existing church-state relations

The responses of Muslim elites by country are indicated in table 1.9. The two most strikingly different patterns are those of French and the British subsamples, each of which overwhelmingly fits into a single category. Although the support of French elites for "secular integration" largely conforms to French norms on church-state relations, the strong support for "voluntarist" policies indicates a distrust of the state and acceptance of the compatibility of French and Islamic values. It is also worth noting that the French sample had the lowest "neo-orthodox response of any of the European groups studied by Klausen. On the other hand, the support of British Muslim elites for the "neo-orthodox" pattern indicates a strong sense of isolation from British norms that makes Britain different from every other country studied by Klausen.

These elite results are important, I would argue, because they represent the attitudinal orientations of the best organized, and in many ways the most accomplished groups among the Muslim population. Therefore, it is important whether they tend to focus on ethnic or religious differences or on similarities.

Thus, the British and American records of economic integration of immigrant populations are far better than that of France. The British record of educational integration appears to have been remarkably successful,

Table 1.9   Policy choice for integration of Islam of Muslim elites, by country of residence

	Denmark %	Sweden %	France %	Germany %	Netherlands %	United Kingdom %	Total %
Secular Integrationist	20.8	37.5	60.0	25.0	13.6	10.7	23.5
Voluntarist	33.3	37.5	30.0	30.6	59.1	17.9	33.8
Anticlericals	33.3	12.5	0.0	22.2	9.1	0.0	14.7
Neo-orthodox	12.5	12.5	10.0	22.2	18.2	71.4	27.9
Total	100	100	100	100	100	100	100

Source: Jytte Klausen, *The Islamic Challenge: Politics and Religion in Western Europe* (Oxford: Oxford University Press, 2005), p. 95.

and the record of the United States somewhat less so; the French record, however, is the worst of the three. Nevertheless, patterns of attitudinal acceptance by both the host population, and by immigrants themselves appear to be far more positive in France than in Britain, indicating a serious gap among different dimensions of integration that challenge assumptions that we often make.

Politicization: The Comparative
Politics of Immigration ·

Although each of the each of the four issues analyzed in the previous section has been important in the politics of France, Britain, and the United States during the past decades and before, the importance has been different in each case, and it has changed over time, in part because of the way that the immigration issue has been politicized in each case. Thus, in Europe concerns about immigration have been politicized in a very different way than in the United States. In many ways the challenges have been similar, but the politics have been different.

Politicization: Conflict, Problem-Solving, Framing

In the literature in political science and public policy "politicization" means a number of related but different things. Most frequently it means increased political awareness or involvement among individuals or groups. In this sense, politicization has been linked both to the politics of development in the developing world,[53] as well as mass participation and involvement in the political process in the developed world.[54] From a different perspective, politicization means conflict. Institutions become politicized when, in their decision-making processes, they evolve toward conflict over problems with which they are concerned. Philippe Schmitter has referred to this as a process that begins with the division among institutional actors about what they see as salient issues, what he calls "controversality," and proceeds by drawing in an expanding "audience" or interested clientele.

Therefore in the politicization of institutions, two dimensions are important, salience and division: the growing salience of issues through which divisions take place; and the growing division of actors around those issues. Thus, public opinion on immigration may be highly negative, but the issue only becomes politically important when it is salient for political actors, and creates divisions among actors either within or between political institutions. The question, then, is how issues become salient for political actors. One process, analyzed in depth by Schattschneider (see below), is the way political actors choose issues to gain advantage in order to mobilize support. Although issues may be driven by forces external to institutions, they are related to division and conflict if the issue is used as a mobilization device among conflicting actors. As Schmitter states: "...as soon as there is evidence of the increase of actor-defined controversiality, the politicization process has begun."[55]

On the other hand, politicization of issues can also be initiated by those who deal with public policy day to day. Policy analysts have demonstrated ways in which issues become salient, not in the service of political advantage, or even in the context of conflict, but in pursuit of solutions to perceived problems. In a seminal work in 1974 Hugh Heclo analyzed the development of the welfare state in Europe in terms of a strong impetus toward problem-solving or "puzzling" as he called it.[56] Policy, then, is the outcome of broad-based collaboration of traditional political actors (elected officials, political parties, interest groups), bureaucratic actors, experts and advocates, who interact in "policy communities". Such communities are characterized by cooperation, rather than conflict, and by problem-solving, rather than advantage.[57] Although this kind of analysis tends to focus on less traditional political actors, what differentiates it from the conflict analysis is less the actors involved than the dynamics and motivation of their interaction—cooperation and learning, as opposed to conflict and winning and losing.

The scope of salience is important for the content of immigration policy. For example, Terri Givens and Adam Luedtke have presented important comparative evidence that when the salience of immigration is restricted to a narrow group of policy-makers and committed, well-organized clients, policy tends to be more open (certainly more open than public opinion would indicate). As the scope of salience of immigration grows however, as media coverage grows and as immigration issues become salient for electoral politics, policy tends to become more restrictive.[58]

Although each of these ways of understanding the development of public policy is not entirely incompatible with the other, each tends to emphasize a different way of explaining policy outcomes and policy change. In the countries with which we are dealing, political advantage is generally sought by political leaders and political parties, and is measured in electoral terms. Problem-solving is usually understood in terms of relating policy to problems that are framed by a broader range of political/administrative institutions.

In this volume, I approach politicization from this top-down institutional perspective. This does not mean that public opinion or organized participation against or in favor of immigration are not important. Rather, they are important insofar as they become salient for the policymaking process. When we refer to the "politicization" of immigration issues, we mean that immigration issues have become part of a public discourse, or are important for electoral purposes; have become issues in political party competition more generally or that they are the subject of proposed or considered legislation about which there is political conflict. I will analyze three related, but analytically separate political processes I believe are essential for understanding politicization. The first is the process of agenda formation: the process through which immigration issues are developed as priorities, and placed on the political agenda. The second is the process through which policy is sustained and developed over time. The third is how policies change in orientation.

By focusing on politicization, my interest is first to understand why immigration policy is different in countries that are similar in many ways; and then to understand why policies vary within countries as well. Thus, the focus is comparative, and is built around three case studies: France, Britain and the United States. The advantage of using three cases that appear to be similar from a socioeconomic point of view, but quite different from a policy perspective, is that we can develop an analysis in considerable depth within a comparative framework. Consider the following: although there are variations, all three countries have become increasingly similar in socioeconomic terms during the past 40 years. All three have developed economies that have moved away from employment in smokestack industry, and with large and growing service sectors. All three societies have relatively low birthrates, with growing post-retirement populations. And all three are more or less dependent on a favorable demographic balance of working-to-nonworking populations for socioeconomic stability. For these and other reasons, all three countries need immigration, and this need seems to be greater for Britain and France (and for most of Europe) than for the United States.

Nevertheless, the United States has developed a more open immigration policy, while at the very same time Britain and France have developed policies of immigration restriction. On the other hand, restrictive policies in Europe appear to be far less effective than they are intended to be, and surprisingly large numbers of immigrants enter Britain and France each year quite legally.

Agenda Formation

Agenda formation implies larger questions of issue formation or agenda-setting. It also is at the core of how issues become politically salient, either through conflict or through problem-solving. Since relatively few issues make it on to the policy agenda, a process through which immigration is presented and defined is related to how it becomes a political priority.

E.E. Schattschneider approached this question through an understanding of political conflict. He associated the initial struggle about policy to the prior question of the way that policy issues are portrayed through the arguments and strategies of political leaders. How issues are defined in policy debates, he argued, is driven by strategic calculations among conflicting political actors about the mobilization of what Schattschneider calls "the audience" at which they are aiming.[59] From this point of view, political leaders skilled in formulating issues to their own advantage strongly influence how (and who in) "the audience"—voters and militants—becomes involved. The motor-force behind policy portrayal is issue-driven conflict among political elites, and different formulations of issues can mobilize different coalitions of supporters, each of which has its policy bias.

The way that these issues are defined by public authorities is a crucial aspect of policymaking that is also linked to which publics are mobilized and within which political arenas policy decisions are taken. The construction of the issue of immigration may be related to pressures of public opinion, to pluralist pressures of organized interests, to initiatives within administrations, or to all three. The point is that issues do not generally just emerge. They are constructed within specific institutional arenas in specific ways for specific purposes linked to political conflict.

On the other hand, an analysis of conflict among political actors trying to gain political advantage does not help us to understand cross-national differences in policy *content*. For example, at various times, in their framing of immigration policy, political party actors in Britain and France, on one hand, and the United States on the other, were all driven by the possibility of electoral advantage. However, the policies themselves were very different in Europe compared with the United States, and the dynamics among the party actors were very different in Britain compared with France.

To understand the orientation of policy, ideas are often important. In his study of race policies in Britain and France, Erik Bleich explains differences in Britain and France primarily by the sharp differences of ideas in the form of "frames" that drove the dominant group of policy-makers in each case. While many differences in policy outcomes can be explained by conflict theory (groups and parties), and some differences in the specific content of policy can be understood through a problem-solving approach that focuses on the role of policy communities or institutionalist perspectives, Bleich sees these as secondary, if what we want to understand is differences in the orientation of policy choices that are made in different countries. He argues that the same kinds of political actors in each country have produced very different kinds of policies because they were operating with very different sets of ideas about the need for policy, its goals and the ways it should be effective.[60] Although questions of agenda formation and framing are often analyzed in terms of winners and losers, the losers do not generally disappear. Schattschneider emphasizes that policy definition is a continuing struggle, often among the same actors in an evolving institutional context. The way that policies are framed, therefore, is important, whether we are dealing with political actors using policy to gain political advantage, responding to conflicting interests, or using policy as a way of dealing with perceived, ongoing problems.

The Political Process of Policymaking

Policy orientations, and the ideas that support them, are perpetuated through the institutional frameworks that sustain them. In this sense, once policy has been defined, it tends to be managed within an institutional framework generally defined by a common understanding of the problem. Theories of path-dependence tell us that the original policy to a large extent determines future policy by constraining institutional choices: "...the range of options available at any point in time is constrained by extant institutional capabilities, and these capabilities are themselves a product of choices made during some earlier period."[61]

The literature on political communities provides us with a more detailed approach to how these constraints are maintained. Although political conflict is not absent from this process, it is constrained by a more or less common assumption about the policy paradigm.[62] The framework has been described as a broad (but limited) coalition of political forces—a network of bureaucracies, interest groups and experts—that constitute a policy network or a policy community.[63] Actors within the policy community share common interests, as well as a more or less common understanding of the problem that the policy is meant to address. The process here is less one of conflict than of problem-solving. Moreover, it is a process that is less politically visible, and while the consequences may be important, it is less politically important in terms of electoral consequences and political mobilization.

Stable institutionalization has also been explained in terms of costs and benefits for institutional actors. Gary Freeman argues that costs of a moderately open immigration policy are diffuse, and born by relatively disadvantaged and poorly organized groups, while the benefits are concentrated among a few groups that are relatively influential and well organized. Thus, business and employers generally benefit from the labor-market impact of immigration: the availability and flexibility of labor, the depression of wages, and the creation of conditions that make it more difficult for trade unions to organize.[64] Indeed, labor market considerations are related to more open immigration policies in the United States over a long period of time, but also to similar openness in France and Britain. In each case, however, the political process associated with such policies has been largely driven by relatively insulated elite decision-makers.

This explanation works best as a way of understanding the perpetuation of more open immigration policies (as in the United States), and leaves open the question of how opposition to immigration can by effectuated politically.[65] In a comparative framework, however, it does not help us understand why any country should have a more exclusionary policy, or why policies should vary, either within countries over time, or among countries across space.

In the three countries analyzed in this study, not only have different policies emerged from different ways of looking at the immigration issue, but the institutional framework, the political actors within this framework, and the dynamics among these actors within which these policies have been sustained are also quite different in each case To some extent, this reflects the differences among political systems in each case, but there are aspects that are specific to the policy process of immigration.

Change

A large part of the story that we tell here is that of change. All of the analyses developed above indicate that existing policy orientations are difficult to change, and that the dynamics of stability are strong. Indeed, none of these theoretical perspectives help us to understand how policies change at all.

Change in policy generally involves a change in how the policy is understood and framed, a change initiated and pursued by actors within an institutional framework. In the cases analyzed in this study, these changes involved an altered institutional context, from administrative institutions to party structures in the French case, and a deep involvement of the president in the congressional decision-making process in the American case. It may make a difference whether the key policy actors are administrative or party-based. Administrative actors are more likely to be "problem-solvers," even as they alter policy in important ways, while party actors are more likely to see issue definition in terms of party competition and the next election (see below). The costs and benefits for party actors are different from those of administrative and group actors.

Thus, both Schattschneider and Lowi see the shift in the policy frame as emerging from the shift in the institutional framework itself, and both strongly focus on the arena within which decisions are made as being decisive for both the policy outcome and the way that it is understood.[66] Each institutional arena provides a different opportunity structure for political actors, but within that structure, a variety of outcomes are possible.

But, how can we understand the dynamics that drive paradigmatic policy change, change that tends to move policymaking from one arena to another? One approach is to explain policy change by the perceived failure of existing policy, either within the policy community itself, within public opinion, or within the larger institutional environment. Failure can take many forms, from war, to a widespread economic crisis, to a social crisis marked by violence. In any of these cases, what are brought into question are the assumptions behind the policy paradigm.[67]

Another approach is to explain policy change by a shift in relative power—and therefore a change in dynamics—among existing institutions, such as the rise of presidential power in the United States during the past century. Change may also involve a change in political actors within the same institutions—different political parties in power, powerful interest groups finding new access points to policy decision-making, and actors exploiting different strategies of using the same institutional framework.

Still another approach is to explain change in policy by variations in the balance among socioeconomic actors within the political system. In fact, although most studies have explicitly rejected this approach for understanding changes in immigration policy in Europe, this has been the dominant approach for explaining policy in the United States.[68]

Change and the Electoral Connection

Finally, we can explain policy change by party competition. The electoral arena is in fact a network of local constituency arenas, each electing its own representative, and each influenced by local political forces. Therefore, it seems reasonable to presume that public opinion, interest pressure and electoral pressure would vary with the variation in the concentration of immigrant populations, since the concentrations of immigrants across spatial areas are also related to political, social, and economic costs and benefits.[69]

Jeanette Money has argued convincingly that the link between local dynamics and the national arena depends on the importance of specific localities for shifting national elections. Therefore, politicization of immigration in Britain and France in the 1960s/1970s was driven by electoral dynamics within spatially defined arenas, areas in which immigrants are concentrated. According to Money's analysis, national party leaders have been drawn to the immigration issue because it can be used to shift voters in constituencies that would be otherwise safe for the other political party (possible swing constituencies), making the issue a useful tool for building national coalitions. Cross-nationally, the common thread is the need for party leaders to build a national electoral majority.

> Driven by electoral competition, local politicians will shift their policy positions in response to changing community preferences, toward either greater openness or greater closure. . . . But immigration control is determined in the national rather than the local political arena. Therefore, it is crucial to understand the conditions under which local demands are successfully transmitted to the national level.[70]

These considerations are of major importance primarily in the context of electoral politics, where policy proposals are developed by political parties for electoral gain. If the main institutional actors are administrative elites, rather than political, these strategic considerations may be of far less importance. They may, however, convince otherwise reluctant party leaders to use the immigration issue for electoral purposes. Thus, the politics of identity, in which immigrants are depicted as representing a challenge to national identity, are imbedded within the dynamics of electoral competition.

However, it does not follow that the immigration issue will necessarily be framed as an identity question for electoral purposes. The way political parties understand "electoral considerations" can involve different kinds of policy considerations, depending on whether they construct the immigration issue as a challenge to identity for voters they anticipate to be anti-immigrant, or as a means of mobilizing a potential immigrant electorate. If the former focus has dominated the thinking of political parties in Britain and France in recent years, the latter focus has been more dominant among political parties in the United States, with very different policy outcomes in each case. If the first pattern has often been identified as the politics of identity, the second has been characterized as ethnic politics, the "pandering" to the sensibilities of ethnic or naturalized voters.

Understanding immigrant populations as potential voters has both policy implications (policies favorable or inoffensive to these groups), as well as organizational consequences for political parties (the choice of political candidates, for example). Clearly, attempts by political parties to mobilize immigrants as potential voters are of crucial importance to immigrant groups. As Richard Alba and Nancy Foner have noted, election of candidates with immigrant backgrounds to political office is a measure of their integration "…in the same sense that entry by minority individuals into high-status occupations is. It is an indication of a diminishment, however modest, in differentials in life chances that exist between majority and minority."[71] Representation also gives them a voice in the distribution of public goods, as well as the ability to control the spatial zones in which they live. Finally, achievement of elective office gives groups control over both patronage and influence over decisions made by civil servants (decisions that are disproportionately important for immigrants). As Alba and Foner argue:

> The Irish of the United States offer a compelling historical example, as they used their leadership of Democratic political machines that ruled many U.S. cities a century ago to bring about massive municipal employment of their co-ethnics.[72]

Policies of Immigration

But what exactly are policies of immigration? Until now, we have alluded to immigration policy, but have not specified what this has meant. Policies on immigration in Europe and the United States have become increasingly diverse over time, in part because they have been defined, not only by legislative and administrative decisions, but also by international agreements and court decisions.

The most basic policies are those that define who may enter and who may stay in a country, which ultimately involves who may become a citizen. By the late twentieth century this took the legal form of visas, both those that permitted the holder to enter for a limited period of time, and for a specific purpose (tourists, students, and guest workers, for example), and those that permitted settlement. When immigration for long-term residence and settlement was formally suspended throughout Western Europe, court decisions compelled that these countries maintain a right to family unification, forcing them to develop immigration policies consistent with these decisions.

A second category of entry policy—this one controlled by international agreement—is refugee and asylum policy. In reaction to the plight of Jewish refugees before and during WWII, a convention on refugees was agreed to at the United Nations in 1951, and then updated by an additional protocol in 1967. Policy on asylum has therefore been developed in the context of these agreements. As restrictions on immigration into Europe increased in the 1970s, applications for asylum increased, further generated by wars, the end of the Cold War, easier transport and organized networks. Confronted with massive numbers of applications of the 1980s and 1990s, European countries reacted by establishing restrictive asylum policies at the national and European levels. There was a similar reaction to asylum in the United States.

A third category of entry policy has been action taken against illegal entry and those who violate the restrictions on their visas. Various kinds of illegal immigrants have been the target of an increasingly large volume of legislation and administrative rules in both Europe and the United States.

Immigration policy, however, has involved more than entry. It has also involved citizenship and integration. Particularly in Europe, the rules of who is eligible for citizenship, under which circumstances, and through which process have changed considerably during the past forty years, and in very different ways. German rules have become more inclusive, but British rules have become very much more exclusive, and French rules have become marginally more exclusive.

Policy on integration has become a major preoccupation in European countries with large immigrant populations. As immigrants have become ethnic groups, and have maintained—or have been forced to maintain—their identity after two and three generations, governments have developed educational, housing and religious policies to encourage various forms of integration. The United States, by contrast, has no national integration policy, aside from the now modified affirmative action policies that were meant to apply to race relations. Often similar policies that are referred to in the United States as policies on race relations, are called immigration policies in Europe. In part because of the federal system, such integration policies that have been formulated, have been developed at the local level, often by local education authorities and local governments.

The Politics of Immigration in Britain, France, and the United States

Questions of immigration first became politicized in each country between the end of the nineteenth century and WWI, and the framing of the problem and the institutional context remained more or less stable until the 1960s. During the decade that followed there were important changes in how immigration policy was framed and how it was developed institutionally in each country. However, in each country both the framing of the issues and the pattern of politicization were quite different.

In France, the first legislation was passed at the end of the nineteenth century. It was not meant to restrict immigration, but to shape and control it through naturalization and citizenship. The problem was defined in terms of French needs for immigrants, but French authorities were always reluctant to encourage the kind of empire immigration and citizenship with which the British seemed far more at ease. As we shall see, the debate in parliament posed a racial/identity definition of the problem against more practical considerations of the need for soldiers and labor. In the end those supporting the latter won, but the former point of view remained important in subsequent debates on immigration.

This orientation of French immigration policy endured until 1974. Indeed, there would be no important legislation on immigration until 1980, and no broad administrative decision until 1945. As in Britain, many important changes were made in how immigrants were admitted, and how they were treated once they arrived in France, but all of these decisions were essentially removed from the legislative arena, and from the context of electoral politics.

In Britain, the question of immigration was separated before WWI from the question of empire citizenship, which, in principle, permitted access to Britain by all citizens of the British Empire. The first restrictive legislation was aimed at Jews who had entered the United Kingdom at the turn of the century to seek refuge from oppression in the Russian Empire. Although the issue was framed in terms of identity, the framing of the problem never took on the deep racial overtones that it assumed in the United States. Restrictive legislation was developed and supported by the Conservative Party (which also strongly supported empire citizenship), but restriction also had some support within the left wing of the Liberal Party as well. In any case, even after restriction, the main sources of British immigration—Ireland and the Empire—remained formally unrestricted, and politically unopposed.

After the third Aliens Act was passed in 1919, there would be no further legislation for almost twenty years, although there would be changes in policy toward immigrants, mostly those seeking asylum from other parts of Europe. During the period between the wars, policy was developed and changed at the ministerial and administrative level, mostly in the Home Office and the Ministry of Foreign Affairs. In this context, decisions were relatively protected from electoral considerations, although decisions made by various interwar governments were sometimes the subject of controversy and debate.

In both Britain and France, the post-WWII question of immigration was framed firmly in terms of identity, and challenges to national identity.

It emerged with the repoliticization of the issue in the 1960s in Britain and the 1970s in France. Redefined in this way, the policy that resulted was one of immigrant exclusion, at least exclusion with regard to immigrants from third world countries, and not simply immigrant control.

In both countries, policy was driven mostly by the dynamics of the party system, but the dynamics were quite different in each case. Exclusionary policies in Britain were first developed by the Conservatives, and deeply opposed by Labour. Within a few years, however, party differences narrowed considerably, so much so that, within less than a decade there appeared to be a broad consensus on both the framework for policy, as well as the broad outlines of a policy of immigration control. Since then, while there have been some partisan differences, the consensus has been more or less maintained. The consensus was based on a compromise through which Labour accepted exclusionary policies, while the Conservatives accepted integration that was based on legislation that prohibited racial discrimination (extended to religious discrimination in 2004).

The changes in Britain, at least from the perspective of the British system, were far more complicated than either in France or the United States. Exclusionary policies emerged out of a wrenching effort to abrogate most of the rights of commonwealth (formerly empire) citizenship. Progressively, British citizenship law excluded citizens of Commonwealth countries, and more or less merged Commonwealth citizens with other aliens in terms of the right to abode in the United Kingdom. This implied a major change for the Conservative Party, which had been an historic supporter of empire and commonwealth citizenship.

On the other hand, in part because exclusionary policy was developed through a redefinition of citizenship, remnants of privileges of empire citizenship have remained in place. Even as entry policy became increasingly harsh, civic incorporation through citizenship rights remained far more generous than comparable policies in France and the United States, at least for immigrants from Commonwealth countries.

In France, the immigration issue has been framed in more or less the same terms as in Britain since 1974, but the dynamics have been quite different. Remarkably, the move toward immigrant exclusion in 1974 was relatively uncontroversial and unopposed; indeed it was not a politicized issue, and was done at the administrative level. Opposition developed first from the courts and then from the opposition Left, not to the suspension of immigration, but to government actions meant to enforce and extend that suspension. Nevertheless, decision-making remained at the administrative level until 1980, when the first postwar legislation was passed (the Loi Bonnet), and then abrogated a year later when the Left arrived in power. Since then, each government has pursued policies consistent with the understanding that immigration must be strongly limited, and that it poses a challenge to national identity.

Despite a convergence of policies on the ground, however, the politics of immigration have been highly polarized between right and left, government and opposition. The Left has tended to emphasize its commitment to "rights"; the right its commitment to "controls"; but both have hardly wavered from an equally firm commitment to halting immigration or to "zero immigration." The result has been a proliferation of legislation that is largely meant to demonstrate differences through small changes embedded in strong rhetoric.[73] In part, what has been driving this political polarization has been the electoral success of the National Front.[74]

In neither Britain nor France have interest groups played an important role in the development of immigration policy. Parties' actions have been driven by the dynamics of the party system and electoral politics, and groups have tended to act in the context of political parties. In fact there are no groups of any significance that are advocating and working for the expansion of immigration in either country, with the exception of some business groups that have been quietly supporting entry for highly skilled immigrants. Such policies have been more successful in Britain than in France, in part because, as we shall see, the British system admits immigrants who can gain work permits, and since 2000 the government has generally conceded to business the initiative for granting these permits.

Since 2000, across Europe, there has been a well-defined opening up of some immigration, although anti-immigrant rhetoric has remained dominant. At the same time that many countries in Europe have begun to open up avenues of access for "highly skilled immigrants, there has been a parallel trend to make other kinds of immigration more difficult, and to impose rules that would carefully differentiate between temporary immigration for work, and more desirable immigration for settlement. Family unification has become more difficult and more painful, and a greater volume of new legislation has been directed against asylum-seekers and undocumented immigrants (clearly the most disdained categories). The French legislation passed in 2007, for example, increases the conditions for family unification and mixed marriages, and abrogates a provision of French law that made it possible for undocumented immigrant living in France for ten years or longer to obtain a residency permit. More emphasis has been placed on stringent rules for integration and citizenship throughout Europe. Most striking, there has been little change in anti-immigrant rhetoric, now largely directed against undocumented immigrants and asylum-seekers.

This mixture of polices, I will argue, can be largely explained by the dynamics of the politics of immigration. France and Britain provide us with two different models of how to develop more expansive policies, while still appearing to pursue more narrow goals of control and restriction. The French pursuit of highly skilled immigrants is thus framed as a way gaining greater control over who enters the country ("chosen, rather than endured"); while the considerable expansion of labor immigration has been pursued quietly through the administrative system by employer initiatives. At the EU level, the limited harmonization of immigration policies has been generally built around restriction, or has been accomplished by framing harmonization in low-saliency terms (integration or anti-discrimination).[75]

Moreover, the development of more explicit integration policies (and integration requirements) has been given increased attention in France and Britain, as well as on the EU level, particularly after a series of episodes of urban violence, beginning in the1980s. In both countries, the development of integration policies has meant centralizing aspects of policy that had been relatively decentralized before (some housing policies and dress codes in schools in France; police powers, anti-discrimination policies in Britain), as well as unending discussions on identity and what it means to be British or French.[76]

Immigration policy in the United States has changed dramatically during the past hundred years, but in ways very different than in Europe. At the beginning of the twentieth century the problem of immigration was defined in terms of national identity, and was far more deeply politicized than in either Britain or France. Indeed, in many ways the emerging definition of national identity was posed in opposition to what was then the "new' immigration from Eastern and Southern Europe.

The issue was shaped and developed at the national level, not by political parties, but by interest groups and congressional committees that had been organized in 1890. Over the following two decades the committees were most successful in passing legislation through which a federal structure was set in place to monitor and control immigration.

Within the Congress, support for and opposition to immigration control was never divided by political party. Enthusiastic support for restriction was strongest among representatives from those regions in which there were the highest proportion of immigrant settlers—the Northeast and the West, and, as the issue was increasingly linked to questions of race, support increased from representative from the South. Nevertheless, it took more than thirty years to develop sufficient congressional support to pass legislation to actually restrict immigration, and when it was finally passed after the end of WWI, there was little congressional opposition.

The opposition to restriction was primarily from presidents of both political parties. Even in this early period, interest groups were important, and support for restriction crossed normal party lines. Business groups generally opposed restriction, and labor supported it. The most powerful restrictionist groups were closely allied with the congressional committees, and their support was far more ideological and racist than economic. By the 1920s, presidential opposition was no longer important (or effective), and debate about the harsh immigration control regime that was set into place was limited to the details.

After 1924, decisions on immigration policy were largely moved to the administrative structure that had been developed by congressional initiatives before 1924. During the next 40 years, however, the main objectives of the quota legislation were slowly undermined through presidential and administrative decisions while the legislation remained in place. Indeed, by 1965 only one in three immigrants entering the United States, entered by the rules established under the 1924 legislation.[77] Political support for quota legislation was gradually undermined by the ability of a succession of presidents, together with congressional allies after WWII to reframe immigration as the core of American identity, rather than a challenge. It was also undermined by institutional change.

Proposals for reform of the immigration regime gained increased support in Congress after WWII, as immigrants and their children began to vote. However, the fate of legislation in Congress was controlled by the committee system that had supported restriction in the first place. Opposition, however, was no longer embedded in the racism of eugenicist ideology, and was instead was more vaguely framed as a challenge to the nation's "cultural and sociological balance by Republicans, and to the defense of segregation by the Southern Democrats."[78] These defenses were severely eroded by the rising tide of the civil rights movement.

Reform was ultimately ensured by a change in the institutional balance at the federal level. Presidential power had severely limited the effectiveness of quotas, and the use of presidential power by Lyndon Johnson in 1964–1965 demonstrated how much had changed in 40 years in the ability of a president to establish and fight for a legislative agenda. Finally, the electoral clout of interest groups, supported by voters who were the sons and daughters of the immigrants that the 1924 legislation sought to exclude, altered the positions of key legislators, who were threatened with defeat after 1964.[79]

The importance of the system set in place in 1965 can be most easily appreciated simply by the fact that immigration ceilings have risen since the legislation was first passed, even though consequences were far different than had been anticipated. Congress, in 1965, anticipated that the main beneficiaries of reform would be Europeans. In fact the largest proportion of immigrants has come from Latin America and Asia.

In the United States, questions of national identity that were at the core of the development of immigration policy at the turn of the last century has played a far less important role in the development of more recent policy. As in Europe, attitudinal opposition to immigration has been consistently present in the United States, but what has increasingly dominated the politics of immigration have been considerations of electoral gain or future party gain as a result of immigrants voting. Defined in relation to a multicultural society after 1965, immigration policy has remained relatively open through good and bad economic times. The core of this policy has resisted nationalist challenges in the 1990s, and the more recent challenge of post–September 11 security. Thus, although policy on both sides of the Atlantic appears to have been driven by electoral considerations, these considerations have been quite different in Europe and the United States.

In the chapters that follow, we will use the framework that we have developed here, and apply it in some depth to the three cases of France, Britain, and the United States. In a comparative framework, we will examine the history and politicization of the immigration question in these three countries. We will also focus specifically on the political process of immigration—immigration politics—in each country. Finally, we will try to explain why the development of a frankly more open policy in the United States has been far easier (and deemed more desirable) than in either Britain or in France.

CHAPTER TWO

Development of French Immigration Policy

Context: The Constitutional and Political System

The present governmental system in France, the Fifth Republic, is the sixteenth formal regime since the fall of the Bastille in 1789. Its constitution was approved by referendum in 1958, and except for the first few years, and a serious constitutional crisis in 1968, the Fifth Republic has proven to be the most stable and accepted regime in modern French history. What sets this republic apart from its predecessors is the institutionalized strength of its executive, the ability of political parties to maintain stable majorities in parliament, and the durability of governments between elections. In this way, the French system came to resemble the British system in terms of executive leadership and stability.[1]

Unlike previous republics, the Fifth Republic is a hybrid between presidential and cabinet government.[2] The president of the Republic—since 1962—has had the mandate of direct election, while the prime minister derives authority through the ability to control a majority in the National Assembly. In practice, the balance between president and prime minister has shifted to the president when both are of the same party, or party coalition, and has shifted to the prime minister, when the prime minister is supported by a majority in the National Assembly that is different from that of the president.

The 1958 constitution vastly diminished the ability of parliament to initiate legislation and to control the political agenda. As in Britain, essentially all control over the legislative agenda has been placed in the hands of the executive (president and prime minister). In addition, the constitution formally differentiated between "rule-making" and "law-making," with the former completely in the hands of the executive. Thus, at least some aspects of policy that would have to be passed by parliament in Britain, can be promulgated as ministerial decisions in France, approved by the Council of Ministers at a weekly meeting, or simply by the minister. Perhaps more to the point, at least some decisions that would have been made by parliamentary vote prior to 1958 are now made by administrative or executive decisions.

Finally, one of the most important innovations of the Fifth Republic has been the Constitutional Council, which has the power to review legislation before it is promulgated. As it has evolved over time, this court has reviewed almost every important law that has been passed, frequently requiring modifications, and sometimes reversing the law itself. However, this evolution has been only a piece of a much larger movement toward what has been termed judicialization[3] in France and in Europe, through which judges have gained a much larger role in both rule-making and law-making.

The Constitutional Council is one of two judicial bodies in France that have played a key role in this process. The other is the much older Council of State (established in 1799), the highest administrative court in France, but which has the power to make judgments about almost all acts of the executive. To this we must add the growing importance of the European Court of Justice, which is part of the structure of the EU, but which is directly linked to the process of judicial decision-making in France; and the European Court of Human Rights, the jurisdiction of which was established by the European Convention on Human Rights (1950), to which France is a signatory.[4]

One additional feature of the French system is important for the understanding of the development of immigration policy. Historically, political and administrative decision-making has been highly centralized, a characteristic of the French State that has endured across 16 different regimes over more than 200 years. In the 1980s, several laws were passed that devolved some political decision making down to regions and localities; and that also transferred some decision making at these levels from administrative to elected bodies. While far from federalism in the United States, and quite different from decentralized decision-making in Britain, these changes did increase the importance of some aspects of local government. They also established a whole new level of the civil service controlled by departmental (county) and regional authorities. In financial terms, however, the importance of the central state is overwhelming, since localities are wholly dependent upon "Paris" for almost any project or initiative that they undertake.

In the making of immigration policy, several aspects of policy have been directly influenced by the institutional framework, while the politics of immigration have been responsible for altering the framework itself. As we shall see, for over a century there was very little legislation on entry policy in France (see table 2.2). While the framework for British entry policy before WWII was developed through legislative acts (see table 5.1), the framework for French policy was developed largely through administrative decisions. This pattern, established when the capacity of political institutions was weak compared with the decision-making capacity of administrative institutions, and entry policy was potentially divisive, endured well into the Fifth Republic. On the other hand, at the same time that the United States was first building the administrative capacity to control immigration, France was able to use its considerable administrative capacity both to exclude and control immigration before WWII, and to permit large-scale immigration after the war.

As French governments became increasingly concerned with questions of integration and incorporation in the 1980s, local administrative and political authorities found that their decision-making authority, already enhanced by decentralization, was further enhanced by the ability to make decisions on housing, education and even entry, under family unification. Indeed, local authorities, concerned on immigration, have helped shape policies in these areas.

The growing scope of judicial decision-making has also been important in shaping French immigration policy. Thus, a decision by the Council of State is largely responsible for the maintenance of family unification, after the French government had decided to cut it back or even suppress it (see further on), while a decision by the Constitutional Council on the asylum policy agreed to in the Schengen Agreement forced the government to amend the constitution in 1993.

Context: France as a Country of Immigration

For at least 200 years, France has been a country of immigration, in the sense that France has generally welcomed immigrants, and has taken a certain pride in its ability to integrate immigrant populations.[5] In the twentieth century, four overlapping waves of immigrants were recruited into France from neighboring countries. The early part of the century was dominated by Italian and Belgian immigration, followed by a period of Polish immigration (and significant "internal migration" from Algeria), and then (after WWII) by a wave of immigration from Spain and Portugal. Since the mid-1960s, new waves of immigrants have been arriving from the former French colonies of North Africa, and more recently from sub-Saharan Africa. (See table 2.1.)

Although each wave of immigration has been seen as a necessity for the labor market, each has emerged in a different policy context, and has been conditioned, and even accelerated, by policy decisions made by a succession of French governments from the nineteenth century until the present. Nevertheless, for each wave of immigration there have been unanticipated consequences, and in fact each has evolved into a wave of settlement and has raised questions about integration and identity.

This general pattern of policy endured from the last quarter of the nineteenth century until the early 1970s. In 1974, France suspended immigration, formally terminating a generally open policy. This decision was made by administrative action, not by law, without parliamentary debate, and without significant dissent. Since then, this policy of exclusion has not—in itself—been brought into question, although many aspects of immigration policy have changed through law, in a flood of legislation

Table 2.1 Foreigners residing in France[a], 1851–2005

Year	Number (thousands)	Percent of Population (%)
1851	381	1.1
1891	1,130	2.8
1911	1,160	2.9
1921	1,532	3.9
1931	2,715	6.6
1936	2,198	5.3
1946	1,744	4.4
1962	2,170	4.7
1982	3,714	6.8
1999	3,263	5.6
2004–2005	3,501	5.6

Note:
a includes those born in France, but not French citizens.

Source: Annuaire Statistique de la France, resumé rétrospectif 1966 and 2000; Report by INED: http://www.ined.fr/en/pop_figures/france/immigrants_foreigners/immigrants_foreigners.

that began slowly in the 1980s and accelerated in the 1990s. The rate of legislation increased as the political salience of immigration grew, and the political salience grew as the percentage of foreigners in the country diminished after 1982. (See table 2.2.)

Thus, the pattern of policy and politics in France is an interesting puzzle. We will describe the evolution of policy and politics in this chapter, and then analyze in greater detail the relationship between the two in chapter 3 that follows.

Policy on Immigration: European Immigration

National Needs, National Identity, and Race By the last decade of the nineteenth century, as a result of demographic stagnation and the catastrophe of the Franco-Prussian War, the need for manpower generally drove the policy-process. Immigration increased, molded and directed by legislation, decrees and various other administrative *circulaires.* Because manpower needs were not simply for temporary labor, but to fill a perceived population deficit that was related to long-term labor and military needs, policy tended to encourage settlement, rather than simply the movement of labor. With a stagnant native population, the number of resident immigrants increased from about 300,000 in the middle of the nineteenth century to just over a million at the turn of the century, to 2.7 million in 1931. Although the majority of these immigrants were single men from Italy, Belgium and Poland (especially after WWI), many of them later

Table 2.2 French immigration legislation

1889	First legislation on naturalization—consolidation and reform of law and practice—as part of a more general effort to control and direct immigrants already within the country. Established *jus solis* as basic principle.
1912	Legislation was passed that required identity documents with detailed pictures and descriptions for resident immigrants.
1927	Law on naturalization that eased the requirement of residency to three years.
1945	Two ordinances established the framework for postwar immigration: conditions of entry and stay; and citizenship and naturalization; work permits and residency permits were entirely separate, making it possible for immigrants to remain in France even if they were not employed; establishment of the *Office national d'immigration*.[a]
1973	Article 23 of Nationality Code—stipulating that Algerians born before independence in 1962 retained French nationality—extended to Moroccans and Tunisians.[a]
1974	Administrative *circulaires* suspending labor and family migration in July; did not apply to European Community (EC) nationals, asylum-seekers or some highly skilled labor migrants.[a]
1977– 1978	Enforcement of suspension of family reunification for three years by decree in November 1977, lifted in December 1978 following a decision of the French Council of State.[a]
1980	Loi Bonnet; tightened entry requirements, and made expulsions of undocumented immigrants easier; abrogated by first Mitterrand government in 1981.
1981	Loi Peyrefitte; stop and frisk laws directed at undocumented immigrants.
1982	New administrative rules requiring a certificate of lodging for visas to visit France.[a]
1983	Loi Badinter; racial criteria approved for stop and frisk.
1984	New long-term visa—voted unanimously—creates a single residency permit, in place of separate residency and work permits, that permits holder to work anywhere in France; visa automatically renewable, unless challenged by authorities.
1986	Loi Pasqua; facilitated expulsion procedures; restricted access to ten-year permits.
1989	Loi Joxe; eased requirements of the Loi Pasqua, but maintained tough entry requirements.
1992	Law establishing detention centers ("waiting zones") at seaports and airports for detention of asylum-seekers and immigrants whose documentation has not been established.
1993 –1994	Lois Pasqua; once again facilitated expulsions; increased to two years waiting time for spouses, and denied legalization if spouse undocumented; restricted claims to welfare benefits for undocumented immigrants; gave mayors increased power to deny a certificate of lodging, and annul suspected marriage of convenience; but, racial criteria for stop and frisk abrogated.
1993	Loi Méhaignerie; modified jus solis for children born in France of immigrant parents—required to request citizenship at age 16–21; abrogated 1973 extension of Article 23, and established extensive residency requirements for Algerians claiming citizenship under Article 23 for their children.
1993	Constitutional amendment approved, enabling restrictions on asylum consistent with Schengen and Dublin Accords.
1997	Loi Debré; increased power of police under Loi Pasqua, and increased residency requirements for naturalization of wives and children of legal immigrants; more difficult to arrange visits of family members of resident immigrants.
1998	Loi Chevenement; substantially restored *jus solis* that had been modified in 1993; reduced power of mayors to reject migrants visiting legal residents; created special visa status for scholars, scientists and highly qualified workers.
2003	Loi Sarkozy I; once again legislation to prevent illegal immigration; eased expulsion process; lengthened period of detention from 12 to 32 days; increased to two years the period that a couple must remain together before claim to naturalization.
2006	Loi Sarkozy II on Immigration and Integration; new rules on marriage and fewer visas available.

Continued

Table 2.2   Continued

2007	Loi Hortefeux: requires "an evaluation of language competence and a knowledge of the values of the Republic" in order to qualify for family unification—the evaluation takes place before permission is granted to enter France; at the request of the applicant, a DNA test may be administered to demonstrate a mother-child relationship; Welcome and Integration Contract now required for all family unification; legal residents now granted an "unlimited resident permit" if in the country more than ten years; there are also provisions for legalization of illegal immigrants; finally, the law provides for questions on race and ethnicity by the census, with the goal of combating discrimination and promoting integration (this decision was found to be unconstitutional).

Note:
a Administrative actions.

Sources: Patrick Weil, *La France et ses étrangers*, 2nd edition (Paris: Gallimard, 2004); Janine Ponty, *L'immigration dans les texts: France, 1789–2002* (Paris: Editions Belin, 2003); *Le Monde*, October 23, 2007.

brought their families. Thus, about 60 percent of this population was active in the labor force in 1931 (about the same percentage as in 1901), and 63 percent of immigrants in the labor force worked in industry and transport (also about the same as in 1901).

In 1889, after immigration had been growing for more than 40 years, France promulgated its first legislation on naturalization—in fact a major consolidation and reform of law and practice—as part of a more general effort to control and direct immigrants already within the country. The legislation was the end product of a long process both to consolidate policy and to consider new needs that had begun to become more evident in the early part of the decade. Its principal concern was to deal with French manpower needs, and to tie immigration to settlement by firmly establishing jus solis as a principle of law.

At least until the onset of the depression, the main concern of French immigration legislation was not to exclude immigrants, but to control their behavior on French soil. In the name of security, requirements became more and more exacting, however, particularly with regard to documentation. In 1912, legislation was passed that required identity documents with detailed pictures and descriptions for resident immigrants, and French administrative authorities could prevent people from crossing the frontier if "...their presence appeared dangerous."[6] However, the ability of the state to mold and control immigration and immigrants was sharply limited by the administrative organization to do so. As Vincent Viet has pointed out, "On the eve of WWI, France had no administrative organization for immigration."[7]

WWI and Manpower

WWI created an overwhelming need for manpower to replace those fighting in the war, but also to man expanding war industries. Thus, both and during after the war, the state itself became increasingly active in man-power recruitment, as well as in the control and direction of immigrants coming into the country. After the war, a larger and better-organized labor movement pressured governments to prevent employers from using immigrant labor to maintain low-wage conditions. Employers, on the other hand, also turned to the state to increase the pool of foreign labor, which they themselves found more and more difficult to do. Moreover, employers needed state help to defend their interests against the efforts by labor exporting countries to impose restrictions and conditions for work-ers leaving for France. Eventually, these arrangements had to be nego-tiated through bilateral state agreements, with the French State as the bargaining agent for the employers.[8]

This post-WWI system of immigration and immigration control was dominated by a manpower recruitment effort that was never legislated. Indeed, between the wars, only two laws on immigration were legislated, both of which were marginal to the system that had been set in place. The postwar system was embedded in a framework of bilateral agreements with Poland, Italy and Czechoslovakia signed in 1919/1920. Within this framework, the French State recruited workers directly for the postwar reconstruction zones, but increasingly recruitment was turned over to a privately controlled agency, la Societé générale d'immigration (SGI). Although specific departments in five different ministries were respon-sible for different aspects of immigration policy and control, SGI had the central responsibility for the recruitment of immigrant workers, recruit-ment that was deemed essential to postwar economic expansion.

The orientation of this policy remained unchallenged until the employ-ment crisis of the depression, when state bureaucracies began to use many of the powers that had been held in abeyance before, in order to limit access of immigrant workers to the labor market. The most effective action by the state was to re-impose the frontier, and severely restrict the entry of immigrant labor. However, as the depression became more severe in 1932, legislation was passed that authorized a complex procedure that offered the possibility of imposing quotas on the employment of immi-grants in various industries (but not in agriculture). The use of such quotas was complicated by the degree to which a number of industries had become dependent on immigrant labor. (See table 2.3.)

In particular geographic areas, concentrations were even greater than for the industry as a whole. In the coal mines of the department of the Nord, 62 percent of the workers (and 75% of underground workers) were immigrants in 1931, as were 70 percent of the iron miners and 90 percent of the workers in certain factories in Lorraine.[9] A great deal has been written about the high concentrations of immigrant labor in specific industries and at specific skill levels in the 1980s.[10] However, the pattern of the 1980s was not substantially different from the one that developed after WWI.

Table 2.3 Percentage of foreigners in specific industries

OCCUPATION	1906 (%)	1931(%)	%CHANGE
Mining	6.2	40.1	548
Steel Mills	17.8	34.8	96
Quarrying	8.7	26.1	200
Construction	10.2	24.1	132
Rubber/Paper	3.6	10.7	197
Chemicals	10	14.7	47
Metal work	4.5	10.5	13

Source: *Résultats statistiques de recensement général de la population*, Vol. 1, No. 5, 1936, p. 51, as reprinted in Gary S. Cross, *Immigrant Workers in Industrial France* (Philadelphia, PA: Temple University Press, 1983), p. 160.

One indication of how severely the labor market had been divided between native and immigrant labor is that, even during the height of the depression, more than 60,000 foreigners (legally) entered the country each year, mostly for labor. In addition, even in the early years of the depression, the government continued a practice that it had initiated during earlier downturns in the economy (and would use again during the period of economic expansion after 1952) of "regularizing" immigrant workers who had found employment by crossing the frontier and finding employment on their own.[11] Moreover, with the notable exception of the construction industry, there were very few requests for the imposition of quotas, either from unions or employers.[12]

As the depression wore on, increasing administrative restrictions were imposed on immigrants resident in France, and as the war approached, restrictions became more severe. Nevertheless, immigrants did not disappear from the labor force. As Cross points out, "...the regulated flow of alien labor became a permanent feature of the economies of France and later of Western Europe....A permanent reserve army of laborers emerged, defined less by their social, educational, or racial characteristics than by their legal status as immigrants."[13]

Although what most defined immigration policy between the wars was controlled recruitment of manpower, manpower evolved slowly into settlement, as workers brought their families or created new ones on French soil. The law on naturalization eased the requirement of residency to three years in 1927, with a result of much higher rates of naturalization, particularly among the more established settlements of immigrants. Nevertheless, the application of this legislation by the administration tended to mold naturalization to perceived ideas of national security and national identity with a bias against Asians, Africans and "Levantines"—Jews (see ch. 4).[14]

In practice, the administration was less favorable to applicants for immigration who could be seen as threats to internal security, and more favorable to applicants who could contribute to conscription.[15] Although there was no requirement for immigrants from North Africa to be naturalized, they were viewed as the least desirable by employers and the administration alike. In 1926 there was a brief, unsuccessful effort to develop an American-type quota policy, that would, in effect, enshrine the notion of desirability in law, yet another example of the tensions in the orientations of a policy of immigration that was determined by the objectives of different ministerial actors.

Settlement and Ghettos

Nevertheless, immigrant communities gradually became settler communities, in ways that were molded by the system of immigration that had been established in the 1920s. Maxim Silverman has analyzed the recent use of the term "ghetto" in the literature on French immigration. There is ample evidence that immigrant concentrations were as normal during the period between the wars as they are now. Silverman cites Noiriel in noting that "[a]ll of the statistics at our disposal from the beginning of the nineteenth century refute the commonly held notion that the constitution of immigrant 'ghettos' is a recent, post-WWII phenomenon."[16] As Noiriel explains:

Each new wave of immigration was translated into the appearance of new "ghettos": in the mines of the Nord and Lorraine, in the Paris region, in the valleys of the Alps and Pyrenees. Some figures illustrate this concentration of foreign manpower: 85% of the immigrants in the department of Loire lived in the arrondissement of St. Etienne in 1930; three quarters of those counted in Meurthe-et-Moselle worked in the arrondissement of Briey; two thirds of the immigrants in Moselle lived in three arrondissements in Thionville and Metz; 90% of the Armenians in the Drôme lived in Valence, etc. At the national level, 1700 [of more than 36,000] communes had a foreign population that approached or exceeded that of the [native] French population during the 1930s.[17]

These concentrations (both industrial and geographic—see table 2.3 above) have been attributed largely to the pattern of state intervention that had begun before WWI—recruitment of groups of immigrant workers from the same areas, who would then be transferred to the same area of France, mostly doing the same work. One consequence of this way of organizing immigration was that there would be high concentrations of immigrants with similar backgrounds and collective identities installed throughout the country, in places where labor was in short supply, and in occupations that native French workers were less willing to fill. Moreover, the way that they were recruited tended to maximize the collective identity of these workers once they arrived in France.

By the post-WWII period—by all accounts—these workers had been integrated into French political and social life. The question is what impact this process had on French political life. Some studies have indicated, for example, that the dynamics of the process of integration of each wave of immigration modified the occupational, geographic, and political structure of the French working class in a somewhat different way.[18] One author has argued that, because of different cultural inclinations of various waves of immigrants, immigration seems to have strengthened the French Communist Party until the 1950s, while it has weakened the party since then.

> We would argue that immigration, by pure ethnological accident, reinforced the Communist Party during the years 1930–1950, and weakened it, within the working class world, during the sixties and seventies.... Each of these groups influenced... the global ideological evolution of the French working class: no immigration is purely passive.[19]

We will look at this question in greater depth in the next chapter. For the moment, it is sufficient to note that the pattern of immigration between the wars was molded by public policy, and it then had an impact on political life in the post-WWII world.

Immigration From Outside Europe

In many ways, nothing much changed after WWII. After a bruising debate within the provisional government, *two ordinances in 1945* established the framework for postwar immigration: conditions of entry and stay; and citizenship and naturalization. After considerable infighting within the government between population demographers and labor-manpower advocates, the first ordinance finally excluded all reference to selection of manpower on the basis of national origin and established rules for entry and *séjour* in France for longer than three months. The second essentially reestablished the naturalization requirements of the law of 1927.[20] Perhaps most important, work permits and residency permits were entirely separate, making it possible for immigrants to remain in France even if they were not employed.

Meeting Labor Market Needs

In principle, French immigration policy after WWII was based on the same problem of labor market needs as it was before the war. It also reflected many of the same concerns as the previous period. Despite the rejection of national origin criteria, the French administration—the demographers in particular—continued to be concerned with the balance between workers arriving from other countries in Europe and those from North Africa, still considered to be the least desirable recruits.

Essentially, the problem seemed to be that the framework that was established in 1945, with the Office National d'Immigration (ONI) at the center of recruitment, failed to provide manpower sufficient for the demands of the French economy. Part of the breakdown appeared to be related to competing ministerial rules and objectives, as well as to the fragility of the infrastructure for receiving large numbers of immigrants, but there were other reasons as well.

After Algerian Muslims gained both French citizenship and free movement in mainland France in 1946 and 1947,[21] there was a surge in immigration from Algeria. In 1946, there were only 22,000 Algerians in France, a mere 1.3 percent of the total number of residents in France from outside of the mainland France, and less than half the total number of North Africans in the country. By 1954, the number had increased to almost 212,000, 13 percent of the number of immigrants (including Algerians), and over 90 percent of the North Africans then in France. It was during this period of strong economic growth, between 1956 and 1962 in France and in Europe, that the French government encouraged immigrants from other parts of Europe to enter the country. This effort was often organized by private employers, and then officially recognized by the state. By the 1960s, perhaps 90 percent of immigration was processed in this way.

That would not last, however, as the economic growth of Western Europe spread to those countries that had supplied the workers to balance those from North Africa. Ultimately, the "internal migration" from North Africa became a foreign migration as decolonization progressed; and the "foreign migration" from Western Europe became linked to the process of European unification and therefore quasi-internal. Nevertheless, the trend that had begun after the war was not seriously altered by decolonization. Immigration from North Africa continued to grow, relative to that of Europe, while immigration from Western Europe grew less rapidly. Italians were replaced by Spanish, and Spanish by Portuguese, and then Portuguese by North Africans. Nevertheless, recruitment efforts in Europe were not entirely unsuccessful.

Beyond considerations of integration into French society, there were also growing concerns about the social costs of immigration. Public officials were concerned about housing shortages in particular, as well as increasing militancy of immigrant workers in the workplace at a time when economic growth was slowing down. Strong efforts to recruit European (and even Turkish) workers, rather than Algerian, reflected both the preferences of employers as well as those of the French administration. During the period after the Evian Accords were signed in 1962, the French and Algerian governments were in constant negotiations over the number of Algerian workers who would be permitted to enter France, with the French trying to reduce the number, and the Algerians trying to increase it. By contrast, during this same period France signed labor recruitment agreements with 16 different countries, with an increasing emphasis on the recruitment of Portuguese.[22] These preferences reflected concerns that had been widespread within the administration since the balance of immigration began to change in the 1960s.

Among the immigrants from the Maghreb, French administrative authorities were particularly concerned about those from Algeria. At the same time that Moroccans and Tunisians had more or less free access to France—and were also given beneficial labor contracts—the French government negotiated agreements with Algeria, in 1964 and 1968, to limit by quotas the entry of Algerian nationals. These agreements were clarified in 1970 by French legislation (that specifically targeted Algerians), and the quotas were reduced by a third agreement in 1972.[23]

Policy Reversal and Immigration Restriction

Unlike Britain and the United States, the French government reversed policy and imposed immigration restriction by administrative action, rather than through legislation: the *circulaires* issued by the Secretary of State for Immigrant Workers on July 5 and 19, 1974. The suspension of labor and family migration took place in July 1974 during the early days of the economic crisis, and from this point of view appears to be a straightforward reaction to the change in labor-market needs. However, the decision was, in fact, far more complicated, and the consequences not at all what policy-makers had anticipated.

The economic and world crisis in 1973–1974—together with a new president and prime minister in France in May 1974—facilitated an action by the government, action that was only partially related to the economy and to labor-market needs. As we shall see in chapter 4, at least as important was the long-standing policy to favor European over North African labor, as well as growing concerns about the broader social impact of large-scale immigration.

At the moment that immigration was suspended, the majority of resident immigrants in the country were still European. In principle, the immigrant population of the country should have stabilized at about 6.5 percent of the population, with about 60 percent of these from Europe (although a lower percentage from the EC, since Portugal was not a member of the EC at the time). In fact, the immigrant percentage of the population did stabilize (and diminished after 1982), but the composition of that population changed radically over the next 25 years.

Unanticipated Consequences

Given the intention of policy decisions that were taken between 1974 and 1977, it is striking that presumably unintended consequences were so profound. The most significant result of the movement toward exclusion was the conversion of an immigrant worker population into a settler population, specifically among those immigrants who were deemed to be the least desirable. Thus, although EC immigrants continued to have the right to cross more or less freely into France, the proportion of these immigrants declined relative to those from outside of the EC. (See table 2.4.)

In addition, because the suspension of family unification was reversed by subsequent administrative *circulaires* and court decisions, the proportion of women to men among non-European immigrants substantially increased by 1982, and then gradually increased to levels approximating those of immigrants from the EC. Another indication of the movement toward settlement has been the growing proportion of children of immigrants (0–14 years of age) in the population.[24]

In the years immediately after the suspension of immigration, the level of immigration dropped rapidly; this was an indication of the ability of the French State to impose a policy decision. (See table 2.5.) It did not stop, however. By the 1980s, the annual level of permanent immigration fell to about half of what it was before 1974, and the largest component became, and remained, family unification, with the number of resident workers about half that of the number of family members. The absolute number of family members arriving had begun to rise significantly after 1968, and then fell slightly after 1974, but the proportion rose dramatically after that.

By the 1980s, the number of family members arriving each year began to drop, although it remained by far the largest proportion of the immigrants arriving each year. Then, after 1993, both the absolute number of family members, as well as the proportion, dropped as well, this time a reflection of policy changes that are described below.

Table 2.4 The changing pattern of immigrant populations resident in France, 1975–1999 (thousands, unless indicated)

	1975	1982	1990	1999
Total # of Foreigners	3,440	3,680	3,580	3,263
—*born in France*	670	830	740	510
—*born outside France*	2,770	2,850	2,840	2,754
Foreigners from EC	1,870	1,580	1,300	1,196
—*ratio of women/men*	82	84	88	88[a]
Foreigners from outside EC	1,570	2,100	2,280	2,068
—*ratio of women/men*	43	61	73	88[a]
Ratio of EC migrants to non-EC migrants	119	75	57	37
Percent of immigrant population in labor force	45%	40%	43%	48%

Note:
a Average for all immigrants.

Sources: INSEE, Census for each year; Annual labor-force survey.

Table 2.5 The flow of foreigners into France, 1974–1999

Year	Immigrants For Family Unification	Total immigration*	% Immigration for Family Unification
1974	68,038	1,32,499	51.3
1975	51,824	67,415	76.9
1976	57,337	84,286	68.0
1977	52,318	75,074	69.7
1978	40,123	58,479	68.6
1979	39,300	56,685	69.3
1980	42,020	59,390	70.8
1981	41,589	75,022	55.4
1982	47,396	1,44,358	32.8
1983	45,767	64,250	71.2
1984	39,621	51,425	77.0
1985	32,545	43,504	74.8
1986	27,140	38,378	70.7
1987	26,769	39,000	68.6
1988	29,385	42,939	68.4
1989	34,594	53,240	65.0
1990	36,949	63,149	58.5
1991	35,625	65,307	54.6
1992	32,665	78,839	41.4
1993	32,435	60,867	53.3
1997	31,000	80,900	38.4
1998	38,300	1,16,900	32.7
1999	38,200	86,300	44.3

Note:

a Does not include additional estimates made by the Ministry of the Interior.

Source: 1974–1993: OMIstats; 1996–99 SOPEMI, *Trends in International Migration, 2002* (Paris: OECD, 2003), p. 175.

Immigration Control: The Search for Consensus

Most scholars have argued that, for at least a decade after the suspension of immigration in 1974, French policy-makers on both the Left and the Right struggled to find a set of policies around which they could build a consensus, similar to that reached in the United Kingdom and the United States during the 1960s. In general, this represented an attempt to create better conditions for integrating those immigrants who were already in the country, while blocking further immigration, at least after 1977. However the attempt to differentiate between immigration control and integration proved to be somewhat elusive, particularly as the political competition between Right and Left sharpened during the 1970s.

Only two pieces of legislation were debated or passed between 1974 and 1981, the year that the Left arrived in power for the first time during the Fifth Republic. The most important and durable of the two had little to do with immigration control. During the 1970s immigrant workers gained more or less full access to trade union rights. Legislation passed by governments of the Right in 1972 and 1975 granted immigrants the right to vote in "social" elections for shop stewards, union representatives and plant committees. The 1975 legislation, moreover, permitted them to stand for election and to hold office in trade unions themselves, provided that they were able to "express themselves" in French and had worked in France for at least five years.[25] Paul Dijoud (Giscard's secretary of state for immigration) referred to the new legislation as a "confirmation of the government's dedication to assuring the equality of social rights between foreign and French workers."[26]

The second law, the loi Bonnet, passed in 1980 during the last year of the Center-Right government, was a result of the sharp change in policy that took place in 1977, when the ambivalence about the suspension of immigration disappeared in the aftermath of the 1977 municipal elections that marked a significant breakthrough for the Socialist and Communist popular front agreements. Although the government coalition at the national level remained in power, Paul Dijoud was replaced by Lionel Stoléru as secretary of state for immigration. Dijoud had been ambivalent about the need for continued immigration, but Stoléru—who was more sensitive to the implications of the deepening economic crisis, and the sharpening political contest with the Left—was firmly opposed to revising the exclusionary policy of 1974.

This shift in policy first became evident in September 1977, when family reunification was suspended for three years, a decision reversed a few months later after a negative opinion by the Council of State.[27] However, after the victory in the parliamentary elections of 1978, the otherwise deeply divided Right (divided between the increasing militant RPR/Gaullists led by Jacques Chirac, and President Giscard d'Estaing's centrist—UDF) could agree on linking the growing unemployment issue to the presence of immigrants in the workforce. In this context, the government sought to encourage immigrants legally in residence to return home, first through simple encouragement, and then by using various means (the possibility of using the quota law of 1932, for example), including payment of thousands of francs and bilateral agreements, to create pressure for the return of "...hundreds of thousands of foreigners selected by nationality, spread out over five years." Although the government spoke of a broad range of targets, in fact, Patrick Weil has argued:

> ...it seems explicit, in the documents that we have consulted, that Algeria constituted the priority target of the French government for several reasons.
>
> —in the first place, the Algerian community of 800, 000 was the largest of the three states of the Maghreb. The realization of the quantitative objectives of return would therefore be easier....

—The trade union involvement of the Algerians was particularly badly accepted by certain French employers.

—The Algerian community, for historic and symbolic reasons, raised the most passionate reactions on the part of those who oppose the presence of foreigners in France. Therefore, the departure of even a part of this community could therefore contribute to diminishing political, social and cultural tensions.

—Finally, the Algerian state seems to be the only one of the three maghreban states to have a structure capable...of organizing the return of a part of their émigré community with effectiveness.[28]

Publicly, Stoléru wrote in June 1979 that "[a] good policy of immigration must be the result of a triple effort [which consists of] preventing all new immigration, encouraging every voluntary departure [and] to adapting renewals [of work permits] to the employment situation."[29] As the discussion continued within the government, however, it became increasingly clear that the objective of proposed new legislation would be a forced return of resident immigrants, with clear objectives each year over a five-year period. In the end, a series of advisory opinions by the Conseil d'État, considerable opposition within the administration, public opposition from trade unions and the Left, and, finally, the public opposition of the RPR, doomed this proposed legislation.

The result was the Loi Bonnet, which tightened entry requirements, but also established rules that made expulsions easier. Not surprisingly, the law became a primary target of the Left, after it gained power in 1981. Although this law gave administrative authorities the right to expel immigrants for a variety of reasons, administration of the law was softened by the Left during its first few years in power, generally by shifting these powers to judicial authorities, and by establishing broader procedural rights. Then in August 1981, the new government declared an amnesty for immigrants who could justify their presence in France—primarily by demonstrating stable employment. All of this was done to firmly establish a difference with the previous policies of the Right that had been strongly opposed by the Left in opposition: "...morally, to repair the 'wrongs' caused to immigrants by the 'Stoléru measures and the Bonnet Law."[30]

On the other hand, the new government passed three measures that confirmed its intention to tighten entry requirements. In October 1981, it increased penalties for employers who hired illegal aliens. Then, a week later it reinforced the conditions for entry that had been established under the Bonnet Law. Finally, in October 1984, the government tightened requirements for family reunification, and reinforced its program for voluntary repatriation.[31]

By 1984, although the gap between Right and Left on how to approach immigration policy seemed to be wide, with considerable bitterness on both sides, there were areas of agreement and common assumptions: there was no serious discussion about reopening the frontier; there was no longer discussion about forced expulsions; nevertheless, both Right and Left were committed to limiting entries and expelling those immigrants who were in the country illegally; finally, there was an emerging understanding that immigrants constituted settler communities, and there were efforts on both sides to assuage the social impact of settlement. Indeed, expulsions would continue under the Left, as would a steady flow of immigrants each year, including immigrant workers (generally about 25% of the total), and family reunification.

Moreover, by 1984 it appeared that both government and opposition were prepared to reach a general understanding about the direction of public policy that Patrick Weil has called a major reference point, "the new republican synthesis" built around a ten-year visa, which, like the American "Green Card" would reduce the movement of immigrants on short-term visas who move from legality to illegality, simply by overstaying their visa limits. The new law, passed in July 1984, created a single residency permit, in place of what had been separate residency and work permits, that also permitted the holder to work anywhere in France. Moreover the ten-year card was automatically renewable, unless it was challenged by the authorities. The law was voted unanimously by the National Assembly.

By the late 1980s there would be little difference between the Right and the Left in terms of actions to maintain the frontier (see below). Both would tend to merge considerations of asylum with the control of entry into the country, and both would systematically reject the vast majority of asylum applications, and would use roundups of immigrants, on the pretext that they were in the country illegally, as a means of intimidation.

Convergence of Policy/Polarization of Politics

The general agreement on the outlines of policy, however, did not at all mean that the rhetoric and portrayal of policy would converge. Although policy itself appeared to be converging, immigration politics after 1984 became less about the struggle over policy, than about politics—the struggle by established political parties on both the Right and the Left to undermine the ability of the National Front to sustain the initiative in defining these issues.

Certainly, part of this effort was for the Right in power to pass high-profile legislation that appeared to tighten already restrictive entry requirements, and for the Left in power, to ease these requirements, while maintaining almost equally restrictive regulations. This resulted in the legislation of 1986 for the Right, that made expulsions easier, and 1989 for the Left, that made them somewhat more difficult. During the election campaign of 1993, the platform of the Right coalition had announced that the new government would pass new, more restrictive legislation that would deal with integration and citizenship.

The new 1993 legislation, presented the year that the Right regained its majority in the National Assembly—the Loi Pasqua—modified the nationality code to make it more difficult for children born in France of non-French parents to obtain French citizenship,[32] resuscitated proposals that gave mayors the right to block family reunification, and facilitated the jailing and expulsion of undocumented foreigners. In addition, the 80 percent majority for the Right in the National Assembly permitted the government to amend the constitution, and to severely restrict asylum applications.[33]

The legislation passed under the stewardship of minister of the interior, Jean-Louis Debré (the Loi Debré) for the Right in 1997, is a good illustration of the short-term and utilitarian role that such legislation was playing during this period. The movement of *sans papiers* (undocumented immigrants) in early 1997, immigrants mostly from West Africa who had been in France for many years, but who were unable to regularize their presence, had raised considerable emotion and support within the Left. The government reacted by passing legislation that would make it impossible for most of the protesters to regularize their status. The law required ten years of residence for children under the age of 16, and a foreign spouse to be in residence for a minimum of two years before they could be eligible for French citizenship. The proposal also required French residents and citizens to notify authorities when they received a non-EU citizen as a guest, and mayors were given extensive powers to regulate the presence of non-French guests in their communes. Perhaps most troubling, the legislation specifically exempted nationals of 30 countries, which specifically left African countries as its target. Although various parts of the proposal were modified and softened during the debate, the debate itself strengthened the tough, exclusionary credentials of the government.[34]

Then, the Left won a surprise victory in the snap legislative elections called by Chirac in 1997, but much of the talk was of the impressive electoral showing of the National Front. In one of his first moves, the new prime minister, Lionel Jospin, announced that he would appoint a commission to study the broad question of immigration legislation, and that he would then quickly decide on what action to take with regard to new legislation on immigration and citizenship.

Within a month of its appointment, the commission issued its report, and recommended that the government try a bold new approach to the immigration issue: to accept with modifications the changes in immigration and naturalization legislation that had been made by the Right since 1993, and to develop an explicit centrist approach that would tend toward consensus and would isolate the National Front.[35]

This centrist approach was rejected by the opposition, and created emotional divisions within the Left as well. Nevertheless, in the debate on the immigration and naturalization proposals by the minister of the interior, considerations of how these bills would relate to the strength of the FN were frequently explicit, and never far below the surface.[36] The spurt of support for the FN in the regional elections of 1998 indicated that in the short-run these efforts were unsuccessful, although the split in the party a few months later seemed to ease the pressure on policy-makers, at least until the shock of the presidential election of 2002. (See ch. 4.)

The 1998 legislation—under a government of the Left—that emanated from the Weil report of 1997, a law on naturalization and a second that modified but did not reject the laws passed in 1993 and 1997, was strongly opposed by the Right opposition as too weak, and by the Left as a betrayal. In fact, the Loi Chevénement changed relatively little. It tightened visa requirements, while easing the conditions for family visits; it somewhat softened requirements for family reunification and removed humiliating requirements for marriage between a French national and a foreigner; but it also increased the number of days that an illegal immigrant could be confined before action on expulsion was taken. In fact, the new legislation was a continuation of the same narrow range of policies that had been developed since the 1980s. In retrospect, the most innovative change in the law was the provision that created a new category of temporary visa for scholars and scientists. Administrative measures later in 1998 also eased entry for computer experts and highly skilled temporary workers, who could then apply for family unification after a year.

However, the parliamentary debate on the legislation reflected far more bitterness than the proposals would indicate. The legislative process, as it had in the recent past, gave both the government and the opposition an opportunity to reinforce their credentials as having a certain kind of toughness on immigration. Although Chevénement claimed to maintain toughness with "humanitarian flexibility," the Right opposition argued that these changes were "irresponsible," and would lead to "profound destabilization of French society". Just before the vote, Jean-Louis Debré complimented his colleagues on the Right for having "... forced the government to emerge from its ambiguity on immigration." While the RPR/ UDF voted unanimously against the Loi Chevénement, the Communists and the Greens (part of the governing coalition) abstained.[37]

So, the accidental victory of the Right in 2002 gave them an opportunity to develop additional credentials before the new cycle of elections began in 2004, not by developing a new approach to immigration, but by somewhat toughening the stipulations of the legislation passed in 1998. The most controversial article of the new legislation increased from 12 to up to 32 days the amount of time that a foreigner without proper papers could be detained before being "escorted to the frontier" or set free. Other parts of the law effectively reinstated the parts of the Pasqua and Debré laws that had been modified in 1998. The law gave power to mayors to refuse entry to visitors from abroad, and required visa applications for applicants from a select group of countries. The new legislation increases from three to five years the waiting period for application for a ten-year *titre de séjour,* as well as proof of "good integration." Similar criteria were applied to applicants for family reunification, further narrowing the fragile right established by the courts. Finally, the law once again adopted many of the strict and often humiliating controls on marriage with a foreign spouse that had been removed by the 1998 law.

The relationship between the 2003 Sarkozy law and those of Pasqua and Debré was alluded to in the consideration of the law by the Constitutional Council. The Council noted that the restored power of mayors had generally worked well between 1993 and 1997, although extended detainments were consistent with practice in other European countries. Thus, the Council, in its consideration of the new law, ruled that it was generally consistent with both past practice and European norms, but struck down the additional burdens imposed for marriage to a foreigner, as well as additional burdens imposed on those with whom visiting foreigners would be living.[38]

Of course, every small change in legislation on immigration has an impact on the fate of those who seek to enter France. Nevertheless, the trend seems clear. Each new government passes legislation that hardens or softens aspects of immigration control, but the commitment to specific forms of control remains firm. At the same time, each government tends to accentuate its policy differences, rather than the similarities, with the majority that preceded it. Despite the recommendations of Patrick Weil, as well as the several attempts (principally by the Left) to reach a working consensus on immigration policy, each government of the Right has tightened existing requirements for entering the country, and facilitated the ability of the state to exclude unwanted foreigners; while each government of the Left has created more extensive judicial oversight over the administration of entry, as well as exclusion.

The narrowness of the legislative changes is in no way reflected in the political debate each time that the legislation is altered, however. As in 1998, the political debate in 2003 was often bitter and hard, and masked the continuing determination by governments of both Right and Left to maintain the frontier, particularly against immigration from Africa. Although the conditions for granting visas to Algerians were somewhat eased in 1998 by the Left, they remained difficult to meet for large numbers of people seeking visas, according to a parliamentary report in 1999.[39] Despite the groundbreaking trip to Algeria by President Jacques Chirac in March 2003, the government remained determined to develop the tightened requirements for visas contained in the 2003 legislation. Thus, once again the debate tended to accentuate the differences between government and opposition over legislation that only modestly modified what already existed.

Thus, France continued to mold a policy of immigration control that was basically one of exclusion, at a time when its own technical reports, as well as reports on the EU level were indicating that France and Europe would need more, rather than fewer immigrants.[40] Indeed, despite the steps quietly taken in 1998, French policy seemed to be increasingly out of step both with its own needs, as well the trends within the European Union, as both Germany and Britain altered their policies to attract skilled workers.

The first tentative steps to reformulate the French view of immigration came in 2006, which moved away from the idea that legal immigration should be terminated, and instead attempted to refocus on more acceptable forms of immigration ("immigration choisie"). The initiative was an extension of the Socialist program of 1998. (See ch. 4). Nevertheless, the 2006 legislation was bitterly opposed by the Socialist opposition, primarily because of the new restrictions that it imposed on family unification and on immigrants already in the country. The law repealed a key section of the 1998 Chevénement law that granted amnesty to illegal immigrants who had been settled in France for ten years, and replaced it with provisions that authorized the government to examine such requests on a case-by-case basis. It also made mandatory for a residency permit that applicants adhere to the CAI ("Welcome and Integration") contract. The contract, which had been initiated as a voluntary program few years before, required parents of children entering France under family unification to take courses on the rights and duties of parents in France.

A year later, after the elections of 2007, the Loi Hortefeux represented the centerpiece of a reorientation of French immigration law. On one hand, the law took some steps to ease integration, and the government announced its intention to "organize economic immigration." For the first time, France established an unlimited residence card to replace the existing ten-year card. In addition, the government announced special provisions that would make it more attractive for professionals and high-end workers to work and settle in France.[41]

On the other hand, family unification became more difficult and more demanding. The CAI became a real contract with sanctions for violation, and those applying for family unification were required to take two-month courses that constituted "an evaluation of language ability and the values of the Republic" in their home countries. The law reduced the time of appeal for those refused asylum to 48 hours, and confirmed that undocumented workers could be regularized only under exceptional circumstances. One of those exemptions would be employment in a profession or an area "characterized by difficulty in recruitment."[42] At the same time the government took steps to increase the pressure on prefects to act against undocumented immigration to meet a stated goal of 25,000 per year.[43]

Immigration Policy: France and Europe

Considerations of French immigration policy are increasingly related to interactions within the EU. Although there is no common immigration policy at the European level, the ability of France to enforce its own policies of exclusion have been enhanced by cooperation among ministries of

justice and home affairs. The arena of policy development within the EU
was and remains relatively protected space, space chosen by ministries of
the interior and justice to avoid many of the national constraints that had
become evident by the 1980s. Therefore, the emphasis on exclusion and
restriction—the "securitization" of immigration policy at the EU level—is
no accident, and directly reflects the preferences of the ministries that control the process and their ability to dominate institutional space. Virginie
Guiraudon, in a comprehensive analysis of the study of the development
of this arena, presents a useful and important way of approaching policymaking at the EU level. She links national and EU politics by analyzing
the movement of the immigration issue to the EU level as initiated by key
national ministries in search of an arena within which they could gain
control over a more autonomous arena of action.

During the 1980s, units of ministries of justice and interior were
increasingly constrained by domestic forces from carrying out policies of
immigration restriction. Court decisions prevented wholesale restriction
of family unification, and made expulsions far more difficult to imple-
ment. They also confronted conflicts with bureaucracies charged with
integration of immigrants already in the country.

> The incentive to seek new policy venues sheltered from national
> legal constraints and conflicting policy goals thus dates from the
> turn of the 1980s decade. It thus accounts for the timing of trans-
> governmental cooperation on migration but also for its character:
> an emphasis on non-binding decisions or soft law and secretive and
> flexible arrangements. The idea is not to create an "international
> regime," i.e. a constraining set of rules with monitoring mechanisms
> but rather to avoid domestic legal constraints and scrutiny.[44]

She describes how justice and interior ministry civil servants gained
monopoly control over the implementation of the Schengen accord
between 1985 and 1990, primarily by defining priorities that linked
immigration to combat against transnational crime.

Although the establishment of the High-Level Working Group on
immigration (1998) resulted in pressures for a more substantial cross-pillar
approach to immigration, which would effectively integrate the interests
of foreign affairs into the mix, Guiraudon argues that the dominant influence is still that of justice and home affairs. As Dietman Herz has noted,
the agenda for decision making by the Council of Ministers on migration affairs is prepared by the Committee of Permanent Representatives
(COREPER), for which the working groups are dominated by civil servants from national ministries of the interior, with participation of staff
from foreign affairs ministries only at the full COREPER meetings.
Perhaps more to the point, the working groups reflect the concerns of
ministries of the interior, and "officials concerned with regular immigration are as yet seldom involved in networks of dense intergovernmental

cooperation."[45] Pro-immigrant NGOs that have battled for access to the decision-making framework of the EU have been forced to seek a different decision-making arena—the rights-oriented framework of "social exclusion." This framework may very well benefit migrants already in the EU, but will have little impact on immigration into the EU.[46]

Nevertheless, it is now becoming clearer that an important challenge to the security framework is the growing need for immigrant labor in specific sectors of the economy, as well as the benefits of this kind of labor for the deficits of the welfare state. Although it is difficult to raise this issue at the national level because of the challenge of the extreme Right in a number of European countries,[47] it may be easier to deal with within an arena of the EU.[48] However, at least for the moment, security concerns appear to have overwhelmed any tentative move in that direction. The European Council of Seville, in June 2002 (immediately after the Le Pen breakthrough in the French presidential elections), refocused on control of illegal migration as a top EU priority. Moreover, as Herz points out, the report of the Working Group of the European Convention that dealt with immigration emphasized that need for immigration policy to remain under the control of member states.[49]

The key indication of the failure of immigration policy to take off at the European level, however, is that no structure has been established that would provide policy-makers with a framework for cooperation, no doubt because national policy-makers are not seeking a more expansive policy within a European framework. One minor exception to this conclusion are the periodic meetings of ministers of the interior of the six largest EU countries (the G6), which have met on security issues, and, more recently on questions of immigrant integration. In March 2006, the G6 initiated discussions among the larger group of EU interior ministers about the development of an EU policy on civic integration contracts for immigrants entering the EU.[50]

Conclusion: Immigration and Policy in France

Immigration policy in France was first codified in law at the end of the nineteenth century, and presents us with some interesting analytical puzzles. Until the most recent period, immigration policy in France was—broadly speaking—a policy of manpower recruitment: recruitment for the armed forces; and, increasingly, recruitment of labor for an expanding economy. Particularly before WWI, French governments were concerned with the lack of growth in the French population. Among the emerging industrial powers of Europe, France was alone in experiencing a declining fertility rate during the latter half of the nineteenth century. As the labor historian Gary Cross notes, this decline was generally seen to have been brought about by deliberate restraint and birth-control (some conservatives characterized this as the "grève des ventres"—the strike of the bellies). Moreover, in contrast to other Europeans, French workers tended not to migrate to where labor was needed, and they tended to avoid difficult and socially unacceptable jobs.[51] Indeed, at the end of the nineteenth century, French workers were being described in much the same way they are sometimes described today:

> The French seldom are willing to be simple laborers or street sweepers, to do certain of the exhausting or painful jobs in the textile mills of the north, in the refineries or olive oil processing plants of the south...Belgians, Italians, and sometimes Germans are needed for all the infinite and essential tasks of civilization. The French people have become a kind of aristocracy among the more primitive peoples of Europe.[52]

Thus, by the end of the nineteenth century, individual decisions by French workers had become a collective demographic choice with policy consequences. Policy choices that would expand the labor market, however, were not necessarily clear, nor was there any single approach developed within the political system.[53]

Ultimately, business interests focused on short-term expansion of the labor market through more open and aggressive immigration policies, but here too the struggle about how to increase immigration was intense. At the end of the nineteenth century legislation was passed to control immigration that had grown since the end of the Second Empire. France passed its first legislation on immigration control in 1889, roughly during the same time period as other European countries and the United States, though not to limit immigration, but to define and control it.

In the twentieth century, particularly after WWI, policy became more active, and focused more closely on the recruitment of labor. Settlement then became a consequence of these policies. Policy orientations were rarely consensual. For example, there was a constant tension between recruitment of immigrants for labor needs, with the idea that this recruitment would vary with the requirements of the labor market, and recruitment for perceived population needs, and therefore would be permanent. Of course, the need represented by these two orientations was linked to the declining birthrate, but the consequences were different. Perceived national needs have also clashed with a racialized vision of national identity. Although the general perspective offered by Rogers Brubaker, that "...the French understanding of nationhood has been state-centered and assimilationist..."[54] is generally true, the immigration debate reflected a strong undercurrent of ethnocultural nationalism.

This tension continued after WWII, but the overwhelming need for labor, at least until the economic crisis of the 1970s, continued to dominate any movement toward exclusion or selection. However, the economic crisis made it possible for considerations of identity and integration to gain ascendance over a need for labor. Although the suspension of immigration in 1974 did not in fact mean an end to immigration, it did mean a movement toward selection and selective exclusion. Although this general movement has been accepted by both the political Right and the political Left, conflict over immigration policy has grown as the political salience of this issue has grown. Thus, as the proportion of foreigners in the country has diminished, the salience of political conflict over foreigners has increased.

The importance of the politics of immigration has been driven by the rise of the National Front, which in turn has both defined the immigration issue as is central theme and its warhorse against the established parties of the Right and Left. The electoral success of FN, and the challenge that represents for all of the established political parties, has made any political consensus on immigration almost impossible to achieve.

Finally, the harmonization of immigration policy has been on the agenda at the European level since 1999. However, the intergovernmental consultations and collaboration around this issue have been dominated by the security concerns of the ministries of interior and justice. Within Europe, these ministries have found a relatively protected arena within which they can develop a thick network of cooperation without being challenged either by governmental opposition or groups that are generally more sympathetic to the needs and concerns of immigrants. Thus, actions at the EU level generally tend to support the more exclusionary policies developed since the 1970s.

CHAPTER THREE

Understanding French Immigration Policy

In this chapter, we examine immigration policy in France from the perspective of the four issues that we analyzed in chapter 1, issues that have concerned scholars and that have frequently concerned policy-makers: why people migrate; control over frontiers; the impact of immigration; and questions of integration and incorporation We will look at how these questions of immigration have been looked at by policy-makers, and how scholars have understood the importance of these policies in France. Then, in the following chapter, we will look more specifically at the politics of immigration in terms of agenda setting, institutionalization and change.

One of the most striking findings in this chapter is that, while scholars and policy-makers have often been concerned with the same issues, they have approached them in different ways. Thus, control over the frontier has been a concern of both, but in different ways. For scholars, frontier control is very much related to the evolving nature of the state, and its continued importance as a political actor. Policy-makers are far more concerned with how they can use the instruments of the state to achieve specific goals—in this case, keeping unwanted immigrants out. For questions of integration, scholars have focused on different models of integration, as well as different patterns of national identity. Policy-makers, however, have been most concerned with integration issues when they have been related to the maintenance of social order, and when they have been able to use integration issues as a means of mobilizing electoral support.

Why Do People Migrate—The Relationship to Public Policy

For more than a 150 years, France was a country of immigration in the sense that formal policies and the behavior of administrative authorities encouraged migration. Indeed, between the wars, and during the 1960s, employers of immigrant labor were encouraged to seek immigrant workers, and French law generally encouraged settlement rather than brief passage on a "guest worker" model. In addition to recruiting immigrants, policy-makers made some effort to encourage those they felt were most desirable, and discourage or exclude those deemed to be least acceptable. As we saw in chapter 2, the tension between recruitment and selection has generally defined French policy since the end of the nineteenth century.

The principal consideration in the legally establishment of *jus solis* in 1889 was to ensure that children of settled immigrants born in France would serve in the French military. The larger impact, however, was to attract family immigration, with less than two-thirds of the immigrant population active in the labor force before WWII.

During the period between the wars, the proactive recruitment of workers through bilateral agreements increased the importance of the "pull" factor, and was the core of a system through which workers were chosen and regulated. In a system in which the demand for labor outstripped the supply, bilateral commissions determined both the number and occupations of workers who would immigrate, with the countries of origin determining where, within each sending country, and among which occupations, recruitment could take place.

As we have seen, even after the depression spread in France between the wars, immigrants continued to arrive to fill jobs in industries and localities in which they were needed. In particular industries, the concentration of immigrants was sufficiently high that, if they were excluded, they could not easily be replaced by native French workers, even if native workers were inclined to take these kinds of jobs.

> As Stephane Wlocewski observed in 1935, 42 percent of the immigrants worked in towns of less than 3000 inhabitants. These workers, in small and often isolated labor markets, could not easily be replaced by natives without great cost and probably greater resistance. Even in Paris, the presumably expendable foreigners were concentrated in trades which could not easily find French applicants...[1]

As we noted in the previous chapter, during the early years of the depression, the government continued to regularize workers who had crossed the frontier to find work on their own, without bothering to go through the official channels.

Thus, between the wars immigrants came because they were sought, and they found settlement in France relatively easy. They continued to arrive, even in hard economic times, generally because they were still needed. This pattern would continue after WWII, but with a new twist, a determined attempt by the French State to balance the free migration from French territories in North Africa with European "Latin-Christian" immigrants. As Vincent Viet concluded:

> During the period that we have just examined, administrative and political authorities strove to attract to France Germans and Italians, while financially encouraging the settlement of their families, in

order to counterbalance Algerian migration. Ultimately, they favored the entry of Spanish and Portuguese. These efforts to attract these kinds of people rested on the prejudice that they were culturally more assimilable than people from North Africa and from countries further away.[2]

Even as French policy appeared to be ad hoc, and the state resorted to frequent regularizations and amnesties, these continuing efforts at ethnic selection were reasonably successful, at least in the short-run. It was only in the 1980s that the number of Portuguese resident immigrants began to fall. Despite widespread perceptions to the contrary, it would not be until the 1982 census that the number of resident European immigrants would be slightly outnumbered by those from Africa and Asia; and not until 1990 that the stock of African (primarily North African) immigrants would absolutely outnumber those from Europe.

By this time, immigrants were arriving in France for reasons that were related to policy, but were different from those of the interwar period. Once immigration was suspended in 1974, the proportion of family members—the major category who could continue to enter the country legally—rose rapidly through the early 1990s (see table 2.5).

What is most striking is that, regardless of the "push" factors that were driving immigration to France during the twentieth century, the "pull" factors of policy generally shaped who arrived. To be sure, some pull factors were not coherently controlled by policy-makers, in particular the private recruitment undertaken during the interwar period and after WWII, as well as the decision by the Council of State to force the state to abandon its plans to limit family unification. Nevertheless, the privatization of recruitment was a policy decision, as was the decision made to regularize undocumented immigrants after the war. At least part of the answer to "why do they come to France" is that it is possible to come, and more possible for some compared to others. On the other hand, why has it not been possible to stop them from coming when that seems to be official policy?

Control over the Frontiers

The ability of France to control its frontiers has been an important issue, both for scholars and for politicians. Arguably, control over the French frontier has been eroded first by the pressures of immigration, both legal and undocumented, second by the constraints imposed by treaty obligations and court decisions, and third by the opening of the internal borders of the Schengen zone countries and by the incorporation of the Schengen agreement of 1985 into the Amsterdam Treaty of 1999. In what sense, then, does France still have a frontier?

I would argue that aspects of embedded liberalism and protections by the legal system can be best understood as a part of the political context that has constrained how the French government controls immigration. Within this context, however, French governments have pursued statist policies that both limit and mold immigration across its frontiers. Governments have become increasingly creative in developing mechanisms of immigration control, most of which have been quite, if not absolutely effective. The overall impact of the development of immigration and asylum rights has been the parallel development of a stronger and more effective state in the area of immigration control.

Indeed, France still has a frontier, although the policing of it may not be simply at frontier crossings. In fact, the formal frontier crossings—the roads and railway border checkpoints—are largely unmanned, and airline flights among the Schengen countries are treated like European domestic flights, without formal passport control. On the other hand, both the external frontier with the non-Schengen world and the internal controls of the non-EU population resident in France has been reinforced substantially. In addition, a significant amount of frontier policing takes place by "remote control,"[3] in countries from which immigrants have come. Finally, rights to immigration (such as family unification) are constantly in flux, and, in significant ways have been reduced.

The impact of decisions taken in 1974 to suspend most categories of immigration was clear, and relatively swift. During the seven years before 1974, an average of 232,000 immigrants entered the country each year. During the seven years after suspension, this average was cut to about 105,000. If we also consider the rates of emigration (much more difficult to know), net immigration moved from an average of 130,000–139,000 to 29,000–40,000 per year.[4] After 1982, net immigration grew to an estimated 65,000 per year, and remained at that level through the last decade of the twentieth century. As one recent report has concluded, "France is certainly an old country of immigration, but for 25 years it is no longer a country of massive immigration."[5] At least by this measure, there was a basic change during the years after the suspension of immigration in 1974.

Much has been made of the decision of the Council of State in 1978 to block the right of the state to limit family unification as the key for understanding the limits inherent in liberal democracy for maintaining the frontier.[6] Indeed, the single largest category of (permanent) immigrants arriving into the country has consisted of various categories of family unifiers, and family unification is generally blamed as the source of unwanted North African immigration (see table 3.1).

However, the role of family unification has been more complicated than is generally acknowledged in the flow of immigration. At least through the mid-1970s, about half of those entering under family unification were Portuguese. Then, after the collapse of fascism in Portugal, this trend quickly slowed to a trickle, accounting for a sharp decrease in family migration (in absolute numbers) during the 1980s and 1990s. Family immigration among North Africans did not increase after 1974, or even after 1978, and diminished during the 1980s (see table 3.1). Nevertheless,

Table 3.1 Immigrants entering France under family unification

	North African (thousands)[a]	Portuguese (thousands)	Total Family Immigration (thousands)	% Family Immigration of total Immigration	North Africans as a percentage of Family Immigrants
1970	12.7	47.0	84.1	—	15%
1971	14.9	46.5	85.5	—	17%
1972	17.3	38.2	79	—	22%
1973	22.2	31.8	78.1	—	28%
1974	23.8	23.4	73.7	51.3%	32%
1975	18.9	18.5	56.1	76.9%	34%
1976	28.8	13.7	63.2	68.0%	46%
1977	26.9	11.0	58.7	69.7%	46%
1978	21.6	7.0	45.7	68.6%	47%
1979	22.0	5.8	45.9	69.3%	48%
1980	24.9	4.9	49.9	70.8%	50%
1981	24.9	4.5	48.7	55.4%	51%
1982	30.0	5.8	56.5	32.8%	53%
1983	26.5	5.8	53.8	71.2%	49%
1984	21.3	4.5	46.9	77.0%	45%
1985	17.0	3.9	38.6	74.8%	44%
1986	15.1	1.6	27.1	70.7%	56%
1987	15.6	0.2	26.7	68.6%	58%
1988	17.4	0.2	29.3	68.4%	59%
1989	21.3	0.1	34.4	65.0%	62%

Note:
a Moroccan generally half or more each year.

Source: ONI and OMIstats.

because of the disappearance of Portuguese immigration, the inflow of family migrants from North Africa (most from Morocco) grew to two-thirds or more of the total of (the now reduced number of) family immigrants by 1990. In this sense it is true that, by 2000, as the proportion of family migrants diminished in general to about 40 percent of total migration (see table 2.5), the steady stream of immigrants from non-European countries were overwhelmingly family members of those already there. In 2001, 70 percent of total third country national (TCN) entrants into France were family members.[7] Therefore, the most that can be said about the Council of State decision in 1978 is that it enabled a steady number of North African family members to enter the country each year.

Probably the best measure that we have of the effectiveness of efforts to control the frontier is the stock of the immigrant population in France since the 1970s. Table 3.2 shows a diminishing immigrant population, as well as a diminishing immigrant population from North Africa, since 1982. The sharpest drop among different immigrant groups has been among Algerians. In 1982, there were more than 800,000 Algerian immigrants in France. This figure dropped to about 478,000 by 1999. About a third of the immigrant population in France is now North African, a proportion which has also been dropping since 1990, and about a third of the entrants each year are North African, although this percentage increased to about 40 percent after 2001[8] (see table 3.2).

In addition to family reunification, the right of asylum, under the European Convention on human rights as well as French law—a right enforced both by French courts and European courts—has been cited as another aspect of frontier control that cannot be easily controlled by the state. Indeed, applications for asylum have generally increased over time, from less than 20,000 in 1981, to over 60,000 in 1989. Within the following decade, applications declined once again to pre-1989 levels, only to increase once again after 1998 to around 50,000 in 2003–2004. At the same time, those requesting asylum changed from predominantly European in the 1970s, to predominantly Asian and African after the 1980s.[9] After 1998, applications for asylum in France increased by more than 50 percent, compared with small decreases in the United Kingdom, Germany, and Italy. In fact, the absolute numbers were even higher than indicated for France because only adults are counted.

Although the administrative structures that were set to deal with these applications were placed under great pressure by these numbers, they were not overwhelmed. In general, the result of increased applications has been

Table 3.2 France: Stock and inflow of North African population

	1964	1972	1982	1990	1999	2001
Total N. African Pop. (*étrangers*)[a]	634,096	1,136,381	1,437,200	1,393,200	1,136,000	1,156,214
Total Imm Population (*étrangers*)[a]	2,214,132	3,705,804	3,714,200	3,596600	3,263,200	3,269,612
% of Imm Population N. African (*étrangers*)[a]	28.64%	30.66%	38.69%	38.74%	34.81%	35.36%
% N African among inflow of immigrants that year	—	—	—	33%	34%	31%[b]

Notes:
a étrangers= noncitizens, residing in France, born abroad or in France.
b 2002.

Source: INSEE census figures and OECD, *Trends in International Migration: SOPEMI 2003* (Paris: OECD Publications, 2004), p. 343.

Table 3.3   Asylum-seekers and recognition rates, 1981–2004

	Number of Applicants	Recognition Rate	Number of Entries as Refugees
1982	19,863	73.9%	14,586
1984	22,350	65.3%	14,314
1987	26,290	32.7%	8,704
1990	61,422	15.4%	8,770
1991	54,813	19.7%	15,467
1999	22,475	22.8%	4,698
2003	52,204	17.0%	9,790

Source: OFPRA.

declining acceptance rates. If we look at table 3.3, we can see that when applications were relatively low in the early 1980s, acceptance rates were well over 65 percent. By the late 1980s, as applications increased, acceptance rates declined to 15 percent, and then climbed somewhat higher as applications declined substantially in the 1990s. Then, acceptance rates declined again as applications increased once again after 1998. Application rates declined once again after 2004, but acceptance rates remained about 18% between 2000 and 2005.[10]

Overall, the actual number of refugees accepted for entry into France is now far lower than it was when there were far fewer applicants in the early 1980s. The number of people residing in France with refugee status was almost halved between 1962 and 1993, while the demands more than tripled.[11] Given the ability of public authorities to adjust acceptance rates to applications, there is every reason to believe that the state is quite capable of controlling this volatile flow.

This leaves us with the question of undocumented or "illegal" immigration. As we shall see, the political question of immigration has focused increasingly on illegal immigrants in France, as it has in the United States. While there are, of course, immigrants who have entered illegally most have entered the country legally, but have overstayed their visas for a variety of reasons. Therefore, there are two dimensions to the status of legality/illegality. The first is the legality of the border-crossing itself. The second is how long the migrant has stayed. As one scholar has emphasized, "An immigrant in a legal situation can fall into illegality from one day to the next. For numerous immigrants, the situation of illegality can represent a temporary phase of the migration cycle, before obtaining a residency permit." This was the case in France in the 1960s, when migrants who had entered the country could legalize their status with a work contract, and has been the case in numerous countries (including France) that have permitted periodic amnesties.[12]

Estimating the number of undocumented migrants in France, or any country, is a formidable task, which always comes with political overtones. The task is complicated by a lack of any good way of knowing how many illegal immigrants have left the country. In addition, government estimates vary with the political climate, and whether it is more politically advantageous to maximize the estimate (to support new budget allocations), or minimize the estimate (to demonstrate the effectiveness of border controls). Nevertheless, by the most recent estimates, in similar political climates, when governments have been responding to charges that they are doing too little, France has one of the lowest rates of illegal immigrants in the OECD. With a claimed estimate of 200,000–400,000 (0.68 percent of the population on the high side), it is considerably lower than that of Britain (550,000, or .92 percent) and far lower than that of the United States (11–12 million, or 3.8 percent).[13] The relatively low proportion of illegal immigrants in France has been attributed—in part—to the fact that illegal immigrants, until 2007, have been able to claim legal residency after ten years in the country. As a result, the number of illegal immigrants who have been legalized under periodic mass amnesties has been far lower than in other countries in Europe. It has also been attributed to the relatively small role that the informal labor market plays in France. "In general, the more a labor market is deregulated," argues François Héron, "the more it attracts irregular migration."[14]

Does this indicate an inability to control the frontier? Of course, it must, at least to a certain extent. However, it is not the frontier that is at issue, since it is widely conceded that the frontier was crossed legally in most cases (90%, according to the Ministry of the Interior), but the ability of the state to keep track of immigrants once they already in the country. In this way, the French capability does not appear to be any worse than it was before the current wave of immigration, and may very well be far better. The agreement to abolish formal border controls within the Schengen area, which went into effect in 1995 in France, does not appear to have diminished French capabilities, and may very well have enhanced them.

Even before the agreement to abolish border controls within the Schengen zone, France began to strengthen its controls at the "external" crossings, particularly at airports, by effectively moving the border to a no-man's land at administrative retention centers. In France, the legal concept of administrative "retention" goes back to 1810; *zones d'attente* (waiting zones) and the *centres de rétention* (detention centers for foreigners waiting to be admitted or deported, where they can be held for up to five days) were created in 1981 and formalized in1992 by socialist governments. In the 1980s there were reported to be seven or eight centers; by 2007 the number had risen to 27.[15]

Some of them already existed in the 1930s or the 1950s, but the newest version was an attempt to prevent asylum-seekers from claiming rights that they would have had once they formally entered French territory, or undocumented immigrants and applicants for asylum whose applications have been refused, but whose cases may be under appeal. Nevertheless, asylum-seekers can be detained for a limit of four days, and then the government must formally bring a request to increase that term before a special judge. In 2001 these requests reached a peak of 12,715, and then fell to 2,400 in 2005. In 2003, 6,765 persons were detained beyond the four-day limit by judge's order, a figure that fell to 2101 in 2005.[16] In part, this fluctuation can be explained by the rise of asylum requests after 1999, and the leveling off of these requests after 2001.

Although advocacy groups have helped to expand the legal recourses available to immigrants and asylum-seekers that have not been permitted to enter French territory, the struggle over rights on either side of a shifting frontier has been ongoing. The conditions in the detention centers under the Left in 2000 were called "the horror of the republic" by a former Socialist minister, and finally opened to surveillance by NGOs by the interior minister, Nicolas Sarkozy, in 2003.[17] For the NGOs that deal with immigration on a daily basis, the conditions maintained in these quasi-prisons seem to be more important than the number of days of permitted detention.[18]

France has also strengthened its control over access to its territory by externalizing many immigration controls to the territory of the sending countries. Thus, most visa applications are wholly process abroad by ministry officials, with variable results. For example, in 2002, 77.3 percent of visa applications in Algiers, 33.7 percent in Bamako, 40 percent in Dakar, and 33.7 percent in Fez were rejected.[19]

In addition, all French governments during the past 25 years have resorted to various forms of expulsion (the most important category of which is "reconduite à la frontière") of those deemed to be in the country illegally. Since the 1980s, the number of expulsions each year has grown somewhat, but the biggest change has been in the number of people who have been detained, but not yet expelled. A major shift in policy took place during Mitterrand's second term, between 1990 and 1991. The number of people detained for expulsion more than tripled, while the percentage of those actually expelled was more than halved. (See Table 3.4) This approach of mass roundups, while expelling about the same number

Table 3.4   Article 22 expulsions ("Reconduites à la frontière")

	Detained for Expulsion	Expelled	Percentage Expelled
1988	8,992	5,863	65.2
1989	7,669	4,808	62,7
1990	9,641	4,567	47.4
1991	32,673	5,867	18.0
2000	36,614	6,592	18.0
2001	37,307	6,161	16.5
2002	42,495	7,611	17.9
2003	49,017	9,352	19.1

Source: Ministry of the Interior, Fichier GASCH3, A. Lebon, *Situation de l'immigration et présence étrangère en France* (Paris: La Documentation Française, décembre 1994); *Rapport de l'Haute Commission à l'Intégration 2002–2003* (la Documentation Française, 2004), p. 44.

of people, has created the impression of greater effectiveness, even if the constraints on actual expulsions have remained the same.

Nevertheless, even if the process remains dubious from a legal perspective, France annually expels more than ten percent of the estimated illegal arrivals. In 2006 Minister of the Interior Sarkozy announced that 20,000 people had been expelled in 2005, double the announced number 2003, and 27 percent more than in 2004. The announcement noted that this was the highest number ever expelled, and also announced a goal of 26,000 for 2006. Certainly, this well-publicized statement was meant to support the emerging presidential campaign for the minister of the interior, but it also demonstrates the ability of the ministry to actually increase expulsions, even with the legal and political constraints in place.[20]

Finally, to strengthen its ability to deal with illegal immigration, the Ministry of the Interior created in 1999 a coordinated police unit to control the frontier: the Central Directorate of the Frontier Police (DCPAF). Although the actual number of police was increased only modestly after 1999 (from about 5,000 to about 5,500, out of a total of 7,327 personnel), the largest increase was in police "walking a beat." Almost half the PAF are posted at airports, with another 30 percent at land posts and maritime ports.[21] However, the concept of "the frontier" has been changing. In 2000, the PAF was reorganized to give it a greater role in neighborhood policing ("police à proximité").

> ... its involvement in urban settings, in the struggle against channels of illegal immigration, as well as its active participation in the removal of foreigners in an irregular situation have led the DCPAF to evolve in a context of growing needs linked to its European commitments, to deal with a strong thrust of irregular immigration, as well as a significant growth of asylum seekers.[22]

Thus, by 2005, the role of the frontier police had changed considerably. It was embedded within a larger Europe, on one hand, but coordinated with the police in urban neighborhoods on the other.

Impact

Public Opinion

One way the impact of immigration can be understood is through public opinion. In general, public opinion, cross-nationally, has been less favorable to new immigrants and increasingly favorable to immigrant groups over time. A certain level of opposition to immigration has been widespread in public opinion for most of the Fifth Republic, although there are indications that the intensity of opposition varies strongly by age. (See table 1.2.) The French public has also consistently differentiated among immigrants from different countries. During the period of postwar intra-European immigration, between 1949 and 1965 "...opposition to immigration remained relatively restrained. Poll results even suggest that enthusiasm for immigration even grew modestly...." However, "French xenophobes seem[ed] more likely to have targeted nonethnic-European immigrants from 1946–1973," and, as patterns began to shift toward higher levels of immigration from the Maghreb, opposition also grew.[23]

During the decade before the 1983 electoral breakthrough of the National Front, public attitudes toward immigrants from North Africa were far different from those toward other immigrant groups—so much so, that these immigrants were clearly set apart. Surveys, beginning in the 1960s, demonstrated that respondents clearly differentiated North African, and particularly Algerian, immigrants from those who came from neighboring European countries. Two dimensions of public opinion referred to in chapter 1 are particularly interesting. The first dimension, "sympathy/ antipathy," can be understood as an inclusive or exclusive attitude. This dimension is reinforced by the attitudes with regard to "integration/ separation," that projects into the future or the past an estimation of the possibilities of including the group in question into the community. In Michèle Lamont's analysis,

> French social scientists often argue that the French political culture of republicanism produces a low level of racism because it delegitimizes the salience of ascribed characteristics in public life, hence facilitating integration of racial minorities. In contrast, my analysis suggests that republicanism has a contradictory impact: it delegitimizes one form of racism, but also strengthens another by drawing a clear distinction between those who share this universalistic culture (citizens) and those who do not (immigrants). This boundary is reinforced by traditional anti-Muslim feelings found in Christian France, by a lasting historical construction of French culture as superior, and by a caste-like relationship of the French with members of their former colonies.[24]

Based on interviews with French workers, Lamont argues that French (white) workers do not disassociate themselves from blacks and the poor; indeed they strongly identify with them. Instead French workers are more likely to exclude from their (moral) community immigrants, especially North African immigrants, while American workers tend to include immigrants (but not blacks) in their moral universe. This way of constructing what Lamont refers to as a moral community implies very special problems for identity on the European side. Nevertheless, it is the United States that has the most dubious historic record in terms of racialized patterns of immigrant rejection. Perhaps one way of approaching this question is by relating attitudinal patterns to the way these patterns are politicized.

Lamont's conclusions are substantially supported by survey data from the 1960s on. During the period before the suspension of immigration in 1974, sympathy for immigrants from neighboring European countries

Table 3.5 Sympathy/antipathy index[a] for immigrant groups, 1966–1993

Immigrant Group	1966	1974	1990[b]	1993[b]
Italians	+47	+75		
Spanish	+36	+80		
Portugese	+30	+63	+71	+76
African Black	+20	+34	+55	+49
North African	−42	−22	+8	+5

Notes:
a Index = "sympathy" minus "antipathy" for each year specified.
b There is no data for Italians and Spanish immigrants for 1990 and 1993.

Sources: 1966 IFOP; 1974 INED; 1990, 1993 CSA—reported in Yvan Gastaut, *L'immigration et l'opinion en France sous la Ve République* (Paris: Éditions du Seuil, 2000), pp. 77–82.

Table 3.6 Integration index[a] for immigrant groups, 1951–1988

Immigrant Group	1951	1971	1974	1984	1988
Italians	+67	+66	+62	+72	+68
Spanish	+44	+45	+52	+72	+61
Portuguese	—	+10	+22	+60	+48
African Blacks	—	−51	−49	−12	−31
North African	−25	−40	−54	−49	−42

Note:
a Index = "easily integrated" minus "difficult or impossible to integrate."

Sources: 1951 INED from Alain Girard and Jean Stoetzel, *Français et immigrés* (Paris PUF, 1953), pp. 38–42. 1971, 1974 INED; 1984 SOFRES; 1988 IPSOS—reported in Yvan Gastaut, *L'immigration et l'opinion en France sous la Ve République* (Paris: Éditions du Seuil, 2000), pp. 83–86.

(as well as Blacks from Africa) generally contrasted with antipathy for North Africans. (See table 3.5.) On the other hand, over time sympathy for all immigrant groups increased. Nevertheless, the striking gap between Europeans and North Africans remained.[25]

We find a similar pattern for the integration/separation dimension, but with far less improvement for North Africans. (See table 3.6.) Even as French respondents became more sympathetic with all immigrant communities, they did not become significantly more optimistic about the ability of North Africans (particularly Algerians) to integrate into French society, at least through 1988.[26]

These patterns are consistent with high (even growing) sentiment that there are "…too many immigrants in France." While this sentiment was never very high with regard to European immigrants since the 1960s, it has remained high, and has even grown, with regard to North Africans.

During the last 35 years, roughly two out of three respondents have agreed that there are too many North African immigrants in France. The key seems to be a strong sense by French respondents of a strong moral difference between them and the Algerian immigrant population resident in France. In 1994, at a time when sympathy for North African immigrants had grown considerably (compared with the 1960s), roughly two-thirds of respondents considered Algerians to be poorly integrated, intolerant, disrespectful of French law and potentially subversive. These sentiments are similar to those expressed in 1965.[27]

Thus, what seems to be driving anti-immigrant sentiment in France is a hard line that respondents draw primarily against Algerian immigrants, but to a lesser extent against Black African immigrants as well. This attitudinal pattern long predates the electoral breakthrough of the National Front, and the success of FN has not significantly deepened that pattern. Nevertheless, we should not confuse this sentiment with the political importance of the immigration issue, or presume that public opposition to immigration is driving policy or the policy debate. We shall see below that in 1984, at a time when opposition to North African immigration was very high, barely 6 percent of voters saw immigration as a priority issue in the approaching elections. Four year later, however, when attitudes toward North Africans had improved somewhat, the percentage for whom immigration was a priority had grown almost four times, and continued to grow until the early 1990s. The question, that we shall examine below, is how public opinion become mobilized for political purposes

Compared with Britain, the impact of immigration on reconsideration of requirements for citizenship in France has been relatively modest. On the other hand, more than in Britain or the United States, there has been a tendency in France, to modify aspects of *jus solis*, to make citizenship more of an earned choice that a simple right. If *jus solis* has meant that there is almost never a "second generation immigrant" in the United States, this is not true in France. According to the 1999 census, 1,310,000 people who were born in France did not acquire French nationality at birth. Of these, 800,000 became French citizens ("French by acquisition"), but the remainder—more than half a million—remained "foreigners" in their country of birth. While the percentage of "foreigners" born in France has declined during the past 25 years, these large numbers of mostly young people have only limited citizenship rights in their native country, and remain subject to some of the harsher aspects of French immigration policy. (See Table 3.7.)

Citizenship

The relationship between immigration and citizenship first became politicized in France in the 1980s.[28] The discussion of these issues very quickly became linked with questions of national identity, and the nationality law

Table 3.7 Foreigners in France

	1982	1990	1999
Born Abroad	2,869,688	2,858,026	2,750,051
Born in France	651,000	737,000	508,488
% of total born in France	18.5	20.5	15.6

Source: INSEE, Recensement de la population.

that defined how immigrants could gain French citizenship. French law permitted the transmission of French citizenship both by *jus sanguinis* (descent) as well as by *jus solis* (territorial birth). Unlike *jus solis* in the United States or Britain at the time, however, French law granted citizenship at birth only to children born in France to at least one French parent. Those born on French soil to parents born outside of France also had a right to French citizenship, but acquired it "automatically" only at the age of majority, provided they were then still residing in France and did not officially decline it.

In 1984, numerous proposals were advanced from various parts of the political right to change that policy in favor of a more restrictive approach, particularly toward young North Africans, born in France. The focus was on the relatively limited question of automatic citizenship at the age of majority. These proposals gained a political arena when the Right took control of the National Assembly in 1986. The Right had a majority to tighten the law, but, in part because of the approach of presidential elections in 1988, Prime Minister Chirac decided to attempt to build a consensus around this divisive issue by appointing a special commission of experts, that crossed political lines, to investigate French nationality law and make recommendations. The most important proposal then being considered was making the acquisition of French citizenship by immigrants born and raised in France conditional upon their actively requesting it, rather than granting it to all but those who actively declined it.

The Nationality Commission held televised public hearings, and collected testimony from a wide range of officials and organizational representatives. The Commission's report aimed at a middle course, between advocates of a greater emphasis on *jus sanguinis* (a more nationalist emphasis), and those that advocated the extension of the rights of noncitizen residents, in particular voting rights in local elections (an emphasis on a postnationalist view of citizenship). The commission argued against relating the process of integration to the multicultural influences of trans-national civil society, and made a case that such an approach only encouraged popular feelings that immigration is linked to a decline of a distinctively French national identity, thereby fueling popular support for the extreme-Right.

It finally published a two-volume report meant to serve as a basis for legislative change,[29] and that resulted in the loi Méhaignerie in 1993, which integrated the commission recommendation that, although *jus solis* should be maintained, its mode of application to second-generation immigrants should be made to depend more on demonstrated choice.[30] Instead of receiving French citizenship automatically at age 18, the new law required that nationality be actively requested between ages 16 and 21. To qualify, those requesting citizenship had to show they had been in France for the previous five consecutive years. According to Miriam Feldblum, the law's main provisions reflected "the new nationalist consensus over citizenship priorities" established during the late 1980s.[31]

The new law went into effect in 1994, but was softened when the Left returned to power three years later. In 1997, the new Socialist prime minister, Lionel Jospin followed a strategy similar to that of his predecessor, by requesting the advice of a commission, headed by political scientist Patrick Weil, to prepare reports recommending revisions to the law. Weil's report showed that in many ways the new law was working in the intended way. Most of those who were eligible were actively requesting French citizenship, often as early as possible, and acquisitions of French nationality increased 21 percent in 1994.[32] On the other hand, some studies of the law also indicated that there were real administrative problems in disseminating information and registering those who would be eligible for citizenship.

Weil finally proposed the retention of part of the 1993 law, but to modify it marginally. The report proposed that young people continue to be allowed to claim French citizenship beginning at age 16. However, if they failed to do so, French nationality was simply to be attributed to them at age 18, unless they specifically declined it. These recommendations were incorporated into the *Loi Guigou* in 1998.

By the end of this long legislative dialogue, the French version of *jus solis* had been generally reaffirmed, with a marginally increased emphasis on an active request for citizenship. However, the real impact of this intense, but constrained discussion was increased pressure on second generation "immigrants" to claim citizenship, and on those born abroad to naturalize. The rate of naturalization increased considerably in the late 1990s, but the number of naturalizations by "declaration" of young people between the ages of 13 and 18, who were born of parents born abroad, almost doubled after the passage of the *Loi Guigou*.[33] Nevertheless, the question of integration has become more important politically, even as the acquisition of citizenship has increased, and as the actual number and proportion of those who are "foreigners" has continued to decline.

The Issue of Integration: The French Model

In France, far more than in Britain or the United States, there has been an explicit model of what it means to be French, and therefore what it means to "integrate". In France, at least in principle, there has been no public support for collective rights for ethnic minorities or communities, no support for multicultural education, and no concessions to customs of ethnic or national groups in the public realm. In fact, the very use of these words has been opposed by French representatives within the institutions of the European Union.[34]

This French view of the process of integration is generally compared with a very different view of the American and British approach to immigrant integration. In France, the American or British pattern of public recognition of collective identities as a basis for public policy is specifically rejected. As Dominique Schnapper has argued:

> The French political tradition has always refused to recognize the American concept of "ethnicity." In the school, the factory, in the union (either in leadership or the pattern of demands), the "ethnic" dimension has never been taken into account, even if social practices don't always scrupulously follow this principle. It is not an accident that there have never been in France real ghettos of immigrant populations from the same country, on the model of Black, Italian or "Hispanic" neighborhoods in the United States, that in poor areas immigrant populations from different countries mix with French people, apparently in the same social milieus. The promotion of Frenchmen of foreign origin comes about individually and not collectively through groups organized collectively.[35]

This perspective is widely shared both by policy-makers and by some scholars. French scholars have also argued convincingly that there are vast differences between the American experience of ghettos and spatial separation of ethnic groups, and the French experience of the expression of identities within relatively integrated urban neighborhoods.[36] The end product is generally seen as effective integration, in the sense that, after several generations, national origin has no meaning.[37]

Of course scholars have recognized that this approach to immigrant integration "...was never a concrete, historical reality either in France or in the colonies. It was never completely enacted, never completely successful." Nevertheless, for many scholars, and for much of the political class, "Its principles continue to inspire government policy towards immigrants." To alter this approach, moreover, "...would break with a long tradition of national integration in France and weaken (and perhaps even dissolve) the social fabric."[38]

There are two problems with trying to understand integration in France in these terms. The first is that the American reference fails to recognize that the United States had explicit state (and national) integration programs for immigrant populations long before these programs were first developed in France. (See ch. 9.) The second is that this model fails to give sufficient weight to the ambiguities in both French rhetoric and practice and the tension between the two. In significant ways, the myth of the

Republican model has deviated from what actually happened, not only recently, but during the previous period of European migration as well.

During the prewar period of European integration, among the most powerful instrument for integrating new immigrant populations were the trade union movement and the French Communist Party. Both the unions and the party sought new members (and eventually electoral support) by mobilizing workers from Poland, Italy, and after WWII, workers from Spain. Part of the effort certainly focused on class solidarity, but mobilization was also based on ethnic and religious solidarities.

Although the efforts of the CGTU (the Communist-dominated trade union confederation between 1922 and 1936) and the party were integrative in the sense that they represented and aggregated the interests of immigrant workers together with those of other workers, they were also supportive of the particular interests of these workers as immigrants, and in this sense contributed to the development of ethnic identity. Both the CGTU and the party organized separate language groups, and, at the departmental and national levels, the party put into place immigrant manpower commissions. Finally, the party supported ethnic organizations and demonstrations among immigrant groups that were both particularistic and more universal in nature.[39] The establishment of communism in immigrant communities altered political party patterns in these same areas, and effectively established local ethnic machines, many of which endured well into the Fifth Republic.[40] (See ch. 4.)

At this (local) level, it is difficult to separate ethnic politics from integration of ethnic solidarities into a larger, more universal political project, but two aspects of this process appear to challenge the conventional wisdom of the Republican model. The Communist Party and the CGTU not only recognized the legitimacy of immigrant collectivities, but also gave benefits to these collectivities at the local level. Even during the "golden age" of the French Jacobin melting pot, ethnic dimensions were clearly taken into account, at least by the Communist Party and the trade unions in ways that were comparable to their American counterparts at the time.

In many ways, nothing much changed with the wave of third world immigration after 1960. Studies on the ground provide clear evidence of the recognition of immigrant collectivities by both political parties and public authorities. As during the previous period, this evidence is more obvious at the local than at the national level. Finally, in official statements of the government and political parties, there has been a reaffirmation of the Republican model as the ideal of immigrant integration.

Nevertheless, there are some differences both in practice and in the expression of the ideal. I will first summarize these differences, and then analyze them in some detail. Most important, there has been far more direct intervention from the central state, in both defining the problem of immigrant ethnic minorities and in elaborating modes of incorporation, and less involvement of intermediary interest groups than during the earlier period. In addition, as we shall see below, the pattern of policymaking has been conditioned by what Maxim Silverman has termed the "racial-ized" view of the post-1960s wave of non-European immigrants in a way that has clearly differentiated them from the waves of European immi-grants that preceded them; and as in the United States in the early part of the twentieth century, the emphasis on race has probed the limits of the integrative capacities of the French version of the melting pot.

In contrast to the tradition of positive solidarity that Communist-governed municipalities had developed toward predominantly European immigrants, by the 1970s many of these same local governments began to treat non-European immigrants (as well as non-white French citizens from the overseas departments,) as temporary residents who must be encouraged to return home.[41] As during the earlier period, Communist municipalities tended to treat new immigrant communities as collectivi-ties, but now in an exclusionary manner.

This pattern was not, however, unique to towns governed by Communists. Virtually every town in the Lyon region, for example, in collaboration with departmental and state authorities, made decisions dur-ing the late 1970s to limit the availability of housing for immigrant families that were based on an understood notion of a "threshold of tolerance."[42] On the initiative of local governments, the state also collaborated in estab-lishing quotas for immigrant children in primary schools.[43]

By the 1980s treating immigrants in a collective manner had taken on positive as well as negative aspects. In 1975, Paul Dijoud, the second Minister of State for Immigrant Workers, was able to secure a major in-crease in housing funding to assist immigrants. Twenty percent of a public housing fund established in 1953 (and paid for by a payroll tax on all companies with more than 10 employees) would be earmarked for immi-grant housing. Although this program was quickly undermined by cor-rupt practices, and was virtually abolished by 1987, it did make limited progress in ameliorating immigrant housing conditions.[44]

After 1981, the newly elected national government of the Left took several unprecedented steps, including the financing of ethnic organiza-tions, that involved central state agencies in ethnic construction, recogni-tion and mobilization (see below). In addition, there was a wide-ranging debate between 1981 and 1986 on the proper model for immigrant incor-poration.[45] After 1986 the dialogue moved back toward a reassertion of the traditional Republican model (see above), but the public discourse continued to be contradicted by relatively open political expressions of ethnic consciousness, as well as public policies that in many ways sup-ported this consciousness. These policies not only tolerated the public expression of ethnic differences, but, as Danièle Lochak points out, also tended to manage and institutionalize them.[46] The most important initia-tive was the law of October 1981 that liberated immigrant associations from pre-WWII restrictions.

Political mobilization on the basis of evolving categories of ethnicity, while not new in France, is now taking place in a different context, largely outside of the organizational framework of established union and party organizations. This phenomenon is similar to the pattern of ethnic organization in the United States. What is also new is the intense involvement of state agencies in France in the development of ethnic organization and ethnic consciousness. Of course it is ironic that this considerable involvement of the state (compared with previous periods) should continue at the very time when such action should be excluded by the reaffirmation of the Republican model.

How then, can we understand the tilt away from a more global perspective? Our comparison with the previous period of immigration indicates that, if we look at the local rather than the national level of policymaking, we can see that other immigrant groups had also been treated in a collective manner. The difference now is the direct intervention of the state in integration policy, not so much through legislation, which has remained generally Jacobin, but through administration, which has become more multicultural in practice.

The weakness of the historic interlocutors for immigrant integration created a new problem for the state, however. For state authorities, it appears that this shift in practice was related to the larger problem of the emerging urban crisis. Urban riots in the Lyons region during the summer of 1981 were largely responsible for the establishment of an *Inter-ministerial Commission on the Social Development of Neighborhoods and the Commission of Mayors on Security. The Neighborhood Commission* recommended more long-term national support for efforts to deal with security and urban problems at the local level. As periodic urban riots continued over more than two decades, the involvement of the state grew, and its efforts contributed to the development of ethnic organization, as state agencies engaged in a sometimes desperate search for interlocutors among what became known as the "second generation."[47]

In a sometimes desperate search for intermediaries (*intérlocateurs valables*) among the "second generation," both local governments and the central state have sought out and have sometimes supported whatever ethnic associations they feel can maintain social order. John McKesson cites a French Senate report on the Lyon region:

> Certain mayors are, alas!, ready to provide everything to prevent cars from burning in their towns. The public powers give in to the blackmail of the fundamentalists, who present themselves as the social actors who are best able to preserve order in difficult neighborhoods where no policeman dares to venture.[48]

In the early 1980s, the involvement of the central state (then controlled by the Left) increased in part because localities (particularly those controlled by the Left) were no longer able to deal with very real problems of ethnic incorporation, problems of education and the outbreak of urban violence. In education, problems of rising dropout rates and student failures among the children of immigrants resulted in the establishment of several programs, the most important of which was the zones of educational priority (ZEP).[49] The designation of these zones—which meant more money from several ministerial sources, more teachers and more experimental programs—relied upon criteria that focused largely on the ethnic composition of an area.[50]

By 1994 it was estimated that somewhat more than 30 percent of those benefitting from the ZEP program were immigrant children.

> Zones of priority, by their global vision of the problem of school failure, indicated that foreign children ought not to be treated "as different". However, the first government *circulaire* of July, 1981, clumsily fixed a "quota" of 30% foreign children as one of the determining indicators of such zones.[51]

Certainly more "disfavored" native children than immigrant children have benefitted from the program, but the point is that the designation of ZEPs was strongly linked to areas of immigrant concentration.

A follow-up *circulaire* stressed that this should be only one criterion among several, but the notion of "determining indicator" stuck, and applications tended to focus mostly on the proportion of immigrants as a basis of need.[52] However clumsy these rules were, they were made necessary by the inability under law for any government to specifically use criteria of ethnicity and race for the development of public policy.[53] This has meant that relatively narrow geographic criteria have taken the place of ethnic criteria. In this way, the Republican model had molded the way that groups are targeted, but has not prevented special programs from being implemented. This became more evident in recent years, when the government has developed pilot programs of affirmative action (*discrimination positive* or *égalité des chances*) using the ZEP program as a framework (see ch. 4).

In fact, as in other countries in Europe, various approaches to discrimination have become integral to policy on integration since 2000. Although the "race-relations" approach to integration has been far more characteristic of the British approach, France has moved in this direction, largely in response to the directives of the EU in 2000. In 2001 and 2002 France passed legislation banning discrimination in employment and housing,[54] but did not pass legislation authorizing an active anti-discrimination agency until 2004. The High Authority Against Discrimination and for Equality (la HALDE) was established in 2005, and issued its first report in May 2006. During its first year, it received more than 2000 complaints from individuals, 45 percent of them complaints of employment discrimination. Although the commission lacks financial resources to investigate discrimination, as well as strong legal means to pursue complaints and enforcement, it represents a new departure to deal with immigrant integration in terms of discrimination.[55]

Two patterns differentiate collective representation of immigrants in the 1980s from the prewar pattern. The first is the greater recognition of these groups as direct intermediaries, relatively unfiltered through institutions *à vocation universelle,* such as unions and political parties. This pattern began in a more or less ad hoc manner in the early 1980s, but was formalized during the same period despite the fact that the Republican model was being officially reasserted. The second is direct subvention by the state to support and maintain links with ethnic associations.

In retrospect, current research in France indicates that something important has changed not only in the practice of immigrant incorporation, but in the ideal of the Republican model as well. During the period of European immigration, the collective mobilization of immigrant groups by political parties and unions tended to incorporate collectivities of immigrants into more universal organizations not defined by ethnicity. It was balanced by state action that did not encourage the ethnic formation. Now, however, ethnic organization is legitimized and encouraged by the state, and ethnically defined groups function as intermediaries within the political arena directly, rather than within unions and parties.

The best Jacobin intentions of French governments have been tempered by emerging realities. Given the decline of the historical agents of integration, there seems to be little alternative to dealing directly with organized representatives of the immigrant communities. This is particularly true when the government wishes to coordinate policies directed toward urban violence with policies to facilitate integration.[56] In addition, if the practice of incorporation has adjusted to new realities, there is also clear evidence that the ideal of the Republican model has changed as well, particularly at the level of administration.

Only in the most formal statements issued by the state does the Republican ideal remain the kind of "program of action" described by Dominique Schnapper. During the 1980s the effective program of action of the state, described in the programs of some state agencies and local governments, has supported a collective approach to immigrant incorporation, and has viewed ethnic identification in positive terms.

Even those government representatives most committed to the Jacobin ideal have been drawn into this contradiction. In 1990, in reaction to the Islamic headscarf affair, Socialist Minister of the Interior Pierre Joxe invited representatives of Islamic organizations to form a Deliberative Council on the Future of Islam in France, an institution that would be the parallel of comparable organizations of Catholics, Protestants and Jews. The hope was that such institutionalized consultation would help to undermine the rise of Islamic fundamentalism. This initiative took almost 15 years to reach fruition, and a process was finally inaugurated by Interior Minister Nicolas Sarkozy in 2003 that would take another two years to work through. *The Conseil Français du Culte Musulman* in itself represented a well-established French approach to dealing with organized religion. Nevertheless, it is clear that, even for most hardened Jacobins, the purpose goes well beyond the coordination of religion.[57]

On one hand, the purpose is to influence the construction of a moderate, domestic Islam in France, and to remove the control of Muslim religious life in France from countries of origin. This represented a change in policy from the 1970s, when French authorities welcomed teachers from North Africa, as part of a program to encourage repatriation. In a speech at the inauguration of a new mosque in Lyon in 1994 Minister of the Interior Charles Pasqua praised the effort to build a "moderate" Islam that would be compatible with the French Republican tradition:

> We need to treat Islam in France as a French question instead of continuing to see it as a foreign question or as an extension into France of foreign problems.... It is no longer enough to talk of Islam in France. There has to be a French Islam. The French Republic is ready for this.

Alec Hargreaves then comments that "Although this is considerably less than the full-blown policy of multiculturalism once apparently favored by some on the Left, it also falls a long way short of the intolerant monoculturalism for which right-wing nationalists have traditionally argued."[58]

On the other hand, it is an attempt to harness the influence of religious interlocutors in order to enhance social control among young immigrants and French citizens of Islamic heritage. As then Interior Minister Sarkozy put it in a speech entitled "Can God Live Without the Republic?"

> When there is a priest or a pastor in the neighborhood to look after young people, there is less despair and less delinquency... Today, our neighborhoods are spiritual deserts... I don't say that the Republic cannot... speak to young people about self-respect and respect for others and for women.... But notwithstanding the ambitions of [nineteenth century educational reformer] Jules Ferry, the Republic is not up to the task and doesn't do it. It is in this sense that religions are a benefit for the Republic. Religions give today's men and women the perspective of fundamental questions of human existence: the meaning of life and death and society and history.[59]

The advantage of this approach is that it falls well within the French tradition of dealing with ethnic groups through religious interlocutors.

France has a large and growing Muslim population—indeed, France has the largest Muslim population in Europe. Not surprisingly, France also has the second largest number of mosques of any European country (about 1,700, compared with 2,300 in Germany), and a younger generation who are relatively more identified as Muslims than the generation that preceded them—according to measures of identity and Mosque attendance. The problem of this approach is that barely two-thirds of those who come from Islamic countries—either immigrants or French citizens—identify as Muslims, and regular mosque attendance is relatively modest, only slightly higher than church attendance of a representative sample of the French population.[60] Survey results indicate that attendance is highest among Moslems of West African origin (39%) and lowest among Moroccans (27%) and Algerians (13%),[61] and practice diminishes as immigrants move out of immigrant and ethnic communities.[62]

The pattern of integration policy in France is sometimes unclear because of the difference between administration and legislation. This is most evident in the recurrent issue of the *foulard* (the head-scarf sometimes worn by Muslim girls) in French schools. From 1989 until 2003, the issue of the foulard came to symbolize the French problem of integrating Muslim populations. It began with the expulsion of three young schoolgirls who were attending a junior high school in Creil for insisting that they wear a *hajib* (a head-scarf, conventionally called a "foulard" in French). The school director defined the problem as a challenge to the accepted rules of religious neutrality—laïcité—of the French school system. The issue quickly became a national "affair," in part because it crossed Left-Right lines, and because it became politicized as part of the question of immigration control and nationality laws.

The minister of education, Lionel Jospin, attempted to maintain flexibility, and restrict the process of politicization, by referring the question to the Council of State for an advisory opinion. The advice of the Council to deal with each case in terms of whether the foulard was an "ostentatious" manifestation of religious symbolism or simply an inoffensive practice (comparable to crosses worn by Christian students, or kippot or stars worn by Jewish students), effectively redirected the question to school directors, and reduced the political pressure for a more general solution to this challenge.[63]

This administrative solution, sanctioned by the Council of State, lasted for fourteen years, but was finally undermined by the very process that it set into motion—"local option." Under pressure from school directors and the well organized teacher's union, the president of the republic finally appointed a commission in July 2003, to examine the problems of applying the principles of *laïcité* to public life. After extensive hearings, the committee issued its report in December, and made a number of recommendations, among which was the passage of a law that would forbid the wearing of "conspicuous" religious signs or clothing, including large crosses, veils or kippot.[64] lthough the report goes to great length to describe the legal and social tensions that exist between the principles of *laïcité* and freedom of religious expression, it argues that these tensions have provided a context for flexible application. One member of the commission argued that the recommendation was based, not only on the reaffirmation of *laïcité*, but on a desire to protect minor girls from pressures (mostly from their families) to do what they otherwise would not do. Perhaps more to the point:

> ... we had to face a reality that was perceived at the local level, but not at the national nor obviously at the international one: wearing

the scarf or imposing it upon others has become an issue not of individual freedom but of a national strategy of fundamentalism groups using public schools as their battleground.[65]

A law, then was thought to be necessary, to prevent fundamentalist groups from trying target schools one by one. Indeed, the essential principles of the recommended law had already been established through a series of decisions by the Council of State during the decade of the 1990s. The law was passed in February by an overwhelming majority, and signed into law the following March. It was also overwhelming approved in public opinion; and, although a small majority of French Muslims opposed the legislation, it was approved by a plurality of Muslim women.[66]

Looking back over past 25 year of French policy on integration, what is most striking is that there has been an evolving policy, and a struggle to define that policy. It has been a policy born of a quest for public order, and has been developed as a result of challenges to that order, from the urban riots that have punctuated French urban life, to the challenges posed by young girls wearing *foulards*. The most flexible policies have been developed locally, through administrative actions. However, periodic laws that deal with integration have tended to reaffirm the principles of the Republican model.

Since 1945, the French Civil Code (Article 21–24) has stipulated that no one can be naturalized without demonstrating his or her "assimilation to the French community" through knowledge of the French language. The Sarkozy law of 2003 requires demonstration of knowledge of rights and duties of French citizens, a requirement that would be strengthened in the legislation of 2006. Nevertheless, the voluntary program put into place in July 2003 in 12 departments in France—the Reception and Integration Contract—was signed by 94 percent of those eligible during the two years that followed. This would impose requirements for knowledge of language and civics that have been imposed in the United States since 1950, and that were legislated in Britain in 2002.[67]

The second characteristic of French policy in this area is that it is constrained—but not prevented—by the often awkward rules of that same Republican model. Thus, it is easier to deal with integration through rules and legislation on religion (permitted as a way of differentiating the population for some purposes) than on ethnicity (officially, not permitted). Affirmative action can be developed by targeting spatial concentrations for education policy (the ZEPs), but any mechanism that would target specific ethnic groups would be a violation of the rules—even if the whole point is to target second and third-generation immigrants who challenge public order. The Republican model has not meant a lack of public recognition of ethnic communities; it has more realistically defined how that recognition takes place.

In fact there has been growing pressure to find a formula that would enable the French State to develop ethnic and racial categories to gather statistics, pursue studies and recommend legislation. The new term that is often used is "visible minorities". In 2006 a French Senate committee (on Laws and Social Affairs) adopted an amendment that would have established "...a typology of groups of people susceptible to discrimination because of their racial or ethnic origins." The amendment, which would have been used to measure diversity of origins in the civil service and some private companies, was rejected by the government, although it was supported by the minister of the interior.[68] Indeed, the Loi Hortefeux, as it was passed in 2007, contained a provision that would permit the census and researchers to pose questions on race and ethnicity; the provision, however, was declared unconstitutional by the Constitutional Council.[69]

Comparing Integration

This policy struggle, combined with periodic urban violence, has left the impression that French immigration policy has failed, in comparison with policy in the past, and compared with other countries (Britain and the United States, for example). Indeed, we have seen that the French economy has been relatively unsuccessful in integrating young people of immigrant origin. In 2004 unemployment rates among immigrants was 75 percent higher than among the population as a whole. Among young people, however (25–34) it was approaching 30 percent—and higher in some localities. (See table 1.3.) No doubt this is linked to the failures of the educational system, where almost two-thirds of immigrants did not attain the level of upper secondary school (see table 1.4), and 48 percent simply dropped out without any degree.[70]

These figures suggest that the ZEP program has been less than successful, and that the efforts at *discrimination positive* may be misplaced. The French record of placement of immigrants in the University system is better than is often assumed (see table 1.4), but that school retention is far worse than is often stated. Therefore, programs to keep immigrant children in school may be more important that high profile programs to place them in elite universities.

On the other hand, by attitudinal measures, French policy has been more successful than is generally acknowledged. If we look at two measures of integration—attitudes toward intermarriage and political commitment—we find that immigrants are generally moving toward integration. Thus, only 15 percent of immigrants of Muslim origin would disapprove of the marriage of a son to a non-Muslim—32 percent would disapprove of marriage of a daughter; about the same percentage of a sample of the general population would oppose the marriage of a child to a Muslim. Among French citizens of immigrant origin, higher percentages than among a general sample think that democracy is working well, that it would be terrible to suppress political parties or the National Assembly, and a far larger percentage (although still a minority) express confidence that they can change

things in the country. On the other hand, the percentage that is not registered to vote (23%) is more than three times the national average.[71]

Among immigrant groups in Europe, French people who identify as
Muslim, appear to be the most "European". As a minority community, they
have the most positive views of their compatriots who are Christian (and
Jewish), and are among the least sympathetic to radical Islam.[72] They are also
the most supportive of the idea that there is no conflict between Islam and
modern society. (See table 1.7.) Moreover, as we saw in chapter 1, French
Muslims are also the most supportive of ideas that are consistent with the
French Republican model. (Table 1.5) Among Muslim elites, there is a consensus about the compatibility of Islam and Western state values, which, in
Klausen's study, clearly differentiates Muslim elites in France, from those in
every other major country in Europe (see table 1.7).

We will come back to some of these issues in our analysis of Britain and
the United States. However, the results of the Pew survey and other recent
studies indicate that within Europe, immigrants in France of Islamic origin have the strongest national identity and are the most inclined toward
integration. Indeed, the sense of alienation that was manifest in the riots
in the fall of 2005 was less a rejection of French society than a demand for
greater and more effective integration.

In many ways the integration problem now confronting French and
other European governments resembles the class crisis of the twentieth century, which posed a constant challenge to the democratic order.
For the organized working class in Europe, there was a constant tension
between those representative groups that sought more effective "integration" through political and social settlements, agreements and access, and
those that sought to opt out of the existing order or promote change
through revolution, or other forms direct worker control. Gradually, a
political compromise that culminated in the "postwar settlement" after
WWII, ensured working class legitimacy through the access of working
class representation within the state.[73]

In the French process, the demands of the population "that has emerged
from immigration" has been for greater inclusion, and French authorities
have been struggling to find the kinds of political and social settlements
and agreements to ease these tensions. Thus, one reaction among young
people in the suburban areas in which the riots had taken place was a
surge in voter registration.[74] The reaction among both intellectuals and
the government has been to focus on questions of discrimination and
employment.[75] Although this focus has been developing for some time,
it indicates a movement toward a focus on ethnic integration typical of
multiculturalism, but a multiculturalism that avoids dispersion and direct
community control.[76]

Politics of Immigration in France

Although France has been a country of immigration—in the sense that the French state has had policies that have encouraged, discouraged and shaped immigration for well over a hundred years—the political salience of immigration issues has been relatively low until recently. Nevertheless, the question of immigration was politicized in different ways during different periods. Until WWII, the issue was framed largely in terms of a need for manpower to defend the state, and after, as a need for labor. However, as the immigrant population changed, the question was increasingly framed in identity terms.

The difference in the framing of the issue was related to important differences in the way that the policy process became institutionalized. After the passage of the law of 1889, the process was confined largely to the administration for the creation of policies of entry. Integration policy, however, emerged from the interactions between immigrant groups and the education system, local governments, trade unions, and ultimately some political parties that created programs to attract and mobilize immigrant groups and potential voters. On the other hand, other political parties also used immigrants as objects, as a way of mobilizing voters on the basis of identity.

Framing the Issue

The first major legislation in France on immigration was the law of 1889 (see ch. 2) The legislation that was passed emphasized the need for reliable manpower to defend a country whose chief rival—Germany—was experiencing rapid population growth. The debate in the National Assembly reflected the concerns of how to frame an issue the importance of which was generally acknowledged. It focused above all on the needs of the armed forces for soldiers, at a time when immigrants were exempt from military service. It also emphasized the need to tie successive generations of immigrants (most recent practice had linked naturalization to *jus sanguinis*) to France and to French national interests.

However, the debate in parliament focused on other ways of framing the issue as well. Although this debate appeared to be settled by the legislation that was passed, it would continue for the next fifty years. Opposed to the proposal were deputies who sought to frame the issue in terms of national identity. They emphasized the racially focused eugenicist arguments, not in an attempt to halt immigration, but to shape it in particular ways. In the end, the need "...to make soldiers" gave additional strength to those who were in favor of firmly imposing the principle of *jus solis* on immigrants who might otherwise seek to avoid military service for their children.[1]

What is most striking about the French legislative debate about immigration that resulted in the law of 1889 was that many of the issues were similar to those that were debated by the United States Congress during the same period, except that French manpower needs finally overrode considerations of race and ethnicity—but not entirely. At the same time that the legislation established the principle of *jus solis*, and therefore integration of generations of children of immigrants born in France, a second principle of inequality was also enshrined: a difference between native and naturalized citizens. The legislation of 1889, (and subsequent legislation in 1927), established a gap in rights between those of born citizens and those of naturalized citizens. Naturalized citizens were temporarily ineligible to vote or run for office, and they were excluded from whole categories of employment. These restrictions would endure in various forms until 1983.[2]

Moreover, at the same time that the legislative debate produced reluctant agreement that immigration and settlement were necessary for the national interest, there was a parallel commitment to the exercise of increased state controls over a growing immigrant population. At the time of the debate about the naturalization legislation there was a continuing discussion within the administration, as well as the National Assembly, about identity cards for immigrants residing in the country, which involved a rivalry between the ministry of war and the ministry of the interior about which administration would exercise control over the alien population. Through a series of decrees and legislation, controls were imposed tboth to serve the interests of security, and to protect parts of the labor market against competition between native and immigrant workers.[3]

During the post-WWI period, there was some legislation, but entry policy was shaped mostly by administrative action in a problem-solving mode that often involved different notions of desirable and undesirable immigrants, and also often constrained the implementation of policy. This thinking was captured in the work of George Mauco, the best known "expert" on immigration during the interwar period. In a report to the League of Nations, Mauco argued that "...among the diversity of foreign races in France, there are some...(Asians, Africans, even Levantines) for whom assimilation is not possible, and is, in addition, often physically and morally undesirable." With the aid of a survey that he had developed, he established a hierarchy of ethnicities, with Swiss and Belgian migrants on top, and North Africans far on the bottom.

Mauco did not draw his inspiration from the eugenics movement so much as a deep strain of cultural racism that presumed an impenetrable barrier to assimilation, as well as a superiority of those closest to French ethnicity. This orientation was close to the liberal perspective on similar subjects in the United States during roughly the same period, and, like his counterparts in the United States, he was optimistic about the prospects of assimilation of the vast majority of immigrants in France.[4] Although the question continued to be framed in terms of French manpower needs, at least until the latter part of the Depression, in 1926 there was an unsuccessful proposal to establish a French quota system similar to the one that had been legislated in the United States two years earlier (see ch. 8). However, in marked contrast with the United States, immigration was not a high salience issue, and the framing of the issue tended to be dominated by administrative concerns.

Once again, in 1945, considerations of manpower needs overwhelmed the concerns of demographers preoccupied with challenges to national identity. Nevertheless, as we saw in chapter 2, without actually altering the framing of the immigration issue, the French administration began to strike a balance between considerations of manpower needs and identity questions by openly encouraging greater immigration from Europe, as opposed to North Africa. Although the debate within the administration was fierce, and reflected deep conflict about the meaning and consequences of immigration, it was hidden from public view At no point did immigration become an electoral issue, but that did not mean that it was not politicized by the definition we gave in chapter 1. By the mid-1950s, administrative authorities were clearly seeking "... immigration of Latin-Christian origin." The result was what appeared to be a period of unregulated entry and post-hoc regularization, but that was undertaken as a way of balancing out the free movement of Algerians.[5] No legislation was passed, nor were there any grand debates in parliament or at party conferences. Policy evolved through a problem-solving approach that was virtually invisible, what Alexis Spire has called "the hidden face of the state."

For 30 years state agencies dealing with immigration altered the way the problem was understood, through several hundred ministerial *circulaires* that were internal directives, rather than documents with the force of law. Through these documents the frame of immigration policy moved from an understanding of immigrants as manpower for settlement, to a concern about ethnic balances, to deep concern about integration, to—finally in 1972–1974—a view that undesirable immigration must be suspended.[6] Through this entire period, questions of immigration were on the agenda of administrative agencies that dealt with the issue, and their changing views of the problem were under the purview of government ministers, but were not the subject of legislative debate.

Re-framing the Question

By the late 1960s, as the pattern of immigration tipped increasingly away from Europe, this implicit attempt at balance became a more explicit attempt to reframe the immigration issue. What appeared to be a rethinking and reframing of the issue of immigration was in fact a reaffirmation of thinking about non-European immigration, however. What had provoked this change was the structure of immigration, not the way policy-makers thought about it.

The first attempts to define a coherent immigration policy for France came after the May crisis of 1968, and is summarized in a report written by Correntin Calvez for the Economic and Social Council in 1969. The report recognized the economic need for immigrant labor, but clearly differentiated European from non-European workers. Europeans were assimilable, and should be encouraged to become French citizens, argued Calvez, while non-European immigrants constituted an "inassimilable island."

> It seems desirable, therefore, more and more to give to the influx of non-European origin, and principally to the flow from the Maghreb, the character of temporary immigration for work, organized in the manner of a rapid process of introduction which would be linked as much as possible to the need for labor for the business sectors concerned and in cooperation with the country of origin.[7]

Calvez's report went somewhat beyond efforts at ethnic balance, since it brought into question whether one single policy on immigration and integration would suffice. The distinction between "good" and "bad" immigrants had been present since before the war, but this report implies a difference between immigration for settlement, and a guest-worker program.

We know from chapter 2 that the framing of the problem of immigration in these terms contributed in important ways to the suspension of immigration in 1974. What is less obvious is that it also contributed to broad agreement around suspension, since the main political actors in both the government and opposition shared this perspective. As in the United States during an earlier period, this perspective informed the discussions and actions of trade unions, political parties, the government and the state; and as in the United States, the emphasis on race probed the limits of the integrative capacities of the melting pot.

Within the political dialogue and in the construction of public policy since the 1970s, "immigrants" have been generally presumed to be people originating in Africa and the Caribbean, regardless of whether they are in fact citizens (either naturalized or born). The "problem" of immigrants, for all practical purposes, did not include aliens from Spain, Portugal (still the largest single immigrant group in 1990)[8] or other European countries, and the "problem" of immigration often seemed to be less that of controlling the frontiers, than incorporating non-Europeans who were already in the country.

Because, from the early years of the non-Western wave of immigration, policy-makers presumed that these immigrant workers were different from those who had preceded them, the idea of difference informed the development and the implementation of public policy. Government and opposition generally agreed with these presumptions, even if they disagreed on their implications for policy. Thus, the Left opposition, on the national level, opposed expulsion of immigrant workers in the country, and generally supported family unification. The Left, therefore, was generally in favor of checking and limiting what they sometimes termed the "racist" labor market policies of the governments of the Right in the 1970s. At the same time, however, representatives of the Left were defining issues and developing integration policies at the local level that were based on similar "racist" assumptions.

Although there were some important large cities with high concentrations of immigrants governed by the Center-Right (including Paris and Lyon), large resident immigrant populations were most characteristic of cities governed by the Left. In contrast to "the tradition of solidarity" that Communist-governed municipalities had developed toward predominantly European immigrants, by the 1970s many of these same local governments began to treat non-European immigrants (as well as non-white French citizens from the overseas departments,) as temporary residents who must be encouraged to return home.[9]

The use of quotas in housing and schools became a widespread practice in the 1970s, the working assumption for which was that "thresholds of tolerance," limited to 10–15 percent of residents or students, were applicable to public policy. Although, the words "immigrants" and "foreigners" were used to describe those against whom such quotas should apply, what was most clearly meant was those perceived as non-white and different. The local policies were firmly rooted in assumptions about difference, and the inability to assimilate these new immigrant populations. Thus in the Fall of 1980, two Communist local housing authorities outside of Paris rejected the applications of citizens from the French overseas territories in the following terms:

…the administrative council has decided to house only native families..[because of] the saturation in our district of applications by foreign families and families from the overseas departments and territories.[10]

A second letter noted that:

We are constrained to limit the housing of persons originating in the overseas territories. In effect, their presence in our buildings provokes numerous problems at different levels…their way of living—frequent and late gatherings, loud shouting and loud music.[11]

More exclusionary policies toward immigrants in Communist-governed municipalities, based on similar assumptions, were developed in quiet collaboration with departmental and national administrative officials. For example, the municipal government of Vénissieux (outside of Lyon) took an initiative to exclude immigrant families from a massive housing development, Les Minguettes, in 1977, with the approval and collaboration of the Lyon regional (COURLY) authorities, state authorities (FAU), departmental authorities, and various public and private companies that were among the eleven participants that constructed and administered the complex. As we noted in chapter 3, however, this pattern quickly became generalized in the Lyon region.[12]

Local governments, by their actions, tended to define the immigrant problem as an ethnic problem, of native Frenchmen against non-Western immigrants and citizens from the overseas territories, and the solutions that they found tended to exclude and limit access for these residents. The role of Communist local governments was important in part because it was not different from that of the others, but also because so many immigrants were concentrated in Communist-governed towns. This automatically meant that these governments were in a position of leadership in policy definition and development.

By the 1980s, however, the framing of the immigration issue in terms of racialized differences had also taken on more positive aspects. As Gary Freeman has noted:

> In a sense, once the state had committed itself to this racially discriminatory policy, it had more incentive than before to increase the effectiveness and generosity of its social policies towards migrants. The fact that a large part of its immigrant population would be permanent persuaded officials that more needed to be done on their behalf.[13]

This way of framing the problem of immigration—as a problem of education through ZEPs or cooptation or integration—implied a change from a simple exclusionary view of the new immigration. It was considerably more optimistic than the formulation of the problem in the Calvez report, while at the same time maintaining a view of the immigrant population as different.

Indeed, by the 1990s, there were a number of reasons to rethink the way the immigration issue was framed. Most of those who were perceived as "immigrants" in France were no longer immigrants, but French citizens, and there was growing recognition within the European Union that Europe in general, and France in particular, was in need of continuing immigration. To portray immigration policy as simply one of exclusion no longer made a great deal of sense. However, as we shall see below, by the 1990s, a different way of looking at immigration and immigration policy was severely constrained because the framing of policy had moved out of the administrative arena, and into the arena of political party competition, primarily because of the political breakthrough of the National Front in the mid-1980s.

The emergence of the National Front altered not only the party system, but also the political salience of the immigration issue. Until the electoral breakthrough, public opinion was negative about immigration and immigrants, but the issue was not especially important for electoral competition (see table 4.1) From 1984 until the early 1990s, the issue of immigration became increasingly important—in relation to other political issues—not only for those who supported the National Front, but for voters of all other parties as well.

The National Front (FN) had been an obscure party of the extreme right since the early 1970s, but achieved an electoral breakthrough in 1983, after it began to focus on immigration as an electoral issue. The success of the FN in increasing the political salience of the immigration issue in terms of immigrants as a danger to French identity did not so much change the way the issue had been framed until then, as much as it did changed both the actors who were defining the issue and the context within which it was being defined. Political party actors became increasingly important, and the dynamics of party and electoral competition formed the core of the political process of policymaking. The results of the role of the National Front can be understood in two related ways. First, it became difficult to depoliticize the issue because in France, unlike Britain in the 1960s, the major parties were unable to develop a consensus about the framing of the immigration issue (see ch. 7). Second, the pressure of the FN made it

Table 4.1 The motivations of voters, 1984–1997[a] (percentage of party voters voting for these reasons)

%	Law and Order				Immigrants				Unemployment				Social Inequality			
	84	88	93	97	84	88	93	97	84	88	93	97	84	88	93	97
PC	9	19	29	28	2	12	16	15	37	59	77	85	33	50	52	46
PS	8	21	24	29	3	13	19	15	27	43	71	83	24	43	40	47
Rt.	17	38	37	43	3	19	33	22	20	41	67	72	7	18	23	21
FN	30	55	57	66	26	59	72	72	17	41	64	75	10	18	26	25
TT	15	31	34	35	6	22	31	22	24	45	68	75	16	31	32	35

Notes:

PC: Communist Party; PS: Socialist Party; Rt.: Right; FN: National Front; TT: Total.

a Since several responses were possible, the total across may be more than 100%. For 1988, the results are for supporters of presidential candidates nominated by the parties indicated.

Sources: Exit Poll, SOFRES/TF1, June 17, 1984, *Le Nouvel Observateur*, June 22, 1984; and SOFRES, *État de l'opinion, Clés pour 1987* (Paris: Seuil, 1987), p. 111; Pascal Perrineau, "Les Etapes d'une implantation électorale (1972–1988), in Nonna Mayer and Pascal Perrineau, Eds., *Le Front National à découvert* (Paris: Presses de la FNSP, 1988), p. 62; Pascal Perrineau, "Le Front National la force solitaire," in Philippe Habert, Pascal Perrineau, and Colette Ysmal, Eds., *Le Vote sanction* (Paris: Presses de la FNSP/ Dept. d'Etudes Politiques du Figaro, 1993), p. 155; CSA, "Les Elections legislatives du 25 mai, 1997," Sondage Sortie des Urnes pour France 3, France Inter, France Info et Le Parisien, p. 5.

difficult to reframe the immigration issue in a way to meet evolving labor-market and demographic needs for more immigration.

Then, in 2006, candidate Nicolas Sarkozy developed what he termed a new departure for immigration policy, by framing it in terms of priorities, rather than exclusion. The focus on "chosen" immigration ("choisie"), rather than "suffered" ("subie") immigration, was a way of emphasizing policy that was already being implemented under the 1998 legislation, but it gave political recognition to immigration expansion, at least in some areas. Indeed, Sarkozy recognized that this frame could be used as a formula for expanding immigration, while at the same time focusing on concerns of National Front voters, those who were most concerned about family unification (see below).[14]

The Political Process of Immigration Policy

Pre-WWII: The Administrative and Political Patterns

As we noted in chapter 2, the system of immigration control after WWI was embedded in a framework of bilateral agreements with a number of labor-exporting countries signed in 1919/1920. Within this framework, French state agencies recruited workers for the postwar reconstruction zones. Increasingly, however, recruitment was turned over to a privately controlled agency, la Societé générale d'immigration (SGI), which then became an agent of the state. Although departments in five different ministries were responsible for different aspects of immigration policy and control, SGI had the responsibility for the recruitment of immigrant workers, deemed essential to postwar economic expansion.

SGI was controlled by a consortium of agricultural and coal mining associations, and sent recruiters directly into villages and mining areas of Poland, and then other parts of Eastern and Southern Europe. Although SGI was private, it was supported by the French state, and its recruitment operations were sanctioned by governments in the regions in which they operated. In theory, workers could migrate to France as individuals, but in order to do so they needed to have work contracts, visas and train fare, all of which was arranged by SGI agents. SGI was a private, profitmaking institution that nevertheless exercised functions on behalf of, and together with, the French state.[15] Medical screening, selection and arrangements for official visas were all done by its agents.

Thus, the initiative for an open immigration policy for the decade of the 1920s was devolved to private interests, with state administrative agencies playing a supportive and/or controlling role. SGI was autonomous, but hardly independent of the French state.

[The] administrations of the Ministries of Labor and Agriculture took great care to define strict rules of control, setting out a compromise between the laissez-faire of the pre-war period and the *dirigisme* that prevailed during the hostilities. If SGI received the support of the French government for its missions abroad, its accreditation carried the obligation to submit to administrative scrutiny: thus, it could only bring in foreign workers after the certification of demand and of contracts by the Ministries of Labor and Agriculture.[16]

Nevertheless, the needs of the labor market appeared to weaken the formal constraints on the SGI, which, at least during the boom years of the 1920s, seemed to function with an independence that dominated its administrative masters.

In general, the result was that policy, and the administration of policy, lacked coherence. It did not mean, however, that there was no policy. Fragmented policy served different political interests in different ways.

> ...although French labor had been excluded from the commanding heights of the policy-making ministries in Paris, it had staked a claim (albeit a weak one) to participate in the local placement offices...[T]he state (largely through the ministry of Labor) chose to accommodate French labor. Departmental placement offices and the Foreign Labor Service attempted to confine job competition to manageable proportions....The Foreign Labor Service anticipated the flood immigrants, controlled the flow at the border, and irrigated the French landscape with them roughly according to the needs of the economy. Finally, a surrogate for the national labor office emerged in a National Manpower Council, which served as sounding board for government policy.[17]

Even with a lack of cohesion, the overall direction of this policy was clear: a controlled open recruitment of immigrants during a period in which there were serious manpower needs.

During the pre-WWII period France also did not have an explicit process for immigrant integration. Schools, churches and political parties, chief among them the local units of the French Communist Party, were the primary instruments of integration. But where the party was successful in mobilizing immigrant workers, it tended to incorporate them by emphasizing collective, rather than individual benefits. In significant ways, the PCF mobilized immigrant workers and their families in ways that resembled those of American Democratic machines during roughly the same historical period. (See chapter 3.)

In areas of immigrant concentration, party mobilization had many of the same characteristics as it did in other industrial areas, with the added ingredients of ethnic bonds. In immigrant areas, it established institutions based on ethnic working class identity. Like the Irish "takeover" of American urban centers from the WASP establishment through the Democratic Party, the Communist victories in these communities (for the most part after WWII) represented a kind of ethnic vengeance of a newly enfranchised electorate that endured in part because the party and the community had been interpenetrated:

> In La Seyne-sur-Mer, among others, the Communist deputy elected in 1947 (and reelected until 1969) is the son of an Italian [immigrant], symbolizing the 'working class revenge of the electorate that is majority Italian'.[18]

For the PCF and the CGTU (the Communist-dominated union confederation), the immigrant communities were an opportunity for growth. After a series of confusing policies, the CGTU, in 1926, developed a position that was highly supportive of immigrant communities. In his report to the 1925 Congress of the CGTU, the national secretary declared that

> If you do not support the foreign workers they will be molded in the hands of the capitalists as a mass of labor which can be used to beat you in all the demands which you make.[19]

By 1926, 16 percent of the confederation's budget was devoted to propaganda among immigrants, mostly to publication of foreign-language newspapers.

Although the efforts of the CGTU and the Communist Party were meant to be integrative, and they aggregated the interests of immigrant workers together with those of other workers, they also mobilized the particular interests of tshe workers as immigrants through separate language groups, and, at the departmental levels, immigrant manpower commissions. Finally, the party supported alliances with ethnic organizations, as well as demonstrations among immigrant groups.[20]

> Although the immigrant workers comprised no more than five percent of total CGTU membership, the construction of an organizational structure dependent on immigrants was more important. The effectiveness of this structure for the PCF only became evident when the party and its electorate began to expand after 1936.
>
> Italians and Poles, above all, often furnished the only party organizations [in some areas], sometimes in liaison with the party through the MOE [*main-d'oeuvre étrangère*] organizations.[21]

The establishment of communism in immigrant communities eventually destabilized older political patterns in these areas, but by establishing local ethnic machines.[22]

During the postwar period, Communist Party and local PCF officials progressively deemphasized the immigrant basis of these communities, and "...by acting in this way, the party tends to eliminate the reasons on which the confidence of the group in itself is based."[23] Nonetheless, the process through which this happened does not seem to have been substantially different from the parallel process in the United States. Both ethnic awareness and ethnic recognition were part of the process, while—at the same time—the melting-pot ideal of the Republican model remained intact.

The Post-WWII Administrative Pattern

Until the movement toward strong immigration control in the 1970s, more open policies were developed within a highly restricted policy community. At the national level, policies on entry continued to be based on the Ordinance of November 2, 1945 until 1980 (without being modified). Practice, however, varied considerably over the years, as policy-makers continued to try to balance labor-market needs against demographic preferences, mostly through a problem-solving approach, the contours of which were related to prewar considerations.

> Between 1945 and 1975, the legislative context of French policy on immigration hardly varied. However, the [administrative] agents of the state did not hesitate to give to this same text changing interpretations over the years.... In the area of immigration, the *circulaire* occupied a preponderant place: the heads of the bureaus of immigration only occasionally referred to the ordinances of 1945 [the legal base, which was also not passed as a law], but preciously conserved the collection of *circulaires* applicable in their area of competence.... The most important permitted the organization of family immigration in 1947, the installation of action on the protection of the national labor market in 1949, the encouragement of regularization of illegal immigrants in 1956, then to slow it down in 1972, and finally the suspension of immigration in July 1974.[24]

The Ordinance of 1945 created the Office National d'Immigration as the key for coordinating its labor recruitment efforts, but recruitment generally lagged. Part of the problem seemed to be related to competing ministerial rules and objectives, as well as to the lack of infrastructure for receiving large numbers of immigrants. But, as we saw in chapter 2, the administration was also concerned about the surge in immigration from North Africa. The government then decided to alter the system, essentially by privatizing it without acknowledgment. During the period of strong economic growth between 1956 and 1962 in France and in Europe, the French government permitted immigrants from other parts of Europe, who had been organized by private employers, to enter the country. Once they gained employment, they were officially legalized through successive amnesties. By the 1960s, as much as 90 percent of immigration was processed in this way.

The generally unregulated immigration of this period has been widely analyzed, and has been related to the pressures of the labor market. Alec Hargreaves, for example, cites Minister of State for Social Affairs, Jean-Marie Jeanneney's statement in 1966, which noted that "Illegal immigration has its uses, for if we rigidly adhere to the regulations and international agreements we would perhaps be short of labour."[25] The need for labor was certainly clear, but before the opening of the frontier to immigrant workers from Europe, much of that need was being filled by migrants from Algeria and other parts of North Africa. As a result of the open door policy, by 1962, the rate of settlement of workers from Europe significantly surpassed that of Algerians.

Strong efforts to recruit European (and even Turkish) workers, rather than Algerians, reflected both the preferences of employers as well as those of the French administration. During the period after the Evian Accords (that granted Algeria independence) were signed in 1962, the French and Algerian governments were in constant negotiations over the number of Algerian workers who would be permitted to enter France, with the French trying to reduce the number, and the Algerians trying to increase it. One result was the 16 recruitment agreements signed by France in an attempt to increase immigration within Europe. This reflected widespread concerns within the administration after the balance of immigration began to change in the 1960s.[26]

Among the immigrants from the Maghreb, French administrative authorities were particularly concerned about those from Algeria. At the same time that Moroccans and Tunisians had more or less free access to France—and were also given beneficial labor contracts—the French government, in 1964 and 1968, established quotas on the entry of Algerian nationals. These quotas were clarified in 1970 by French legislation and were reduced by a third agreement in 1972.[27] As we shall see, there were several reasons why Algerians were subject to special treatment that went well beyond concerns about integration.

The suspension of immigration in 1974 by administrative action was not a highly charged political decision. Nevertheless, there were indications that immigration was becoming more politicized, and that containment within the administrative framework was becoming more difficult. The best example is the reaction to the Marcellin-Fontanet circulars in 1972, which simply halted the long period of regularization of illegal immigrants once they had obtained employment. These administrative decrees instead required that potential immigrants obtain the commitment of employment before their arrival or face expulsion. Employers strongly opposed the measures, and ultimately so did the unions, as immigrant workers confronting expulsion, demonstrated in front of union offices. In the end, the Minister of Labor, George Gorce, reversed Marcellin-Fontanet, and granted amnesty to over 50,000 illegal immigrants in the second half of 1973.[28]

The Dynamic of Partisan Competition

By 1980, the Left was firmly building a position against expulsions, and at the same time emphasizing its differences with the (Right) Government still in power. Without much fanfare, this marked the end of immigration decision-making confined within the administration, and the beginning of a more contentious process of partisan conflict. The decision by the Right to try to develop harder legislation on expulsions in 1978–1979, and counterpressures from trade unions and civil rights groups on the Left also made it more difficult to confine decision making to administrative decrees.

The politicization of the process, however, was greatly accelerated by the electoral breakthrough of the National Front in 1983–1984, which ensured that, in decision-making on immigration, the electoral context could not be ignored. Indeed, increasingly after 1984, it appeared as if immigration policy was far more polarized than it was (see ch. 2). Although very little separated Left and Right governments with regard to policy on immigration, the electoral stakes made immigration politics one of the great dividers between Left and Right. As the National Front gained in electoral support, the story of immigration politics after 1984 became less about the struggle over policy orientation itself, than about the struggle by established political parties on both the Right and the Left to use policy to undermine the ability of the National Front to sustain the initiative in portraying and defining these issues.

Of course, this does not mean that the electoral breakthrough of the National Front was important only in terms of rhetoric. Since the mid-1980s, governments of the Right and the Left have been sensitive to the policy positions advocated by FN. While the more extreme positions have been resisted, other hard FN positions have been enacted into law or promulgated by administrative actions. A 2005 analysis notes the following areas in which more restrictive policy has been linked to FN pressure: more restrictive rules for family unification and marriage, more restrictions on tourist visas, increased levels of expulsion of illegal immigrants, greater restrictions on the right of asylum, and greater requirements for naturalization.[29] Of course the problem is that it is difficult to know if at least some of these more restrictive policies would have been enacted even without FN pressure. Nevertheless, at least some policy changes can be linked more directly to the competitive dynamics of electoral and party competition.

Both the RPR (the Gaullists) and the UDF (the Centrists), the main parties of the established Right, were deeply divided internally in their competition with FN for voters who were frightened by the problems of a multiethnic society. There was intense conflict between those who advocated cooperating with FN and accepting their issues in more moderate terms, and others who were tempted to try to destroy their rival on the Right through isolation and rejection of their portrayal of these issues altogether. Each time the Right felt it had succeeded in outmanoeuvring the National Front (the legislative elections of 1988, the municipal elections of 1989, and the immigration legislation of 1993—see below), it was reminded that the challenge would not disappear (the by-election victories of the FN in Marseilles and Dreux in December 1989, the legislative elections of 1993, the presidential and municipal elections of 1995, the legislative elections of 1997, and finally, the regional elections of 1998). More and more, the electorally weak parties of the Right needed the 10–15 percent of the electorate that voted FN nationally, and locally the challenge was even more severe.

As for the Socialists, until the legislative elections of 1993 (and while they were still in power) they struggled to defuse the rhetoric of the National Front with a variety of approaches: by policy initiatives (strengthening border controls, at the same time that they tried to develop a policy of integration) when they controlled the government; by agreeing with the established Right when they were electorally threatened by the opposition, as did Socialist Prime Minister Laurent Fabius, while debating with the then leader of the opposition Jacques Chirac in 1985, by arguing that "the National Front poses some real questions…"; and, more generally, by alternating between the pluralist rhetoric of a "right to difference" approach to immigrants and an individualistic "right to indifference" approach.[30] It was a minister of justice of the Left who in 1983 proposed and passed legislation that gave the police the right to use skin and hair color to decide which people to stop for identity checks; and it was the Left that first established rules in 1984 that made family reunification far more difficult, by requiring approval of applications in the country of origin, far from political pressures of metropolitan France.

These rules were then further tightened by three Left governments between 1988 and 1993. The restrictions were then codified in the *Lois Pasqua*, passed by the Right in 1993/94, which added teeth to the regulations first formulated in 1984, by giving the prefect the right to challenge and withdraw the *titre de séjour* (the right to abode) of any family member.[31] On the other hand, the *Lois Pasqua* also stipulated that identity checks by the police should *not* be based on race or national origin.[32] In this way, despite the confusion, the dynamics of party competition gave teeth to the broader definition of the issue of immigration in national politics: from a labor market problem, to an integration/incorporation problem; to a problem that touches on national identity, to problems of education, housing, law and order, to problems of citizenship requirements.

This politics of party competition is illustrated well by events in the spring of 1990, concerning how the immigration issue should be framed.

The (Socialist) Rocard government attempted to develop a Left-Right consensus about the portrayal of the immigration problem. Using as a pretext a disturbing report by the National Consultative Committee on the Rights of Man, the prime minister called a meeting of all political leaders, except those of the National Front, to develop a program to combat *racism*. The RPR–UDF opposition, however, rejected this definition of the problem, and organized their own meeting (March 31/April 1) the weekend preceding the meeting with the prime minister to discuss problems of *immigration*. When they met with the government, the opposition came armed with four propositions for changing immigration policy. They were able to extract from the Rocard government a commitment for a second meeting that would deal with opposition initiatives, preceding a general parliamentary debate on racism *and* immigration in May 1990.[33]

Behind most of this activity was the continuing pressure of the National Front, which was holding its National Congress while the government and the Centre-Right opposition were developing their positions. The opposition groups (that is the Right) had never come closer to agreement on a unified approach to the politics of immigration, and their propositions represented a way of differentiating themselves from the Socialist government while tentatively approaching some of the ideas of the National Front. The clearest statement was made by former president Valéry Giscard d'Estaing, who was quoted as saying: "The foreigners can live in France with full rights ["dans le respect des droits de l'homme"] but they cannot change France." Giscard promptly launched a national petition to hold a referendum to make naturalization legislation more restrictive (one of the proposals agreed to by the opposition and eventually passed in 1993, though by legislation, rather than referendum).[34]

Not all the actions of the Socialist governments emphasized consensus. As prime ministers, both Michel Rocard and Edith Cresson also attempted to portray their approach to immigration as "hard" and decisive, and when the Socialists were in power after 1988 there was a steady increase in the number of foreigners detained because of invalid documents: the number of foreigners detained rose two and a half times from 1989 to 1991, but the percentage of those detained who were actually expelled (some after hearings) declined from over 60 percent to 18 percent. (See table 3.6) The government was clearly making a point at a time when it was under considerable pressure from the opposition, and when the National Front was doing well in by-elections.

Therefore, any attempt to develop a core consensus among the established parties was undermined in important ways by the electoral success of the National Front (mostly in by-elections during the period we are considering here). In this kind of environment, it seems unlikely that any kind of *expression* of consensus could develop. As *Le Monde* noted at the time, "...political leaders are convinced that the issue is too important for partisan quarrels.... They vie with each other to accentuate their divergences as if to mask their agreements."[35]

The importance of the FN challenge was demonstrated by the end of the electoral cycle in 1995. Immigration themes played almost no role in the presidential election campaign that year. Both candidates of the Right, Balladur and Chirac, appeared to presume that the legislation passed in 1993 would defuse the issue, while the Socialist candidate, Jospin, in a brief paragraph in his election program, indicated that he would ease the requirements on the children of immigrant parents born in France imposed by the 1993 legislation. Only Le Pen, the leader of the National Front, spoke of going further.[36]

After Le Pen's impressive showing in the first round, however, both Chirac and Jospin attempted to attract FN voters without making obvious overtures to Le Pen. Jospin spoke approvingly of proportional representation, which would have increased the representation of the National Front, while both Chirac and Juppé (who would be named prime minister) spoke darkly of problems of law and order and "...the confiscation of the maintenance of order by ethnic or religious groups."[37]

The campaign and results of the municipal elections in June 1995—in which the National Front won in several important towns (including Toulon and Orange)—once again focused attention on immigration issues. Le Pen promised to use the new local power of the FN to emphasize "national preference" in all policy areas. Clearly, this new tilt of the immigration issue posed a challenge for the newly elected president, Jacques Chirac. The president created a full ministry to deal with questions of immigration and integration, with the awkward name of the Ministry of Integration and the Struggle against Exclusion. In a series of dramatic moves, the government rapidly moved against undocumented immigrants and announced a program to move "delinquent families" (generally considered a codeword for immigrant families) out of slum neighborhoods, presumably into other slum neighborhoods.[38] Then, in reaction to the victories of the National Front in the municipal elections, as well as to a new wave of bombings by Algerian dissidents, the president suspended the implementation of the Schengen Accords—which would have opened French borders to the free movement of people within most of the EU—in July.[39] In an interview with a German newspaper, one of Chirac's chief aides argued that "Europe works for Le Pen," and he suggested that the Le Pen challenge might be met by derailing Schengen and returning to a hard-line Gaullist support for the nation-state.[40]

A now forgotten incident in April 1996 well illustrates how local support for the National Front served as a spearhead for national influence over policy. Thirty members of a National Assembly committee recommended new immigration legislation that would limit access of undocumented immigrants to hospitals and schools, and that would facilitate expulsion of minors from French territory. The recommendations were widely opposed, even within the majority—opposition included former hard-line interior minister, Charles Pasqua—and the proposal never gained government support.[41] Nevertheless, immigration legislation was now back on the political agenda, placed there by committee members who were particularly vulnerable to the FN pressure. In the districts of 9 members of the committee, the National Front was the second party in the 1993 legislative elections; and in 22 of 30 districts, the FN vote was well above the 1993 national mean for the party.[42]

The relationship between the pressure from the extreme Right and the need for each government to maintain its credentials for being tough on immigration effectively prevented a succession of governments of the Right and the Left from considering changes in immigration policy that would provide for easier entry.

All major proposals of this kind have ultimately failed. For example, in October 1999, former Prime Minister Alain Juppé, in an interview in *Le Monde*,[43] argued that this was a good moment to open a new page on the immigration debate, and that, along with the European Union,

> We must define common criteria to welcome new foreigners into the EU. I believe, in effect, that 'immigration zéro' does not mean much: family unification is a right, and Europe will need foreign manpower, if we take account of demographic trends.

The moment was right, *Le Monde* noted in its editorial, because the weakness of the extreme Right (the National Front had split in a bitter dispute between its two leaders nine months before), and the victory of the French "multicolored" soccer team in the World Cup the previous June had given a boost to a new effort to recognize that immigration continues, that France remains "the champion of mixed marriages, [and] is strengthened by this mix". Nevertheless, the proposal was opposed by most of the leaders of the Right, including former minister of the interior Jean-Louis Debré, as "inopportune," and died quickly.

Because the vote for the Left was splintered among several candidates in the first round of the presidential elections of 2002, Jean-Marie Le Pen, the candidate of the National Front came in second. The Right was divided as well, with the result that Jacques Chirac placed first, but with the lowest percentage of votes of any leading candidate in the history of the Fifth Republic, and only 2 percent ahead of Le Pen. In the second round, Chirac won with the support of the Left, and with more than 81 percent of the vote.

Nevertheless, for the Right, the electoral lesson seemed clear—never in the future to permit its support to be undermined by the immigration issue as used by the National Front. Thus, in the years that followed 2002, the constraints imposed by the National Front remained, and were even reinforced by what had happened.

The strategy of the Right to deal with the challenge of the National Front included a combination of hard policy and actions that would demonstrate the effectiveness of the state in dealing with illegal immigration. The immigration legislation in 2003, with its emphasis on stricter visa requirements and the experimental integration contract focused French legislation on interests close to those of National Front voters, while Minister of the Interior Nicolas Sarkozy, periodically employed extreme Right discourse and took action that would indicate that this government was serious about controlling the frontier. (See ch. 3.) By 2005, Sarkozy was given credit by officials of the majority Right UMP (the designation since 2002 for the governing coalition of the Right) for the relatively poor showing of the National Front in elections at the end of 2004 and early 2005.[44]

This success provided an opening for the recognition and elaboration of a new departure in immigration policy in 2006, termed by Sarkozy as *immigration choisie*, as opposed to *immigration subie*. It was a call for an increase of high-tech immigrants in place of those who arrive for family unification, but was also a step away from the *immigration zéro* rhetoric of a decade earlier (see ch. 3). This new orientation, in part first elaborated under the socialists in 1998, was integrated into the 2007 legislation. It is unclear whether such a policy can be made to work, or whether reduction of family unification is even legal under existing international agreements. Indeed, the goal (that half or more of immigrants fit this category of *immigration choisie*), acknowledged as difficult to achieve, was termed "mission impossible" by one noted scholar.[45]

It is clear, however, that this is an approach that Sarkozy understands and explains in terms of the dynamics of the electoral challenge of the National Front.

> *Immigration choisie* is practiced by the quasi-totality of democracies in the world. And in these countries, racism and the extreme right are less strong than here. In short, this [proposal] is a rampart against racism. This should make us think. I want a calm and lengthy debate about the theses of the extreme right, which makes every foreigner into a delinquent, and the extreme left, for which to speak of immigration is the equivalent of xenophobia.[46]

While it is certainly true that every country has made some effort to "choose" those that it accepts for settlement, it is less clear that this has made them more resistant to the success of the extreme Right. On the other hand, the statement should probably be read for what it hypothesizes about the importance of this policy for France.

The New Interest Group Universe

Although the dynamics of party competition have been most important for understanding the development of immigration policy in France, the changes in the interest group universe has also played a role. Prior to the 1980s, the interests of immigrant groups were mediated either through more universal associational interest groups (unions or church groups, for example), many of which were, in turn, dominated by political parties, or by the representatives of foreign states from which immigrant groups had come.

In the 1970s, when policy-makers assumed that there was a real possibility that North Africans would return home, a policy consensus developed around state aid for programs that would encourage them (or at least permit them) to do so. Immigrant groups, legally excluded from forming their own associations since before WWII, were never involved in the development of these programs. The Ministry of National Education cooperated with numerous Socialist and Communist local governments in developing Arabic language classes within the normal curriculum and special language and culture classes outside of the normal curriculum. These programs were established through agreements with the countries of origin, and the teachers were recruited by the countries themselves. By the early 1980s, such programs were attracting about 20 percent of foreign students and 10 percent of Algerian students in France, but, despite the hopes of the government, they were never important in encouraging the return of immigrants to their home countries.[47]

One of the most important decision of the Left when it came to power in 1981 was to pass a law in October 1981, that liberated immigrant associations from pre-WWII restrictions, and placed them on the same legal footing as other associations in France. Most important, immigrants could now administer their own (and French) associations, and receive public funding. This change in the opportunity structure, in turn, coincided with a reaction among young immigrants against discriminatory practices during the decade before. Roughly speaking, the mobilization of immigrants during the 1980s has many of the same roots as the mobilization of similar associations in the United States in the 1930s.

By the mid-1980s, these associations had become a network of established intermediaries for immigrant populations that negotiated with trade unions, political parties and the state at the local and national levels. By the end of the decade they numbered between three and 4,000, ranging from about a thousand Islamic associations, to the better-known national groups such as SOS-Racism and France Plus.[48] Although the Socialists attempted to bring the main associations within the orbit of the Left, in contrast to earlier periods of immigration, these associations operated outside the established network of intermediary groups, which were forced to recognize their independent existence. Even when established, more universal intermediary groups did succeed in incorporating the leadership of these associations, their leaders continued to maintain considerable independence.[49] As one scholar has put it:

> The progressive fusion of successive immigrant generations with native French people of the same social stratum cannot be seen to the same degree as before. Diverse components of the working class

increasingly refer to their national, ethnic or religious origins, and refer less and less to the social condition that they share.[50]

During the early 1980s, many of these groups focused on the "right to be different," a goal that was then consistent with the main thrust of government policy. However, as the rise of the National Front distorted and transformed the political meaning of diversity, the most important immigrant associations shifted their goals toward integration into the national community. In the process, however, they emerged as ethnic lobbies, and began to use national origin and religion to mobilize for political stakes.[51] The literature that has emerged from research during the past decade devotes considerable space to comparing the differences between ethnic mobilization in France and in the United States, but the essential point is that, as we have seen, political mobilization on the basis of evolving categories of ethnicity is hardly novel in France. The question is, what about it is new?

We have seen in chapter 3 that such ethnic mobilization is now taking place outside of the organizational framework of established union and party organizations. We have also seen that there is more intense involvement of agencies of the state at the very time when such action should be excluded by the reaffirmation of the Republican model. This involvement can be understood in terms of the breakdown of traditional agencies of immigrant incorporation.

The state has tended to be surprisingly dominant, and that these associations have proven to be remarkably ineffective in the political process. They have clearly not functioned as political and electoral entrepreneurs in the American sense. Part of the reason is certainly that political parties have made little or no effort to co-opt potential ethnic voters (see below), and associations have made little effort to become political entrepreneurs in the electoral process. At the 2006 meeting of the Union of Islamic Organizations of France (UOIF) there were no important political figures who spoke, and not a single deputy of the Left attended.[52]

Immigrant organizations have been hesitant to pursue an American style multicultural political campaign. Indeed, there are many indications that the values of the Republican model have been important for the children of immigrants. At the above cited meeting of the Union of Islamic Organizations in France, the president of the French Muslim Students Association noted that: "The young Muslims have passed the stage of a 'vote communautaire' in favor of a personality who claims to represent them. Their preoccupations are those of all of French society."

Another reason may be that these associations are largely dependent on state and local government financing, and therefore are less likely to be effective negotiators. In Jocelyne Cesari's study of Marseilles, she found that the state and the municipality were overwhelmingly important in constructing and defining patterns of associations. In 1990, 29 immigrant associations received substantial financing from the city government, and shared 3 million francs from Fonds d'Action Sociale (about 25 percent of the total FAS budget). The result was that these were not advocacy groups and political entrepreneurs, but ethnic beneficiaries of state funding. Although most decisions about subventions are made annually, the groups that received grants had remained stable since 1985, and the pattern of financing had both legitimized and encouraged ethnic-based association:

> The FAS or the municipality only give subventions when individuals from North African immigrant groups are organized in associations. For this reason, young people who are often mobilized without reference to ethnic identities as...neighborhood groups, slowly develop a presentation of themselves as young "beurs" or franco-maghrébins, which favors [them in] the allocation of resources.[53]

The Politics of Change

There has been only one major change in policy orientation in immigration policy during the past century—the suspension of most immigration in 1974. Although this change has been explained in terms of the dynamics of group politics, as well as electoral competition, neither of these explanations seems to have been the basis for the decision.

Jeanette Money, presents interesting evidence that as early as 1971 the right-wing national majority began to take immigration control and the "problem" of immigrants seriously at the local level , as part of a strategy to defend their majority against the resurgent Left.[54] She demonstrates that there were a high proportion of potential swing electoral constituencies in departments with high concentrations of immigrants (generally, where the Left was strong), and that the right-wing majority targeted anti-immigrant appeals to those constituencies. These appeals were widespread during the municipal elections of 1971, the legislative election campaign in 1973, and were even more widespread during the presidential election campaign in 1974. Thus, although immigration was certainly not an important national issue in these campaigns, it was of far greater importance at the local level, in swing constituencies controlled by the Left and seen as vulnerable by the Right.

There is no question that immigration issues were important to Communist and some Socialist mayors in towns with large immigrant populations during this period. Communist mayors in particular anticipated political reactions to North African immigration, and right-wing rivals saw this as an issue that could be exploited. Nevertheless, there was no clear evidence of pressure from the voters themselves, and attempts to mobilize voters around immigration were not successful. By the late 1970s, Communist local governments were trying to limit access of immigrant residents to local services, and were pressing the national government to impose local quotas on the immigrants resident in these towns. This was capped by an anti-immigrant campaign by the Communist Party during the presidential election of 1981. However, this campaign faded quickly when it failed to resonate among voters, and after the PCF lost support in the towns that had been the focus of this campaign.[55]

In fact, in the 1973 legislative elections the Right lost support in constituencies where the Left was strong, many of which were those swing constituencies with high immigrant populations that had been targeted by the Right. Thus, although there was certainly political pressure from some local governments in areas of high immigrant concentrations, this is quite different from electoral or public pressure. Furthermore, it is important to differentiate between voters' concerns and the priorities of voters' concerns when they actually vote. Indeed, as late as 1984 (at the point of the breakthrough of the National Front), only 6 percent of the French electorate gave immigration as a motivation for the electoral choice. It was only after immigration policy had been changed that the issue became highly politicized and important in electoral terms, even at the local level.[56] We will return to the electoral issue below.

Another way of understanding the policy change is that it was a result of a shift in the balance of interest groups supporting and opposing the more open policy of the postwar period.[57] There was little opposition to suspension from trade unions (with the partial exception of the CFDT). The employers' association opposed the suspension, and employer federations that most depended on immigrant labor were most vocal (la Fédération Parisienne de Construction in particular). Nevertheless, employers had traditionally favored European workers over those from North Africa, and European immigration would continue, and even increase for some time (from Portugal in particular). The suspension of immigration was not widely discussed, and did not become the subject of legislative debate, since no legislation was involved.

The suspension of immigration in some ways seemed to represent a radical change in policy, albeit consistent with similar moves toward exclusion that were taking place in other European countries at the same time (Germany suspended immigration in November 1973). However, at least at first, it was less radical than it may appear. First, the suspension would not apply to immigrants from countries of the European Community, since they were in France under special EC regulations. Second, emigration from Algeria, the largest sending country outside of Europe, had been suspended by the Algerian government itself, following a series of incidents in September 1973. Third, prior to 1973–1974, French policy had tended to be selective, with a bias against Algerian immigration. Fourth, although specifically interdicted by the decree of July 1974, family unification continued (although at lower levels), until attempts to enforce the suspension of family migration was specifically forbidden by the French Conseil d'État in 1978. Finally, in July 1974, the option of lifting the suspension remained open, and would for some time.

Indeed, for several years the process of change seemed to reflect an administrative rebalancing rather than a shift in interest group support. The new Secretary of State for Immigration, Paul Dijoud, defined what he called "a new policy of immigration," which in fact seemed similar to the old one:

> Immigration is still an economic necessity, since the degree of development of our economic system of production, and the unequal development of sectors and regions would seem to require appreciable contingents of immigrant manpower for several more years....

The fears seemed similar as well:

> [However] the equilibrium of our collective existence is in question. When the proportion of foreigners reaches 20% in certain departments, 40% in certain cities, 60% in certain neighborhoods, exceeding certain thresholds of tolerance creates the risk of the phenomenon of rejection, compromising social peace.[58]

It appears that the economic crisis permitted the administration to do what it had been prone to do before, since it was now less constrained by pressures from the labor market.

It gradually became clear over the next decade, however, that in fact the orientation of French policy had changed in a significant way in 1974. Before suspension, French policy was open to immigration, with a tilt toward ethnic balancing in favor of Europeans. After suspension, French policy became increasingly exclusionary, with significant—and unsuccessful—attempts to limit access of non-European migrants. Although, over the next decade, it gradually became clear that immigration in various forms was continuing, the larger public believed that it had been stopped, creating a gap between perception and political reality that fed into the eventual politicization of the immigration.

In these ways, the decisions reached between 1974 and 1978 were quite different from parallel decision on policy made in both in Britain and the United States. As we shall see, in these countries the change of policy was the subject of legislative action and widespread legislative debate. In the French case, the change of policy only developed over a long period of time, without legislation and without public debate.

In recent years, there have been other attempts to once again alter the paradigm of immigration policy, without success. In fact, the struggle for change continues, and has focused on a tension between two strategic understandings of immigration. The first, which sees immigration as a challenge to national identity, is a reaction to the pressure of the National Front, and emphasizes using the immigrant issue as a way of mobilizing voters opposed to immigration and immigrants (this is the issue as defined by Jeannette Money above). The second and far less dominant strategy in France sees immigrants as a political resource (as ethnic voters), and focuses on mobilizing immigrants as a way of changing the electoral balance among political parties.

Electoral Strategy

Thus, the politics of French immigration policy have been defined by an identity approach to immigration, which has been driven by electoral competition. The effects of the electoral weight of the National Front have been particularly important for the Right, and have effectively constrained its ability to pursue alternative electoral strategies. This does not mean, however, that alternatives have not been considered. The first indication of this was in the period after the split in FN in 1998–1999, when an opportunity seemed to open up that permitted the Right to consider other alternatives. In addition to the policy initiative, Juppé saw his approach as a way of attracting immigrant voters to the Right:

> In general, politicians are accused of not being concerned about the preoccupations of citizens, and when they try, let us not accuse them of electoralism. I have concluded simply that numerous people who are descended from immigrants [*issues de l'immigration*] have been disappointed by the left, from which they expected a lot. It is our task to address them today.[59]

This version of the electoralist approach was a substantially new way to look at immigration, at least for the Right in the French context, and particularly for a leading conservative politician. In many ways it was similar to the approach that was finally pursued by the Republican Party in the United States after 1996, when the Bush team concluded that they could not afford to simply concede the new immigrant voters to the Democrats in 2000 (see ch. 10). In France, however this approach did not attract any support among the established parties of the Right. By 2002, with the reappearance of the challenge of Front National, this initiative had been long forgotten, and the Right was firmly committed to dealing with immigration in terms of its electoral competition with the National Front, as an identity issue.

However, as we have noted above, gradually after 2002, Minister of the Interior Nicolas Sarkozy attempted to redefine the issue of immigration in a way that would change the orientation of policy from exclusion to an acknowledgment of controlled immigration. In a speech before the National Assembly, as he presented his 2003 legislation, he noted: "We have created as an objective the myth of zero immigration. This myth makes no sense at all. It is contrary to reality."[60]

At the same time that his rhetoric was used to attract working class voters to the majority UMP from the National Front, he made gestures toward immigrant communities calculated to attract immigrant voters. By June of 2005 the Socialists were sure that "...immigration would be at the heart of the presidential campaign of the Right for the presidential elections of 2007," even though there was no increase in public opinion that indicated that immigration was a priority issue.[61] As it turned out, they were correct, but it played out almost entirely within the Right. The political context for the debate on this approach was the struggle for leadership of the majority Right between Nicolas Sarkozy and Dominique de Villepin.

The initiatives by Sarkozy were meant to stake out a position on immigration that would clearly differentiate him from de Villepin, his archrival within the majority. As interior minister from March 2004-May 2005, de Villepin supported a policy on immigration that was tougher than that of Sarkozy (who was minister of finance during the same period). He established courses in language, law, and civics for prospective Muslim clerics. He also took the initiative of establishing a private, association-based Muslim foundation in 2005 as a symbolic alternative to the mosque-based council supported by Sarkozy. He also proposed—unsuccessfully—that all services concerning immigration be regrouped under the authority of the ministry of the interior, but did succeed in centralizing and strengthening the Frontier Police Force (PAF—see ch. 3).[62] Finally, his successful expulsion of a radical imam from Lyon in October 2004, who had preached the legitimacy of violence against adulterous women, created a considerable stir. Imams had been expelled before, but only because they had supported violence associated with jihad.

Thus, in June 2005, in the aftermath of the failure of the French electorate to approve the referendum on the European Constitution, when Sarkozy was appointed minister of the interior in a government that was led by de Villepin as prime minister, a struggle to redefine immigration policy became very quickly became a centerpiece in their rivalry. Sarkozy was determined to present strong immigration legislation that would, for the first time, define the objectives of French immigration policy in terms of his 2003 statement.[63] The principle point of disagreement, however, focused on integration policy, rather than on policy of entry.

The new departures proposed for integration policy represented a challenge to dominant ideas, and returned to the failed Juppé initiative. The minister of the interior (Sarkozy) first proposed legislation that would permit the direct financing of mosques, and then resuscitated proposals he had made in 2003 for "positive discrimination," proposals that had been opposed by de Villepin in 2004.[64] To Sarkozy's vague proposals for positive discrimination, Chirac and de Villepin countered with a focus on anti-discrimination legislation that would promote equality of opportunity.

Within a month, the debate about republican principles had been elevated to a struggle between two different models of integration. Responding to a question from a reporter, de Villepin emphasized that affirmative action was not especially successful in the United States:

> Don't mistake the meaning of the words: positive discrimination provides a position for someone as a function of race or ethnicity...which is not at all the philosophy of equality of opportunity, which is at the heart of the republican pact. It is not in the name of membership of a minority, of a group, because someone is of a certain race or of a certain ethnicity that one is going to get a job or a place in this or that school. It is because one deserves it, because someone makes the necessary effort...We support the defense of merit.[65]

While this debate was a high-stakes political contest within the governing Right, it was reflected by a parallel debate within the Socialist Party, where a report was circulating (written by the national secretary for social questions) that—together with proposals for multilevel visas that would appear to permit the recruitment of guest-workers—advocated the use of quotas for more effective integration. Here too, the American reference played a role, and deeply divided party leadership.[66] While the debate itself was important in policy terms, and indicated the importance of integration policy on the political agenda, the consequences were far less important in political terms than they were for the Right.

By the autumn, Sarkozy pushed the differences further by opening up the possibility of the right to vote for immigrants, the revision of the law of 1905 on the separation of church and state to make it possible to finance the construction of mosques, and by once again focusing on positive discrimination.[67] At the same time he began to formulate legislation (passed in July 2006).[68]

Thus, by October, Sarkozy appeared to be dominating the immigration agenda. While reaching out to ethnic communities through a variety of proposals that would recognize a major change in the Republican model of integration, he developed proposals that were calculated to attract the working class voters that had flocked to the National Front in increasing numbers. This was a bold attempt both to neutralize the National Front, to deprive them of their ability to arbitrate both elections and policy, and to alter the electoral attraction of the Right for newly enfranchised immigrant voters. In a more complex way, Sarkozy's political approach to immigration was the parallel of that of George Bush in the United States.

It was an attempt to deprive rivals on the Left of immigrant votes by using a different kind of electoral strategy, one that focuses on immigrants as electoral actors or potential electoral actors; a strategy that sees immigrants as ethnic voters. It is clear that Sarkozy has devoted considerable energy to organize his official activities around this strategic approach since 2003. Some of this effort appeared to be undermined by the month of riots in November 2005, but this effort remained undiminished in the months since.[69] What is less clear is whether this strategic approach will have a long-term electoral payoff.

Since the 1970s, the political geography of immigration in France has changed substantially. Areas of immigrant population have become more concentrated, while the political domination of these areas by the Left has been reversed. With almost 60 percent of all immigrants in France, the percentage of immigrants in the Paris region (*the Ile de France*) grew from 13.3 percent of the population in 1982 to 14.7 percent in a decade (double the national average). Meanwhile the percentage in other regions has continued to decline.

By 1999, only 17 percent of the electoral circumscriptions (districts for National Assembly elections) in France had immigrant populations of more than 10 percent. More than 70 percent of these circumscriptions were in the Paris region, with most of these in the suburbs. However, a majority of them were represented by the Right—everywhere except in the city of Paris itself (see table 4.2).

This shift is indirectly related to the success of the National Front, because of its growing ability to mobilize working class voters. Even where the National Front was eliminated or withdrew in the second round in elections in the 1980s, most of these voters never shifted back to the Left. Although the normal vote of the Left has declined by only a few percentage points in elections since the 1970s, it has declined far more in the 32 *départements* in which there is the highest concentration of immigrants than in other *départements*, indicating a reaction from voters and potential voters of the Left.[70] In this way, voter reaction to immigrant presence seems to provide a key to the realignment of the party system, as well as a powerful argument against pursuing a positive strategy to mobilize immigrant voters by national parties.

Table 4.2 indicates that higher concentrations of immigrant populations offer the possibility of politicization, *but in which way?* How should the policy problem be framed, and how should policy be developed? Some towns governed by the Left (generally the Socialists) have seen immigrants

Table 4.2   Percentage of respondents who claim there are "too many Arabs in France"[a]

% Immigration in Commune/ Party ID	None	1–4%	5–10%	10%+	Total
Communists (PC)	66.7	70	31.6	25	41.2
Socialists (PS)	75.9	54.5	46	26.5	47.5
Centrists (UDF)	83.3	70	92.3	72.7	77.3
Gaullists (RPR)	80	85	81.3	71.4	80
National Front (FN)	100	95.5	92	85.7	92
Total	74.2	64.4	62.8	46.9	60.9

Note:

a Does not include smaller parties and non-identifiers.

Source: CSA survey 9662093, November 1996, Q5246/RS12/ETR.

Table 4.3   Circumscriptions in France (métro) with 10 percent + population immigrant (1999), by the party of the deputy

	Paris (city)	Suburbs of Paris	Provinces	Total
Right	9	**24**	**17**	50
Left	**11**	22	10	43
Total	20 (22%)	46 (49%)	27 (29%)	93 (100%)

Note: Circumscriptions = 555.

Source: INSEE Circonscriptions législatives: résultats du recensement de la population de mars 1999.

as a political resource and as concentrations of immigrants increase, voters of the Left have tended to have more favorable attitudes toward their presence. On the other hand, in towns governed by the Right, voters have been generally prone to see immigrants as a challenge to French identity, and increased immigrant presence appears to have no significant impact on the already negative orientation of voters of the Right. Both of these local orientations are reflected in table 4.2.

However, with so few circumscriptions with concentrations of immigrants more than 10 percent, and with most of these circumscriptions dominated by the Right, there appears to be little incentive to frame the problem of immigration in more positive terms by political parties in national elections. Thus, the political advantage of a more positive approach to immigration nationally is limited, since there are few electoral constituencies in which there are large numbers of immigrants who could represent a potential gain in electoral support. Moreover, the political will to do so is substantially reduced as these areas have become dominated by the Right, which tends to see immigrants as a problem rather than as an electoral potential. (See table 4.3.)

Despite the rhetoric cited above, them has been little attempt—either on the Left or on the Right—to mobilize these voters and potential voters, either on the local or the national levels. Studies indicated that there are few representatives at the local level who have been recruited from ethnic communities, and virtually none at the national level. During the period between 1995 and 2001, there were on average just over three percent of municipal councilors from ethnic communities in towns of 50,000 or more, where there were most likely to be higher concentrations of immigrants . The percentage did not rise beyond that in such cities as Marseilles and Paris, where there were very high levels of immigrant populations and which paid greater attention to immigrants, and here France compares poorly with the United Kingdom, where immigrant representation was far higher in London boroughs.[71] Perhaps more striking, even these small numbers did not translate into any national representation. Some research clearly indicates that reluctance to name minority candidates has been related to pressure from the National Front.[72]

However, published research indicates that the Socialist party has frequently resisted naming minority candidates both at the local and national levels for reasons that have less to do with the National Front than with the maintenance of established local elites and the balance of power within the party. In comparison with the British Labour Party (see ch. 7), the French Socialist Party has been less inclined to see immigrant voters as a political resource, in part because decisions on candidates are made beyond the neighborhood level, and are often dictated by national priorities. Indeed, one study by Garbaye attributes the relative success of Roubaix in electing an unusually high percentage of minority candidates to party *weakness*, and the strength of community organizations.[73]

Conclusions

In France, the pressure that drove the immigration issue toward a restrictionist orientation in the 1970s came from the national administration and governments of the Right, but also from localities dominated by the Left, pressures that were moderated by their national parties. From the early 1980s, the issue was driven by constituency level competition between the established Right and the National Front. Thus, there is little objective pressure for a more positive electoral strategy in France.

In addition, there is little pressure from below—little demand—for this kind of strategy. Although there was an important surge of "immigrant" registration during the months after the widespread rioting in the fall of 2005, this registration was not related to a larger mobilization movement; indeed, it was not generally the result of political party initiatives.[74] Indeed, we have seen that immigrant associations appear to have made little effort to construct their demands in terms of "deliverable" votes. In France, as in Britain and the United States, there are groups that have fought for immigrant rights, and they have had some notable successes, particularly in the courts and in the streets. In the courts, the decision by the Council of State in December 1978 to mandate family unification (see chapter 2) was the result of a case brought by an immigrant rights group (G.I.S.T.I.) and two trade unions (the CFDT and the CGT). In the streets (and churches), periodic movements of resistance by undocumented immigrants to increasing expulsions have been widely supported—often with some impact. However, little of this has been translated into political power; nor has it had much of an impact on the programs or actions of political parties.[75]

The absence of a positive electoral strategy that would deal with immigrants as potential voters is often blamed on political culture—the Republican model of integration. However, if we consider the role of the Communist Party during the pre- and postwar periods with European immigrant groups, it is obvious that ethnic political mobilization can be effectively reconciled with the Republican model. The change has been explained as a result of the weakening of the structures that have served traditionally to incorporate immigrant groups, the Communist Party in particular. This explanation makes considerable sense, but we must add that the weakness itself can be understood in part by the inability of unions and the parties of the Left (specifically the PCF) to incorporate the recent wave of immigrant workers.[76] In addition, the racialization of the new wave of immigration that we analyzed above has created new socio-political cleavages that were reinforced by the emergence of the National Front in the 1980s.

And yet, there are clearly reasons to pay more attention to a political strategy that would mobilize immigrant and ethnic voters. Although the distribution of immigrants by circumscription does not give much political weight to these potential voters, their social weight indicates greater potential. A recent official report notes that among the 95 metropolitan departments in France, 25 percent have youth populations above the national average, and almost 15 percent of the age cohort 0–24 years are children of immigrants. Almost 60 percent of the departments have significant immigrant youth populations of 9–10 percent or more of the youth population. This more widely distributed concentration of immigrants among youth is potentially dangerous if alienated, but also indicates a political resource that is growing and not being tapped.[77]

CHAPTER FIVE

Development of British Immigration Policy

Context: The Constitutional and Political System

The present governmental system in Britain began to develop during the second half of the nineteenth century, as universal suffrage developed in stages, and as political parties emerged as the primary organizers of British political life. By the early twentieth century, what became known as the Westminster model had emerged. Unlike France or the United States, this model was not embedded in a written constitution, and did not represent a sharp break with the past. As Richard Rose has pointed out, the rule of law was firmly established by the seventeenth century; the accountability of the executive to parliament by the eighteenth century; the establishment of political parties in the nineteenth century; and universal suffrage well into the twentieth century.[1]

Although modern Britain is often thought of as a single entity—a unitary system—governed from London, this unity has never existed in the sense that there has been a "one and indivisible" French Republic. Scotland was united with England in 1707, when a common parliament was created in London, and the United Kingdom of Great Britain (England, Scotland and Wales) and Ireland was created in 1801, the end-product of an expansion from England that began in the middle ages; when Ireland broke away in 1921, the name of the country was changed to the United Kingdom of Great Britain and Northern Ireland. Indeed, when there is finally a settlement of the Irish question, the name of country may be changed once again. In 1997, after approval by Parliament in London, Scotland and Wales each approved by—referendum—the devolution of limited powers to regional assemblies (each with somewhat different power). In Northern Ireland, a Parliament governed through home-rule provisions until 1972, and after the "Good Friday Agreement" in 1997 Protestants and Catholics shared power in a new Northern Ireland Assembly.

Thus, although the United Kingdom is juridically a united country, with all power officially emanating from Parliament in London, the centralization of institutions differ, and decentralization has been reinforced by devolution. This juridical complexity is matched by a complexity of identity. Most people in the United Kingdom, in fact self identify as English, Scottish, Welch or Irish, rather than British.[2] In addition, there has never been any agreement about the meaning of what is British, or for that matter English. Indeed, as we shall see, at least until after WWII this was further complicated by an expansive concept of citizenship, which incorporated the entire population of the British Empire.[3] Even today, after citizenship has been redefined through fifty years of legislative change, resident aliens from former empire countries retain citizenship rights that comparable aliens do not have in the United States or other parts of Europe. As a result of immigration from what are called New Commonwealth countries, about 8 percent of the population of the United Kingdom is now nonwhite. The political process through which immigration policy has developed is therefore embedded in complex territorial structure, and an increasingly multiracial society.

The governmental structure is defined by the strong control that any British government has over its legislative agenda. Unlike the United States or France, there are no obvious constitutional constraints on government action. The sometimes-cited "unwritten constitution," a collection of parliamentary acts, accepted conventions about the political process and some judicial decisions is sufficiently vague to be reinterpreted with relative ease through new acts of parliament. Parliament is sovereign in interpreting law, and no judicial authority has the prerogative to declare an act of parliament unconstitutional, although this has been somewhat complicated by The Human Rights Act in 1998 that incorporated the European Convention of Human Rights into British law.

At the core of the British government is the Cabinet, appointed by the Prime Minister from among his senior party colleagues, generally serving in the House of Commons. Members of the Cabinet head government departments, and, by tradition, share collective responsibility for all government decisions. Cabinet meetings are held with some frequency, but, as the role of the Prime minister has become ascendant during the period after WWII, government decisions are no longer made as a result of long Cabinet debates and consultation. Members of the Cabinet remain the key decisions-makers for their own departments, but the Prime Minister increasingly dominates the overall direction of the government.

For policymaking in Britain, the political party provides the context for understanding the development of important policies, as well as policy alternatives. Individual ministers, both as members of the government and as party leaders, are key players in framing policy alternatives and in setting the political and legislative agenda, although the large policy debates take place within the context of political parties that are either governing or are in opposition. The success of individual ministers in getting their priorities on the agenda is an indication of their reputation and importance. In these ways, policymaking is inherently partisan, less dominated by independent administrative forces than in France, and less linked to policy communities than in the United States.

This does not mean that interest groups are not important in the British system. Because there is a only one center of power, however, it does mean that interest groups seek influence in parliament, and, above all, in the ministries—and among the ministers—where policies are developed and decided.

Ministries and ministers are also important because of the well-established political principle of ministerial responsibility. In France, and in the United States, well-placed higher civil servants often play an independent role in the development and framing of political issues. In Britain, however, civil servants must work within the confines of ministerial responsibility, since ministers are held responsible for all actions and decisions within their departments. This very much circumscribes the role of civil servants as independent actors, capable of moving and maneuvering policy within the political system.

Thus, as we can see from table 5.1, the core of British immigration policy has been developed through a series of legislative acts, rather than through administrative actions. During the past century, the rules of entry

Table 5.1 Legislation on immigration and citizenship in Britain

1905	Aliens Act; first structure for organizing and limiting immigration of aliens (not Empire and Commonwealth citizens)—bureaucracy of immigration inspectors was provided with discretionary powers; authorized to forbid entry to aliens judged to be without "decent" support, or who :appeared likely to become public charges" because of disease or infirmity; legislation provided for possible deportation of aliens; affirmed right to asylum.
1914	Alien Restriction Act; Home Secretary was given the power to completely restrict the landing of immigrants, deport them, to require them to live in specific areas, the force them to comply with registration, to require or prohibit them from changing residence and to restrict travel.
1919	Aliens Restriction Act; prohibited aliens from sitting on juries, and made it a criminal offense for any alien to promote industrial unrest in any industry in which he had not been legally engaged for more than two years.
1948	British Nationality Act; establishes two categories of citizenship—citizens of the United Kingdom and the colonies (CKUCs) and citizens of the Commonwealth; both with unrestricted rights to enter and reside in the United Kingdom.
1953	Aliens Order; recognized a need for labor by creating a link between entry and work permits issued by the Department of Employment, which in turn were based upon local labor conditions; permits were valid for a year, and then extended up to four years, after which restrictions were generally removed.
1962	Commonwealth Immigrants Act; entry of Commonwealth citizens and CUKCs with passports issued outside of the United Kingdom subject to immigration and labor market controls; also establishes criteria for deportation.
1964	Nationality Act; established an ancestral right to recover UK citizenship—the Natal formula—for settlers in Africa; could now reclaim UK citizenship, providing that they had a father or grandfather born or naturalized in the United Kingdom (or existing colonies or protectorates).
1965	First Race Relations Act; outlaws racial discrimination in public places; establishes Race Relations Board and National Committee for Commonwealth Immigrants to oversee.

Continued

Table 5.1   Continued

1968	Commonwealth Immigrants Act; passed in response to East Africa Asian crisis; applies Natal formula—restricts free entry and settlement to "patrials," those with a continuing relationship to the United Kingdom demonstrated by one of parents or grandparents born in the United Kingdom, or by five years of settlement. Initial quota for immigration control set at 1,500 heads of household.
1971	Immigration Act; consolidates previous legislation, and generalizes "patrial" category for free entry; affirms right of family unification for wives of resident immigrants.
1976	Second Race Relations Act; Commission for Racial Equality established.
1981	British Nationality Act; Creates three categories of citizens—British citizenship, British Dependent Territory Citizens, and British Overseas Citizens—with only British citizens free to enter and abode; *patrials* redefined as British citizens; *jus solis* designation for citizenship restricted to children of settled immigrants and British citizens.
1988	Immigration Act; right of family unification legislated in 1971 stricken from the legislation; all family unification would now be subject to demanding administrative rules.
1991	British Nationality (Hong Kong Act); grants 50,000 Hong Kong residents and families access to British citizenship.
1999	Immigration and Asylum Act; provides for the dispersal of applicants, and imposes new restrictions on work.
2002	The Nationality, Immigration and Asylum Act; introduced tests in English language and citizenship ceremony, as well as demonstration of sufficient knowledge of life in the United Kingdom; applicants for asylum are forbidden to work legally; established and expanded asylum reception centers.
2004	The Asylum and Immigration Act; creates a new category of offence to enter the United Kingdom without proper documents; substantially increases the police power of immigration officials to act without warrants; if asylum is denied, family support can be withdrawn and applicant can be removed to a third (safe) country.

have been set mostly through legislation, and British citizenship has been also redefined through a series of legislative acts. In this way, the entry of Commonwealth citizens into Britain, previously separate from immigration, has come to be controlled by immigration law.

Nevertheless, as we shall see in this chapter and the two that follow, administrative decision-making has been important in British immigration policy. In contrast to France, however, this decision making has been constrained by ministerial responsibility. Ultimately, it is the minister (usually of Home Affairs) who is responsible for the rules that are developed and the actions undertaken by his or her department.

Context: Britain as a Country of Immigration

Unlike France and the United States, Britain has not been a traditional country of immigration. Indeed, until well after WWII the United Kungdom was clearly a country of net emigration. (See table 5.2) Between 1871 and 1931, there was a net outflow of population of more than 3 million people,

Table 5.2 Immigration and emigration to and from the United Kingdom since 1890

Year	Emigration (th)	Immigration (th)	Net (th)
1890	218.1	109.5	-108.6
1900	168.8	97.6	-71.2
1910	397.8	164.1	-233.7
1920	285.1	86.1	-199
1930	92.2	66.2	-26.0
1938	34.1	40.6	+6.5
1950	130.3	66.0	-64.3
1960	88.7	80.2	-8.5
1970	290.7	225.6	-65.1
1980	229.1	173.7	-55.4
1990	231	267	+36.0

Source: B.R. Mitchell, *International Historical Statistics, Europe, 1750–1993*, 4th Edition (London: Macmillan Reference, 1998), Table A9.

Table 5.3 UK Population born abroad, by origin and percentage of population

	Foreign countries (th)/%	Old Common-wealth (th)/%	New Common-wealth (th)/%	Republic of Ireland (th)/%	Total born-abroad (th)/%	NCW as % of born abroad	Irish as % of born abroad
1931	347/ 0.8%	75/ 0.2%	137/0.3%	362/0.8%	921/2.0%	14.9%	39.3%
1951	722/1.5%	99/0.2%	218/0.4%	532/1.1%	1,571/3.2%	13.8%	33.9%
1961	842/1.6%	110/0.2%	541/1.1%	709/1.4%	2,202/4.3%	24.6%	32.2%
1966	886/1.7%	125/0.2%	853/1.6%	732/1.4%	2,596/5.0%	32.9%	28.2%

Source: *Social Trends* No. 2, 1971 (London: Her Majesty's Stationary Office, 1971), pp. 54–55.

mostly to the colonies.[4] Nevertheless, Britain has also been a country of immigration, to which successive waves of migrants have come, even as greater numbers were leaving.

The composition of the immigrant population has also been different from that of France and the United States. While, until the 1960s, the overwhelming proportion of immigrants into France and the United States has been from "foreign" countries (generally European), the highest proportion of immigrants into Britain has been overwhelmingly from former colonies—even before WWII. This balance has changed since the 1960s, but what has changed most is the mix of immigrants from former colonies. The proportion of entries from Ireland (and the "Old Commonwealth"—Canada, Australia and New Zealand) has declined, while that from the "New Commonwealth" (primarily India and Pakistan) has proportionately increased. (See table 5.3.)

By separating considerations of immigration control from the larger consideration of citizenship, British policy-makers defined two different kinds of policy problems, at least until the 1960s. By then, the citizenship problem had come to dominate policy-makers' thinking about immigration. Although these two tracks had their parallels in France and the United States, the track of citizenship continued to dominate British immigration policy until the British Nationality Act of 1981 essentially ended a process of redefining citizenship, and finally redefined all entries of noncitizens as immigration control.

The Meaning of Commonwealth Citizenship

Although, until recently, roughly two-thirds of those who entered the United Kingdom, did so as Empire/Commonwealth citizens, there was no legislative definition of what this meant until 1948. Throughout the nineteenth century British subjects had the formal right, established by custom, to move freely within the empire and dominions. Even after the establishment of Irish Republican citizenship in 1921, the border between the two countries remained uncontrolled; and even after the Republic left the Commonwealth in 1949, controls were not reimposed. The reason usually given (for example in the debate on the Commonwealth Immigrants Bill in 1962) is that it was too difficult to control this frontier, but that controls had been established in other ways.[5]

A decade before WWII, at the beginning of the Great Depression, almost 40 percent of the those born abroad, and resident in the United Kingdom, were from the Irish Republic, and only a third were foreigners that were neither from areas now known as the Old or New Commonwealth or Irish. Although access from the Old Commonwealth (or "Old Dominions") was relatively easy, it was far more difficult, however, to enter Britain from what are now known as the New Commonwealth areas of India/Pakistan or the Caribbean. Perhaps one way of understanding why the openness of empire/commonwealth citizenship was not challenged long before the 1960s, is that—with the exception of the Irish—relatively few immigrants succeeded in entering Britain through this route until the 1950s. (See table 5.3.) Inflow from the Empire, and then from the Commonwealth, was limited by a lack of supportive networks in Britain, as well as by popular and administrative behavior at the water's edge. In fact, policies to limit entry from the New Commonwealth were applied as far back as the nineteenth century, and were clearly related to the more explicit legislation developed in the 1960s.

At no time were "coloured" British subjects considered to be welcome in the home country.[6] Most of the immigrants from the Indian Subcontinent and the Caribbean at the end of the nineteenth century were seamen on British ships. Although, as British subjects, they formally had a right to remain in Britain, they were frequently subject to administrative/police controls and deportation. Early in the nineteenth century legislation was passed, and administrative rules were set in place, to ensure that seamen from the Subcontinent and the Caribbean ("lascars") were returned to their home ports By the end of the nineteenth century, all "destitute" Indian seamen were subject to repatriation.[7] R.G. Spencer argues that, between the two world wars,

> ...the government applied a de facto immigration policy which was specifically directed at limiting the growth in numbers of "coloured" seamen, whose communities had already become established in a number of UK ports... The policies were implemented without any public announcement through administrative measures, by government circulars, by intergovernmental arrangements or by confidential letters from the Home Office to Chief Constables. At the same time the imperial rhetoric of "equal rights for all British subjects" and *civis Bitannnicus sum* was maintained. The policies of the inter-war years constituted an undeclared immigration policy whose intention was to keep out Asian and black settlers.[8]

In general, two methods were used to restrict entry into Britain, both of which effectively did so by restricting exit based on criteria of class: by using such requirements as affidavits of support, bond or cash deposits; and by requiring passport endorsements. These restrictions were imposed by the commonwealth or colonial government authorities, thus obviating the need by the UK government to discriminate at the port of entry. Indeed, those who wished to leave were generally not informed that they had a right to enter the United Kingdom as British subjects.[9] Although some coloured subjects did indeed manage to settle in the United Kingdom, in general they were treated as if they were aliens—or worse.

A variety of studies indicate that the small number of Blacks and Indians present in Britain at the end of the nineteenth century suffered both from popular discrimination, and from "...an increasing tendency to racialise the two groups. At a scientific level, this emphasis on race was particularly evident in the Anthropological Society of London, which was founded in 1863." On the other hand, for more privileged immigrants from India—those with higher class or professional status—there were probably more opportunities in Britain than there were in India.[10]

Perhaps the most significant challenge to free Empire/Commonwealth entry occurred just after WWI, during the hot summer of 1919, with the most serious racial attacks against nonwhite residents in the United Kingdom that had occurred up to that date. The attacks against Blacks and Chinese (but also against some Irish) in such dispersed cities as Cardiff, Liverpool, Hull, Glasgow, and London, were not the first disturbances of this kind, but they were certainly the most extensive. The riots added to the pressure for passage of the 1919 Aliens Act, but Commonwealth immigrants were also dealt with more informally through administrative actions. Coloured residents were encouraged to leave, at times with travel subsidies, and repatriation committees were set up in major cities. These efforts, however, failed to induce many to leave, and, in the end, "...the

India Office and the Colonial Office were both sensitive to the possible political repercussions of pressing the question too hard."[11] At least for the moment, the interests of the Colonial Office, which was concerned with the preservation and perpetuation of the Empire, prevailed over those of the Home Office, which was concerned with the maintenance of order in the United Kingdom.

The broad ideal of Empire citizenship was deeply undermined by its discriminatory administration from the very beginning. As a result, it is surprising that those born in what became known as the New Commonwealth comprised even as much as 15 percent of non-UK residents in Britain at the beginning of the Great Depression. The right of Empire citizenship appears to have had only a minor impact on patterns of immigration, but the maintenance of this myth could endure—despite the practice—because the regulation of this migration was informal, administrative, and in many ways opaque. Thus, before WWII, Britain had an open-door policy for the Empire, through which few entered, as well as a policy of restriction for other countries that severely limited access to those who sought entry.

Nevertheless, even with a need for labor, the United Kingdom remained a country of emigration, rather than immigration. Through the nineteenth and into the twentieth century, a continuous stream of (mostly) young men from the British Isles emigrated to North America, the British colonies and other parts of the world. At the highpoint of British emigration to the United States, 1890, there were almost 1.3 million U.S. residents who had been born in Britain, Scotland and Wales, and another 1.9 million from Ireland.[12] Based on estimates of national origins, well over half the immigration quota for the United States set under the authority of the 1924 Johnson-Reed Act was from the United Kingdom.[13] This trend continued from the end of WWI to the onset of the Great Depression.

Although immigration into the United Kingdom grew after WWII, net immigration was less than 10,000 per year through the 1960s. In the 1970s, the United Kingdom once again became a net exporter of population, and in the 1980s, there was a net outflow of population of more than 50,000 people per year, on average, as families migrated under arranged passage to Australia, New Zealand and South Africa. "Since 1901, more people have emigrated from the United Kingdom than immigrated. By 1997, a net exodus from the United Kingdom of 15.6 million had occurred."[14]

The year 1962 marked the beginning of the end of the special system of Commonwealth entry. As we shall see, the restrictive legislation passed in 1962 applied to all Commonwealth immigrants, but was widely perceived as being directed specifically against those from the New Commonwealth (NCW—here and below, NCW also implies "coloured," and therefore has a racial connotation). Subsequent legislation specifically targeted NCW immigrants with formulas that merged them with aliens for purposes of immigration control.

The control over alien entry, as opposed to Commonwealth/Empire entry, into the United Kingdom goes back to roughly the same period when such entry was restricted in both France and the United States. However, while early French and US legislation was passed to shape immigration that was needed or wanted, early British legislation was passed to halt unwanted immigration. Let us first look at legislation to restrict immigration from non-commonwealth countries, and then return to commonwealth restriction.

Policy on Immigration

Immigration and Immigration Restriction before WWII

At the end of the nineteenth century, there were no formal restrictions on immigration into the United Kingdom, and even before this, legislated restrictions were limited to reactions to specific revolutionary events on the continent. This nonrestrictive policy, however, was changed by legislation passed in 1905, primarily in reaction to the first wave of primarily Jewish immigration from Russia and Eastern Europe. As in the United States, immigration began to accelerate slowly after 1880. At least until the end of the1890s, about 2500 Jews, immigrants often on their way to the United States, decided to stay in Britain each year. This number increased rapidly, however, as war and pogroms pushed an increasing number of Jews to immigrate to Britain. By 1914, 120,000 Jews had settled in the United Kingdom.

The first legislation formally controlling immigration was passed by a Conservative government in 1905, after an unusually long process that lasted several years (see ch. 7). The new law set up the first structure for organizing and limiting immigration of aliens, though not for Empire citizens. In addition, a bureaucracy of immigration inspectors was provided for, with a considerable range of discretionary powers. Aliens were permitted to land only at authorized ports, and immigration officers were authorized to forbid entry to aliens judged to be without "decent" support, or who "…appeared likely to become public charges" because of disease or infirmity. These criteria applied only to "undesirable aliens," that is steerage passengers on immigrant ships. In addition, the legislation provided for deportation of aliens if, during their first year in the country, they received charity relief, or were found living in unsanitary conditions.[15]

In contrast to harsher legislation that had been considered in 1904, however, the law contained provisions that were more "centrist" in terms of policy that would unite the Conservative Party, and that would be less offensive to the Liberal Party opposition. So, for example, an otherwise harsh piece of legislation affirmed the right to asylum (an important declaration at a time of war and pogroms). As we shall see, many of the same conditions imposed by the 1905 act had already been imposed by American authorities by this time.

Administrative discretion narrowed considerably as war approached, and the powers of the 1905 act were extended considerably after the outbreak of the war. Less than a week after the declaration of war on July 28 1914, the Alien Restriction Act of 1914 was rushed through parliament in a single day. The Home Secretary was given the power to completely restrict the landing of immigrants, to deport them, to require them to live in specific areas, to force them to comply with registration, to require or prohibit them from changing residence and to restrict travel.

The 1919 Aliens Restriction Act confirmed most of these powers of the Home Secretary, but also had stipulations that applied to aliens already in the United Kingdom. It prohibited aliens from sitting on juries, and made it a criminal offense for any alien to promote industrial unrest in any industry in which he had not been legally engaged for more than two years. This provision paid political homage to the prevailing fear of radical anarchists. Although it seems not to have been enforced, in remained in force until 1971.[16] Thus, the 1914 wartime measures, together with the Restriction Orders (in Council) based on the legislation, became the fundamental law for immigration control. It was extended and enhanced at the end of the war, and then again each year (with some amendments) until it was replaced by the Aliens Order of 1953.

The 1914 and 1919 acts had made no reference to the long tradition of asylum in the United Kingdom, and this tradition more or less merged with administrative discretion, as the depression deepened at the same time as the Nazis tightened their grip on Germany.[17] Moreover, as Jews attempted to flee, political pressure, often driven by anti–Semitism, forced a tightening of restrictions against asylum-seekers, restrictions supported by both the Conservative and Labour Parties. In practice, the Home office exercised considerable discretion in the admission of aliens and refugees.[18]

After the war there was little change in the legislative rules governing admission of aliens, but labor-market needs had changed. The 1953 Aliens Order represented a small change in policy, by recognizing a need for labor by creating a link between entry and work permits issued by the Department of Employment, which in turn were based upon local labor conditions. Although such permits had been issued between the wars, the process became more systematic after 1953. Permits were valid for a year, and then extended up to four years, after which restrictions were generally removed. This system was then extended to Commonwealth citizens by the legislation passed in 1971.

Therefore, immigration control until the 1960s followed two separate tracks: the regulation of access from the Empire/Commonwealth; and the restriction of immigration of aliens. Each was effective in keeping the inflow of immigrants from either the Colonies/Commonwealth or from other countries at low levels, at the same time that net outflow continued to dominate. In practice, executive and administrative discretion tended to dominate in each area.

Commonwealth Immigration and the Redefinition of Citizenship

Although British immigration policy during the postwar period seems to be a continuation of the prewar pattern, in fact it involved a radical change in orientation. The shift in orientation was primarily a reaction to a sharp change in immigration patterns—resulting from a breakdown in the subtle controls of the prewar period. Although New Commonwealth immigrants were still a minority of immigrants entering the country, the growth of this immigration began to accelerate in the late 1940s. As immigration from other sources began to level off in the early 1960s, NCW immigration continued to grow even more rapidly. Thus, the controls that had limited "coloured" immigration from the commonwealth were increasingly less effective. At the same time there were few formal restrictions in place to limit such immigration.

The British Nationality Act of 1948

This first postwar legislation on immigration had little to do directly with the actual entrance of either aliens or Commonwealth citizens into the United Kingdom. The legislation was a reaction to the independence of India and Pakistan, as well as Canadian legislation on immigration and citizenship passed in 1946. At its core, the Nationality Act was a reaffirmation of an open notion of British "subjectship," based on allegiance to the Crown. The Canadian legislation had violated an idea of subjectship within the British Empire that had existed since the seventeenth century, that a person was a "subject" of the Crown as a privilege granted by the sovereign, not as a claimed right of citizenship. Since the Canadian legislation had first defined Canadian citizens, and then declared that "a Canadian citizen is a British subject," it had changed the rules by which subjectship had been defined.

The 1948 act defined five categories of British subjects. The first, Citizens of the United Kingdom and Colonies recognized, for the first time, a distinctive British citizenship. The second, Citizens of Independent Commonwealth Countries, recognized the action that had been taken by the Canadian government (and soon to be taken by other independent Commonwealth republics). The third, Irish British subjects, anticipated the movement of the Irish Republic toward full independence. The last two categories separated out a category of British subjects without citizenship, British Protected Persons who were aliens, but with a protected status; and finally, aliens.

The first two categories enjoyed broadly identical rights to enter the United Kingdom, to work, to vote and to stand for Parliament. The third gave special recognition to Irish subjects, in the event that Eire became a republic (as it did a year later). Irish citizens could then retain their status by making a request of the British government, although any Irish citizen born in the United Kingdom (i.e., in Ireland before 1922), or whose father was born in the United Kingdom, was automatically a British subject. The fourth category of British subjects was meant to protect British settlers in other countries who might want to reclaim their subject status at a later date.[19]

Thus, the act defined an open subjectship, linked to a relatively open citizenship, with almost no restrictions for those subjects of the colonies and Commonwealth—about 25 percent of the population of the world—who wished to enter and reside the United Kingdom. Moreover, by creating broad citizenship rights for subjects as well as citizens, the act did not clearly differentiate between the two.

Scholars who have been critical of the BNA of 1948 have a point when they argue that the act was

> . . . an emphatic reaffirmation of the unity of empire, in which the maintenance of non-national subjectship, defined by allegiance to Crown, was consciously held against the nationalisms of the periphery. In refusing to devise a concept of national citizenship, the British Nationality Act created the core dilemma for all immigration laws and policies that followed: not to dispose of a clear criterion of belonging.[20]

Nevertheless, by differentiating between citizens and subjects for the first time, the act created categories that would become important in the future for immigration restriction.

The Commonwealth Immigrants Act of 1962

The 1962 legislation has been generally portrayed as a turning point toward immigration restriction in the United Kingdom. In retrospect, given the scope of conflict about the 1962 proposal, the legislation seems like a surprisingly hesitant first step in the direction of abandoning the special status of citizens of the Colonies who resided outside of the United Kingdom and citizens of recently established Commonwealth countries. Instead of simply legislating that such citizens would be subject to the same immigration legislation as other aliens wishing to enter the United Kingdom, the law maintained numerous aspects of special status.

Perhaps the most tortured part of the new law, was that it differentiated British citizens of the United Kingdom from those who resided in the few remaining colonies. The passports of all British subjects who were Citizens of the United Kingdom and Colonies (see table 5.4) were the same, except for one thing—the stamp of the authority under which they were issued. The legislation differentiated between British subjects whose passports were issued under the authority of Her Majesty's Government *in* the United Kingdom (HMG-UK), who had free entry into the United Kingdom; and British subjects whose passports were issued under the authority of Colonial Government in any one of the colonies, who would

Table 5.4   Changing categories of British citizens and aliens, 1948–1981

	Free Entry	Citizenship privileges, but restricted entry	Citizenship privileges, and unrestricted entry	Restricted entry	Restricted entry
British Nationality Act, 1948	Citizens of the United Kingdom and Colonies (CUKC)		Irish British Subjects ——— Citizens of Independent Commonwealth Countries	British Protected Persons (aliens)	Aliens
Commonwealth Immigration Act, 1962	CUKC–HMG-UK	CUKC–Colonial Govt. ——— Commonwealth citizens	Irish citizens		Aliens
Nationality Act, 1964	"Natal" principle: Citizenship based on ancestry				
Immigration Act, 1971	CUKC–HMG-UK ——— CUKC+CW citizens with "patrial" rights	CUKC–Colonial Govt. ——— Commonwealth citizens	Irish citizens		Aliens
Immigration Act, 1981	Citizens of the United Kingdom	British Dependent Territory Citizens		British Overseas Citizens	Aliens

no longer have free access. As Randall Hansen emphasizes, it was the *authority*, rather than the actual place of issue that was crucial.[21]

In this complex way, some subjects of the colonies were separated from fellow passport holders of the United Kingdom, even if they resided in the United Kingdom. For subjects of the colonies with passports that were issued under the authority of colonial governments, the legislation made entry into the United Kingdom dependent on labor skills and the needs of the labor market, thus applying the same principle of entry as for Commonwealth citizens without UK passports (and that had been previously applied only to aliens).

Nevertheless, subjects in the colonies retained UK nationality, as well as UK passports. As colonies became independent, the situation became more complicated. For example, large numbers of Asians were given the option of UK citizenship by the Kenya Independence Act of 1963 "...on exactly the same basis as the European settlers," and similar provisions were made when Uganda became independent. Under the 1962 act, all of these people were entitled to enter the United Kingdom freely, and began to do so as "Kenyanisation" policies were adopted by the new government, and as similar national preference policies were put in place in other parts of East Africa.[22] The impact of this provision would be felt within a few years.

Meanwhile, some of the restrictive aspects of the legislation were cushioned by the fact that there was widespread (if declining) need for immigrant labor. It was also cushioned by other aspects of the law. Entrance was restricted to those Commonwealth citizens who held Ministry of Labour employment vouchers. However, if a Colony or Commonwealth citizen entered the country without such a voucher, and could evade discovery for more than 24 hours, that person could remain. Evasion of control in itself was not a legal offense, and, moreover, case law established that the burden of proof for establishing that an immigrant was in the country less than 24 hours was on the Home Office.[23] Commonwealth and colony citizens could be deported if they were convicted by a court, and there was a recommendation for deportation made by the judge, but deportation was limited to those who had been resident in the United Kingdom for less than five years (in effect giving automatic naturalization to colonial citizens after five years of residency, since they held British passports).[24]

The Labour opposition had strongly and emotionally opposed the legislation while it was being debated, and promised to repeal it. Nevertheless, after returning to power in 1964, it administratively implemented more demanding controls in 1965, by reducing the number of Ministry of Labour vouchers for new immigrants, and ending vouchers for unskilled labor entirely.[25] At the same time, the Labour Party sponsored the *Nationality Act of 1964* that initiated a process that would make it possible to differentiate between white and nonwhite UK "nationals" living in former colonies. This little-noticed legislation established an ancestral right to recover UK citizenship. White settlers in Africa, who had been pressured into accepting the citizenship of their newly independent countries, could now reclaim their UK citizenship, providing that they had a father or grandfather that was born or naturalized in the United Kingdom (or existing colonies or protectorates). This "Natal formula" carefully differentiated between white and Asian settlers in the African former colonies, without at all making direct reference to the differentiation.[26]

The Commonwealth Immigrants Act of 1968 and the Asians Crisis

The Commonwealth Immigrants Act of 1968 is something of misnomer. In fact, the new law was primarily another redefinition of citizenship, and citizenship rights. The legislation passed in 1968 by a Labour government anticipating a negative public reaction to the arrival of large numbers of Asians from East Africa, created a blunt instrument to deal with a specific and pressing problem. The Asians who fled to the United Kingdom from East Africa after 1964 were British nationals who held what appeared to be valid UK passports under the 1962 legislation. Although they were effectively asylum-seekers who were fleeing from oppressive governments in newly established states, they were claiming what appeared to be their rights to enter the United Kingdom.

The Asians from East Africa had every reason to believe that they could legally enter the United Kingdom. This was in part an accident and in part based on an anticipated commitment made by the Conservative government. Because most Asians resident in Kenya (and other East African countries) were not automatically granted Kenyan (and other) citizenship at the time of independence, they chose to retain their UK passports (as CUKCs). Hansen demonstrates that the possibility that these Asians might not be accepted for entry into the United Kingdom had been anticipated by the Conservatives, nevertheless, and that "At least three archival documents demonstrate both that the Asians' position was recognized and accepted, before and after the 1962 Act, and that at least one promise was made to members of the Kenyan Asian community."[27]

Thus the new law—passed with great haste—incorporated the Natal formula as an instrument to deny entrance, and, at the same time, to further refine the meaning of citizenship. The Asians from East Africa retained their British nationality, but this no longer entitled them to enter the United Kingdom, except by special vouchers. On one hand, their British nationality was a pretext for denying them work permits in the countries where they lived; on the other hand, their ancestry did not permit them to enter the country for which they held a passport. By comparison, most white settlers in East Africa—who held the same passports as their Asian neighbors—had no problem meeting the Natal criteria for free entrance into the United Kingdom.

The Immigration Act of 1971

In their election manifesto in 1970, the Tories promised, at long last, to establish a single system of immigration. In fact, the 1971 legislation fell considerably short of that objective. The heritage of the 1948 categories proved to be insurmountable, and the new legislation proved to be yet another exercise in honing the rights of entry and abode of different kinds of British citizens. Instead of simply defining British citizenship, with a free right to enter, the new legislation once again reiterated the privileged status Citizens of the United Kingdom and Colonies born in the UK, as well as that of CUKCs (and their wives) resident in the United Kingdom for more than five years, who had free entry into the United Kingdom.

For citizens of independent Commonwealth countries, as well as CUKCs with passports issued in the remaining colonies, access would be defined by a variation of the Natal criteria first used in 1964. In 1971, the "right to abode" in the United Kingdom for these categories was limited to those with a parent born in the United Kingdom. In 1973, the criteria for these "patrials" were altered by administrative rules to include grandparents. Thus CUKCs with non-UK issued passports retained their UK citizenship, but only patrials retained a right to entry and abode. The objective of the modified rules, of course, was to maintain privileged access for the white immigrants from the Old Commonwealth. However, the new law did create a statutory right for family unification for wives and children of settled male immigrants (Section 1–5), though not for husbands. This question was more or less resolved in 1988, when the same restrictive rules were applied both to husbands and wives.[28]

Nevertheless, both Independent Commonwealth citizens, as well as CUKCs with limited passports, who did enter retained a surprising number of citizenship privileges that sharply differentiated them from aliens from other countries. After some hesitation, the requirement for registration with the police for these immigrants was dropped in committee. Once they registered to vote, Commonwealth citizens, citizens of the colonies, and citizens of the Irish Republic resident in the United Kingdom were eligible to vote in all UK elections, as well as for deputies for the European Parliament. Another way to understand this is that citizens from 54 Commonwealth countries and Ireland, as well as immigrants from 15 Dependent Territories could vote (and run for office) in the United Kingdom.[29] All of the Commonwealth immigrants remained citizens of their home countries, but they gained these British citizenship rights by virtue of residence in the United Kingdom. It was not until 1981 that the question of UK citizenship was directly addressed and defined.

The British Nationality Act of 1981

The legislation of 1981 appeared to finally do away with the ambiguities of the 1948 definition of Citizens of the United Kingdom and Colonies. After 1983, there were only citizens of the United Kingdom, all of whom had the right to enter and abode—and others. The CUKC category was formally abolished, and the much-maligned patrial definition was abandoned (or rather subsumed under the broader category of British citizens). Almost all CUKCs who had the right to abode under the 1971 legislation now became British citizens. This included most patrials, except for those who resided in the Commonwealth and whose only ancestry claim was to the colonies.[30] On the other hand, CUKCs who were Commonwealth citizens, who were also patrials under the 1971 legislation with ancestors from the United Kingdom, retained their right to abode; those born in the Commonwealth after the 1981 law was in effect—from parents born in the United Kingdom—now had the right to dual citizenship.[31]

Those who had had UK nationality with a nonresident CUKC passport, or who were British subjects under previous legislation, were now called something else: British Dependent Territory Citizens (BDTC) and British Overseas Citizens (BOC). The former were mostly citizens of

Hong Kong, but included citizens of thirteen other colonies or dependencies; and the latter gave truly meaningless protection to essentially stateless persons, who had been denied citizenship by other members of the Commonwealth.

Thus, the BNA finally appeared to formalize the changes in entry requirements for citizens of the Commonwealth and Colonies that had accumulated since 1962. It also created a single category of British citizenship, under which all citizens had the right to enter and abode. On the other hand, it made access to that citizenship more difficult by modifying the rules of *jus solis* established by the British Nationality Act of 1914. The broad privilege of automatic citizenship to any child born in the United Kingdom (formerly the United Kingdom and Empire) was narrowed to children born in the United Kingdom of a British mother or father, or of non–British parents settled (legally resident, without restriction on the right to abode in terms of time) in the United Kingdom. Nevertheless, the right to citizenship of children born to parents who did become citizens or registered for settlement, or of those children who remain in the United Kingdom for ten years under certain circumstances, was ensured under the law.

The major losers were children of illegal aliens, as well as children whose parentage was not clearly British (under the new legislation). Perhaps the greatest losers were the British Dependent Territories citizens, and British Overseas citizens who were already resident in the United Kingdom. Previously, they had automatically acquired the right to abode after five years of residence, but now would have to conform to a more demanding process.[32] Thus, while there is no specific reference to race, the patrial aspects of the legislation facilitated entry and citizenship for those born in the Old Commonwealth, while making it more difficult for NCW citizens and Asians in the colonies.

This substantial change in British nationality law, which stands in marked contrast with similar legislation in the United States, nevertheless left the United Kingdom with arguably the most liberal citizenship law in Europe. Even with the requirement of what amounts to modified, double *jus solis*, the British criteria remained more liberal than those of modified *jus solis* in France.[33] French law, for example, does not provide for *jus solis* rights for children of legal, long-term residents. Moreover, the remaining *jus solis* provisions guarantee that a multiethnic British population will be perpetuated into future generations

Nevertheless, the 1981 BNA was the culmination of a process of withdrawal of citizenship rights, which progressively restricted citizenship to those born in the United Kingdom and their direct descendants. In the end, policy-makers, who were driven primarily by considerations of immigration and immigration restriction, were moved to expand instruments of ancestral connection (*jus sanguinis*), in order to differentiate among claims for the right of entry from the declining British Empire. Although the *jus sanguinis* rights under British legislation after 1971 were certainly less expansive than those of German law,[34] they came from a similar racial idea of what constituted the British nation—an idea that was in contradiction with the multiethnic British society that was being perpetuated by *jus solis*. Moreover, as we saw above, the legislation did not address the extraordinary rights retained by citizens of the Commonwealth, the Dependent Territories, as well as the Irish Republic to vote and run for office.

The long 20-year process narrowed the concept of citizenship, increased the number of people who were defined as aliens, but did not much alter the requirements of *aliens* to enter the country. By 1983, there were five kinds of aliens: citizens of the Irish Republic, with exemption from controls and the right to abode within the "Common Travel Area" that includes the United Kingdom; citizens of the European Union, with the right to enter and work in the United Kingdom under the "free movement" provisions of the Treaty of Rome; citizens of independent Commonwealth countries who are able to assert patrial claims that entitle them to enter and abode; citizens of British Dependent Territories and British Overseas citizens, some of whom could make claims for privileged entry (see below); and, finally, ordinary immigrants, which included the residual categories of Commonwealth citizens and citizens of British Dependent Territories without special claims. Of the five, then, four retained at least some special rights of entry, as well as at least some voting rights.

For ordinary immigrants, except for the alteration of *jus solis* in the 1981 BNA, there was little change in the rules governing alien admissions that were in force before 1962. However, there have been continuing changes that have taken place through administration, Thus, through the Highly Skilled Migrant Program, it has been possible for non-EU migrants with high education levels and special skills to enter the United Kingdom, and, for the first time since 1965, a new Sector Based Scheme was introduced to deal with shortages in unskilled labor in a number of sectors.[35]

The BNA of 1981 was the last major piece of comprehensive immigration legislation that was passed in the United Kingdom. Legislation was passed in 1987 and 1988 to fine-tune the framework in place, in 1990 and 1997 to deal with the reversion of Hong Kong to China, and in 1993 to deal with asylum.

Some of these changes, however, were quite important, and reversed previous decisions that had been made. Thus, in 1988, in response to a decision by the European Court of Human Rights that ruled that—because it applied only to wives—the statutory right of family unification legislated in 1971 was discriminatory, the right was simply stricken from the legislation. After 1988, all family unification would be subject to demanding (and demeaning) administrative rules that created an assumption of intent to defraud on the part of the applicant.[36]

On the other hand, in 1998 (the year after Hong Kong was returned to China), the British Government announced that all dependent territories would be renamed overseas territories, and that former citizens of these territories would receive British citizenship, with a right to enter the United Kingdom, restoring a right last held in the 1950s. This followed the British Nationality act of 1990, which, after long discussion, granted full British citizenship to up to 50,000 citizens of Hong Kong (based on a Canadian-style point system), and then in 1997 to some BOC (mostly ethnic Pakistanis) in Hong Kong.[37]

New Departures: Liberalization, Privatization and Rhetoric

Although no major pieces of legislation have been passed in Britain since 1981, this does not mean that there have been no new departures. On one hand, legal immigration has grown, encouraged by important new administrative initiatives to recruit immigrant labor. On the other hand, the number of asylum-seekers has first risen, and then declined because of legislative and administrative actions both to discourage applications and to minimize acceptance of those who apply.

After 1981, a steady stream of immigrants entered the United Kingdom under the work-permit program. By 2000, there were more than 1.1 million foreign nationals working in the United Kingdom, and the foreign population had increased significantly (see below). Rather than respond negatively to this trend, the Labour government after 1997 began to respond to the demands by employers for more skilled labor. Prior to the 2001 elections, the Education Department initiated "fast-track" entry into the United Kingdom for people with skills in information technology, and relaxed rules for entry for nurses and teachers. In 2002, the government launched a broader program to recruit skilled workers through the Highly Skilled Migrant Program based on a Canadian-style point system. Individuals who accumulate sufficient points, by scoring well on such criteria as educational qualifications, work experience and professional accomplishment are then free to look for a job, and are thus free to enter the United Kingdom without a guarantee of employment.[38]

This approach, however, has quietly shifted the initiative for labor migration from the state to employers. The Economist, looking back on immigration policy after 2000, concluded that:

> Over the past five years, the government has quietly liberalized the work-permit system: businesses, which used to have a tough time getting permits for foreigners, now find that applications go though pretty much on the nod. By and large, it is the employers who determine what kind of immigrants get jobs. They ask for permits, and the government responds, usually positively.[39]

However, by early 2005, with an election coming up (see chapter 7) the Labour government was under considerable pressure to demonstrate that it maintained control over the flow of immigration, and under new rules, it determined that it would set the priorities of the kind of workers that the economy needed.

As in France, the real targets of government initiatives were asylum-seekers and illegal immigrants. In a survey commissioned by *The Economist*, only 7 percent of those who thought that there were too many immigrants cited those who entered with employment permits, while 85 percent cited asylum-seekers and those in the country illegally.[40] The reaction was largely due to the sharp rise in asylum applications between 1996 and 2002. These applications then sharply declined after 2002.

The legislation that was passed after 1981—aside from the incorporation of some provisions of free movement of Schengen in 1988, and the Hong Kong Act of 1990—dealt with the tightening of rules that applied to asylum seekers. The Asylum and Immigration Act of 1993 was meant to accelerate asylum decision-making; and the Immigration and Asylum Act of 1999 provided for the dispersal of applicants, and imposed new restrictions on work. By 2005, with surveys indicating that voter concerns about illegal immigrants were on the rise,[41] even more restrictive conditions were being considered by both the Labour government and the Conservative opposition. The Conservative proposals would have exported hearings for asylum-seekers abroad, and would have imposed an overall quota on admissions. These schemes, admitted the Conservative home affairs spokesman, would violate the 1951 Geneva Convention on refugees, as well as the European Convention on Human Rights.[42]

An Evaluation

As in France, the long-term trend in British immigration policy was to minimize entry into the United Kingdom of colonial peoples that policy-makers believed to be to different to be integrated. This was countered until the 1960s by the constraints imposed by the heritage of a large empire and by an expansive, multicultural concept of citizenship. Unlike France, there was no strongly held belief in a need for labor immigration or migration to augment the armed forces and the defense of the nation. On the other hand, emigration from the United Kingdom exceeded immigration until the 1980s, and the balance is still negative each year (with occasional exceptions) for British citizens. In a large sense, immigration of all kinds still compensates for the outflow of British nationals.[43]

Indeed, although the objectives of citizenship and immigration policy have certainly been to exclude immigrants from the New Commonwealth, and existing literature argues that these objectives have been pursued with considerable determination and zeal by administrative authorities, the overall results do not reflect this. Inflows of immigrants from New Commonwealth countries have increased by about 50 percent since

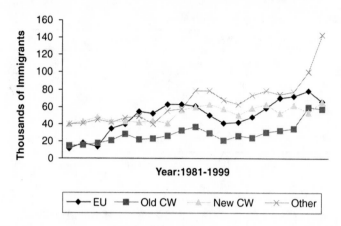

Figure 5.1   Migration flows into the United Kingdom

Source: Janet Dobson, Khalid Koser, Gail Mclaughlan and John Salt, "International Migration and the United Kingdom: Recent Patterns and Trends," Final Report to the Home Office, December 2001. (RDS Occasional Paper No. 75), p. 39.

1981 in absolute numbers. Indeed, the net inflow of migration from Old Commonwealth countries, EU countries and other foreign countries, have all increased. (See figure 5.1.) The *net* inflows for NCW immigrants, however, have been far greater than for Old CW or EU immigrants, since the yearly outflow numbers for the former is about ten percent of entries, compared to half to two-thirds of the entries of the latter. As a result, the stock of foreign population from South Asia, Africa and the Caribbean has grown considerably, as has that from EU countries, since the mid-1980s, at the same time that the stock of population from Ireland has diminished.

By 2002, foreign residents in the United Kingdom from South Asia, Africa and the Caribbean outnumbered those from Ireland for the first time. During this same period, the stock of foreign residents grew by almost 50 percent. (See table 5.5.)

Therefore, if we consider these results, it appears that the administration of immigration legislation seems at variance with the understanding of that legislation by large numbers of scholars and journalists. Christian Joppke, for example, entitles his tightly argued chapter on British immigration policy "Zero Immigration Policy: Great Britain". He argues that: "If, for different reasons, Britain shared with Germany a penchant for zero-immigration, the question arises why she has been so much better at realizing it." In fact, none of these statements seem to be true.

First, unlike France, where the rhetoric of zero immigration was widespread by the early 1990s, the rhetoric of public officials and political leaders in the United Kingdom (some of it quoted by Joppke) was more culturally racist ("keep out the coloured subjects of empire, toward whom

Table 5.5 Stock of population born abroad

Born in:	1986		1996		2002	
	1000	*% total*	*1000*	*% total*	*1000*	*% total*
Ireland	586	31	441	23	411	15
South Asia, Africa and the Caribbean	276	15	348	18	487	18
EU	791	43	792	41	949	35
Total	1820	100	1934	100	2681	100

Source: SOPEMI, *Trends on International Migration 2004* (Paris: OECD, 2004), p. 350.

there were not ties of belonging; embrace the descendants of British set-tlers, who mostly happened to be white") than "zero immigration" in content. Nevertheless, by some measures, it would appear that the United Kingdom has been more successful than most countries in Europe, espe-cially Germany, in limiting immigration. In 2001, the stock of foreigners in the United Kingdom, as a percentage of the population, was lower than in almost every EU country, and far lower than in Germany. On the other hand, the immigration flow into the country was only slightly lower than Germany in 2001, and higher (normed to the population) than France and the United States. In addition, the flow of asylum-seekers into the United Kingdom in 2002 was higher in absolute numbers than German, France, and the United States.

More to the point, however is that while the stock of foreigners had either stabilized or diminished in all other major countries, relative to the population, in the United Kingdom it grew by almost 50 percent. Moreover, entries of immigrants and asylum-seekers during the last decade of the twentieth century doubled in the case of the former, and grew four times in the case of the latter. In the case of France, immigra-tion entries stabilized (well below the UK level) and asylum-seekers grew, but remained half the UK level. In the German case, immigration rates diminished by 50 percent, and asylum rates fell to less than a quarter of their levels, in the early 1990s. Therefore, if the objective of British policy was to reduce immigration toward "zero," it would have to be judged a failure, a far greater failure in terms of trends than policy in Germany or France.

CHAPTER SIX

Understanding British Immigration Policy

The issues analyzed in the first chapter, and then applied to the French case in chapter 3 (why people migrate; control over frontiers; the impact of immigration; and questions of integration and incorporation), look somewhat different from the perspective of the British case. Thus, unlike France, Britain was a country of net emigration until the end of the twentieth century. Nevertheless, large numbers of immigrants arrived all during that period, and their arrival was shaped—if not controlled—by evolving British policy. By and large, the frontiers of Britain are often said to be better defined, and more easily controlled than those of France—but are they? Until well after the post-war period, the frontiers of Britain were embedded in the Empire and then the Commonwealth. Indeed, these frontiers have still not been entirely separated, even after legislation that has more of less resolved the question of UK citizenship.

The impact of immigration on British political and social life has been similar in some ways, and different in others, from the impact in France. On one hand, the general impact on public opinion has been similar. Reactions in public opinion polls against third world immigrants from the former Empire and Commonwealth have been largely negative (as in France), but the political consequences have been different. In part, these reactions, and anticipated reactions, have forced a succession of British governments to rethink and fundamentally redefine British citizenship, but often in unanticipated ways. On the other hand, there has been no serious political party challenger from the extreme right that has success-fully exploited these reactions.

Finally, Gilbert and Sullivan aside, the meaning of being British has never been a preoccupation in Britain. As long as Britain was embedded within the Empire, and there was no explicit British citizenship, this did not much matter much. However, with the establishment of British citizenship in 1981, and the reaction against third world immigration in public opinion, questions of integration have been increasingly tied to those of "Britishness," in much the same way that they have in rest of Europe.

Why Do People Migrate?

Because Britain has been, historically, a country of emigration, it is not at all surprising that the problem that has dominated British policy has been quite different from the demographic/labor-market-driven problem that dominated French policy. At the beginning of the twentieth century, both France and the United States still had a demographic/labor market need for immigrant labor. On balance, Britain did not. Thus, France and the United States were engaged in a policy struggle to balance these needs with the challenge that immigration posed for national identity. This struggle was not entirely absent from policy considerations in Britain—in particular with regard to "internal" Irish migration—but the need for labor was balanced against the larger consequences of empire.

On the other hand, people did come, both through "internal" migrations within the empire, and through international immigration. Two-thirds of those who migrated to Britain before WWII came through empire migration, despite the restrictions noted in chapter 3, with the largest proportion from Ireland. Although net emigration continued to dominate until well into the 1980s, post-war labor needs opened opportunities for immigration that were greater than those that existed before.

The tensions between existing public policy and understandings, and labor market needs can be seen in the reaction to the arrival, in June 1948, of 492 Jamaicans aboard the *Empire Windrush*. These black immigrants had arrived uninvited, and their arrival was noted by the Cabinet Economic Policy Committee. The committee urged the Colonial Office to prevent such "incidents" from happening in the future. Nevertheless, Prime Minister Atlee wrote to a group of concerned Labour back-benchers that:

> It is traditional that British subjects...of whatever race and colour...should be freely accessible to the UK. The tradition is not to be lightly discarded...It would be fiercely resented in the Colonies themselves and it would be a great mistake to take any action which would tend to weaken the loyalty and goodwill of the Colonies to Great Britain.[1]

Due to the growing labor shortage, the cabinet committee no doubt understood the need for immigrant labor, but they were concerned by this large arrival of non-white workers. A year later, this need for labor prompted the Royal Committee for Population to recommend recruitment of 140,000 young immigrants "...of good human stock and...not prevented by their religion or race from intermarrying with the host population and becoming merged in it." The Ministry of Labour specifically ruled out recruitment of West Indian colonial immigrants, but also noted that the 350,000 Europeans who were eventually recruited would not be guest workers on the German model, but would be welcomed for permanent settlement.[2]

Between 1948 and the beginning of the end of free Commonwealth immigration in 1962, there was hardly a rush of immigration from the New Commonwealth countries. During a period when the labor market very much needed additional workers, most of this need continued to be recruited from Europe and Ireland (see table 5.3). Nevertheless, the proportion of immigrants from the New Commonwealth did continue to grow, and by 1961, the percentage of NCW residents among all foreign residents in the United Kingdom had increased to almost 25 percent. Those who were least wanted increased the most.

This increase in NCW immigration, however, served to alter the context within which the politics of immigration was organized. The political reaction to non-white immigration that surfaced with the landing of the *Windrush* in 1948 was further strengthened by the reorganization of the politics of immigration a decade later. In ways that we shall explain in chapter 7, mass opposition to non-white immigration was then linked to diminishing support for Commonwealth preference across the political spectrum, to produce legislation that essentially redefined the line between British subjects and aliens.

There are clear parallels between attempts by France to shape immigration in the 1950s, by encouraging European rather than North African immigration (see ch. 2), and British policy during the same period. Ultimately, the British were more successful (see tables 3.4 and 5.3), in part because of the continuing high levels of Irish immigration. Nevertheless, what is striking is that well into the post-war period, there were, in fact, two parallel policies. After WWII, even when public policy reflected a need for increased immigrant labor, it also continued to perpetuate emigration policies that went back to the nineteenth century. At the same time that Britain was recruiting foreign labor, the government helped organize the emigration of 760,000 UK residents to the colonies to keep the Empire British![3]

Compared to France,[4] as well as other countries in Western Europe, total net immigration into Britain remained relatively low until 1991. Even though inflows were high (see table 5.2), outflows were high as well. After 1991, however, inflows have almost doubled at the same time that outflows increased more slowly. Thus, in 1993 inflows and outflows were about even; a decade later, there was a net inflow of between 150 and 170,000 people, considerably higher than France (although the figures are not entirely comparable), and clearly due to vastly increased inflows, rather than any decline in outflows (which were also rising).[5]

What table 6.1 demonstrates is a shift of immigration patterns from the 1960s. British citizens are continuing to leave, in numbers that are smaller than they were forty years ago, although in a steady stream. At the same time, the net arrivals from non–EU countries continue, but at higher levels than the period when citizenship laws were first changed to exclude New Commonwealth citizens.

Table 6.1 Net migration in and out of the United Kingdom (thousands of people)

	1996	1997	1998	1999	2000	2001	2002
British Citizens	−35	−34	—	−23	−57	−53	−91
Non-British/EU	30	29	43	8	6	11	11
Non-British/Non-EU	61	65	91	178	214	214	233

Source: OECD, *Trends in International Migration*: SOPMI, 2001 (p. 255), 2004 (p. 284) (OECD: 2002, 2005).

Net immigration is not calculated for France (exit figures are not calculated). However, during the nine years between 1995 and 2004, the Ministry of Foreign Affairs estimated that the number of French citizens living abroad increased from about 900,000 to almost 1.2 million, an average increase of about 33,000 per year. These are substantially lower than the British exit figures (for citizens), even during a period when the French economy was growing at a lower rate than the British economy.[6] Nevertheless, the balance of migration has shifted from net emigration to net immigration in Britain, while the pattern of net immigration seems to have continued in France.

It is difficult to explain shifting patterns of exit, but entry increases appear to be related to a shift in British policy. The Highly Skilled Migrants programs, as well as other similar programs that were meant to attract more immigrants to Britain (the British version of *immigration choisie*), chosen by skills and potential to strengthen the economy, did not replace family immigration, which has remained the largest single category of those admitted for settlement (about 40 percent). However, these programs have certainly increased migration from India, the largest single country as a source of labor immigration. Between 1999 and 2002, the number of work permits doubled, but for Indians, they went from 5,700 to 19,000.[7] The shift in initiative for labor immigration from the state to employers has introduced a new dynamic into the system that serves to increase, rather than limit total immigration—a clear lesson for France. As in France, push factors continue to be important, especially for asylum. The pull factors of policy, however, continue to shape who actually arrives, and who is accepted for immigration.

Control over the Frontiers

As in France, the question of the frontier is important both for scholars and for policy-makers. During the parliamentary election campaign of 2005, control over the border was emphasized by the failed Tory campaign in two ways. First, Michael Howard, the Conservative leader, noted that "We face a real terrorist threat in Britain today—a threat to our safety, to our way of life and to our liberties....But we have absolutely no idea who is coming into or leaving our country." He then pledged to establish a new, consolidated police force, which would bring together police from Customs, Special Branch, ports police and police that now work British border controls (about 7400 officers, backed by about 16,000 staff). On the other hand the Tories also pledged to cut the immigration and asylum budget in half![8]

These perceptions that the UK border is insecure have been fed by stories of the smuggling of illegal immigrants into the country, and above all, by the thousands who "hitched" rides through the Eurotunnel. During the first six months of 2001, Eurotunnel officials intercepted 18, 500 people attempting to make the crossing. Many of these people had come from a Red Cross aid center at Sangatte (near Calais), on the French side of the English Channel, and the ensuing publicity and tension between Britain and France finally led to an agreement to close the center in December 2002. As we shall see below, however, these perceptions ran counter to reality by 2005.

As we have seen, the frontiers of the United Kingdom for purposes of immigration have been complicated, and have been the subject of considerable debate. The British frontier before 1962 was embedded in the Commonwealth. Although entry into the United Kingdom was controlled for aliens, it was open to citizens of 55 countries of the Commonwealth, Ireland, as well as residents of 15 dependent territories. As we saw in Chapter 5, movement within the Empire and the Commonwealth was controlled through a variety of mechanisms. Nevertheless, the borders of the United Kingdom remained relatively open. Even after border controls for all entries were established through progressive steps after 1962, ambiguities remained. Free entry continued for citizens of Ireland, and citizens of the Commonwealth and dependent territories that were granted entry retained a privileged status as UK residents.

In addition, although Britain remains one of only two of the Europe 15 countries that have not signed on to the Schengen Accords, citizens from the Europe 15 have relatively easy access to Britain, and can work in Britain with few problems, because of the right to free movement for work required by the EU. Of course, the understanding is mutual, and large numbers of UK citizens now work freely on the continent. Nevertheless, inflows from the EU remain flat and relatively modest. As we can see in table 5.5, foreign residents in the United Kingdom who were born in other countries of the EU are the largest single component of those born-abroad, but they have continued to diminish as a proportion of the total population born abroad. The relatively free entry of EU citizens was reinforced by British policy that extended free movement entry to the ten new members of the EU without delay in May 2004—one of only three EU countries to do so (the others were Ireland and Sweden).[9]

Nevertheless, by some measures and within these constraints, the United Kingdom has made stronger efforts to control its frontier than either France or the United States. Between 1999 and 2002 asylum applications doubled over the previous years, and, rose higher than those for

France or the United States (although US applications declined after 1996—see below, Chapter 9). As in France, however, increased applications resulted in sharp declines in recognition rates (see table 6.2). This decline is even more marked, if we consider that after 2000, most asylum admissions were granted as emergency or humanitarian "leave to remain" for a temporary period (ELR, HP and DL).

Illegal immigration has become the major immigration issue during the past decade, but there is no indication that it is in any sense out of control. Unlike France, Britain does not have a coordinated frontier police force. Like France, however, Britain both detains and expels those it deems to be in the country illegally. Prior to 2002 there were two kinds of detention centers: removal centers for those the government was in the process of expelling; and removal prisons for the detention of detainees whose claims were being processed.

The power of the government to detain immigrants without limit was provided by the Immigration Act of 1971, although this power was used sparingly until recently. A new, more comprehensive "reception center" was introduced by the Immigration and Asylum Act of 2002, with the aim of providing services as well as forcing detention with a limit of six months. As late as 1995, as few as 250 people were being detained; this number rose to 1445 by 2002, and 2000 by 2005, about the same level as detentions in France (see ch. 3).

Expulsions from Britain, however, have been far higher than from France. The goal of 25,000, announced by the French interior minister in 2006, was already exceeded in Britain in 1999, with 37,800 people removed. This number has continued to rise, and in 2002, 65, 500 people were removed, more than 8 and a half times the figure for France in the same year.[10] These expulsions have included far more people than asylum seekers whose applications have been refused. Indeed, only about 20 percent

Table 6.2 Asylum-seekers and recognition rates: 1997–2004

	Number of Applicants	Percent granted Asylum	Percent granted ELR, DL, HP	Percent of Applicants Admitted
1997	32,500	11%	9%	20%
1998	46,015	17%	12%	29%
1999	71,160	36%	12%	48%
2000	80,315	13%	13%	26%
2001	71,025	11%	17%	28%
2002	84,130	12%	25%	37%
2003	49,405	6%	11%	17%
2004	33,960	4%	8%	12%

Source: Home Office statistics, reported in Esme Peach and Rachel Hanson, "Key Statistics About Asylum Seeker Arrivals in the UK" (ICAR/2005). See www.homeoffice.gov.uk
*Exceptional Leave to Remain, replaced by Humanitarian Protection and Discretionary Leave on April 1 2003.

of those removed are in this category. Others included a variety of people who had been in the country illegally.

Nevertheless, the government has estimated that there are about 550,000 illegal immigrants in the United Kingdom.[11] That estimate, which is about 0.98 percent of the population, is considerably higher than in France, but far lower than the United States. As we noted in chapter 3, with regard to France, the relatively high figures for Britain may be related to the openness of the labor market. As in the United States, employers are relatively free to employ undocumented workers. Despite the wide-ranging powers to punish employers who employ these workers, there were only 17 convictions during the seven-year period from 1998–2004, the seven years after new rules went into effect in January 1997 under the Asylum and Immigration Act of 1996 (8 of them in 2004). We can compare this with thousands of convictions in France by the early 1990s.[12] Undocumented workers continue to be punished in unprecedented numbers though expulsion, but the "pull" of the market continues to be strong.

Impact

Public Opinion

The imposition of immigration controls after 1962 has often been depicted as a reaction to an upsurge of anti-immigrant public opinion. The story told generally relates public opinion to the restrictionist policies first initiated by the Conservatives in the 1960s. Most of the vast literature on immigration control written by both UK and U.S. scholars generally agrees that restrictionist policies were first introduced in response to rising public opinion against non-white immigration, provoked in part by riots in the Notting Hill area of London and Nottingham in 1958. Indeed, it is clear that public opinion was strongly opposed both to immigration and to immigrants.[13]

During the period leading up to and coinciding with the imposition of restrictive immigration controls in Britain, public opinion patterns were superficially similar to those in France. There was an unbroken public consensus that antedated the imposition of restrictions that too many immigrants had been permitted to enter Britain. Well after restrictive legislation had been passed, a somewhat smaller percentage supported the notion that "fewer" immigrants should be admitted, or that the number of immigrants presently accepted is "too high." Perhaps the biggest change, however, is that opinion has become increasingly bipolar, with the number of those who disagree increasing substantially (see table 6.3).

As in France, moreover, public opinion varied considerably by immigrant group. On average, between 1983 and 1989, 67 and 62 percent of those surveyed preferred less settlement of Indians and Pakistanis and West Indians, compared with 32 percent for immigrants from Australia.[14]

Table 6.3   Opposition to immigration in Britain

		1963 %	1966 %	1970 %	1983 %	1986 %	1989 %	1992 %	1994 %	1997 %	2000 %
"Too many immigrants let in Britain"	Yes	83	81	85	—	—	63	—	64	61	66
	disagree	12	14	10	—	—	18	—	33	35	—
"Admit…"	fewer	—	—	—	54.4	54.4	52.8	—	—	—	—
	more	—	—	—	6	6	6	—	—	—	—
"Number of immigrants too…"	high	—	—	—	—	—	58	52	—	—	—
	low	—	—	—	—	—	6	6	—	—	—

Sources: Anthony M. Messina, Race and Party Competition in Britain (New York: Oxford University Press, 1989), p. 12; Rita J. Simon and James P. Lynch, "A Comparative Assessment of Public Opinion Toward Immigrants and Immigration Policies," International Migration Review, Vol. 32, No. 2, Summer, 1999, p. 46; Rita J. Simon, "Immigration and Public Opinion," (unpublished, 1995), p. 7. MORI/Socioconsult/Readers' Digest, 1989–2000: http://www.ipos-mori.com/polls/2000/rd-july.shtml

Nevertheless, once again as in France, there is data that indicates that positive receptivity towards immigrants increases considerably over time and hostility declines, although the gap between immigrants from Australia/New Zealand and India/Pakistan/West Indies remains.[15]

Anthony Messina adds that public opinion with regard to immigration was more important than in some other policy areas.

Unlike equally or more salient economic issues, which the electorate has often viewed as beyond the competence or control of the [political] parties… non-white immigration, race relations, nuclear disarmament, and EEC membership, have been perceived by the public as politically manageable and the responsibility of parties and government.[16]

Yet, how salient was the issue of immigration over time, and how important was it in relation to other issues? Ultimately, it is the priority of issues that tends to force them on the political agenda. Here the answer is more nuanced.

Once the initial legislation was passed between 1962 and 1974, the issue seemed to fade as a priority political question in public opinion (see figure 6.1). Compared to other "hot-button" political issues— crime/law and order/violence (Cri), the economy (Eco) and poverty (ov)—immigration and race-relations(Rac) had only rarely risen to one of the three most important issues that concerned voters, and, at least until 2000, was a priority in public opinion only twice, each

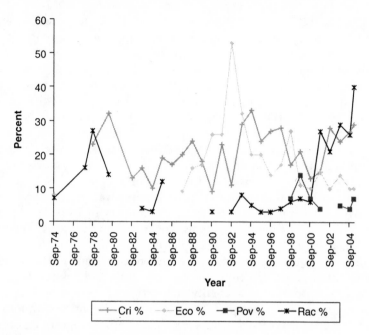

Figure 6.1 The most important issue/other issues facing Britain
Source: Data from MORI Issue Surveys, 1974–2004.

time fleetingly. The first peak corresponds to the run-up to the bitter elections of 1979, in which immigration was briefly used as a wedge issue by the Conservative Party under Margaret Thatcher. The second period corresponds to reactions to urban unrest during the fall of 1985.

In early 1978, it was generally presumed that national elections would be called after the summer, and the opposition Tories began to gear up for the elections in February. The new Tory leader, Margaret Thatcher raised the issue of the impact of immigrants, and in a television interview called for an end to immigration. (See ch. 7.) Her comments were condemned both by leaders of her own party, and by the Labour government, and within a few months she dropped the issue, without specifying any follow-up policy changes.[17] All of this is remarkably reflected in the trend of the Mori survey. The priority of the immigration issue moves up rapidly in early 1978, and then sinks rapidly by early 1979.

Similarly, until the riots in Birmingham and Brixton in September 1985, immigration was a priority issue for only 5 percent of those polled. Then, in September it jumped to 12 percent, to 17 percent in October, and down to 9 percent a month later. Indeed, in the press and in comments by the government this was seen as a race issue (included in the issue category by MORI). If in the first instance, the priority of immigration was generated by a brief attempt by the Tory leader to develop a wedge issue for the anticipated elections; in the second instance, it reflected both the real events on the ground, and the intensity of press and government discussion about these events.

Then, in the spring of 2000, the priority of immigration as an issue began to increase once again. This time the pattern was similar to what had happened in 1985, in reaction to what was perceived as a flood of asylum-seekers and illegal immigrant from the Sangatte refugee aid camp on the French side of the Channel Tunnel. As the number of asylum-seekers grew after 1999, and as the publicity about Sangatte grew, the priority of theissue of immigration increased as well. Indeed, by 2005, as figure 5.1 indicates, immigration was perceived as one of the two most important issues facing the country by over 29 percent of those polled, at a time when it was a priority issue for only 13 percent of the EU 15, and at a time when the priority of the issue was declining in other European countries.[18] A clue to the concerns that emerged after 2000 is contained in a survey done for the Economist in early 2005. Public opinion is generally supportive of those who immigrate to Britain to work, is not concerned about immigrants taking jobs that might otherwise go to British workers, and there appears to be little concern about racial balancing.

> The newcomers that grate are those who strain the delicate British sense of fair play: 85% cite either asylum seekers or illegal immigrants as the main reason the country is being overrun. They are thought to be bad news not because they take jobs or commit crimes, but because they compete unfairly for public services.[19]

The most rejected immigrants in the poll that is cited are no longer the West Indians, but overwhelmingly those immigrants or asylum-seekers perceived as dangerous (Iraqis and Pakistanis) and those seen as living off the state (Romanians).

Indeed, these reactions reflected an increasingly divisive party debate about these very same issues. Particularly in opposition, the Conservatives have attempted to use immigration, increasingly defined as asylum-seekers, as a wedge issue with which to upend the Labour government. This was clear in 1978, but also in 2001 and 2005. On each occasion, the Tories were encouraged by reactions of public opinion, but each time, the issue failed to resonate in electoral terms. (See ch. 7.)

All in all, through the twists and turns, the fact that immigration has been such a continuing concern in British politics has not meant that it has been a continuing policy priority. Prior to 2000, the importance of immigration for voters was small compared to other issues. Since then, more or less redefined as an asylum question by political party actors, the issue has gained in importance, fed by election rhetoric in 2000–2001 and 2004–2005, and intra and inter-party conflict between elections.

Attitudes in Britain, while superficially similar to those in France with regard to immigration, actually appear to be far less hard with regard to immigrants than those in France. The "hard line" of attitudinal patterns that we found in France (see ch. 3) with regard to Algerian and other North African immigrants, is far less evident in Britain. The most negative attitudes are reserved for asylum-seekers and the newest wave of immigrants. Since 1999, the most important increase of immigrants has not been from either the NCW countries of the Caribbean or from South Asia, but from Africa and the Middle East. The number of people either accepted for settlement, or whose applications for asylum have been accepted, has doubled for both categories. Africans from such countries as Ghana and Nigeria are now the largest single category of immigrants entering into Britain during the past five years.[20] Indeed, the most unpopular immigrants now arriving in Britain appear to be Iraqis, Africans (as opposed to West Indians) and Romanians. Among the older NCW immigrants, the Pakistanis are the most unpopular (behind the Iraqis), and appear to be the closest to French reactions to Algerians.[21]

British respondents are generally more sanguine about the changes that are being brought by immigration than are their French counterparts, and the perceived challenge to British identity appears to be less important. (See table 6.4.) They tend to worry about the loss of British culture, but see a multi-cultural Britain as a good thing, and are not at all concerned by its consequences. They seem relatively unconcerned about mixed marriage, or about having non-white bosses in the workplace. In these ways, they seem to be more optimistic than the French about integration.

Citizenship

Part of the reason is probably that perceptions of British identity have been changing along with changes in citizenship (see below). The slow movement towards a legal concept of British citizenship, that began in 1948

Table 6.4 Attitudes toward immigrants in Britain

Question:	Agree	Disagree
"I am concerned that Britain is losing its own culture" (2003)	57	29
"It is a good thing that Britain is a multi-cultural society" (2003)	70	16
"It would upset me if a close relative married a person of Asian or Afro-Caribbean origin." (2000)	12	75
"It would upset me if my neighbor was of Asian or Afro-Caribbean origin" (2000)	8	80
"It would upset me if my boss was of Asian or Afro-Caribbean origin." (2000)	6	80

Source: MORI, "Britain Today—Are We An Intolerant Nation?," October 23, 2000; "British Views on Immigration," February 10, 2003.

and was not finalized until 1981, was in fact a continuing parliamentary debate about criteria of belonging to a changing national community. Indeed, this question is not yet settled, since criteria for civic participation in the electoral process remain far broader than criteria of citizenship. French discussions about belonging tend to focus on language, culture and increasingly on shared civic values. British discussions, however, are far closer to those in the United States. Unlike France, a notion of multi-culturalism is broadly accepted. Acceptance of diversity among new immigrant groups appears to be an extension of the acceptance of what is understood as diversity within the United Kingdom itself.

As Labour Prime Minister—then Chancellor of the Exchequer—Gordon Brown said in 2006:

> While we have always been a country of different national, and thus of plural identities—a Welshman can be Welsh and British, just as a Cornishman or woman is Cornish, English and British—and may be Muslim, Pakistani or Afro-Caribbean, Cornish, English and British—there is always a risk that, when people are insecure, they retreat into more exclusive identities rooted in 19th century conceptions of blood, race and territory—when instead, we the British people should be able to gain great strength from celebrating a British identity which is bigger than the sum of its parts, and a union that is strong because of the values we share and because of the way these values are expressed through our history and our institutions.[22]

Brown's statement on identity is verified by the multinational identities revealed in a survey published by Richard Rose 25 years ago, at the very moment when the issue of British citizenship was finally settled by legislation. The collective identity of "British" was a minority identity everywhere in the United Kingdom, including England. In the context of complex multicultural identities, immigration appears to pose much less of a challenge to identity than it does in France.

When Brown actually sought to identify what it means to be British, he did so in civic culture terms that would be familiar to most Americans—"... not just on institutions we share and respect, but on enduring ideals which shape our view of ourselves and communities—values which turn influence the way our institutions evolve." Brown's sanguine views of multi-culturalism would change in the months following this speech (see below).

The core of the statement remains relevant for understanding the struggle over the definition of what it means to be British. Nevertheless, it is important to point out that the broad acceptance of ethno-territorial identities (English, Scottish, Welsh etc.) is not the same as the acceptance and promotion of multiculturalism based on ethnic and religious identities that are not based on the territorial components of the British Isles. We shall see below that the "new" multiculturalism represented a sea-change from what had preceded it.

The impact of immigration on citizenship was also quite different in the British case than in the French case. As we saw in the last chapter, changing patterns of immigration were certainly a strong motivating factor in the reconsideration of British citizenship, but not the only one. The changes in citizenship laws grew out of post-war decolonization, and were also a reaction to the establishment of national citizenship status in each country of the Commonwealth. Nevertheless, a desire to discourage NCW immigration also shaped the way that the legislation was formulated. As we have seen, the exclusionary definitions that were built into the legislation after (but not including) 1962, applied to those who were, for the most part, defined as citizens residing outside of the United Kingdom, but with the right to enter freely. The consequences of the 1962 legislation applied equally to citizens of the Old and New Commonwealth, but subsequent legislation did not. As a result, Britain, a country with a long tradition of *jus solis* as a basis for citizenship, relied increasingly on *jus sanguinis* as a principle for deciding who could freely enter the United Kingdom as a British citizen. The cumulative changes in British citizenship law were contained in the 1981 legislation.

> The 1981 legislation created a British citizenship. It automatically attributed *jus solis* to children born in the UK of a British citizen or of a non-British permanent resident born in the UK. Otherwise, a minor could acquire British citizenship if he resides in the UK for ten continuous years prior to applying. In addition, British citizenship is automatically attributed through *jus sanguinis* to the first generation born abroad. At the next generation, the descendant of the British citizen has to settle in the UK; otherwise he loses his British citizenship.[23]

The requirement of being born of at least one British citizen parent, or of one parent who was a permanent resident of the United Kingdom established *jus sanguinis* as an important principle for the citizenship of children of immigrant parents born in the United Kingdom. This requirement was not different from requirements in France, but substantially different from those in the United States, where, under current interpretations of the 14th Amendment (1868), anyone born on U.S. soil (*jus solis*), is automatically an American citizen.

The novelty in current British law is the advantage of automatic citizenship (and right of settlement) that is given to the children and grandchildren of emigrants—an important bias against immigrants from the NCW. In this way, a desire to promote immigration from the Old Commonwealth, and discourage it from the NCW shaped the 1981 legislation.

Integration and Incorporation

The Race Relations Act of 1965 provided an institutional base for integration that was agreed to by both major political parties. The extension of this legislation in 1968 and 1976 then provided substantial depth to this approach that secured a bipartisan approach to immigration, race and multiculturalism.[24] By 1968, the race relations approach to integration, with its acceptance of ethnic pluralism, promotion of multi-culturalism and structures to combat discrimination, had begun to take on a life of its own.[25] By the time the third Race Relations Act was passed in 1976, there was considerable partisan contention and disagreement about its more far-reaching provisions (including "positive action provisions"), but not about the race-relations approach to integration.[26]

The concept of "race," in Britain was applied to virtually all "New Commonwealth" immigrants (primarily those from Pakistan, India and the Caribbean, as opposed to those from Canada, Australia, and New Zealand) in political debates about "coloured" immigration from the 1950s on. This way of looking at non-European immigrants was not essentially different from the way similar immigrant populations were viewed in France or Germany. The difference was in the formal policy framework that was developed to incorporate them.

> The emphasis on assimilation was... rapidly abandoned in favour of "good race relations," namely peaceful coexistence through tolerance, diversity and pluralism. There is an obvious contradiction between the belief in stringent immigration control and in diversity as contributing ipso facto to social order, but the compromise was driven by party-political necessity.

While in France, acceptance of this kind of pluralism (often called "insertion") is seen as a substitute for full participation in society, in Britain it is understood as an important dimension of such participation.[27]

The articulation of a positive approach towards multiculturalism, although it began with race-relations, very quickly evolved into a broader understanding of multiculturalism. Thus, Roy Jenkins, Home Secretary at the time, noted in 1966:

> I do not think that we need in this country a melting pot.... I define integration therefore, not as a flattening process of assimilation but as equal opportunity, accompanied by cultural diversity, in an atmosphere of mutual tolerance."[28]

Jenkins perspective was reinforced by a series of reports on education, beginning with the Swann Report in 1985. The Swann Report (*Education for All*) strongly advocated a multicultural education system for all schools, regardless of institutions, location, age-range or ethnicity of staff/pupils. The report made a link between education and multiculturalism by noting that racism had an adverse effect on the educational experiences of black children in the United Kingdom. These conclusions have been reaffirmed by numerous reports since then.[29] Perhaps most important was the

1997 report by the *Commission on the Future of Multi-Ethnic Britain*, which reaffirmed United Kingdom as "community of communities." The net effect was what one author has called "a conceptual shift,"[30] that disassociated questions of integration from those of immigration—the management of arrivals—and, as Tariq Madood has observed, recognized integration as a two-way process of dual responsibility, in which:

> ...members of the majority community as well as immigrants and ethnic minorities are required to do something; so the latter cannot alone be blamed for "failing to or not trying to integrate." The established society is the site of institutions—including employers, civil society and the government—in which integration has to take place and they accordingly must take the lead.[31]

Thus, the British version of multiculturalism in public policy evolved on the assumption of "equivalent groups," the identity of which is defined in cultural terms.

Because of the multicultural approach to integration, Britain has generally avoided the kinds of integration struggles over dress codes and religious organization that have taken place in France. The constraints on categorization and information-gathering that have marked French efforts to deal with integration in terms of discrimination—especially in employment and housing—have been absent in the British case.

The focus on racial discrimination has left the question of religious discrimination more ambiguous. Most Muslims in Britain are also members of ethnic minority communities, and have therefore been protected "indirectly".[32] Although the courts have been less active than in United States in developing criteria of discrimination, British judges have applied the European Convention on Human Rights to integration issues. In 2005, for example, a British court of Appeal judge ruled that a decision by a school in Luton, requiring that all students wear uniforms, failed to consider the human rights of Muslim girl who insisted on wearing a *jilbab* (a long and shapeless robe). The decision, in a school in which almost 89 percent of the students are Muslim, but come from 21 ethnic groups, was taken in consultation with parents and Muslim organizations.[33]

In addition, other issues of integration of immigrants and ethnic communities remain important. With roughly the same rhythm as in France, riots have erupted in major British cities with high concentrations of immigrant populations (1981, 1991–1992, 2001) The British riots have had many of the same characteristics of their French counterparts, except that they have been more violent in terms of personal injury to residents and the police. The most important difference has been the political consequences of the riots in each case. The first post-WWII civil unrest in Britain was in 1948–1949 in Liverpool, Deptford, and then Birmingham, but the riots in Nottingham and Notting Hill in London in 1958 were the first serious riots. As we saw in chapter 3, the reaction of French authorities to the first urban riots in Lyons in 1981 was to frame the problem in terms of social control and education. They expanded state involvement in neighborhood organization and in educational integration, an orientation that remained at the core of the French integration effort over the next two decades.

The British reaction to the riots in 1958 was to frame the problem in terms of race relations. At first, it was seen as a "race problem," the solution for which was to limit immigration, "and prevent a British Little Rock."[34] By 1964, however, the 1958 events—still seen in terms of race relations—became the basis for race relations legislation.

Although Labour's initial response to the riots was confused, by the end of September (one month after the onset of the disorders) it had issued a policy statement committing itself to legislate against racial discrimination. Having formulated a pro-legislation policy, Labour followed through by urging the Conservative government several times during the next few years to pass antidiscrimination legislation. . . . [T]he social disorder exhibited during the 1958 riots engendered a sense within the Labour Party that the state needed to take action to preserve the peace.[35]

Similar to the French initial integration efforts, the British approach was rooted in a need to maintain public order: "For [Home Secretary] Soskice, race relations legislation was in large part related to concerns of public order, a lesson first learned by the [Labour] party in 1958." As Soskice said in the House of Commons:

> Overt acts of discrimination in public places, intense wounding to the feelings of those against whom these acts are practised, perhaps in the presence of many onlookers, breed the ill will which, as the accumulative result of several such actions over a period, may disturb the peace.[36]

By 1965, Labour was able to get the agreement of the Tory opposition to this strategic formulation, and it became the core of the British approach to integration policy. Indeed, this approach endured, and was strengthened even after three additional rounds of serious riots between 1981 and 2001, as well as the attacks on the London underground in June, 2005.

Nevertheless, as in many countries, including France and the United States, there has been growing pressure to assert the limits of multiculturalism, and support a stronger sense of collective identity. By 2001, in the aftermath of urban riots in the summer and the attacks in the United States in September, government reports indicate the beginning of a reassertion of policies of civic integration into a society based on shared values. The Cantle Report,[37] which was being drafted at the time of the attacks in the United States, linked the summer riots to highly segregated communities.

> The report's conclusions centred on the need to redress this situation through a "greater sense of citizenship," the identification of "common elements of nationhood" and the need for the "non-white

community" to use the English language and "develop a greater acceptance of, and engagement with, the principal national institutions."[38]

The Home Secretary then called for an "honest and robust debate" on race relations, This was followed by a Home Office report in 2002, *Secure Borders, Safe Haven: Integration with Diversity in Modern Britain*, which re-associated immigration with integration by arguing that immigration should be contingent upon increased civic integration and "shared values."[39]

Thus, the attacks in London in 2005 accelerated a process that had begun four years before. Although the actual policy requirements in place by 2007 were not as coercive as those in France or the Netherlands, they were moving in the same direction.[40]

The most important symbolic change in this direction has been the initiation of a citizenship test and a citizenship ceremony under legislation passed in 2002. Beginning November 1, 2005 all applicants for naturalization were required to pass a "Life in the UK" examination, together with certification in the English language. Although the Home Office denied that this was a "Britishness test," it was widely referred to in those terms by both the prime minister and in the press. In fact, the mix of questions on history, politics and society generally resembled the questions on the citizenship examination in the United States.[41] Together with new citizenship ceremonies that include a pledge of allegiance, the civics and language tests are meant to create a meaningful gateway for integration, the kind that has never existed before in Britain.

The tensions between manifestations of multiculturalism and the pressures to develop policies that focus on a common identity are most apparent in education, particularly in debates about the National Curriculum. The profound impact on teachers can be seen in two recent government reports on education and curriculum. An April 2007 report from the Historical Association noted that some schools were avoiding teaching controversial history subjects, including the slave trade and the holocaust because "...they do not want to cause offense," and, indeed, teachers are mandated to be aware of the sensitivities of their diverse populations.[42] When the report was commissioned in 2006, the Schools Minister Lord Adonis said the national curriculum encouraged teachers to choose content "likely to resonate in their multicultural classrooms," but some found it difficult to do that. A few months earlier (in January 2007), a report to the education secretary emphasized that the school curriculum should teach "core British values" alongside the multicultural curriculum, with an emphasis on history and civic values.[43]

As in France, there is considerable concern in Britain, especially after the June 2005 attacks, about patterns of segregation among ethnic minorities. Indeed, in Britain, multiculturalism has been cited as an excuse for not dealing effectively with questions of discrimination. In 2004, the Chairman of the Commission on Racial Equality warned that multiculturalism "is in danger of becoming a sleight of hand by which ethnic minorities are distracted by tokens of recognition, while being excluded from the real business [such that] the smile of recognition has turned into the rictus grin on the face of institutional racism".[44]

As in France, increased attention has been given to questions of discrimination and affirmative action that would create greater opportunities for young and ambitious youth in ethnic areas of large cities. A 2005 report of the British Commission for Racial Equality has suggested a somewhat different program—gerrymandered catchment areas to integrate schools and universities—to deal with these problems.[45]

In fact, after 2005, British governments devoted greater attention to what has often been phrased as a "hearts and minds" approach to Muslim communities, by government attempts to enlist Muslim individuals and community organizations in their efforts to enhance security. These outreach efforts have been far more extensive than similar programs in France or the United States, and have been most explicit in the announced programs of the Foreign and Commonwealth Office and the Department of Communities and Local Government, and are aimed mainly at engaging with Muslim communities to prevent radicalization and promote voices of mainstream Islam among Muslim youth.[46]

Recent reports, however, suggest the limitations of the British approach. Even Muslim community leaders who have been most cooperative with government efforts have been reluctant to get involved in developing programs for the operation of mosques,[47] for example, or to set standards for the recruitment of Muslim prison chaplains. A series of measures proposed by Ruth Kelly, the Secretary of State for Communities and Local Government, to give civic training to imams and to encourage "…a message about being proud to be British, proud to be Muslim…," has received little support among Muslim leaders.[48]

Nevertheless, these government-sponsored efforts have been continued, even reinforced under the new government of Gordon Brown, who placed emphasis on the importance of civic education programs at his first press conference in July 2007. It is estimated that 100,000 children attend religious education classes at mosques, and civic education has been integrated into religious classes.[49] The government is also pursuing cooperation at the EU level that began with the French initiative at the meeting of interior ministers (G6) in March 2006. At that time, Home Secretary Charles Clarke noted that he supported a more muscular integration contract that would ensure that "…new immigrants live up to the values of our society," and that they could be expelled if they did not.[50]

Although integration concerns in both Britain and France have increasingly focused on questions of ethnic, racial and religious discrimination, British governments have focused on these efforts far longer than their French counterparts, and with far more effective instruments according to recent scholarship.[51] To the extent that integration problems in both Britain and France have become racially based, the American experience with racial integration has some mixed lessons. On one hand, affirmative action has contributed towards the development of a large and success-ful black professional and middle class in the United States, and has also brought large numbers of racial minorities into the political system. On the other hand, at the same time, unemployment rates among young black men in the United States have grown by almost 50 percent during the past 25 years, far more than among whites and Hispanics.[52]

Comparing Integration

A substantial problem for both countries, and for long-term integration, may be concentrations of poverty among those in ethnic communities who are left behind and do not benefit from either positive discrimination or more integrated schools. Table 1.3 indicates that immigrant unemploy-ment rates in Britain are far less severe than in France, and that the gap between immigrant and native unemployment rates, while greater than in the United States, is better than in France. However, the gap in unem-ployment between the most successful ethnic groups (Irish and Indian) and the least successful (Pakistani, Bangladeshi and Black Caribbean) is far greater than in the United States (see ch. 10). The former have unemploy-ment rates of 4–7 percent, compared to 11–15 percent for the latter.[53]

As in the United States, educational attainment brings unemployment rates down for immigrant populations, and therefore appears to be an important key to integration. (See table 1.5.) Therefore, the high rates of university education for immigrant populations (higher than for the native population) are a good index of successful integration. Perhaps more important is the relatively low rate of educational failure among immigrants (see table 1.4), higher than the United States but lower than France. Indeed, as we noted in chapter 1, the percentage of immigrants without any educational qualification is about 10 percent in Britain, com-pared with about 50 percent in France.

Finally, compared to France, Britain has had some modest success in integrating immigrants into political life (see table 1.6) In contrast to France and the United States, immigrant populations from the NCW in Britain are potentially part of the electorate as soon as they establish resi-dency in the United Kingdom. Thus, their percentage of the electorate is about as large as their percentage of the voting age population. At about 6.6 percent of the electorate, over 80 percent of immigrant minorities are in the electorate, compared to only about half in France (2.7 percent of the electorate—based on census data).[54] (See ch. 7.)

Although Britain has had considerable success in integrating their immi-grant populations by important measures, indeed far greater success than France, immigrants of Islamic origin have been among the least successful. Moreover, there are strong indications from the Pew surveys in 2006 that, among British citizens who identify as Muslim, their Muslim identity is far stronger than their British identity; their inclination to adopt "national" customs is far less than their French counterparts; and their toleration of their fellow citizens is considerably lower than Muslims in France. (See tables 1.7 and 1.8) Perhaps more telling, they are alone among Muslim groups in Europe to be as concerned with the decline of religion and with the influence of pop culture, as with problems of unemployment.[55] British mass publics seem to be no less accepting of Muslim immigrants than other European mass publics, and are somewhat more accepting of expressions of Muslim identity and multiculturalism (table 1.6).

Not surprisingly, such contradictions give considerable support to government civic education programs, if only because they force an explicit formulation of what British values are. Similarly, the discussions about the National Curriculum that focus on the need to teach "core British values," also stimulate discussion of what those values are, without at the same time denying the value of multiculturalism.[56]

CHAPTER SEVEN

Politics of Immigration in Britain

Compared with France, both the framing of the immigration issue, and the process of politicization was markedly different before and after WWII. Until the 1950s, immigration was understood primarily as the arrival of foreigners from outside of the British Empire and Ireland. Defining immigration in these terms in fact excluded considering the notion that most of the people from areas that were not part of Great Britain—in particular people from Ireland—were immigrants. Between the late 1950s and 1981, the immigration issue was framed in different terms that did—in fact—consider entry from the colonies and Commonwealth. However, because of the complexity of British citizenship, the issue was framed in terms of the revision of citizenship laws to exclude unwanted immigrants from New Commonwealth countries and from former British colonies in Africa and Asia. Since the late 1990s, the immigration issue has been complicated by questions of asylum and illegal entry.

Throughout this long period of time, the politics of immigration has continued to be structured by party competition and, at times, electoral politics. Although events and tendencies in the political environment have certainly influenced both the framing of immigration issues, and their salience in party competition, parties have generally controlled and constructed both. Intra-party struggles have been important in this process, and inter-party struggles have finally been resolved through policy changes.

However, unlike France, after a policy orientation has been put in place, there has been a rapid tendency toward policy consensus, which has facilitated long periods of administrative policy-making; and unlike the United States, interest groups politics have been relatively unimportant in determining policy outcomes. Periods of policy reorientation, on the other hand, have been times of strong political tensions, and high levels of issue salience for immigration that have been manifested in party electoral competition. The task, then, is to explain how immigration issues become highly salient, and how this salience is dealt with politically.

Framing the Issue

In contrast with France, the issue of immigration in Britain in the early years was framed primarily in a conflictual context. Political reaction against immigration began to develop within the Conservative Party in the 1890s in ways that are strikingly similar to those of the period after WWII. The issue of restriction was first formulated as an identity issue by several Tory (Conservative) leaders, despite the relatively small immigrant population. Although the issue was developed in terms consistent with racial and identity fears, it was not framed in the kind of pseudo scientific eugenicist language used in the American case (see Chapter 10). The debate also lacked the balance of demographic need that was evident in the French case (see Chapter 3). What was most interesting, however, was that in the framing of the immigration issue by the Tories, there seems to have been no reference whatsoever to immigration from non-white countries of the Empire. The focus was mainly on Jews.

Before WWII

The Royal Commission on the Aliens Question was established to investigate the question of immigration, which had been developing as a problem within the Conservative Party for more than a decade, largely under pressure from the back-benches of the party (see below). In effect, temptations of electoral advantage were pitted against a problem-solving approach both within the Conservative Party, and between the Conservatives and the Liberals during this period. The members of the commission ranged from radical restrictionist (William Evans-Gordon) to supporters of continued Jewish immigration (Lord Rothschild), and the testimony and discussion was often bitter. The commission report in 1903 was a mixture of analysis and evaluation, on one hand, and policy recommendations on the other. It focused most specifically on the impact of immigration on employment and wages, rather than on integration itself, although there was considerable testimony on the question of Jewish integration (including testimony by Theodore Herzl, who spoke about anti-Semitism and the Zionist solution to the Jewish problem).[1]

The commission analysis found that there were very few immigrants that had entered the country, compared with immigration into other countries at the time (0.69 percent of the population, compared with 1.4 in Germany, 2.7 in France, 2 in Austria, and 9.6 in Switzerland), that foreigners were not taking the jobs of English workers, that they were not a source of infectious disease, and that they were exploited in the housing and job markets. Moreover, almost half of the 287,000 aliens in the United Kingdom lived in London, with the rest dispersed elsewhere in relatively small numbers.

Thus, the commission seemed to provide a very weak basis and rationale for restrictive legislation. Nevertheless, it recommended that a highly restrictive control regime be established (see below). Although the legislation that was finally passed was far more modest that what had been proposed, the principle of restriction was clearly established, indeed hardly challenged. In the end of the party dialogue in 1905, the issue of immigration was largely framed in terms of class, rather than race, although anti-Semitism continued to hover in the background of the debate. Indeed, as we have seen, with the pressure of WWI, restriction was strengthened against aliens, but the principle of empire citizenship and access was not challenged. This orientation remained intact for the entire period between the wars.

After WWII

During the post-WWII period, the major political parties tended to frame the issue of immigration in roughly the same way. For both parties this meant a continuation of the distinction between aliens and empire citizens (increasingly, citizens of the British Commonwealth). This distinction became increasingly problematic, however, as the ties of empire declined with independence, and as Commonwealth countries established their own citizenship laws. Although different classes of citizenship were formally established under the British Nationality Act in 1948, it has been argued that the intention was meant to preserve the pre-1946 system. Nevertheless, several M.P.s recognized the potential consequences of differentiating among classes of subjects.[2]

In 1948, the British faced a policy dilemma that was quite different from the one faced by postwar France. French policymakers generally agreed—and had for a long time—that France faced a severe labor-market problem that necessitated immigration. On the other hand, demographers in particular remained concerned—even preoccupied—with the balance between workers arriving from other countries in Europe and those from North Africa, still considered to be the least desirable recruits. At its core, this was an issue of identity and how and whether policymakers understood immigration to be a challenge to national identity. In the end, the French were neither willing to openly restrict immigration, nor to set national quotas, nor to define immigrant workers as "guest-workers" and in this way restrict their stay, at least in theory.

British policymakers, by contrast, expressed no overt concern that continued open immigration from the colonies and Commonwealth (as opposed to immigration from countries outside of the colonies and Commonwealth) would be a challenge to British national identity. Indeed, the notion of national identity that was expressed by leaders of both political parties virtually necessitated this kind of open immigration policy. Joppke notes that

> There was consensus between the Conservative and Labour Parties not to restrict free movement within the realm of empire, now

democratically refashioned as the British Commonwealth of Nations. As the Tory Sir Maxwell Fyfe said... "We must maintain our great metropolitan tradition of hospitality to everyone from every part of our Empire".[3]

Although there was partisan dispute about whether that hospitality should be contained in open citizenship (the Labour preference), or "subjectship" (the Tory preference), Labour agreed that this kind of openness would "give the coloured races of the Empire the idea that ...they are the equals of people in this country" (Labour Home Secretary Ede). For the Tories, the maintenance of "subjectship" represented, at the same time, the tradition of empire and inequality of status. For Labour, the maintenance of broadly defined citizenship represented a high degree of equality for citizens of the United Kingdom, the Commonwealth and the colonies.

The consensus, based on a uniquely elite sense of empire identity, rested on the ability of the state to continue to limit immigration from the Commonwealth. When this assumption began to break down within the next decade, not only the policy, but the manner of framing the policy would be strongly contested. In chapter 6, we saw how the growth of NCW residents during the decade between 1951 and 1961 altered the context within which the issue of citizenship was being considered. It was in this context that ideas about national identity began to change, and that the defense of empire openness gave way to narrower ideas of UK identity.

Reframing the Question

It was during the discussions and policy negotiations leading up to the legislation in 1962 that the Tories first reframed the immigration issue. Jeannette Money argues that the decision to introduce immigration control legislation that would be applicable to Commonwealth citizens was based on electoral considerations, which focused particularly on marginal constituencies represented by the Tories, with relatively large immigrant populations. However, as she notes, the Conservative Party had passed resolutions in favor of Commonwealth immigration control in 1958 and 1960. The electoral incentives that she analyzes were important for Tory M.P.s that represented the constituencies cited above, but it can hardly be argued that they feared an anti-immigrant campaign from their Labour rivals (who were most unlikely to organize anti-immigrant campaigns). In fact, it appears more likely that the Conservatives were reacting to problems that had been perceived over a number of years, and a debate on these problems within its own ranks, that finally culminated with a decision by party leadership to adopt a position that had widespread support among back-benchers.[4]

Although the legislation applied to *all* members of the Commonwealth, it was clear from the beginning that its primary impact would be on potential immigrants from the New Commonwealth countries. Therefore, while the impact of the Commonwealth Immigrants Act of 1962 was relatively modest, the importance of the legislation was to establish the rationale and the principal mechanisms for exclusion in the years to come. As Paul Gordon argues, "The Commonwealth Immigrants Act1962 was the start of a process; and increasingly restrictive controls followed." The problem after 1962 was that the legislation was relatively ineffective in limiting access to the NCW immigrants that were its intended target. In fact, the proportion of the NCW population resident in the United Kingdom increased by 58 percent between 1961 and 1966 (see table 5.2).[5] Labor force surveys on dates of arrival indicate that although immigration from the Caribbean declined dramatically during the decade after the Commonwealth Immigrants Act of 1962 came into force, immigration from India and Pakistan grew proportionately more.[6]

The Labour Party had opposed the 1962 Act, and quite unexpectedly had become the defender of an open empire/commonwealth citizenship. However, within two years, the way the party framed the issue began to change rapidly. Indeed, this change in orientation was taken specifically to depoliticize the issue. Richard Crossman—Minister of housing, and then leader of the House of Commons in the Labour Government after 1964—argued in his memoirs that the restrictionist decisions of the Labour Government in 1965 were taken to bring Labour closer to the Tory position: "Politically, fear of immigration is the most powerful undertow today....We felt we had to out-trump the Tories by doing what they would have done and so transforming their policy into bipartisan policy"[7] This same orientation was carried over to the decision-making on the Kenyan Asian crisis in 1968.

Home Secretary Callaghan also defended the legislation in terms of race relations.

> Our best hope of developing in these Islands a multi-racial society free of strife lies in striking the right balance between the number of Commonwealth citizens we can allow in and our ability to ensure them... a fair deal not only in tangible matters like jobs, housing and other social services but, more intangibly, against racial prejudice.[8]

Race tensions, he argued, would be an inevitable result of large-scale Asian entry into the United Kingdom. Such tensions could only be avoided through an exclusionary policy based on race. Of course the word "race" was not part of the legislation, but it did emerge in debates and discussions, and was certainly central to the understanding of the Commonwealth Immigrants Act of 1968.

But party differences can be important, even in the context of policy consensus. In the parallel conflict in 1972, when Uganda announced its intention to expel all Asians, a Conservative government redefined the issue, and treated this crisis in terms of asylum, rather than immigration.

In this way, the Tories did not abandon their commitment to restriction, but also did not abandon the Ugandan Asians (see below).[9]

Thus, by 1965, both major political parties were edging toward a consensus on immigration restriction, the objective of which was to convert Commonwealth citizens (as well as citizens of colonies still in existence) into full-fledged foreigners, subject to immigration law. The progress along this road, however, was far slower and more incomplete than the rhetoric would indicate. Part of the explanation for this slow change was that the core objective of more than 20 years of legislative efforts after 1962 was to redefine British citizenship. However, instead of doing this directly, by nationality law, new citizenship was progressively defined in terms of immigration law.

> Usually a state allows its own nationals free access to its territory and the immigration laws regulate entry and residence of non-nationals. Not so in the UK. One of the notable features of recent UK immigration law has been its divergence from British nationality law.[10]

Even after almost 20 years of legislative effort to remove the differences between Colony/Commonwealth citizens and aliens, the former still retained privileges denied to the latter. In numerous ways the retention of even diminishing nationality rights for citizens of the Colonies and Commonwealth would create loopholes into which immigrants from these areas could enter the United Kingdom. The use of immigration law to redefine citizenship also meant that once immigrants from the colonies and Commonwealth actually managed to enter the United Kingdom, they more easily gained citizenship rights that were available to their counterparts in France (and most other countries) only through naturalization.

The Political Process

Pre-WWII: Political and Administrative Patterns

Initiated by the Conservatives in 1899, legislation directed specifically against Jewish immigration (although it applied to all aliens) was passed by the House of Lords, but was never accepted for consideration by the House of Commons. As we have seen above, the real battle for restrictive legislation developed in 1902–1903, as agitation for restriction grew among backbenchers of the Conservative Party, this time with support from within the leadership, and received considerable sympathy within the cabinet of Prime Minister Arthur Balfour.[11]

Sir Howard Vincent, an influential member from Sheffield, whose constituency was virtually devoid of foreigners, teamed up with Major William Evans-Gordon, a backbencher from Stepney, an area on the East End of London with a large and growing Jewish population. Together, they began to pressure the party from the outside, by mobilizing street demonstrations, and pushing a seemingly reluctant government into creating the *Royal Commission on the Aliens Question* in 1903. Evans-Gordon served as an effective advocate for immigration restriction, while Lord Rothschild (a leader of the Jewish community) provided an effective counterweight. Using the commission recommendations (rather than its analysis), the government proposed restrictive legislation to a divided Conservative Party.

The alien legislation proposed in 1904 was formulated to unite a Conservative government that was badly divided over questions of "cheap labor" and tariff reform (that would finally force Balfour's resignation in 1905). Some of these same issues found resonance among the opposition Liberals, who were also concerned with the question of "cheap labor," and were concerned about losing votes in the East End of London to the Tories by opposing the government initiative.[12] In the end, after a fierce internal battle, the Liberals opposed the bill, and Tory enthusiasm waned sufficiently—evidently because of the passion of the anti-Semitic campaign of the Tory radicals—to force the tabling of the legislation until the next parliamentary session of 1905. As we saw in chapter 5, when the legislation was re-proposed, it contained provisions that were more "centrist" in terms of Tory sensitivities, and more attractive to the Liberal opposition.

The Liberal government elected in January 1906 declined to repeal the act, but also declined to enforce it with vigor. Given the amount of discretion that the legislation had left to inspectors, the instructions given by the new government remained a key to the effectiveness of the law. Thus, after the Liberals won a much reduced, slender victory in 1910, the new government began to enforce the law with greater vigor.[13] Pressure for strong enforcement grew considerably as the war approached, and the powers of the 1905 act were extended by the 1914 legislation after the outbreak of the war, and by the 1919 legislation after the war.

Nevertheless, even after 1919, there was sufficient administrative discretion left to permit the Home secretary to exert considerable control over entry and entry criteria. By the 1930s, the context of immigration had changed significantly, and there were no proposals to change the restrictive orientation of the legislation. In the growing refugee crisis of the 1930s, the Home Secretary exercised administrative discretion to develop a modified frame for understanding the immigration question, a frame that was a reaction to refugee pressure.

In the early 1930s, preference for entry was given to refugees—mostly Jews—who were either on their way to somewhere else, or those who were wealthy or well connected. By the late 1930s, the Home Office began to distinguish between aliens and refugees, with a reluctance to admit more refugees. After *Kristallnacht*, in November 1938, the government relaxed restrictions, but also began to look for other places within the Empire to which Jewish refugees could be sent.[14] After the limitations of that policy became evident, the government softened its admissions policies.

Government options were limited less by the legislative context than by the international political context—by reports of Jewish-Arab communal tensions in the British mandate of Palestine. At the very moment when Jews from central Europe were seeking refuge, the 1937 Peel Commission recommended that no more than 12,000 Jewish refugees each year be admitted to the mandate territory. Two years later, a policy white paper recommended admission of 75,000 over five years, but with no further admission without the agreement of Arabs already in Palestine. Official acceptance of these recommendations, however, did little to alleviate the problem. The attempt to internationalize the refugee question at the Evian Conference in 1938 was a failure. As a result, the British Government responded to the growing pressures by easing admission to Britain, rather than Palestine.[15] By the time the war began, about 50,000 Jewish refugees from Nazi Germany had entered Britain.

Post-WWII: Administrative and Political Patterns

Discretion in the administration of immigration legislation remained the center-piece of immigration control. The 1953 Order in Council see Chapter 5, provided a core policy. It stipulated that:

> . . . any alien can be refused entry into the United Kingdom at the discretion of an immigration officer; that in general, he shall not be allowed into this country for more three months unless he holds a Ministry of Labour permit for work or has visible means of financial support; and that any alien can be deported either by the courts or by the Home Secretary when "he deems it conducive to the public good."[16]

Thus, the admission of aliens was also governed by prerogative powers of the Crown which went beyond the statutory authority of the code: ". . . it meant that the immigration authorities could act even more arbitrarily against aliens than was provided for in the Aliens Order of 1953." Ian Macdonald has demonstrated that British courts have given broad scope to the administration of Royal Prerogatives to restrict immigration, although they have been somewhat less generous about deportation.[17] In contrast to legislative rules, the exercise of Royal Prerogatives is less subject to judicial constraints. Nevertheless, if we compare the use of administrative authority before WWII and after the war, it becomes clear that arbitrariness can be used to soften admissions (before the war), or to make admission more difficult (after the war). Although new legislation in 1948 redefined citizenship categories, patterns of policy-making on immigration changed little until the early 1960s.

The changes in policy in the 1960s required a sharp re-framing of the immigration issue, in order to focus on immigration from the colonies and the Commonwealth, rather than from immigration sources that had been the target of previous legislation and administration. It required a re-definition of citizenship. How then can we understand the changing politics of immigration through which this took place?

Unlike France, the structure of immigration politics did not change. Policy continued to be developed within the framework of party competition. However, the dynamics of party competition were reoriented by changes within the Conservative. These changes were only minimally related to labor market requirements, and were related far more to the changing balance among ministerial actors.

Until the early 1960s, there was considerable support among business and political elites for increasing, not decreasing, labor market immigration.

> As late as 1965, the government predicted labor shortages of two hundred thousand annually. Declining industries, especially the northern textile companies, relied on immigrant labor to maintain their competitive advantage. And the British government itself was actively involved in recruiting immigrant labor for the London Transport and the National Health Service. The British Hotels and Restaurants Association also actively enlisted Commonwealth immigrants.... The newly arrived immigrants found housing in inner city areas that were vacated when the native workforce moved to more desirable suburban locations.[18]

Randall Hansen argues that what was weakening the support for maintaining free NCW immigration was the growing gap between two ministerial actors: the Ministry of Labour and the Colonial Office provoked by what turned out to be a small increase in unemployment. In fact, although unemployment rates hovered around historic lows until 1974—lower than 2 percent until 1962, and under 3 percent until 1971—rates had begun to edge up between 1955 and 1958, and then declined once again, only to rise slightly after 1961.[19]

Unemployment among NCW ("coloured") immigrants, however, had begun to rise once again in late 1959, according to the Ministry of Labour. Hansen's archival material indicates a real anxiety in that ministry,[20] which was monitoring declining needs for immigrant labor in specific areas, and had found as early as August 1958, "...that employment prospects for immigrant workers were deteriorating rapidly. It put pressure on the Colonial Office, which had the greatest responsibility for the West Indies and the greatest interest in avoiding migration control." The Ministry of Labour suggested to the Colonial Office that the West Indian governments be convinced to withhold passports from those who were seeking employment in the United Kingdom, a continuation of policy that had been in force since 1955 for Indians and Pakistanis.[21]

However, this policy—a clear extension of pre-war colonial policy—appeared to be less and less effective, and sub-continent immigration began to increase after 1958, despite the arrangements in place. For example, the arrangements were severely undermined in 1959, when the Indian Supreme Court declared exit controls to be unconstitutional, which forced India, and then Pakistan to relax these efforts.[22] Although the effectiveness of the policy of home-country restriction varied between 1958 and 1962, the more the Colonial Office relied on informal restriction to defend its position, the more it lost ground to the Ministry of Labour.

The decline of the influence of the Colonial Office in this policy arena is related to the more general decline of support for an economically integrated, multicultural Commonwealth. This view became more difficult to sustain, as European economic integration progressed, and as the independence of former colonies increasingly engaged in alliances of their own gained momentum. Moreover, although the Colonial Office tended to favor Commonwealth immigration as a matter of principle, its policies also reflected different racial assumptions about immigrants from different sources, specifically about differences between immigrants from the Subcontinent and those from the West Indies. If the former were "lazy, feckless and difficult to place in employment," the latter were "industrious, reliable and talented."[23]

In this context, the policy challenge was initiated within the Conservative Party. It then quickly became an issue between the Conservatives and Labour. Although Labour had bitterly opposed the 1962 legislation, by 1968, the party had come full circle—both in the way that it was framing the issue (see ch. 5), and in the policies that it pursued. Thus, the 1968 Commonwealth Immigrants Act—passed by the Labour Government—drew a line in the sand. There were two aspects of the 1968 legislation that were of overriding importance for the future. The first was a clear and open affirmation of consensus on immigration policy with the Tories. The second was an affirmation by the Labour Government that it intended to apply exclusionary immigration policy *specifically* against non-white immigrants.

In 1962 there were clear differences between the two major parties with regard to immigration/citizenship legislation. By 1965, these differences had become far more ambiguous. Thus, the legislation passed by Labour in reaction to the Kenyan Asian crisis in 1968 effectively broke a promise that had been made by the Tories, and, in retrospect, seems unusually harsh for a government of the left. (See ch. 5.) A similar crisis broke out in 1972, when Idi Amin, who had recently staged a coup against Milton Obote in Uganda, announced the expulsion within three months of all Asians in Uganda. This time the Conservative Government, led by Edward Heath, pursued a course that was quite different from its Labour predecessor. Heath was under considerable internal pressure from an anti-immigrant wing of the party led by Enoch Powell. The Government, nevertheless, decided to take "full responsibility" for the

Asians. It negotiated resettlement agreements with several countries, but ultimately accepted 28,000 of the 50,000 for settlement in the United Kingdom. By treating this new crisis in terms of asylum, rather than immigration, the Tories maintained their commitment to restriction, but did not abandon the Ugandan Asians, even under pressure from Powell.[24] Nevertheless, the fundamental commitment to restriction by the party was reaffirmed in the Immigration Act of 1971, and in the legislation of Natal criteria for entry into the United Kingdom.

During the following 25 years the policy consensus has remained more or less intact, but this does not mean that immigration has not been a salient political issue. As in France, agreement on policy has often been masked by intense political struggle. Thus, the lack of important policy differences has not prevented the use of immigration for political purposes, particularly around elections. An early clash, without policy consequences, occurred during the run-up to the parliamentary elections of 1979. Margaret Thatcher's 1978 comments, that Britain would be "swamped by people of a different culture," a clear reference to non-white immigrants, and her call for "an end to immigration, drew immediate condemnation from the Government, and from leaders of her own party.[25] Nevertheless, within days, the balance of support in the polls moved from a small Labour lead to an 11 point Tory lead.[26] By summer, Thatcher had dropped the immigration issue, and by the time that the elections finally took place in May 1979, the immigration issue had been definitively displaced by issues of the economy and Labour's control over strike action.

As we noted in chapter 6, there were similar patterns in 2001 and 2005. As the Tories turned their public attention to the question of asylum seekers and illegal immigration in the run-up to the parliamentary election in June 2001, the immigration issue, defined in this way, began to look more and more like the wedge issue that they had been toying with since the Thatcher period. Focusing on asylum-seekers, the Conservative leader referred to Britain as a "foreign land" early in the campaign. Comments of other Tory leaders tended to reflect the more racist thinking of the Tory right-wing.

> As the numbers [of asylum-seekers] grew, so did the press coverage...
> Tory politicians and newspapers focused on "bogus" asylum-seekers who were coming to Britain to live off the fat of the land.

But that was only part of the story:

> Labour, defensive, turned on the foreigners too; Barbara Roche, the immigration minister, for instance, described the begging techniques of asylum-seekers as "vile."[27]

In the end, raising the issue resulted in no important benefits for the Conservatives, and the issue faded in political discourse, but not in public opinion after the elections. At the moment when it might have disappeared as a priority for voters, it was reinforced by the attacks of September 11, 2001. Thus, reinforced by the discussion of new anti-terrorist legislation, and the terrorist attacks in Madrid, immigration as an issue remained high on the political agenda in 2002–2004, despite the efforts of the Conservative Party to move in a very different "compassionate conservative" direction, led by their new shadow home secretary, Oliver Lewin. When Lewin was replaced in the run-up to the 2005 election, the Tories were once again tempted by surveys that indicated that the issue had not diminished in importance.[28] (See ch. 6.)

Nevertheless, the basic framework of understanding has endured. Indeed, it is important to note that there have been no proposals to alter either the basic labor market criteria for entry, or the privileged rights of Commonwealth and Irish immigrants who establish residency in the United Kingdom. The general partisan consensus that has been established has permitted a high level of administrative discretion. What continues to characterize immigration policy is the degree of discretion that has been attributed to administrative authorities to establish and change rules of admission and abode, without the constraining role of constitutional rights.[29] Thus, while administration of family unification has been hard and restrictive, new rules established in 2002 that initiated a Highly Skilled Migrant Program have made it possible for non-EU applicants with high education levels and specific skills to enter the United Kingdom without any guarantees of employment. Moreover, for the first time since 1965, a new Sector Based Scheme was introduced to deal with shortages in unskilled labor in a number of sectors. (See ch. 5.)

The Politics of Change

While this analysis the political process of immigration policy-making may give us some insight into how policy is made, it gives less insight into why policies change. During the period between 1962 and 1971 British policy on citizenship and immigration changed in a dramatic way. While there were no claims about "zero immigration" as there were in France, there were claims that undesirable immigration from the NCW would be severely restricted by changing the rights of Commonwealth citizens, and by defining a new UK citizenship.

There is a considerable body of literature that argues that the change in policy is related to a racist reaction among policymaking elites to the increase of NCW immigration in the 1950s. This reaction was fueled by fears of social instability and public opinion. Public opinion on this issue was then manipulated to support a change in policy. In this way, public opinion reaction was inflated and exaggerated and used to justify the imposition of increasingly restrictive immigration controls.[30]

In his study of British immigration policy, Randall Hansen argues that public opinion appears to have needed little manipulation in its opposition to immigration and its support for restrictive legislation. Indeed, as in France and the United States, political elites who favored relatively open immigration could draw little comfort from the low levels of mass support. More to the point, there is no indication that variations in policy were driven one way or the other by public opinion.[31] Public opposition to immigration appears to have been less a driving force for policymakers than a constant resource that varied in saliency. (See ch. 6.) Hansen then makes a convincing case that the decline of the Colonial Office as an institutional support against immigration restriction from the NCW is the key to understanding the change in immigration policy in 1962. (See above.)

On the other hand, this does not mean that racism among policy-making elites was not important in the development of immigration policy in Britain, or that a racist construction of the immigration issue by political elites did not happen or was not important. Indeed, despite Hansen's robust defense of policy-makers against charges of racism, his archival materials reveal a pattern of racial concerns in the construction of the immigration issue. Both the Ministry of Labour and the Colonial Office began to make their cases in racialized terms—especially after the riots of 1958. As in France, what most concerned policy-makers well before the initiation of restrictions were racial tensions and the perceived problems of integrating non-white immigrant groups. Although there was clear conflict within each political party, even before 1962, about the need for immigration restriction from New Commonwealth countries, the core of the dialogue in each case turned on racial differences and race-relations.

Moreover, public opinion did not give any support to the notion of a Commonwealth people. Rising public opinion against immigration in Britain did not perceive any common national bond with New Commonwealth immigrants, an assumption that had been at the heart of the approach to immigration before the passage of the 1962 legislation, and that was the approach that had been advocated by the Colonial Office. Public opinion perceived them simply as foreigners, indeed among the least desirable foreigners in the country. Under these circumstances, a simple merger of all non-UK resident-citizens into the category of aliens (and therefore immigrants when they crossed the frontier) would probably have been strongly supported by public opinion, and would have been closer to the approach taken by France 12 years later.

A different approach to understanding change is provided by spatial analysis. Thus the dynamic of change depends on the importance of specific localities for shifting national elections. In contrast to France, where immigrant concentration was strongest in localities dominated by the Left, at least during the period when immigration restriction was initiated, two-thirds of the 106 constituencies with at least 5 percent foreign-born population in Britain were held by the Conservatives after the 1959 parliamentary elections. About a third of these were classified by the Tories as swing constituencies, according to Jeannette Money.[32]

Money argues that this provided an incentive for the Conservatives to initiate legislation for immigration restriction as a response to voter sentiment in key constituencies, and as a way of seeking to win in marginal constituencies in which Labour M.P.s were vulnerable on the immigration issue. This analysis is more convincing in explaining Tory attempts to win in marginal Labour constituencies than in explaining why Tories should try to use this issue for electoral purposes in constituencies that they controlled, since it was not likely that they would be challenged with anti-immigrant campaigns by their Labour rivals. In any case, as in France, the political gain nationally was minimal, and the Tories lost the 1964 election. In the end, although anti-immigrant attitudes were certainly widely held, they proved to be less salient, compared with other issues.

Still, there was clear electoral pressure in some Labour-represented constituencies with high immigrant populations, where Butler and Stokes estimate that Labour lost three seats and was prevented from winning others.[33] In Aston (Birmingham), the sitting Labour candidate lost his seat in 1964 after he refused to shift his stand on immigration—even though the party itself supported the Tory legislation of 1962 that it had vehemently opposed at the time. And then, of course, there was the shock of Smethwick, a safe midlands constituency where Patrick Gordon Walker—Labour's shadow foreign secretary—was overwhelmed by his anti-immigrant Conservative opponent; he then lost again in a by-election a few months later, when the party gave him a safe seat to bring him back into the cabinet. Anthony Messina argues that "The extent to which the electoral outcome at Smethwick altered the major parties', and especially Labour's, perception of the race issue cannot be overstated." Ten years later, Labour leader Richard Crossman would summarize the problem:

> Ever since the Smethwick election it has been quite clear that immigration can be the greatest potential vote-loser for the Labour party if we are seen to be permitting a flood of immigrants to come and blight the central areas in all our cities.[34]

Thus specific electoral pressures appear to have played an important role in the reorientation of immigration policy for Labour. However, there is at least some evidence that the electoral pressure played differently for the Tories than for Labour; that far from attempting to outbid one another to "…shift their policy positions in response to changing community preferences," each party was seeking to mobilize different kinds of voters in areas of high immigrant concentration, and that each party understood the problem of immigration in a different way at this level.

In a survey taken in 1969, among MPs representing constituencies with high immigrant concentrations, the differences between the two major parties could not have been starker. Labour MPs from these constituencies strongly opposed restriction. The commitment of Tory MPs in these constituencies, on the other hand, was to go much further down the road of restriction, even after the most restrictive legislation had already been passed—and even during a period when policy agreement between national Labour and the Conservatives appeared to be strong. By 1969, well over half of Tory MPs were prepared to agree with the most radical anti-immigrant propositions, with the percentage increasing with immigrant concentration. (See table 7.1.)

Therefore, immigration appeared to be essentially a Conservative issue, useful against Labour, but one that divided Conservative politicians, far more than an issue that divided the left. For each set of MPs the problem aspects of the immigration issue went far beyond simple electoral incentives. There is plenty of evidence of electoral pressure at the constituency level, but the impact of that pressure was different for each of the major parties. What seems to have happened in Britain is that national parties assumed relatively moderate national positions on immigration restriction, isolating the more radical MPs from their constituency organizations. The political dynamics were also different. In France the positions of the national and local parties of the Right were similar, while some local parties of the Left appeared to be more favorable to restriction (though not voters of the left) than the national parties (Socialist and Communist).

For the Tories, a move toward immigration restriction was a useful, but limited position, limited specifically by the sensibilities of MPs from areas in which there were few if any NCW immigrants. For Labor, it was more difficult to support restriction, but such a position could be rendered more acceptable by support for anti-racism legislation. Thus, Labour first challenged the 1962 legislation because, as Gaitskill said, it carried racial overtones, and then linked their support for even tighter immigration restriction with the Race Relations Act of 1965.

Table 7.1   MPs attitudes on immigration and repatriation in 1969 (percentage)

1969: Britain must completely halt all colored immigration, including dependents, and encourage the repatriation of colored persons now living here.

	Agree	Disagree	Strongly Disagree	Don't Know	Total
Labour MPs from high immigrant areas	4%	29%	66%	—	100%
Labour MPs from low immigrant areas	6	38	54	2	100
Conservative MPs from high immigrant areas	50	7	36	7	100
Conservative MPs from low immigrant areas	37	45	13	5	100

Source: Robert C. Frasure, "Constituency Racial Composition and the Attitudes of British MPs," *Comparative Politics*, January 1971, p. 206.

Moreover, for the Tories, immigrants represented an object of advantage in emphasizing identity politics. For Labour, immigrants represented a potential new electorate, a political resource, whose support could give Labour a marginal political advantage in some constituencies.[35] The problem is that, in Britain, as in France, the incentive to pursue immigrants as a political resource was not strong because of the distribution of immigrant communities.

Electoral Strategy

Although the political geography of immigration has changed substantially in France since the 1960s, the change in Britain seems somewhat more limited. As in France, the areas with immigrant concentration have remained concentrated in a few areas. However, in contrast to the 1960s, we can estimate from the most recent census data available that the number of electoral constituencies with more than 10 percent New Commonwealth immigrants has increased by a factor of four. Money estimates that there were about 33 (our of 630) constituencies with 10 percent or more NCW immigrant alien immigrants in 1966, or just over 5 percent.[36] There are now 128. Table 7.2 summarizes the results of parliamentary constituencies in which the non-white population is greater than 10 percent, together with the party affiliation of the MP elected in 2001. Of the 641 UK constituencies for which we have census results, 128 (20 percent) have non-white populations of 10 percent or more. Of these, as in France, most are concentrated in two very limited areas: 54 are in London, 19 in the West Midlands, and 12 in the remainder of the Northwest (primarily the Manchester area). Two-thirds are either in London or the West Midlands.

However, there may or may not have been a shift in political representation in these areas, which are now overwhelmingly Labour. In the 1960s Money reports that 17 percent of the electoral constituencies had immigrant populations of 5 percent or more and of these, two-thirds were represented by Tories. On the other hand, Frasure's estimate of representation

Table 7.2 British constituencies with 10 percent or more non-white ropulation, by political representation

	London and W. Midlands	Outside	Total
Labour	73	41	114
Conservatives	8	2	10
Lib-Dem	4	0	4
Total	85	43	128

Source: Census results for the United Kingdom for 2001; results of elections for 2001, House of Commons: Total constituencies = 641.

during this period, based on different estimates, gives the clear advantage to Labour.[37]

In 2001, of the 128 local authorities with 10 percent or more immigrants, 114 are represented by Labour. They are in the same areas cited by Frasure. This would appear to increase the incentives for Labour for a positive orientation toward immigrants (or non-whites), as well as incentives for their electoral mobilization at the local level.

The incentives, however, remain relatively limited. In contrast to France and the United States, immigrant populations from the NCW are potentially part of the electorate as soon as they establish residency in the United Kingdom. Thus, their percentage of the electorate is about as large as their percentage of the voting age population. At about 6.6 percent of the electorate, over 80 percent of immigrant minorities are in the electorate, compared to only about half in France (2.7% of the electorate).[38] Immigrants in Britain have been most successful at the local level. Alba and Foner have observed that, where there are concentrations of immigrant groups, they have been far more successful in winning local office than in France. In the London boroughs, 10.6 percent of the local councilors in 2001 were (mostly Asian) ethnic minorities. They also conclude that in all of the authorities in Britain where ethnic minorities exceeded 10 percent, "...the Asian community achieved a position close to parity," and in more than a quarter exceeded parity.

Representation at the national parliamentary level, however, has been far less impressive. As we noted in chapter 6, in the House of Commons elected in 2005, there were 15 minority M.P.s (of the 630 members), about a third of what we might expect, normed to the proportion of the population. Since no minority candidate was elected in France in 2002, the comparison is relatively favorable, but it is about half that of the United States (for Hispanics).

As in the French case, for our purposes, the question of representation is less important than how these patterns are related to the way immigrant populations are understood politically, and how this is related to the development of immigration policy. To the extent that immigrants are understood as a political resource, rather than a challenge to identity, representation is a reasonable index of how much they are mobilized for electoral purposes, generally by political parties, but also by community organizations that often serve as political entrepreneurs with political parties, as well.

If in the French case, the relative success of recruitment of minority candidates at the local has been attributed both to party decentralization and to the weakness of parties, the relative success in the British case can be related to the ward-based system of candidate designation in the Labour Party, which both empowers local ethnic politicians and accentuates the advantage of concentrated ethnic votes in a single member district.[39] Thus, compared with France, local level political influence of immigrants voters can be translated into influence over national representation through the Labour Party, and has been in a limited number of cases.

On the other hand, there is no evidence that the recruitment of minority representation has had any influence over the orientation of the Labour Party (or the Conservative Party) toward immigration policy. The presence of minority legislators may have some influence over party policy, but, at least at key moments of change, does not seem to influence party decision-making about public policy priorities. In the mid-1970s, argues Erik Bleich,

> ....although the issue was salient enough to rally significant electoral support, within the [Labour] party there was a tendency among some to blame "Powellism" for what they viewed as Britain's distasteful immigration and race policies. Segments of Labour thus attempted to rethink the party's strategy and to develop an alternative to the prevailing anit-immigrant rhetoric. This new philosophy was reflected in policy documents such as Labour's 1972 Green Paper on Citizenship, Immigration and Integration and in their 1973 Party Programme. In spite of this activism, the party chose first to omit and then to marginalize promises to legislate on race in its February and October manifestos, suggesting that pro-reform members lacked the clout to parlay changing attitudes into a Labour commitment to act.[40]

Thus the politics of immigration in Britain has moved some distance toward an understanding of immigrant populations as a political resource, with all that implies in terms of influence over policy. This approach is consistent with the very large proportion of the immigrant population that is in fact part of the electorate, as well as with the multiculturalist British approach to integration. This perspective, however, is limited by two other political realities. First, concentrations of immigrant populations are limited to a very small part of political space, to constituencies that are relatively safe for Labour, from which it is hard to leverage national influence. Second, in the results of recent surveys, it is striking how weak key civic values are among the Muslim population that forms a large percentage of immigrant voters now in the electorate. In table 1.8, only a sixth of British Muslims are as likely as their French counterparts to see their identity as citizens of their country, rather than simply Muslim; and are only half as likely to make the adoption of "national customs" a priority.

Therefore, we are confronted with an unusual contradiction. In France, where the importance of civic values is relatively widespread among the immigrant populations, immigrants are not regarded as a political and electoral resource, even by the parties of the left that are relatively favorable to their interests, and to which they tend to give their votes.[41] In Britain, where the importance of civic values is relatively weak among immigrant populations, immigrant voters have been relatively more successful in integrating into political life.

Conclusion

This brings us back to the question of how we can understand the change in immigration policy in Britain that moved sharply toward restriction between 1962 and 1971. Although electoral considerations appear to have been important both for the Conservatives, who initiated the change, and for Labour that accepted it, the key appears to be the change within the Conservative Party with regard to the defense of Commonwealth citizenship. This broad citizenship had been under pressure since the war, and became increasingly untenable as NCW immigration increased sharply during the 1950s. The conflict between the Ministry of Labour and the Colonial Office was finally resolved in favor of the former within the Conservative Party. Once the issue was re-framed in terms of immigration and identity, it then became more difficult for Labour to defend a more open citizenship, and hence a more open immigration policy, particularly after the bitter 1964 election. Nevertheless, the decision of Labour to fall back on race-relations legislation indicates the different way that the issue played within the party, compared with the Conservatives. Although the pursuit of immigrant voters became marginally more important for the Labour Party in the 1970s, its position in favor of restrictionist policy then remained unchanged.

While the structure of the political process of immigration policy has remained essentially the same over the last century, the dynamics that have driven the process have changed in fundamental ways. The reframing of the immigration issue in identity terms, first by the Conservatives, and then by Labour, very much resembled what would happen in France a decade later. However, because the issue was shaped in the context of citizenship, rather than simply immigration, the results were different in essential ways. In part because of the heritage of empire, the reframing of the issue never involved a rejection of a multicultural society by either of the major parties.

Indeed, in defending restriction, Labour in particular emphasized the importance of the maintenance of "balance" in order to preserve a multicultural society. While it is true that this view was challenged from the extremes of the Tory right and the British National Front,[42] it remained at the core of the understanding between the two major parties. By the 1970s, these concerns—at first linked to Labour's support for restriction—had been separated from questions of entry, and instead were more closely linked to the emerging autonomous sphere of discrimination within Britain.[43] The focus on discrimination enabled the Labour Party to seek to augment its electoral support among minorities, and to assuage its own left wing, without however altering its position on immigration restriction.

The legislation of immigration restriction, by altering citizenship, also had other consequences. Alien legislation was made somewhat more restrictive in 1988 and 1999 (see ch. 5), but—remarkably—it has never abolished the advantages of citizenship rights still attributed to the very NCW immigrants against whom restrictive legislation was directed in the first place. Indeed, although restriction in Britain has often been harsh (particularly the administration of family unification), the rhetoric of "zero immigration" has neither been important nor applied, and the rights of immigrants in the country have been far more extensive than in France, and better protected through anti-discrimination legislation. At the same time, however, surveys cited above indicate that these policies may be less effective in terms of integration than in France.

Finally, the dynamics of the party system were very different than those in France. Although the challenge of the British National Front in the 1970s appeared to have had some influence on the rhetoric surrounding the immigration issue, the party did not provide the same kind of electoral challenge as its counterpart in France. As a result, there was not an electoral dynamic to radicalize the movement toward restriction, and even in the relatively few constituencies with a high proportion of immigrants, the radicalization of the immigration issue has remained limited, and has not provided a challenge to the prevailing consensus. On the other hand,there has been only a limited tendency within the Labour Party to support a more open immigration policy, or to promote minority candidacies—in order to attract immigrant votes. Therefore, presence of immigrants within the electorate, has played a far less important role in the determination of immigration policy than in the United States (see ch. 10).

CHAPTER EIGHT

Development of U.S. Immigration Policy

Context: The Constitutional and Political System

What most differentiates the United States from France and Britain is the organization of its political system. Austin Ranney has pointed out that, even though the United States has been referred to as the "first new nation," it is in fact older than most modern states of Europe. Indeed, in terms of the organization of its constitutional system, it is far older than France and—arguably older than Britain as well.[1]

If both France and Britain have evolved into different kinds of unitary, parliamentary systems, the American federal system is strikingly different in terms of its territorial and government organization. While the process of governmental decision-making under federalism has changed in the United States over the years that immigration policy has evolved, it remains an important consideration for the understanding of the politics of immigration since the nineteenth century. Similarly, while the organization of national government, and the relative balances among national institutions has also evolved, the complex organization of national government has been a key factor for understanding both the content and the politics of immigration policy.

In the American federal system the individual states have had broad authority to develop immigration policies of their own. Until almost the end of the nineteenth century, this included policy on admission of immigrants, and the processing of applications for entry. At the same time the federal government in Washington developed broad policies that shaped the flow of immigration for settlement. In most areas of policy and policy-making, federalism in the United States has never meant a division of powers. Instead it has generally been a sharing of the power of policy-making between the states and the federal government. At times, however, national policy and state policies have been directly in conflict. For example, the Burlingam Treaty between the United States and China in 1868 facilitated Chinese immigration into the United States, where they made a major contribution to railway construction and commerce.

However, ferocious anti-Chinese sentiment in California—where many of the Chinese immigrants settled—resulted in anti-Chinese state legislation that undermined Chinese settlement. Similarly, relatively open national immigration policy after 1965, combined with weakly enforced prohibitions on the employment of undocumented immigrants, resulted in a (successful) campaign in California in the mid-1990s (Proposition 187) to deny welfare benefits to illegal immigrants. While federalism has generally enhanced the ability of the states to resist policies, it has also made it more difficult for the federal government to develop coherent national policy.

The political importance of the states has been enhanced within the national government through representative institutions that overrepresent the relatively scarcely populated states. Thus, in the U.S. Senate, the representation of each state is equal, and in the House of Representatives, even though representation is roughly proportional to the population, each state is guaranteed at least one representative, regardless of population. Moreover, the popular election of the President of the United States is filtered through an electoral college that gives relatively greater weight to smaller states. Thus, from time to time, an American president is elected with fewer popular votes than his opponent (as in the election of President Bush in 2000).

In the United States, political parties are of limited importance for understanding the process of policy development. Although the two-party system has proven to be surprisingly durable since the end of the Civil War, the Democratic and Republican parties are highly decentralized, and have provided only a weak bridge among the structural divisions of American federalism. Parties dominate the organization of the House and the Senate, and modern presidents have each forged a national organization to support their election campaigns. Nevertheless, even when both houses of congress and the presidency are controlled by the same political party, agreement among these three decision-making institutions on important policy initiatives usually requires substantial compromise.

Unlike in France and Britain, winning majorities for the passage of legislation generally include representatives of the minority party. In Europe, parliamentary parties have high and enduring party cohesion. The proportion of party representatives voting together on almost every issue approaches 100 percent. While members refuse to vote with their party from time to time (an increasingly frequent occurrence in recent years), this is a generally rare and noted event, a deviation from the norm. By comparison, in the United States Congress, cohesion reaches 100 percent only on the votes for the organization of each house, at the beginning of each session. Otherwise, cohesion indices are rarely higher than 60–70 percent.[2]

Since the end of WWII, mixed party government at the national level has been the rule, rather than the exception (see table 8.1). During the 60 years between 1947 and 2007, there was unified party government

Table 8.1 Unified party-control of government institutions in the United States, 1947–2007

Years	President	Party
1949–1953	Truman	Democrat
1953–1955	Eisenhower	Republican
1961–1963	Kennedy	Democrat
1963–1969	Johnson	Democrat
1977–1981	Carter	Democrat
1993–1995	Clinton	Democrat
2003–2007	Bush	Republican

during only 22 (37 percent) of those years. Although the Democrats dominated the Congress until 1994, they did not always control both houses. If "cohabitation" in France under the Fifth Republic has meant prime ministerial domination of the political process, mixed party government in the United States has sometimes meant partisan and institutional polarization (1995–2001), and sometimes bi-partisan coalition-building across a wide range of issues (1953–1961). On the other hand, even during periods of one-party domination, conflict between presidential priorities and congressional resistance has been normal. One important study of the period 1946–90 has shown no difference between the rate of legislative production during periods of one party and mixed party control. Indeed, Republican President Eisenhower probably had an easier time working with a Democratic congress than did Democratic President Clinton.[3]

The modern policy-making process in the United States generally requires presidential leadership, which in practical terms means well-formulated presidential proposals, follow-through by a well-organized presidential staff, and cooperation with congressional leadership. Within both houses of Congress, committees and committee and subcommittee chairs are key figures in policy development and the mobilization of winning coalitions. In the Senate, with 21 standing committees, 68 subcommittees and numerous other special committees and joint committees, almost every one of the 100 senators chairs a committee or a subcommittee, as do about a quarter of the members of the much larger House of Representatives. Under the rules of each house, chairs can often prevent legislation from ever reaching the floor for a vote, and committees often have ongoing relationships with both major interest groups and administrative agencies, in their policy area. Members of both houses of Congress tend to build their influence and power within the committee system through seniority.

Samuel Beer has argued that two kinds of vertical (national) bureaucratic hierarchies have become a main feature of American federalism. In key areas of public policy, people in government service—the "technocracy"—tend

Table 8.2 U.S. legislation on Immigration and Citizenship

1790:	First national naturalization legislation; "free white persons," resident at least 2 years; swear loyalty to US Constitution
1798:	Alien and Sedition Acts; authorizes president to deport "dangerous" foreigners; 14-year residency requirement; amended in 1802 to five years
1819:	Passenger Act: Set minimal standards for immigrant ships; first federal regulation of immigration from Europe to the United States.
1875:	Supreme Court decides Henderson vs Mayor of New York; held that the regulation of immigration is federal regulation of foreign commerce
1882:	Chinese Exclusion Act; suspends immigration of Chinese labor for 10 years; extended in 1892; made permanent in 1902; Chinese ineligible for naturalization.
1882:	Immigration Act; under pressure from the State of New York, congress "nationalized" state regulations for admission of immigrants; implementation still in hands of states
1891:	Immigration Act: Assigned responsibility for immigration to federal government, establishes post of Superintendent of Immigration in Treasury Department, immigration centers at Ellis and Angel Islands.
1906	ability to speak and understand English required for naturalization
1907–8:	by Gentlemen's Agreement with Japan, Japanese laborers not issued travel documents in Japan for emigration to the US (except for Hawaii; separate executive order banning migration from Hawaii to mainland).
1917:	Literacy requirement for all new immigrants (required to read 40 words in any language); Asia designated a barred zone for immigration.
1918	The Passport Control Act required people entering the United States to first obtain visas from American consulates abroad, and that these visas be stamped in valid passports.
1921:	Emergency Quota Act; admission from European countries restricted to 3 percent of each foreign-born nationality in 1910 census; Western Hemisphere unrestricted (except by literacy test); total immigration limited to 375,000.
1924:	Johnson-Reed Act; total immigration (non-Western Hemisphere) limited to 150,000; temporary quota of 2 percent of foreign-born nationality resident in US according to 1890 census; commission set up to develop formula for determining quotas based on national origins of US population.
1929:	National origins formula for quotas agreed to; quotas distributed by estimated origins of white US population in the 1920 census. No quotas for Western Hemisphere.
1942	The Bracero Program agreed to with Mexico, and passed as Public Law 45 in 1943. The agreement provided for Mexican contract workers to work in the United States for limited periods, supervised by both the Mexican and the U.S. governments. Similar contract labor agreements were made with other governments in the Caribbean. The program endured until 1964
1943:	Chinese Exclusion Act repealed
1948	Displaced Persons Act. The first refugee legislation enacted in the history of the United States. It provided for the admission of more than 400,000 displaced persons through the end of 1951, by mortgaging future quotas.
1952:	Immigration and Nationality-McCarran-Walter Act; revised 1929 quotas, with minimum annual quotas for all countries, ending most racial restrictions; ends ban on non-white naturalization; priority given to skilled workers and relatives of US citizens; requires ability to speak, understand, read and write English for naturalization; restrictions on the entry of communists.
1965:	Immigration and Nationality-Hart-Celler Act; Abolished national origins system, together with all race restrictions to immigration; set limit of 170,000, with 20,000/ country limit, for Eastern Hemisphere, and 120,000 for Western Hemisphere (no country limits); created preference system for visas, emphasizing preferences for those with family connections and work.

Continued

Table 8.2   Continued

1978:	Amendments to Immigration and Nationality Act; combined ceilings for a total of 290,000 worldwide, with limit of 20,000 per country.
1986:	Immigration Reform and Control Act; focus on undocumented immigrants; amnesty: legalization of seasonal agricultural workers who were employed at least 90 days the year before; and others in continuous residence since 1982; outlawed hiring of undocumented workers, with mild employer sanctions. Provided for limited special agricultural worker program
1990:	Immigration Act; increased immigration limit to 700,000 per year; provided for highly skilled immigrants
1996:	Illegal Immigration Reform and Immigrant Responsibility Act; increased appropriations for border controls; easier deportation for illegal aliens, even immigrants with long residence; income restrictions for bringing relatives; limited due-process rights for immigrants; citizenship required for public benefits.
1997–98:	Congress restored access to benefits for categories of immigrants who had been receiving them prior to 1996; increased number of visas for skilled temporary workers.
2000:	Legal Immigration Family Equity Act; made it possible for immigrants to adjust legal status, with employer and/or family sponsors; increased ceiling for skilled temporary workers; automatic citizenship for foreign adopted children.
2005	The Real ID Act of 2005 required that drivers' licenses issued by the states conform to national standards. Among the requirements for issuing a license is proof that the applicant is a legal citizen or resident or alien in the United States.

to initiate policy, and form alliances with their functional counterparts in state and local government. At the national level, they link the executive with congressional committees, as well as key associational interest groups in durable policy communities. Their territorial check and counterpart has been the "intergovernmental lobby" (IGL) of governors, mayors and other local officeholders—elected officials who exercise general territorial responsibilities in state and local governments. If the interests of the technocracy vary by the function of government for which they work, the intergovernmental lobby focuses on how policy costs and benefits are distributed among territorial units. The IGL links state and local governments with their elected officials in the House and the Senate. From the perspective of federalism, this evolution has been both centralizing, because it creates a national network for local elected officials with territorial interests, and decentralizing, because it has enhanced the ability of local officials to defend their local interests at and from the national level.[4]

The need for coalition-building in the policy-process in the United States has resulted in long cycles between the initiation of policy proposals and their successful approval. The first proposals for broad immigration control were made in the1890s, but not finally approved in law until 1921 and 1924, and then implemented in 1929. The first important bills for revision of the quota system of 1924 were proposed in 1948, but not voted into law until 1965. Even when there are strong congressional majorities in favor of legislation, the threat (and reality) of a presidential veto can delay legislation for many years (as happened with the exclusionary legislation of 1924). In addition, even when there are favorable congressional majorities, as well as presidential support, committee resistance can also prevent legislative enactment (as was the case with the 1965 legislation).

Thus, in contrast to France and Britain, the American federal system is replete with veto points that can both prevent and delay policy change. But, similar to France and Britain, the administrative process can both enhance and undermine the implementation of legislation that has been approved.

Context: The United States as a Country of Immigration

In many ways the pattern of immigration policy in the United States appears to be unique, and to follow a logic that is not related to other countries. Throughout the nineteenth century, the United States was a country of immigration that welcomed millions of immigrants and what would now be called asylum-seekers, with little restriction at the borders. A United States government document on immigration has estimated that during the century between the fall of Napoleon and WWI, 30–35 million immigrants came to the United State, a number that is four-times greater than the U.S. population in 1815.[5]

Immigration contributed in a major way to the growth of the American population during the nineteenth century. Indeed, between 1850 and 1920, the percentage of foreign-born residents constantly hovered around 14 percent of the population. This was never the case for either France or Britain.

The flow of immigrants into the United States was high, and continued to increase—both in absolute and relative terms—until the 1920s, when immigration regulation began to go into effect. After 1930, with

Table 8.3 Importance of immigration in the United States

Decade	% Population Growth	% Population Growth due to Immigration	Foreign-born as a % of the Population
1840–1850	35.9	10.0	9.7
1850–1860	35.6	11.2	13.1
1860–1870	26.6	7.4	14.0
1870–1880	26.0	7.1	13.3
1880–1890	25.5	10.5	14.7
1890–1900	20.7	5.9	13.6
1900–1910	21.0	11.4	14.6
1910–1920	14.9	6.2	13.1

Source: U.S. Department of Commerce, Bureau of the Census, *Historical Statistics of the United States, Colonial Times to 1970* (Washington, DC: UGPO, 1975), Part 1, pp. 8, 117.

the impact of the imposition of the regulations from the 1924 legislation, combined with the impact of the Great Depression, it then fell to historically low levels. Neither France nor Britain ever experienced this level of influx of foreign populations. In terms of needs on both sides of the Atlantic, the trends in immigration were highly complementary:

> The mass migration of the 19th century was the result of a near perfect match between the needs of a new country and overcrowded Europe. Europe at this time was undergoing drastic social change and economic reorganization, severely compounded by overpopulation. An extraordinary increase in population coincided with the breakup of the old agricultural order which had been in place since medieval times throughout much of Europe... At approximately the same time, the industrial revolution was underway, moving from Great Britain to Western Europe, and then to Southern and Eastern Europe. For Germany, Sweden, Russia, and Japan, the highest points of emigration coincided with the beginnings of industrialization and the ensuing general disruption of employment patterns. America, on the other hand, had a boundless need for people....for settlement, defense, and economic well-being.[6]

Although the closing of the American frontier was signaled by the census of 1890, the need for labor-related immigration continued unabated, through the rapid expansion of industry between 1890 and WWI.

Of course the pressures within Europe varied considerably. Thus, as we have seen, the United Kingdom of Great Britain and Ireland was a major country of emigration to the United States, Ireland in particular. Great Britain, on the other hand, also provided incentives for the emigration to other parts of the British Empire. German emigration to the United States was about as high as that from Britain, but by the end of the nineteenth century, after the establishment of the German state and a burst of population growth, was far higher. On the other hand, even after the disruptive beginnings of French industrialization at the end of the nineteenth century, official American figures on migration indicate little immigration from France. The population grew only modestly in France during the nineteenth century, particularly in comparison to its adversaries, Britain and Germany. Not surprisingly, the percentage of foreigners residing in France almost tripled between the middle of the nineteenth century and the end of WWI. (See Table 2.1.) In general, the main trends of emigration towards the United States from Europe can be understood, not only by the relative openness of the America frontier, but also by the population growth and the population policies of the countries of origin.

Thus, in terms of the results, the United States was by far the most important country of immigration until WWI. On the other hand, the United States was also the first major country to impose highly restrictive

Table 8.4 U.S. immigration and rates of immigration, 1840–1920

Decade	Number of Immigrants (average/yr. in thousands)	Inflow of Immigration (per 1000 residents)
1841–1850	171	8.6
1851–1860	260	9.6
1861–1870	232	6.4
1871–1880	282	6.2
1881–1890	525	9.2
1891–1900	371	5.3
1901–1910	769	9.0
1911–1920	1563	15.6

Source: U.S. Department of Commerce, Bureau of the Census, *Historical Statistics of the United States, Colonial Times to 1970*, Part 1, pp. 8, 105–106.

legislation to control immigration, and for reasons that had little to do with labor market needs. The first and most serious restrictions were applied for reasons of national origin—first against Chinese, and then against other immigrants from Asia. However, these harsh restrictions were somewhat softened by citizenship policy. No restrictions were ever placed on the *jus solis* principle of citizenship, even when those who benefited from it were the children of those who were either not wanted or those who had arrived illegally.

As it turned out, the Chinese Exclusion Act of 1882 was not an isolated legislative case, but became a model for restriction (or exclusion) based on national origin that was shaped at the end of the nineteenth century, and then passed after WWI. This approach to exclusion and control was not unknown in Europe, and indeed, was discussed by French policy-makers at about the time that the 1924 Act was passed in the United States (see ch. 4), but this approach never gained much traction in Europe.

In the 1920s, when countries in Europe were welcoming, even seeking, immigration, the United States virtually closed its doors to immigration from Europe. Then, again, during the period after WWII, when countries in Europe were once again seeking immigrants for their undermanned labor markets, this exclusionary policy was maintained, but with many modifications related to the American need for labor and the evolution of the cold war. While America continued to exclude most immigration from Europe and Asia, however, it did not restrict immigration from the Western Hemisphere in the same way, and even created a guest-worker program for Mexicans.

During the forty-one years between 1924 and 1965, immigration slowed to a trickle, and the proportion of foreign-born declined from almost 15 percent of the population to less than 5 percent (the lowest level since 1830), at the very same time that the foreign-born population in Western

Europe was rising rapidly. The legislation passed in 1924 had the explicit goal of freezing the ethnic composition of the United States (ultimately around "national origins" established by the 1920 census). Although countries in Western Europe were sensitive to the challenges of diversity, and in practice acted to created "balances" among immigrant groups, the seemingly rigid and discriminatory option created in the United States was explicitly rejected in favor of more open immigration policies.

In the 1970s, when doors to immigration were closing all over Europe, the United States altered its basic policy on immigration control. It then maintained and even expanded a more open immigration policy that had been passed in 1965. As policy became increasingly exclusionary in Europe, American immigration policy became increasingly open. As European policy was increasingly oriented towards the exclusion of third-world, non-white immigration, American policy tended to favor immigrants from Asia and Latin America, many of the same immigrants that had been excluded under the legislation of the nineteenth and early twentieth century. Indeed, one of the primary goals of the 1965 legislation—amended by the Immigration Act of 1990—was to maintain diversity of immigration through the admission of "diversity immigrants" from under-represented countries.

Thus, the policy exceptionalism of the United States, far from being recent, has been typical, in different ways, of the past hundred years. What we will describe in this chapter, is the policy orientation of the United States during the past two centuries, the change in policy, and primarily the change in orientation of that policy.

Immigration Policy: The Nineteenth Century–1921

Shaping Immigration: Population Policy

It has sometimes been argued that prior to 1882, the United States did not have a policy on immigration, and that the invisible hand of the international labor market dominated transatlantic flows.[7] However, this is only true in the most formal way. First the federal government played an active role in setting the context for immigration. Second, both the states and the federal courts dealt directly with questions of immigration control from the earliest days of the republic. Finally, the dynamics of the federal system influenced the development of restrictionist immigration policy at least as much as any decision by the national government.

It is indeed true that for almost one hundred years the federal government of the United States played only a small role in directly controlling immigration. Nevertheless, immigration was part of what Aristide Zolberg has called "a comprehensive population policy" that was meant to stimulate economic growth and expansion.[8] The federal government, according to Zolberg, generally tended to create a framework for immigration that was both expansive and encouraging. (See ch. 10.) Federal policy created both positive incentives to attract immigrant settlement, and attempted to reduce the barriers in Europe that would prevent exit.

The federal government also attempted to control some aspects of immigration. The Passenger Act of 1819 attempted to discourage the immigration of paupers, and this legislation was echoed by some state governments that passed restrictive legislation against paupers and other "morally undesirable" immigrants.[9] During the Civil War, the Republican administration took steps to ensure continued expansion. The Homestead Act of 1862 opened cheap land to immigrant settlers (the legislation offered 160 acres of land free to both citizens *and* aliens).

While the federal government attempted to shape immigration in various ways, it was the states that took the lead in restriction, first by resisting some expansive federal policies, then by mobilizing against them. (See Chapter 9.) State regulation was not a simple matter. Along the Eastern seaboard, numerous states attempted to restrict the entry of paupers and "undesirable" immigrants, attempts that were generally unsuccessful, in part because of differences in state legislation.[10] Perhaps more important, the administration set in place by the states that received immigrants (New York, which received the majority of immigrants, Massachusetts, Pennsylvania, Maryland and South Carolina) generally consisted of volunteers who were often from charity organizations that were favorably disposed towards immigrants, "protective charity foundations," that were unlikely to enforce restrictive measures with great vigor.[11]

Finally, the ability of the states to regulate was constrained by the courts, which also shaped, but did not forbid state regulation.[12] State and federal courts often acted as a brake on individual state action, and routinely struck down state legislation that was applied in a discriminatory fashion against particular nationality groups. For example, in 1874, the United States Supreme Court confirmed the right of the individual states to exclude immigrants who were criminals and lepers, but argued that they "...cannot discriminate against citizens of a foreign treaty power as a class."[13]

The initiative for immigration policy appeared to move definitively to the federal level on March 20, 1876, when the U.S. Supreme Court ruled that the regulation could no longer be controlled by the states as ordinary police power, but instead came under the formal jurisdiction of the federal government to regulate commerce (including "human commerce").[14] Nevertheless, federal power to regulate immigration remained limited to the provisions of legislation passed in 1875, which voided contracts for the importation of prostitutes and excluded convicted criminals from entry into the United States. For the first time, provision was made for federal inspection of ships carrying immigrants, and for federal deportation of undesirable aliens.[15]

Despite the shift in authority indicated by the court decisions, there was relatively little impact on policy at the national level. It is clear that forces proposing immigration control (let alone restriction) were insufficiently strong until the 1880s to enact any important federal role in immigration regulation, even when the state alternative was eliminated by the Supreme Court, and when the Court strongly urged the federal government to assume control. (See Chapter 10.) For six years the directors of local charities were left without funding, although immigration control was still their responsibility, and they lobbied intensely for federal legislation.

Eventually, the federal government did take action, under federal legislation passed in 1882 (the *Immigration Act of 1882*), in which the secretary of the treasury was given responsibility for collecting a head tax on immigrants and excluding classes of people previously excluded by state law. The actual inspection of immigrants entering the country, however, was still left to under-manned and under-financed state commissions, which often farmed these obligations out to the same charitable organizations that had administered them before.[16] Therefore, it is not surprising that in 1889, a select committee of the House of Representative (the Ford Committee) found that all of the categories of immigrants that had been excluded by previous legislation were able to gain entrance into the United States with little difficulty.

Chinese Exclusion

The Chinese Exclusion Act in 1882, and its follow-up legislation in 1888 and 1892, was the most draconian exclusion legislation ever passed in the United States. It not only suspended and then excluded immigration from China, but went further by excluding naturalization. The 1888 legislation (the Scott Act) prohibited entry to any Chinese person (not just laborers), and excluded reentry of those who had been able to legally reenter under the 1882 act. (To reenter, they had to demonstrate that they had left behind *both* family *and* property valued at over a thousand dollars.) Finally, the Geary Act in 1892, which reimposed what had been a 10-year suspension for ten more years (it was later made permanent), imposed humiliating conditions on those Chinese legally resident in the United States. The law denied bail to Chinese in *habeas corpus* cases, required them to carry a certificate of residency and required them to prove with a white witness that they had resided in the country prior to 1882.[17]

The federal courts, which had previously acted to protect open immigration from Europe from incursions by the states, now moved in the opposite direction. The federal courts not only supported the rights of the federal government to impose harsh conditions upon and reduce the established rights of Chinese residents, but also established a "plenary power doctrine," which stated that:

> ...not only has [the federal government] the power to regulate immigration, but that the political branches could exercise this power without being subject to judicial scrutiny. Congressional authority to regulate immigration was based on the imperatives of national security, territorial sovereignty, and self preservation.[18]

Justice Stephen Field, who wrote the opinion in the *Ping* case,[19] further elaborated:

> [If Congress] considers the presence of foreigners of a different race in this country, who will not assimilate with us, to be dangerous to its peace and security...its determination is conclusive upon the judiciary.

In subsequent decisions, the court extended and deepened this doctrine to virtually all federal officers, and made deportation equal with exclusion.

Nevertheless, the Chinese did manage to find some success in the state courts of California, where through a creative use of documents, they forced the otherwise unsympathetic judges to certify residents who had dubious credentials. Thus, at least at the margins, the well-organized Chinese community learned to use the court system to prevent strict enforcement of the Chinese Exclusion Act.[20]

An Accelerated Process

By 1889 both houses of Congress had established special committees to deal with immigration, and very quickly after, Congress acted to consolidate control over immigration. For the first time, under the *Immigration Act of 1891*, the Federal government assigned the Bureau of Immigration to assume effective control over the entry of immigrants into American ports (and built a new facility on federally-owned Ellis Island in New York harbor).

During the 25 years between the end of the Civil War and 1890, three general, pieces of legislation were passed that did not basically alter the relatively open system. Of far greater consequence, in terms of previous tradition, was the Chinese exclusion of 1882. After the establishment of the Congressional committees, hardly a year passed without consideration of major legislation on immigration at the national level. Indeed, new legislation was passed in 1891, and again in 1893; and literacy legislation was passed in 1896—then vetoed—then re-proposed in 1898, passed by the Senate, but rejected by the House of Representatives. Literacy legislation was passed two more times (1913 and 1915) and vetoed, before it was definitively passed over President Wilson's veto in 1917.

Congress acted to limit and shape immigration as best it could during the period before WWI. As well shall see in Chapter 10, Congress was most successful in establishing national structures that would later be used to enforce restriction.

Thus, in 1906, *the Naturalization Act* was passed, requiring the knowledge of English for naturalization. However, far more important from the perspective of policy development, it also established the Federal Division of Naturalization to supervise the process, and restricted naturalization to certain courts.[21] The overall effect was to limit and shape naturalization, but in a way that was acceptable to political reformers.

During this period, the list of those excluded for specific reasons also grew. Anarchists, epileptics and beggars were added in 1903, and people with TB, and mental or physical defects were added in 1907. Through a "Gentleman's Agreement" between the United States and Japan, the Japanese were placed in the same category as the Chinese.

Finally, *the Immigration Act of 1917* established the requirement of a literacy test, a requirement that prohibited the entry of aliens over the age of 16 who were unable to read in any language. Interestingly, President Wilson vetoed the legislation as a violation of the traditional American commitment to political asylum (the law, however, specifically excluded those fleeing religious—but not political—persecution). The law was passed over his veto. The new legislation also increased the list of "genetic" conditions for which an alien could be excluded, and most notably established an Asian Barred Zone to include "Hindu and East Indian labor."[22]

By the time of American entry into WWI, the principle of immigration exclusion based on racial and identity considerations was firmly established, but used only for an expanding category of Asians. Controls of European immigration were also in place, but relatively loosely administered, and were based on individual characteristics, rather than racial categories. Nevertheless, eugenicist thinking was sufficiently strong in the policy-making institutions of Congress that it was highly likely that it would frame public policy on immigration from Europe during the postwar period, and indeed it did.

During the war, however, restrictionists won a significant, if temporary victory. The federal agency given responsibility to decide admission at the gates of entry—the Immigration Bureau—was generally distrusted by restrictionists, and was generally assumed to have the same pro-immigrant biases as the social service agencies that it replaced.[23] *The Passport Control Act of 1918* required people entering the United States to first obtain visas from American consulates abroad, and that these visas be stamped in valid passports. More to the point, gate-keeping was transferred from the Bureau of Immigration to the State Department, which worked more closely with restrictionist interests in congress. The "temporary" visa requirements were made permanent by the Johnson-Reed Act in 1924.

Thus, at least until WWI, in a more chaotic process that was shaped by federalism, American policy-makers wrestled with many of the same problems as their counterparts in France. A perceived need for manpower—for settlement and labor—was always in tension with questions of identity and rejection. In France, national needs of the armed forces and the labor market assured that immigration would remain open and that naturalization would remain easy. On the other hand, fears that immigration would dilute national identity resulted in severe restrictions on naturalized citizens (see ch. 2). In the United States, until after the Civil War, there were clear political majorities in favor of open immigration.

However, this began to change after the war, as the immigration issue was framed increasingly in terms of identity, and less in terms of manpower needs. (See ch. 10.) The first indication of change in the political balance was the ability of Congress to override President Wilson's veto of the Immigration Act of 1917. A more definitive sign, however, was the passage of the Emergency Quota Act of 1921.

Immigration Restriction

The Emergency Quota Act of 1921

By the end of WWI, restriction on immigration was politically inevitable. Over 800,000 immigrants entered the country in 1921. This was certainly not a record, but it did approach the peak years of the period before the war. By 1920 the political climate had changed. The combination of a surge in unemployment and the post-war "red-scare" lent considerable public support to the restrictionist cause. Indeed, within the House immigration committee, there was a consensus on restriction. The real issue was what form it would take. While the House committee was in favor of a total suspension of immigration—as a reaction to the perceived emergency—the Senate committee was more influenced by business interests that sought to keep immigration open, and sought a compromise.

The compromise was presented by Senator William Dillingham, the chairman of the pre-war U.S. Commission on Immigration (see ch. 10), who convinced the committee to adopt a proposal that he had made before the war, to limit immigration to a percentage of the foreign-born populations in the country in 1910. The percentage finally accepted in negotiations with the House committee was 3 percent, with a total ceiling of 350,000. The bill passed both houses with overwhelming votes. After the outgoing President Woodrow Wilson refused to sign it, it was re-passed by even larger margins and approved by the newly elected President Warren Harding.[24]

The 1921 legislation was meant to be temporary. However, this should not obscure the fact that it represented a turning point in American immigration policy. The turning point was not so much that immigration was restricted, but rather in the way that it was restricted. By restricting immigration through quotas, its objective was to freeze the composition of the American population, and to ensure that immigration from southeastern Europe would be limited. This concept of shaping the composition of immigration along national and racial lines (all Asians remained eliminated from consideration) then remained the principle of immigration control for the next 44 years. During the next two years, the level of immigration was cut in half, although there was a final sharp peak in 1924, in anticipation of the legislation passed that year.

The temporary legislation was extended until 1924, while discussions within congress continued on how to make the system both permanent and more restrictive. The principle of quotas that reflected existing population distribution was already in place. What had not been finally resolved was how these quotas would be calculated. For the moment, it was possible to use a proportion of those born abroad already in the country, but this permitted a level of immigration from Eastern and Southern Europe that proved to be politically unacceptable. With 150,000 entries in 1922 from Southern and Eastern Europe, immigration was continuing at a level that was unacceptable to developing congressional sentiment. Between 1921 and 1924, the political pressures no long revolved around whether there should be restriction, but rather the formula that should be used.

The Johnson-Reed Act of 1924

The "permanent" legislation passed in 1924 was also a compromise of sorts. On one hand, the total ceiling each year was reduced from 350,000 to 150,000. More important, the base year for calculating quotas was changed from 1910 to 1890, and the percentage was temporarily reduced from three to two percent, until a new formula based on national origins of the total population could be devised.

The core principle integrated into the 1924 legislation was that of "national origins," the idea that immigration should be shaped to perpetuate the ethnic composition of the United States at the time of the founding of the Republic. The formula that was adopted was complicated: "...a number which bears the same ratio to 150,000 (the legislated ceiling as the number of inhabitants in the United States in 1920 having that *national origin*, going back to the date of the founding of the republic, bears to the number of white inhabitants of the united States in 1920, with a minimum quota of 100 for each nationality."[25] Since the 1921 legislation was based on a percentage of the different foreign-born populations, the principle of national origins (if it could be calculated) gave far more weight to the larger native population.

For two years a debate raged about the base year for this calculation, whether it would be 1890 or 1920 when the immigrant and naturalized proportion of the population was larger. This decision was of some importance for determining the differences between the number of Eastern and Southern Europeans, but far more important for determining the differences among the more acceptable countries of Northwestern Europe. When the decision was finally made to choose 1920 as a base in 1927 (a very small victory for those who opposed restriction) it had been calculated by a specially appointed committee that 44 percent of the population consisted of the descendants of "native stock," descendents of those present in the United States in 1790, and 56 percent of the descendants of "immigrant stock" those who arrived after 1790. The quotas that were finally decided were based, not on a percentage of the proportion of foreign-born population the United States in 1920, but on a proportion of the estimated number of citizens of a specified national origin.[26]

Because the Anglo-Saxon population had been dominant in 1790 and German immigration had been important during the earlier years of the nineteenth century, the formula strongly favored the quotas from these countries. However, the 1920 base year also favored British over Germans quotas. One unanticipated consequence of this decision would be to allot fewer places to German-Jewish refugees after Hitler came to power. When the national origins formula was finally implemented in 1929, about 58 percent of the 150,000 places were allotted to Great Britain, Northern Ireland and the Irish Free State, and another 15 percent to Germany. The remainder of the places was distributed among 58 countries, the vast majority of which were given 100 places.[27] The Johnson-Reed Act then became the basic framework for American immigration policy until 1965.

Changing Johnson-Reed

During the years after the quota system was implemented immigration into the United States fell to its lowest point since the decade of the 1830s. Just over half a million people entered during the entire decade of the 1930s, including an estimated 250,000 refugees from Nazi persecution.[28]

Although refugee pressure increased substantially through the decade of the 1930s, the liberalization of immigration legislation was impossible during a period when the country was suffering from the worst economic depression in its history. Once the United States entered the Second World, however, the economic environment was substantially altered in a number of ways. War production finally ended the depression, and wartime exigencies gave the State and War Departments more clout. In 1943, in deference to our Chinese allies, the Chinese Exclusion Act was repealed, and a small, symbolic Chinese quota was established.

At the same time, a new contract labor program was agreed to by the Department of State and the Mexican government to meet the wartime needs of agribusiness in the southwest, *The Bracero Program of 1943*, which would endure until 1964. It provided for temporary labor for agriculture, with apparent safeguards to prevent abusive acts that had taken place before. The program, which had its roots in a similar program during WWI, authorized the entry of 4–5 million temporary workers, and bypassed the legal requirements of literacy. At the insistence of the Mexican government, safeguards were negotiated that would require wages and social services comparable to native American workers. The Mexican government would supervise recruitment, and workers were assured that they would not "... suffer discriminatory acts of any kind." On the other hand, the U.S. government was assured that the contract workers would return home, because a portion of their wages was to be deposited in a Mexican bank until their return.

In practice, none of the protections was honored, and massive illegal entry was tolerated during crop season.

Mexican braceros routinely received lower wages than domestic migrant workers and endured substandard living and working conditions. Contrary to the bilateral agreement, the INS permitted employers to recruit braceros at the border. If they did not allow employers to recruit their own guest workers, one INS official recalled, "a good many members of Congress would be on Immigration's neck."[29]

Thus, while the restrictive quota system remained in place as the framework of American immigration policy, the number of exceptions to the legislation ("non-quota entry status") increased progressively. Two legislative efforts are indicative of this trend. The first consisted of two laws in 1945 and 1946 that contributed to the establishment of the principle of entry based on family unification. The *War Brides Act of 1945, and the Fiancés Act of 1946* gave foreigners who would or did marry an American GI non-quota entry status. The second, the *Displaced Persons Act of 1948*, was the first legislation in the nation's history to deal with refugees. It ultimately provided for 400,000 places for displaced persons from Europe (Poles accounted for a third of those admitted, followed by German ethnics) over the next three years. However, the restrictions in the legislation—for example, preference for those having been engaged in agriculture, and the requirement that visas could only be secured by applicants having entered Western zones of occupation before December 22, 1945—were deeply biased against Jewish refugees, and the law was only reluctantly signed by President Truman.[30] These restrictions were removed in new legislation passed in 1950, giving new impetus for a liberal immigration reform coalition. This small victory, however, also served to mobilize the restrictionists in congress, particularly those on the Senate Judiciary Committee, and their allies on the House Immigration Sub-committee.

The McCarran-Walter Act

The restrictionist coalition first succeeded in increasing restriction, by including in the Internal Security Act of 1950 authorization to exclude aliens who had been communists at any time, and/or belonged to organizations that were deemed "front" organizations. It also provided for the expulsion of any non-citizen residing in the United States who had been a communist or had engaged in 'subversive" activities.[31] Thus, congress took the initiative in once again reinforcing an isolationist trend, and linking aliens and immigration to danger to the security of the United States.

In the ensuing congressional debate on the 1952 McCarran-Walter bill, the case for maintaining the 1924 framework was made primarily on grounds of national security, but also on the grounds of ease of integration; the racial theories of the 1920s remained in the background. This proposal called for some reform around the edges. The quota system would be maintained, but within each quota, preference (50%) would be given to those with higher education and "exceptional abilities," with the remainder of the places allocated to specified relatives of U.S. citizens and permanent residents. Asian exclusion and the Asiatic Barred Zone would be abolished, but only a small quota would be established for a vast Asian-Pacific Triangle that extended from India to Japan and the Pacific islands. Perhaps most important, the bar on Asian naturalization would finally be lifted.[32] On the other hand, the law confirmed the quota system as well new categories that reinforced the exclusion of "radicals".[33]

The Democratic House and Senate overrode the veto by President Truman, and rejected a parallel proposal for more liberal reform. Nevertheless, support for more liberal immigration reform remained important, and many of the reform leaders who were on the losing side of that issue in 1952, would remain in congress to continue the struggle. Indeed the struggle continued in a variety of ways. In passing the 1952 legislation, congress had framed the issue in terms of national security and integration, frames that were more easily challenged than the original racist frame of science and eugenics. The outgoing Truman administration began to build a new frame for immigration control by establishing a Presidential Commission on Immigration and Naturalization in 1952 that specifically challenged the methodology and conclusions of the pre-WWI Dillingham Commission.[34] (See ch. 10.)

In addition, the existing system was increasingly challenged by a growing number of non-quota admissions of refugees from communist countries under a series of refugee acts, and by special presidential exemptions ("parole powers") that had been authorized under the McCarran-Walter Act. Although each exemption had to have a specific reason, by 1965 only one in three immigrants was entering the United States under the quota provisions of the framework act of 1924. In 1964, more than half the British quota and a third of the Irish quota remained unused, while there were long waiting lists in Italy and Greece. A congressional report argued in 1965 that

> [T]he national origins system has failed to maintain the ethnic balance of the American population as it was designed and intended since the nationals favored with the high quotas have left their quotas largely unused. Immigration statistics establish that only one of every three immigrants, during the last two decades, actually was admitted to the United States as a quota immigrant under the national origins system.[35]

The political struggle to reform immigration nevertheless endured long after it was evident that the system was no longer working. Indeed, as we shall see, without the pressures created by the civil rights movement, and ultimately, what one scholar has called "the Great Society Juggernaut," reform might have been delayed well beyond 1965.

The New System

The Hart-Celler Act of 1965

The Immigration and Nationality Act of 1965 was formally an amendment to the legislation passed in 1952. A decade later it was seen as "...the most far-reaching revision of immigration policy in the United States since the First Quota Act of 1921."[36] Nevertheless, at the time, both President Johnson and some of the act's key sponsors saw the impact of the legislation as relatively marginal.[37] The new law recast the framework for immigration and immigration control. It incorporated some of the principles already in McCarran-Walter, but more fundamentally, it abolished the national origins quota system.

In place of preferences based on nationality and ethnicity, the law established a system based on family unification and needed job-skills. It established a preference system of seven categories, beginning with unmarried adult children of citizens of the United States, then spouses and unmarried children of legal residents. No limit was placed on spouses, parents and unmarried minor children of U.S. citizens. Preference was also given to married children and adult brothers and sisters of U.S. citizens. Finally, preference was given to gifted intellectuals and skilled workers. For the first time, refugees were also given a preference category. All in all, 74 percent of admissions were given to family immigrants, 20 percent for employment and 6 percent to refugees. A ceiling was established at 170,000, with a limit of 20,000 per country for the Eastern Hemisphere; for the first time a limit was placed on the Western Hemisphere of 120,000, with no country limit. This total ceiling of 290,000 doubled the existing ceiling, and it would continue to rise over the next 25 years.

In 1976 and 1978, the system was somewhat modified, and the separate ceilings between the Eastern and Western Hemispheres were collapsed into a general ceiling of 290,000. Of far more significance was the Immigration Act of 1990, which reaffirmed the expansive system of 1965, significantly increased the ceiling, and put in place important new rules for entry.

The Immigration Act of 1990

As we shall see in chapter 10, by the late 1980s it was clear that the dynamics of the politics of immigration were vastly different from what they had been before 1965. The great debate over Americanization and the assimilability of a diversity of immigrants appeared to have changed substantially. In the 1980s, although there was some negative reaction to immigration from Latin America and Asia, restrictionists were unable to gain sufficient political support to limit immigration. The best they could do was to place the same per-country ceilings on Western Hemisphere immigration (in 1978) that had been applied to the Eastern Hemisphere.

Instead, at a time when all major countries in Europe were debating how, not whether, to reduce immigration, the debate in the United States was focused on how, not whether, to expand legal immigration. Republican interest in expanding the number of skilled workers for business merged, somewhat uneasily, with Democratic interest in expanding entry for Irish immigrants. The result was the Immigration Act of 1990. The fears of the Asian and Latin American lobby groups that family unification entries would be sacrificed to employment entries resulted in the overall increase of the ceiling to 675,000, with the possibility of "piercing" that ceiling for immediate relatives of citizens. Family-based visas increased modestly, and employment based visas substantially. The Irish interests were accommodated by a program of "diversity visas," that would eventually provide for the admission, on an annual basis, of 55,000 immigrants from "under-represented" countries. (See chapter 9.)

Dealing with Illegal Immigration and Asylum

By 1990, immigration legislation that dealt with legal immigration had been separated from legislation that dealt both with refugees, and with illegal immigration. A decade before it was not obvious that the tracks of each category would diverge. After all, refugee admission had been folded into the Immigration Act of 1965, and by the 1970s illegal immigration appeared to be the leading edge for the mobilization of a new restrictionist movement.[38]

The separation of these issues was largely the work of the Select Commission on Immigration and Refugee Policy (SCIRP), established in 1978, in the aftermath of the refugee crisis engendered by the chaotic end of the war in Vietnam. SCIRP conducted hearings on how to deal with immigration and asylum. In many ways, this commission was the parallel of the pre-WWI Dillingham Commission, in the sense that it served to define what the problem was, and what were the legislative choices (see ch. 10).

We will look at the report of the commission more carefully in Chapter 10, and analyze its importance for framing the issues of immigration. Here, however, it is important to note that the final report in 1981, *Immigration Policy and the National Interest*, strongly supported both an expansive immigration policy and a compassionate refugee policy in the national interest. On the other hand, the report strongly condemned the adverse impact of illegal entries, and urged that such entries be dealt with through strong employer sanctions, border enforcement and the initiation of a national identity card. It argued that "illegality erodes confidence in the law generally, and immigration law specifically". The precondition for increasing legal immigration was to effectively control illegal entry.[39] In the end, Tichenor argues, one important impact of the SCIRP report was to separate out the policy tracks of legal and illegal immigration, which made it far more difficult for restrictionists to use one against the other.

Asylum legislation was also separated out. In 1980, the United States passed the *Refugee Act of 1980*, the most important comprehensive refugee legislation in the history of the country. For decades, waves of refugees who had fled various communist regimes had been accepted for entry into the United States, generally under special legislation, and special presidential "paroles" that had been authorized under the McCarran-Walter Act. A notion of a "normal flow" of refugees was established at 50,000, a number which could be increased when necessary, and that was separate from other categories of legal immigration. The legislation provided for full legal residency after one year, as well as settlement and welfare assistance. Perhaps most significantly, it created an expansive definition of "refugee" that went beyond the Cold War definition of those fleeing from Communist regimes, and that accepted international criteria defined under the United Nations Refugee Convention of 1951 and the 1967 Protocol. A refugee was now defined as

> ...a person who is unwilling or unable to return to his country of nationality or habitual residence because of persecution or a well-founded fear of persecution on account of race, religion, nationality, membership in a particular social group, or political opinion.[40]

The new legislation was immediately challenged by the Mariel Boatlift, when Fidel Castro ordered the mass expulsion of 125,000 Cubans. The Cubans, and a smaller number of Haitians arrived in Florida and demanded asylum, but the Carter administration refused to classify them as refugees (under the 1980 act this decision was made by the attorney-general). Their status was not finally settled until 1986. At the same time, more than 200,000 Indochinese and other refugees were accepted for settlement under the new legislation.

The Immigration Reform and Control Act of 1986 (IRCA)

For almost 15 years, legislation on illegal immigration had been debated in Washington. The 1986 legislation was the end-product of bipartisan efforts by Congress under four presidents. The first bill had passed the House of Representatives in 1972. Considering that the Select Commission on Immigration and Refugee Policy (SCIRP) had recommended strong means to control illegal immigration (which it considered a danger for growing legal immigration), that these recommendations had been generally accepted, and that public opinion was overwhelming in favor of stopping illegal immigration, the 1986 legislation was surprisingly weak and virtually unenforceable.

The new legislation proposed to deal with illegal immigration in two ways. First, it provided for employer sanctions, certainly the most controversial provision, but one that had been recommended for many years.

Penalties would be imposed on employers who knowingly employed aliens who were not authorized to work in the United States. However no identification system was established under the law, and the sanctions program had little support in both Congress and the administration, and was never fully funded, particularly under the Reagan administration, which was far more interested in deregulation of business than in imposing additional regulations.[41] IRCA also provided additional funding for expansion of the border patrol.

Second, the law contained provisions that would grant the largest amnesty in American history (far larger, in fact than had been granted by any European country), would make it easier for aliens to become permanent residents, would establish a new farm-worker program, and would give greater legal protections to aliens working in the United States. The amnesty applied for one year to illegal immigrants who had been in the United States prior to 1982. Eventually more than 3 million illegal immigrants would benefit from IRCA, in part because the courts overruled attempts by the INS to establish restrictive rule of implementation.[42] That total was also increased by the "late amnesty" agreement in 2000 between President Clinton and Republican congressional leaders, which permitted amnesty for illegal aliens who had been part of lawsuits claiming eligibility to reinstate their claims under IRCA.

Under the provisions for the farm-worker program, up to 350,000 workers would be granted temporary residency permits for three years, if they worked in agriculture for at least 90 days each of those years. After four years of farm labor, aliens would be eligible for permanent residency permits. This concession to agricultural interests, together with the amnesty, was meant to create a more secure, legal agricultural work-force, and to undermine the basis of illegal immigration. Nevertheless, the number of illegal immigrants continued to grow unabated by IRCA.[43]

In fact, the section of the legislation that proved to be least effective was the section most directly related to its original intentions, employer sanctions for employing illegal immigrants. Although this provision was popular in public opinion, its actual enforcement was difficult, and was strongly resisted by both pro-immigrant groups and by employers associations. For both of these reasons, the issue would continue to reverberate, making illegal immigrants the target—*faute de mieux*—of political actors whose real target was sometimes legal immigration.

Thus, a decade after IRCA, with the apparent success of Proposition 187 in California and the report of the Jordan Commission urging reduction of immigration ceilings, the country seemed to be going through a backlash against immigration (see Chapter 10, pp. 237–274), but the principal victims were illegal immigrants. *The Illegal Immigration Reform and Responsibility Act,* passed during the election campaign of 1996, once again bolstered border control, tightened asylum procedures, and generally made life more difficult for illegal aliens. Welfare legislation passed at the same time, however—*The Personal Responsibility and Work Opportunity*

Act of 1996—also blocked a range of welfare benefits for legal residents for five years after their arrival. As we shall see, one important consequence of the legislation of 1996 was a massive naturalization campaign, and a vast increase of Latino voters that benefited the Democratic Party. (See Chapter 10.) On balance, the net result of the reaction of the 1990s was a reaffirmation of expansive immigration policy. A decade later, the number of illegal immigrants was double that of 1996, but the same issues were being debated in much the same way as they had been before.

Since 2001, political concerns about illegal immigration have overlapped with growing concerns about national security. One result was *the Real ID Act of 2005.* The new legislation required that drivers' licenses issued by the states had to conform to national standards. Among the requirements for issuing a license is proof that the applicant is a citizen or legal resident or resident alien in the United States. While states were not obliged to conform to these standards, after 2008 non-conforming licenses would no longer be accepted by any federal agency (including airport security) as valid identification. Perhaps the most controversial aspect of the new law, however, was the severe limit that it places on judicial appeal. Appeals to federal courts about provisions of the act were limited to constitutional issues. It also barred non-citizens from the right of habeas corpus review for most detention and deportation orders, tightened requirements for asylum, and facilitated deportation by defining a range of activities linked to "terrorism". Finally, the law authorized the construction of new border barriers, and then waived all laws that interfered with this construction. The construction was under the authority of the Attorney-General, but waivers were to be decided by the Secretary of Homeland Security. Thus, while the new law specifically targets illegal immigrants and border control, it also has consequences for immigrants who are legally in the United States.

New immigration legislation was proposed by President Bush to deal with the massive presence of illegal immigrants, estimated at almost 11 million in 2006.[44] At the heart of the president's proposal were some familiar ideas: a temporary worker program would be linked to an amnesty program. The temporary worker program "would create a legal path for foreign workers to enter our country in an orderly way, for a limited period of time. This program would match willing foreign workers with willing American employers for jobs Americans are not doing." Thus, the agricultural worker program created by IRCA would be expanded to other parts of the workforce, but this time temporary workers would not have a path to permanent residency, and would be required to return home. This would be enforced with the use of a "tamper-proof" identity card, presumably related to the license required under the Real ID Act. Finally, the president proposed a pathway to legality (he specifically denied that this would be the equivalent to "amnesty") for those who met specific requirements, as a means of reducing the unprecedented number of illegal immigrants already in the country.[45]

In the run-up to the mid-term congressional elections of 2006, the debate in congress was sharply divided, with the Republican majority in the House of Representatives taking the lead in focusing on the presence of illegal immigrants in the United States, and the weakness of border controls, while most Democrats supported the Kennedy-McCain proposal (see below). In December 2005, the Republican-controlled House passed legislation that would make illegal presence in the United States a criminal offense, that would eliminate diversity visas and that would authorize the construction of additional barriers along the border with Mexico. The bill contained none of the key provisions advocated by the president.[46]

Five months later, the Republican-controlled Senate passed very different legislation—a bi-partisan proposal supported by Democrat Edward Kennedy and Republican John McCain—that contained most of the president's proposals. The bill would have provided for 200,000 new temporary guest-worker visas a year, and created a separate guest-worker program for farm workers. The bill also divided the illegal immigrants into three groups.

> Those here five years or longer would be allowed to stay and apply for citizenship, provided they pay back taxes, learn English and have no serious criminal records. Those here two to five years would eventually have to return to another country and apply for a green card, which could allow their immediate return. The roughly 2 million immigrants who have been in the United States illegally for less than two years, would be ordered home, and be subject to deportation. Illegal immigrants convicted of a felony or three misdemeanors would be deported no matter how long they have been in the United States.[47]

Legislation that would authorize extension of the border fence was passed and signed by the president in October 2006. However, as the mid-term elections approached, no compromise appeared to be possible on the remaining bills, and the issue was put off until the next session of congress in 2007, where it quietly died. The House never passed the McCain Kennedy bill, and it died a slow death, as the presidential race began in earnest in 2007.

Thus by early 2007, the decoupling of legal and illegal immigration had led to a passionate debate about the rapidly increasing population of illegal immigrants that even the conservative Republican House leadership agreed could not be deported.[48] On the other hand, these same Republicans were willing to defy their own president to prevent legislation that would contain even partial amnesty. For their part, the Democrats and allied Republicans supported a partial amnesty and guest-worker program that could alleviate the immediate pressure of more than 11 million illegal aliens, but would probably do nothing to prevent the continued flow of illegal immigrants into the United States. None of the proposed legislation seriously increased employer sanctions, the enforcement of which had been declining for many years. The enforcement provisions in the IRCA legislation were relatively weak, but the 20-year history of declining audits, warnings and fines collected was a clear indication that there was no political will to use even these meager tools. As a result there was no incentive for employers not to hire illegal immigrants, and no deterrent to the pull of employment in the United States.[49]

CHAPTER NINE

Understanding U.S. Immigration Policy

In this chapter, we will examine the four issues that we analyzed for France and Britain in chapters 3 and 6: why people migrate; control over frontiers; the impact of immigration; and questions of integration and incorporation . Compared with France and Britain, the United States has always been seen as a country of immigration.[1] The United States accepted—indeed encouraged—immigration at a time when the country was expanding westward, and the economy was growing rapidly. As we have seen (table 8.2), the result was that between 1840 and 1920, a more or less consistent 14 percent of the population was born abroad. However, this very real openness did not necessarily mean that immigrants were unequivocally welcome in the United States. Negative reactions to immigration and immigrants were clear as soon as immigration began to increase in the 1840s.[2] Indeed, political and social reactions to immigration have been deeper and sometimes more violent than in either France or in Britain, and the political reaction developed far earlier than in either European country. The first major anti-immigrant political party emerged in the United States in the 1840s (the American Party), and the most severe legislation based on race and national origin was passed first in the United States and not in Europe.

The severe restrictions that were imposed on immigration after 1929, combined with the difficulties of getting out of Europe as depression and war spread there during the 1930s, effectively and rapidly reduced the arrival of immigrants to the United States. From over a million immigrants per year, during the years before WWI, to more than 300,000 per year during the decade after the war, immigration was reduced to about 35,000 per year during the decade before WWII. In addition, the idea that America was a "country of immigration" became a controversial subject, a recognition of what had happened rather than a continuing public philosophy, at least until the late twentieth century.

On the other hand, the negative impact of the opening up of immigration after 1965 has been less severe in the United States than it has been in Europe. In is important to note that the impact of the "new" third world immigration since 1965 has been far less negative than was the impact of earlier immigration from Europe. Compared with a century ago, the focus of restrictionist movements are on illegal rather than legal immigration, and there is little support for the kinds of ethnoracial restriction that dominated the politics of immigration during the previous period.

Integration efforts in France and Britain have moved rapidly toward the kinds of explicit requirements for entry and citizenship that were more characteristic of the "Americanization" programs in the United States a hundred years ago than they are now. Support for multiculturalism and diversity is stronger and better institutionalized in the United States now than it is in either European country. As a result, the question of integration, as it has been politicized in the United States, generally tends to focus on language ability and civics, rather than on broader cultural questions of integratability.

Why Do People Immigrate?

The question of why people immigrate to the United States has been the subject of considerable debate. On the other hand, Aristide Zolberg has carefully documented how in the nineteenth century, federal policy on immigration control tended toward the creation of positive incentives for the attraction of labor that were more or less effective. These incentives took two forms: the first was a network of international agreements in which support for immigration was embedded; the second involved a more direct shaping of immigration itself. It its way, this federal action was similar to the French legislation in 1889, which had similar intentions.

> They actively recruited those considered most suitable, kept out undesirables, stimulated new immigration flows from untapped sources, imported labor, and even undertook the removal of some deemed ineligible for membership. On the positive side, American policy initially extended well beyond laissez-faire to proactive acquisition, reflected in multiple initiatives to obtain immigrants from continental Europe by insisting on their freedom of exit at a time when population was still regarded as a scarce, valuable resource preciously guarded by territorial rulers.[3]

The federal government was not inclined to control and restrict immigration. The Alien and Sedition Acts of 1798 asserted the right of the United States to deport undesirable individuals (a right sometimes contested by European countries), but the federal government maintained no agency to control, regulate, or even monitor the flow of immigrants into the country (except for the bureau of the census, beginning in 1820). Thus, throughout much of the nineteenth century, federal policy supported relatively open immigration. At least until 1808, the Constitution restricted the ability of the Federal government from controlling the entry of migrants (or slaves) into the United States. The Supreme Court affirmed this right, however, in 1824, and specifically noted that Congress now had the right to legislate on immigration. Nevertheless, legislative action remained limited.[4]

What the newly established republic did do was to campaign throughout Europe to lift exit barriers that were widespread in the early nineteenth century, and encourage those who were leaving to come to the United States. Although emigration from Europe was limited in terms of numbers, and the British in particular made attempts to divert emigration away from the United States and toward Canada, this campaign was largely successful by the 1830s.

Railroad and shipping companies then actively promoted emigration from northern Europe, "...and, in many cases, the multiplying U.S. consulates functioned in effect as labor-recruiting and land-selling agencies, eventually reaching all the way to remote Norway. Simultaneously, American entrepreneurs enticed newcomers from across Western Europe by way of private missions." To a remarkable degree, the United States established networks of recruitment that took advantage of expanding railway networks in Europe, and the increasing speed and capacity of transatlantic shipping.[5]

To a more limited degree, the federal government also attempted to shape immigration. Zolberg makes a convincing case that the first legislation regulating immigration, the Passenger Act of 1819, was meant to discourage the immigration of paupers and servants by limiting the number of passengers aboard ships (by specifying the ratio of passengers to tonnage). The state governments along the Eastern seaboard, however, approached this problem more directly by legislating restrictive legislation against "morally undesirable" immigrants.[6] (See Chapter 8.)

The federal government began to take a far more active role in both immigration recruitment and regulation after 1860. During the Civil War, the Republican administration took steps to ensure continued westward expansion. Even before the war, during the presidential campaign of 1860, the Republican Party had inserted into its platform promises of legislation favorable to immigration, to attract votes of large German, Swedish, and Dutch constituencies in the Middle West. The loss of life during the war accentuated this commitment. In the hands of Secretary of State William Seward and Secretary of the Treasury Salmon Chase, the Homestead Act of 1862 was used as a tool to actively recruit European emigrants.

> Some U.S. consuls hired full-time agents to attract prospective settlers with free land.... While Western states and territories continued to use immigration agents and publicity campaigns to induce immigration from Europe, railroad companies sent agents to Germany to recruit farmers to develop vast railroad lands.[7]

After the 1864 election, the Republican congress responded to a request from President Lincoln, and passed legislation ("An Act to Encourage Immigration") that created a Commissioner of Immigration and a Bureau of Immigration to recruit immigrants in Europe. It also created the equivalent of a "guest-worker" program, with contracts that would last one year. The contract provisions were abolished by the Reconstruction Congress in 1868, but in fact the law had already provoked the establishment of two private companies that specialized in immigrant recruitment (the American Emigrant Company and the Foreign Emigrant Aid Society), that in turn fostered immigration for many years after. In this same direction, the United States negotiated a treaty with China to foster trade, but also to ease Chinese immigration. The Burlingame Treaty guaranteed the right to move from one country to the other, as well as the right of Chinese residing in the United States to "the same privileges, immunities and exemptions" as citizens of the United States.[8]

The abrogation of the Burlingame Treaty by the Chinese Exclusion Act of 1882 thus marked the beginning of a change in national policy, but a change that would evolve over a long period of time into a pattern of incentives that would be very different from what existed before 1882. Until then, national incentives were formulated to attract labor immigration and settlement to support an expanding country and a rapidly growing economy. Employers recruited labor in Europe and the Far East, aided by U.S. consuls and benefits available to immigrants in the United States.

After 1882, national policies were increasingly vulnerable to state and local reactions to immigrants and immigration. These reactions began in California in the 1870s, and then spread to New England by the 1880s. The movement toward immigration-control evolved as a movement toward limiting, but also shaping continuing immigration. By 1917, all Asians were barred from entry into the United States (with the exception of Filipinos), and from naturalization. Entry from other parts of the world required minimal literacy that nevertheless restricted the most impoverished from entry.

The quota legislation of 1921/1924 permitted relatively large quotas of immigration from those countries in Europe from which there would be the least push-pressure to migrate to the United States in the years that followed, and severely restricted entry from countries for which "push" would be relatively strong. In theory, "national origins" could be consistent with the "chain" of family unification. However, the concept of national origins gave preference to distant family connections that went back more than a century, to the country's origins. After 1929, there was no year during which the quotas that went into effect that year were actually fulfilled. By the end of the decade only a third or fewer of the quota places for entry into the United States were filled.

Even before the end of WWII, incentives began to change, primarily in response to the war and then foreign policy requirements. First China, then Eastern Europe, and finally the Caribbean benefited from nonquota exemptions. In addition, selected groups of refugees from Europe gained special entry into the United States during the years after the war. As the rules changed after 1945, the number of nonquota entries increased in response, and the number of those entering increased dramatically.

By the time that the new immigration regime was approved in 1965, about 300,000 immigrants were arriving each year, double the number of the immediate postwar period, most of them nonquota, and an increasing proportion from outside of Europe, primarily from the Western Hemisphere. This significant rise of immigration was due in part to the admission of immediate relatives of U.S. citizens, as well as to admissions of refugees and displaced persons (400,000 under the legislation of 1948 and 1950).[9] However from the mid-1950s on, the persistent growth of immigration can be attributed above all to the arrival of nonquota immigrants from the Western Hemisphere, overwhelmingly from Mexico and the Caribbean. Until then, most of the arrivals from the Western Hemisphere were from Canada, and most migrants from Mexico were temporary non-immigrants. (See table 9.1.)

Until the 1965 legislation was passed, immigration from the Western Hemisphere was not regulated by the regime set in place in 1924, although it was constrained (in principle) by the literacy requirements of the Immigration Act of 1917, as well as by other financial requirements. Nevertheless well before WWII two separate and different immigration regimes were in place. The first regime, which was controlled by the Department of State, screened Europeans who applied for entry under the quota system. The second, controlled by the Immigration Bureau, screened mostly Mexicans who entered as temporary labor for growing agribusiness (see ch. 10).

If immigration from Europe was (see chapter 10) framed in terms of identity and a challenge to "Americanism," immigration from other

Table 9.1 Changing immigration patterns after WWII

Year	Total Immigration (quota and nonquota)	Total Immigration from Europe (quota)	Percentage of quota immigrants from Europe	Percentage from Western Hemisphere (nonquota)
1938	67,895	42,499	62.6	21.2
1946	108,721	29,095	26.8	27.1
1948	170,570	92,526	54.2	22.3
1950	249,187	197,460	79.2	14.2
1953	170,435	84,175	49.4	39.4
1955	237,790	82,232	34.6	39.6
1957	326,867	97,178	29.7	41.3
1959	260,686	97,657	37.5	26.2
1961	271,344	96,104	35.4	41.6
1963	306,260	103,036	33.6	48.2

Source: U.S. Bureau of the Census, *Historical Statistics of the United States* (Washington, DC: USGPO, 1975), p. 105 and 113.

countries in the Western Hemisphere was understood in terms of labor that was necessary for the stability of the American economy.[10] If anti-immigrant movements that emerged from state politics tended to oppose immigration from Southern and Eastern Europe (as well as Asia of course), often the same state interests (primarily agricultural) strongly supported labor immigration from Mexico, Central and South America. Indeed, the incentives in place tended to encourage, rather than restrict, this stream of immigration.

The frontier ports through which European immigration was controlled were strengthened at the end of the nineteenth century, and a first layer of controls (visa requirements) was moved to consulates in Europe during WWI. What Zolberg has called "remote control" border control—the movement of controls to the countries of origin—was established in law in 1924, and consulates in Europe assumed primary responsibility for issuing entry documents.[11]

Europeans, Mexicans, and Asians

Europeans were accepted as immigrants for settlement, but Mexicans, although seen as unfit and inassimilable, were always seen as temporary labor. They were encouraged to come to work by direct recruitment during WWI, and immigration for labor from Mexico increased substantially after the war ended. In fact, the line between legal and illegal entry remained blurred, and the southern border remained only lightly patrolled. The efforts of the Border Patrol (established in 1924) were directed more toward undesirable Europeans and enforcement of prohibition, rather than against Mexicans.[12]

At least until the mid-1950s migrant workers from Mexico were also encouraged to return home, through formal and informal means. During WWI, money was held back until Mexican workers returned home. After the war there was a surge of Mexican immigration for settlement, both legal and illegal, comparable to the surge in the 1950s. With the onset of the depression, and growing pressure from the American Federation of Labor, the Immigration Bureau initiated an effective crackdown on undocumented Mexicans in 1929. By 1931, the combined effects of the crackdown and the depression had reduced even legal Mexican immigration from over 40,000 to just over 3,000.

During WWII, a second guest-worker agreement with Mexico was concluded (the Bracero Program—see ch. 8), and similar agreements with a number of Caribbean countries were negotiated. The Mexican government would recruit and select the workers. In practice, however, the terms of this contract labor program—in particular the guarantees of comparable wages and against discrimination—were regularly violated. "The alliance of agricultural growers, Southern and Western 'committee barons,' and immigration officials would permit the easy flow of Mexican labor immigration for most of the century."[13]

The system remained remarkably stable until the mid-1950s, when immigration for settlement from Mexico and Latin America began to grow rapidly. One sign of this increase was the parallel increase of illegal immigration. Although there was considerable resistance in Congress to react to either the legal or illegal surge, the Eisenhower administration, for political reasons, ordered a roundup of undocumented Mexicans in 1954, which was dubbed "Operation Wetback" (see ch. 10). The INS claimed that more than a million illegal immigrants had been rounded up and sent back to Mexico. In fact, many of those rounded up were in the country legally, and still others were quietly permitted to remain as legal workers under the Bracero program.[14]

In any case, the number of Mexican immigrants (for settlement) and their proportion among total immigrants continued to grow, recruited by agribusiness in the southwest, and attracted by the prospect of work and long-term settlement. Although the two systems of immigration control became more explicit and better coordinated after 1965, the incentives for immigration, and the political system that supported these incentives, remained in place even after the new legislation was passed. Agribusiness has continued to provide incentives for Mexicans, and Latin Americans who arrive through Mexico, to enter both legally and illegally.

What has changed is that this immigration is no longer temporary, and can no longer be seen as a guest-worker program. At the same time, much of the immigration for settlement is undocumented. Indeed, as in Europe, the "perverse effect" of state action against undocumented immigration has forced temporary workers to remain in the United States, either for long periods of time or permanently, because of fears that they will not be able to return if they go home. Therefore, it is hardly surprising that one result of the change in the immigration regime inaugurated by the law of 1965 was a continued growth of both legal and undocumented immigration from Mexico and Latin America. Mexicans, whose surge in immigration to the United States had begun a decade before the change in the migration regime, were particularly well positioned to take advantage of both the second preference, spouses and unmarried children, and the fifth preference, brothers and sisters of U.S. citizens.

More surprising was the relative and absolute growth of immigration from Asia, particularly from China and Korea. The congressional committee staffs that prepared the 1965 legislation noted that there were relatively short lines for visas to the United States in countries in East Asia. Of course the tiny quotas for Asian countries before 1965 were a clear disincentive that was removed when quotas were replaced by preferences. In addition, as David Reimers has carefully noted, the chain effects of preferences 2 and 5 were underestimated by Congress. Within a decade after the new law went into effect in 1968, these miscalculations had become evident.[15]

On the other hand, the new immigration regime significantly reduced immigration from countries in Northern and Western Europe that had previously benefited from virtually open admission under the quota system. Professionals from Britain and Germany now competed for preference admissions with those from Asia; and prospective Irish immigrants lacked the kinship ties and/or the professional qualifications required by the new system. Eventually, these "deficits" were dealt with through the "diversity visas" created by the Immigration Act of 1990. What was originally intended to benefit potential Irish immigrants who could not qualify under the preferences set by the 1965 act, in fact opened the door to all countries that were underrepresented through the application of these preferences (see ch. 8).[16]

By and large the pattern of incentives set in place after 1965 tended to attract immigrants in a predictable way in terms of the preference categories. (See table 9.2.) What was less predictable was how this immigration would be distributed among different countries in different regions. Mexican immigration had begun to rise well before the new immigration regime, and continued to rise more or less in proportion to the total increase after 1968. The increase in Asians entering the country, however, was far out of proportion to the total increase. First, there was a surge of applications by Asian professionals under the sixth preference, and then a growth of applications under the second and fifth preferences. The absolute number of Europeans entering the United States also increased, but, in proportion to the total number of immigrants, was cut in half under the new system.

Although the inflow of immigration into the United States is generally larger than the inflow into France and Britain, what is most evident is that the patterns are very different. Family immigration is higher in the United States than in either of these two European countries. (See table 1.1.) While family immigration into France and Britain is overwhelmingly "non-discretionary," (that is the immediate family of residents by right—spouses and children), in the United States, family immigration is mostly discretionary (that is parents and other relatives), and is accounted for by public policy that favors family arrivals. Therefore, the comparative differences

Table 9.2   U.S. immigration by classification of admission

	1990	1994	1996	1998	2000	2002	2005
Total Immigration	136,483	804,416	915,900	660,477	841,002	1,059,356	1,122,373
Total Family and Immediate Relatives	448,640	463,608	596,264	475,750	581,442	670,556	649,201
Total Employment	58,192	123,291	117,499	77,517	106,642	173,814	246,878
Refugees	97,364	121,434	128,565	54,641	62,928	125,798	142,962
Others[a]	932,287	96,083	73,572	52,565	89,990	89,188	83,332

Notes:
a Mostly related to IRCA amnesty adjustments and diversity.

Source: U.S. Census Bureau, *Statistical Abstract of the United States*, (Washington, DC: USGPO, 2000), p. 9; (Washington, DC: USGPO, 2006), p. 9.

Table 9.3 U.S. immigration by region

	1966	1981–1990	1991–2000	2001–2005
Total (000)	323.0	7,256.0	9080.5	3,779.7
Europe (%)	35.8	9.7	14.4	15.4
N. America[a]	37.9	43.1	43.1	37.1
S. America	12.4	6.3	5.9	7.1
Asia	12.4	38.8	31.8	33.5
Africa	0.6	2.7	4.2	6.1

Notes:

a includes Canada, Mexico, Central America, and the Caribbean.

Source: U.S. Census Bureau, *Statistical Abstract of the United States*, 2000, p. 9; 2006, p. 9.

among France, Britain, and the United States are related to explicit policy choices. Almost 40 percent of U.S. entries are in this discretionary family category, compared to only 6 percent for France and 18 percent for Britain.

Control over Frontiers

It is now commonplace to assume that the United States has lost control of its frontier. Well over a million people are apprehended each year for being in the country without proper documentation, and most of these have crossed the southern frontier without authorization. Moreover, apprehensions have grown more than tenfold since 1965, and have remained high despite massive efforts to strengthen the border. The events of September 11, 2001 only reinforced the political importance of the question of frontier control. On the other hand, the "war on terror" has made it more difficult for asylum-seekers to pursue their claims, and has made it easier to place them in detention. In 2004, the Intelligence Reform and Terrorist Prevention Act limited the grounds for asylum and expanded the bases of detention.

Two frontier issues have preoccupied European governments during the past decade: asylum-seekers and undocumented immigrants. In contrast with Europe, Americans have been relatively less concerned about these issues. Although there has certainly been more concern about asylum-since September 11, 2001, the number of those considered each year has not declined during the past decade. Perhaps more to the point, the percentage of those accepted has increased considerably. There was a drop in both applications and acceptances in 2001/2002, but the normal application number was resumed by 2003, and the acceptance rate increased rapidly (see table 9.5).

If we use the index of both unauthorized frontier-crossing and the presence of undocumented immigrants in the country, the frontiers of the United States are by far more poorly controlled than any country in

Europe. Moreover, by these measures, the effectiveness of border controls appears to have grown worse since a greater effort was invested in border control almost 25 years ago. The estimated 11–12 million undocumented immigrants now in the United States (3.8% of the population) are four times that of Britain, as a percentage of the population (550,000 or 0.92%), and 5.6 times that of France (200–400, 000, or 0.68%).[17]

Illegal immigrants are about 30 percent of the foreign-born, are more numerous than the number of legal permanent residents, and are increasing by about 500,000 per year. More than 7 million are now employed (almost 5% of the workforce), and they constitute 24 percent of all workers employed in farming, 17 percent in cleaning, 14 percent in construction and 12 percent in food preparation.[18] These figures are even more impressive if we consider that they do not include temporary workers, and that children born of illegal immigrants (more than 3 million) are in the country legally as U.S. citizens.

One way to understand the growth on this undocumented population is to examine it historically. Until the 1990s, border enforcement along the long borders with Mexico and Canada was not particularly directed toward the exclusion of undocumented immigrants. As we have noted above, there was no formal federal border patrol until 1924, and even after that, efforts were not directed against Mexicans or Canadians. They were aimed at European "subversives" attempting to infiltrate across the northern and southern borders of the United States, and at alcohol smugglers during prohibition. By 1930 there were 875 men assigned to the Border Control, with a mission of patrolling more than 8,000 miles of border.[19] All efforts by labor leaders and restrictionists to enforce restrictions on entry from Mexico between the wars were unsuccessful, adamantly opposed by the same immigration committees that had voted restrictions on immigrants from Eastern and Southern Europe, and that blocked the admission of refugees from Europe.[20]

Cycles of Enforcement

After the war, even with the Bracero Program in place until 1964, Mexican workers continued to arrive illegally. Constrained by the influence of agribusiness, only sporadic efforts were made to enforce controls on the Mexican border in cycles of enforcement with similar dynamics. These cycles usually begin with pressure from border area politicians, pressure that generally creates a context of political salience. Action by federal authorities is directed toward the reduction of this salience, or use of it for other political objectives; and the cycles generally conclude with pressure from businesses whose interests have been hurt or undermined. Each of these cycles has left the system intact. The first such effort was "Operation Wetback," a military style operation during the summer of 1954, led by Attorney-General Herbert Brownell and the new head of Immigration and Naturalization Service, retired General Joseph M. Swing. While enforcement was emphasized along the border, thousands of Mexicans—mostly in the southwest, but in other parts of the country as well—were rounded up and sent back to Mexico. Beyond the glare of the cameras, however, some of those rounded up were "dried out"—permitted to become legal Bracero workers. In its 1955 annual report, the INS claimed that "...the so-called 'wetback' problem no longer exists...the border has been secured."[21] Indeed, the number of apprehensions understandably declined after the summer of 1953.

Enforcement, however, was only part of the explanation. The government also increased the Bracero contracts from just over 200,000 in 1953 to 400,000 by 1960.[22] The Bracero program ended in 1964, however, and the new legislation that brought the Western hemisphere under immigration controls came into effect in 1968. By 1976, the limitation of 20,000 immigrants per country was applied to all countries, including Mexico, increasing pressure on the southern border.

Although unauthorized entries along the southern frontier increased rapidly after 1965, the border was not as open as it has often been depicted. By the1980s, Border Patrol apprehensions had gone from a low of 72,000 in 1956 to a bit more than a million. By 1986, both apprehension and expulsion had reached 1.6 million, and then declined to under a million in the 1990s.[23] Most of those who were apprehended were sent back with little delay in a process called "voluntary departures."[24]

The general balance between apprehension and removal seemed to indicate that the border was never out of control, but was controlled in a particular way (see figure 9.1). Each year, those crossing illegally were not prevented from crossing, but were apprehended after they had already crossed, overwhelmingly in the area just north of the southwestern border with the United States. They were then "voluntarily" returned to Mexico, although many often returned to the United States again.[25]

After 1993, resources at the border were vastly increased. The Clinton administration, in reaction to the anti-immigrant movement in California, decided to emphasize high profile border enforcement. During the decade after 1993, spending on border enforcement more than tripled, and the number of officers in the Border Patrol more than doubled to almost 12,000.[26] The border was further reinforced in May 2006, when President Bush announced that he was sending 6,000 National Guard troops to provide logistical support for the Border Patrol for two years.[27] The increase in resources was reflected in an increase of border control activity, in the rapid rise of both apprehensions and removals. Indeed, since the end of the nineteenth century, there were only two years (1953 and 1954) when removals even approached the average levels of the period since 1976.

However, the large increase of resources at and near the border seemed to make only marginal difference, either in the pattern of apprehension, removal, the general balance between the two, or the entry of illegal immigrants. Moreover, even as the border was strengthened with greater budget resources, more personnel and more technology, the number of illegal immigrants successfully crossing that border actually increased. The Pew Hispanic Trust estimated that about 400,000 per year arrived between 1990 and 1994; between 1995 and 1999, annual unauthorized arrivals increased to about 575,000 per year; and between 2000 and 2005 to about 850,000. The net increase (after accounting for those who left and those who died) was lower, which accounts for the current estimated net increase of about 500,000 per year.[28] Since apprehensions and expulsions peaked in 1986, the number of unauthorized immigrants living in the United States is estimated to have almost tripled. (See table 9.4.)

Compared to France and Britain, the United States has more effective capabilities to maintain its border. The frontiers of France are embedded into the Schengen arrangements, and those of Britain are in many ways dependent on cooperation with its partners in the European Union, Ireland in particular. As Rey Koslowski has noted, the collective border authorities of the EU have greater resources than the United States, but these authorities are primarily under national control, with cooperation limited to information sharing and (mostly) bilateral arrangements.[29] The apprehension and expulsion rates of the United States indicate reasonable effectiveness compared with Europe. The formal removals, that have increased to more than 200,000 per year, are proportionately far more than the 25,000 that Nicolas Sarkozy claimed was his goal as minister of the interior. Nevertheless, the successful entry rate of illegal immigrants is an indication of the failure to secure the borders. How then, can we explain these discrepancies?

One clue seems to be what Peter Andreas has called the paradox of "a barricaded border and a borderless economy."[30] Andreas's conclusion is strongly supported by the report of the French Senate, as well as by data cited by other scholars on the enforcement of employer sanctions in the United States.[31] Wayne Cornelius, for example, notes that the other side of the border enforcement strategy that was initiated in 1994 was the collapse of employer sanctions and worksite enforcement. While there were almost 10,000 agents at the border in 2001, a mere 124 immigration agents were assigned to enforcement at the workplace. "This token level of worksite enforcement is the fundamental reason why much tougher border controls in the last 10 years have had such a weak deterrent effect."[32]

Table 9.4   Millions of unauthorized immigrants living in the United States

January 1982	June 1986	June 1989	October 1992	October 1996	April 2000	March 2005
3.3	4.0	2.5	3.9	5	8.4	11.1

Source: Jeffery Passel, "Size and Characteristics of the Unauthorized Migrant Population in the US" (Washington, DC: Pew Hispanic Center, 2006), Figure 2.

Table 9.5   Asylum applications and acceptance in the United States[a]

Year	Received	Granted	Acceptance rate[b]
2006	54,432	13,343	24.5%
2005	50,753	11,737	23.1%
2004	56,609	13,015	23.0%
2003	66,931	13,376	20.0%
2002	74,627	10,977	14.7%
2001	61,939	10,001	16.1%
2000	51,967	9,236	17.8%
1999	54,916	8,421	15.3%
1998	71,729	7,291	10.2%
1997	84,904	6,559	7.7%

Notes:
a Does not include refugee applications from outside of the United States.
b Includes conditional acceptances.

Source: U.S. Department of Justice, Executive Office for Immigration Review, Office of Planning, Analysis, and Technology, Immigration Courts, annual statistics.

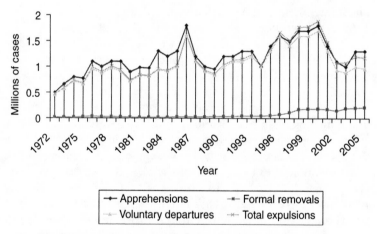

Figure 9.1   U.S. apprehensions and expulsions: 1972–2005

Source: U.S. Department of Homeland Security, Office of Immigration Statistics, 2005 Yearbook of Immigration Statistics (Washington DC: USGPO, 1966), pp. 91, 95.

Enforcement of employer sanctions rests on a weak legal basis, but studies clearly show that even these weak tools have been employed with declining frequency, and principally during cycles of enforcement. Thus, between 1990 and 2002, employer audits (usually random investigations, but some as a result of a "lead") declined 77 percent from a high of 10,000. There was a similar drop in sanctions: warnings to employers dropped by 62 percent and fines by 82 percent. In 2003, only 124 employers received fines for employing illegal immigrants.[33] Criminal prosecutions declined from 182 in 1999 to 4 in 2003.

After 2003, a new cycle of enforcement began, and then in 2006, during the ongoing debate on the proposed immigration bill, there was a surge of high profile raids on employers throughout the country. In 2004, the government won 46 criminal convictions against employers; in 2005 it was 127. A surge of raids in 2006–2007 resembled a series of similar high profile operations during other cycles of enforcement: Operation Wetback in 1954 and Operation "Hold the Line" in 1993 focused on the Mexican border; the Vidalia raids in Georgia in 1998, and Operation Vanguard in 1999 focused on meatpacking plants in the Midwest.[34] Each of these "operations" represented less a change of policy, or a broadly thought-out plan, than a political demonstration of the will of the federal government to maintain the integrity of the border. In fact, cycles of enforcement appear to be an integral part of the maintenance of a relatively fluid border with Mexico. Each time that there has been a surge of enforcement, there has been a mobilization by some state governments (Texas in particular) and organized agribusiness to restore the political balance.

The surge of enforcement in 2006–2008 was both determined and brutal. The government emphasized criminal charges against both employers and immigrant workers, and formal removals (as opposed to voluntary removals), which increased by 12 percent in 2006.[35] As opposed to the crackdowns of the 1990s, the scope of these raids was national, and struck several different kinds of industries. At the beginning of December 2006, Swift and Co. (meatpackers) plants were raided in five states, and 10 percent of the workforce was arrested.[36] A few months later, in Illinois and Michigan, managers of two cleaning companies were arrested for criminal offenses with significant jail-time.[37] Small family farms were raided in western New York State; a job agency was raided in Baltimore and a company that manufactures backpacks for the U.S. Army was raided in New Bedford, Massachusetts.[38] As in other operations, many of the victims were legal immigrants. Legal children were separated from their illegal parents, and legal immigrants were mistakenly rounded up and sent back to Mexico. Immigration agents conducted announced and unannounced raids even on companies that had been cooperating with federal efforts to identify undocumented immigrants.[39] By the summer of 2007, the government was demonstrating its resolve by focusing more resources on fixing employer responsibility for ascertaining the legal status of the workers that they hire, with an emphasis on criminal charges against employers.[40] By 2008, large numbers of immigrant workers were forced to serve prison time before they were formally removed.[41]

As in the past, however, this cycle of enforcement represented a limited effort, with a limited political objective. The not-so-hidden agenda of the Bush administration was to gain support for its immigration proposals by encouraging business interests to increase their pressure on Congress.

As the Secretary of Homeland Security expressed it, there is a direct link between the increased enforcement and the president's immigration proposals. On one hand, he argued that:

> It would be hard to sustain political support for vigorous work-site enforcement if you don't give employers an avenue to hire their workers in a way that is legal, because you are basically saying, "You've got to go out of business." [Nevertheless] businesses need to understand if you don't...play by the rules, we're really going to come down on you.[42]

To reinforce this point, he told protesting farmer groups and employers that hired low-wage labor that they should focus their attention on Congress: "We can be very sure that we let Congress understand the consequences of the choices that Congress makes."[43]

The surge of enforcement, moreover, does not alter the basic structure of the relatively open American labor market, as well as the willingness (or determination) of employers, agribusiness in particular, to employ undocumented workers. After Operation Wetback, the Bracero program was vastly expanded to appease agricultural interests. After the raids in 1998 and 1999, their scope was cut short as the agribusiness employers complained that plants were forced to close in the Midwest, and crops rotted in Georgia.[44]

In 2006–2008, press reports indicated that farmers would continue to hire illegal immigrants to fulfill their labor needs, given the very limited availability of guest workers.[45] Farmers openly said what they have always said about illegal Mexican labor: "We would rather use legal workers...but if we don't get a reasonable guest-worker program we are going to hire illegals."[46] In addition, there are indications, reminiscent of 1998–1999, that political coalitions that unite business interests with human rights advocates could effectively block draconian enforcement—in Texas for example.[47] After the failure to pass comprehensive immigration reform legislation by the summer of 2007, Congress then quietly began to find bipartisan support for more limited, piecemeal legislation that would achieve some of the objectives and constrain the enforcement surge that was progressing at the same time. It appeared that there was a reasonable chance that a limited amnesty bill would pass—giving a path to citizenship to high-school graduates who are illegal, if they complete two years of university or military service. Bipartisan negotiations also began for a temporary worker program for agriculture.[48] The urgency of the problem was accentuated by the surge in demand for food in 2008, but most of these initiatives were put on hold as the presidential race began to heat up in 2008.

Therefore, given past experience, it seems probable that the 2006–2007 enforcement surge was probably limited in time and space. In addition, as we shall see in chapter 10, some of the actions of the federal government to enforce restrictions against illegal immigrants have been met with resistance from states. The lack of action on comprehensive reform, however, has also prompted an unprecedented output of state legislation that deals with a range of issues, from health education and benefits, to voting and employment, some of which is aimed at restricting illegal immigrants, some at providing additional support and services[49] (see ch. 10).

Illegal immigrants in the United States seem to have no problem finding work. Not surprisingly, 94 percent of male undocumented immigrants are employed, compared with 86 percent of male legal immigrants and 83 percent of the native male population. They are a self-selected group of young men, fit for work, and often willing to work for the lowest wages.[50]

Another explanation for the massive number of illegal immigrant resident in the United States is the absence of amnesty or regularization programs since IRCA in 1986. The IRCA legislation eventually resulted in the legalization of almost 3 million immigrants who qualified in the two routes to regularization that it authorized; 90 percent of those who applied were approved.[51] Since then, however, there has been no way for unauthorized immigrants to regularize their status, except for special legislation.

By contrast, until July 2006, French law provided for regularization of undocumented immigrants who had integrated into the workforce and/or had integrated into the community through family and residence. British law was less generous, with a regularization program in 1998 that provided for regularization only of domestic workers. Other European countries have had programs that have ranged between one-shot regularization under specified conditions to more extensive and periodic programs.[52]

A British policy debate on amnesty was postponed by the 2005 parliamentary election. However, by June 2006, the Ministry of Immigration was suggesting the possibility of a broad amnesty that could be applied to as many as 450,000 undocumented immigrants, most of whom were estimated to be either asylum-seekers or immigrants who had overstayed their visas. The process would be to grant them Indefinite Leave to Remain, which would make them eligible for citizenship after a period of time. However, by that July, the ministry dropped the idea because of opposition within the government.[53]

Nevertheless, the British debate suggested some of the pitfalls for the parallel debate in the United States. For example, the Minister of Immigration estimated that it would take a full ten years to deport the estimated 550,000 illegal immigrants then in the United Kingdom. The ministry also estimated that the process would be expensive—about 11,000 pounds for each deportation. Of course, the minister may have been attempting to build support for a possible amnesty, but the discussion itself focused on topics that are rarely approached on the U.S. side of the Atlantic: the feasibility and the cost of massive expulsions, as well as the costs to the economy.[54]

Finally, it has been argued that illegal immigrants who would normally return home after a period of work in the United States are now more inclined to remain because of the difficulties of crossing the frontier.[55] Of course, this was exactly the unanticipated result of the suspension of immigration in France in 1974, and the new restrictions on immigration imposed by Britain after 1962 (see chs. 2 and 5). One clear result of the border enforcement has been the dramatic increase of deaths along the Mexican frontier since 1993. As frontier crossing has moved from more populated areas to more remote mountainous and desert areas, the number of reported deaths has increased from 180 in 1993 to a peak of 370 in 2000; since then there has been a slight decline reported by the Border Patrol. In fact, 1993 represented a low-point, a decline from a high of 355 in 1988. However, while environmental exposure accounted for relatively few deaths before 1993, this has become the major cause since then.[56]

Impact

Public Opinion

As in France and Britain, public opinion on immigration in the United States has grown increasingly negative since immigration began to increase after 1965. Nevertheless, patterns of public opinion have varied considerably more than in Europe. At least until the mid-1990s, negative orientations toward immigration were less pronounced than in Europe, although low levels of positive receptivity were generally comparable (see table 9.6). In the period prior to the liberalization of immigration in 1965, there was no surge in public opinion that could explain liberalization; however, opposition was relatively low and, in this sense, permissive. As immigration from Asia and Latin America increased after 1965, negative attitudes began to harden, and by the mid-1990s opposition had doubled, only to sharply diminish after 1995. By 2001, public attitudes were more positive than they had been in decades.

In 1995, 65 percent of Americans polled by Gallup felt that immigration should be decreased compared with 41 percent in 2001. Only 24 percent felt that present levels were acceptable in 1995, compared with 42 percent in 2001. Indeed 14 percent of Americans polled support increased levels of immigration on 2001, double the percentage of 1995. Therefore, 56 percent of those polled in 2001 supported either existing or increased level of immigration. Only a minority of those polled felt that immigrants "cost the taxpayers too much," only 13 percent felt that they "take jobs that Americans want," and a large percentage felt that immigrants "mostly help the economy."

Although the reaction to immigration provoked by the events of September 11, 2001 brought a spike of opposition (by October, those who thought that immigration should be decreased rose to 58%), this reaction began to subside within a year, to pre-2001 levels. There was a parallel trend in other measures of approval. If we compare these measures in

2005 with those in 1993, we find a general trend toward acceptance (See tables 9.6 and 9.7).[57]

Within these general trends, these measures are considerably higher among Hispanic-Americans. Black Americans, however present more a more complex attitudinal pattern. On one hand, they are more supportive of increased immigration (18% *v.* 14% for non-Hispanic whites in 2005), and favor making it easier for illegal immigrants to become citizens (30% *v.* 19% for non-Hispanic whites in 2005); on the other hand, they are more inclined to see immigrants hurting the economy (66% *v.* 52% for non-Hispanic whites) and are less inclined to see immigration as a good thing for the country (55% *v.* 60% for non-Hispanic whites in 2005).[58] This implies that although Black Americans tend to see immigration as an economic threat, they are inclined to support immigration and immigrants in the context of civil rights.

Although, there has been considerable variation in attitudes toward different immigrant groups, the gap between attitudes toward European immigrants and those from non-Western countries appears to be narrower than in France and Britain. Thus a survey in 1982, at a time when opposition to immigration was increasing rapidly, immigration from China and Japan was seen as having been slightly less "beneficial" than immigration from Poland and Italy; and Jewish immigration was seen to

Table 9.6   Opposition to immigration in the United States

	1953 %	1965 %	1977 %	1986 %	1993 %	1995 %	1999 %	2001 %	2002 %	2005 %
"Should immigration be decreased"	39	33	42	49	65	65	44	41	49	46
"Increased"	13	7	7	7	6	7	10	14	12	16

Sources: Roper Poll, 1953; Gallup Poll:1965–2006.

Table 9.7   Immigration and public opinion in the United States, 1993–2005

Do you feel that immigrants ? (percent):

Year	Pay fair share of taxes	Cost taxpayers too much	Both/neither/no opinion
2005	49	44	7
1993	37	56	87

Do you feel that Immigrants help or hurt the economy? (percent)

Year	mostly help	mostly hurt	neither	both	No opinion
2005	42	49	3	3	3
1993	28	64	2	2	4

Source: Gallup Organization Polls on Immigration.

have been slightly more favorable than immigration from Germany, and almost as favorable as British and Irish immigration. All of this is quite remarkable, if we consider that the United States excluded Chinese and Japanese immigrants during the earlier wave of immigration, and denied naturalization to those already in the country. The limited survey material available appears to support the hypothesis of Rita Simon and Susan Alexander that:

> The responses show that immigrant groups who have been in the United States longer tend to receive more positive evaluations than do recent immigrant communities, even if the earlier ones had been feared, opposed, and disliked at the time of their arrival. Note, for example, that the Chinese and Japanese, whom we once passed special legislation to exclude received more positive than negative ratings, as did Jews, Italians and Pole, against whom the quota acts of the 1920s were largely directed.... The more recent the arrival, the higher is the percentage of respondents who rate them as bad for the United States.[59]

This pattern of narrowing differences over time is similar to that of France and Britain, but the differences are now narrower in the United States, and the time for narrowing appears to be more rapid than in Europe. The level of "too many" has declined rapidly for what are perceived as recent immigrant groups (Latin American and Asian), and has begun to decline even for immigrant groups that are perceived as most associated with terrorist activities since 1993 (Arabs).

This difference may be related to a growing acceptance of "diversity" on a cultural level in the United States compared with Europe (see table 9.8 and 9.9). There is also some evidence that contact with immigrant populations by native-born populations increases sympathy rather than hostility. We saw a similar phenomenon in France (see table 4.2), where antipathy

Table 9.8   Do you think that the number of immigrants now entering the United States from each of the following areas is too many, too few, or about the right amount?

Region	Year	Too many	Too few	About right
Europe	2002	25	12	53
	1993	33	10	52
Latin America	2002	46	5	41
	1993	62	5	29
Asia	2002	39	5	47
	1993	62	4	29
Arab countries	2002	54	5	33
	1993	64	6	24

Source: Gallup Organization Polls on Immigration.

Table 9.9 In your view, does the increasing diversity in the United States that is created by immigrants mostly improve American culture or mostly threaten American culture?

Year	Improve	threaten	both	neither	No Opinion
2006[a]	45	—	—	—	—
2001	45	38	4	5	8
1993	35	55	3	3	4

Note:
a Slightly different question in *America's Immigration Quandry*, Pew Hispanic Center, March 30, 2005, p. 3.

Source: Gallup Organization, Polls on Immigration.

decreases with increased immigrant concentration. In the United States, there is also an unexpected *inverse* relationship between the recognition that the problem of immigration is "big" and the perception of immigrants as a "threat" or a "danger." Thus, in communities where there are high concentrations of immigrant populations, native respondents are both more likely to see immigration as a "big" problem, and are *also* more likely to be sympathetic to immigrants (see table 9.10).

On balance, patterns of public opinion on immigration in the United States are similar to both France and Britain: variable but strong opposition to increased immigration; a difference between opposition to immigration from old sources of immigration and more recent sources; and evolution of relatively more favorable attitudes over time. There are significant differences, however, between trends in France and Britain as opposed to the United States. Although, in ways similar to France and Britain, more open policies initially increased opposition to immigration, in contrast to France and Britain, this opposition shifted after the mid-1990s toward more favorable and receptive public sentiment.

In any case, how salient are these attitudes politically? As we noted in chapter 6, ultimately, it is the way that issues are prioritized that tends to force them onto the political agenda. In surveys, priorities can be estimated in two ways: either by asking respondents an open-ended question, such as "which are the most important problems facing the country today;" or by presenting the issues on the presidential/congressional agenda, and asking respondents "which they think is a top priority". By both of these measures, the question of immigration has been of relatively low priority in terms of public opinion, but its political priority has grown as legislation has been debated in Congress. (See table 9.11.)

The politicization of immigration has also been shaped by changing settlement patterns of recent immigrants. Census figures published in 2006 indicate that immigrants comprise not only a growing proportion of the population, but also a more dispersed population that is growing in regions like the northern Midwest, New England and the Rocky Mountain States.[60]

Table 9.10 U.S. attitudes toward immigrants and concentrations of immigrant populations

	Hi Concentration[a]	Medium Concentration	Lo Concentration
Immigration is a "very" or "moderately big" problem in your community	54%	40%	28%
A growing number of newcomers to the United States threaten American customs and values	47%	46%	60%
Immigrants today are a burden because they take jobs and housing	47%	55%	65%
They strengthen the United States with their hard work and talents	47%	39%	27%

Note:

a *Percentage of foreign-born in respondent's zipcode; respondents include only those whose parents were born in the United States.*

Source: *America's Immigration Quandry*, Pew Hispanic Center, March 30, 2006, pp. 3, 5.

Table 9.11 The political priority of immigration issue

A. Most important problems facing the nation (open ended)

	November 2005	March 2006	May 2006
War in Iraq	29	20	18
Govt. and Politics	7	10	13
Immigration	2	4	10
Economic Issues	24	22	27
Health care	5	6	4

B. Top domestic priorities for Bush and Congress (Percent considering each a "top priority")

	January 2001	January 2002	January 2003	January 2004	January 2005	January 2006
Defend **United States** against terrorism	—	83	81	78	75	80
Improve education system	78	66	62	71	70	67
Strengthen nation's economy	81	71	73	79	75	66
Secure Social Security	74	62	59	65	70	64
Reduce crime	76	53	47	53	53	62
Protect environment	63	44	39	49	49	57
Reduce budget deficit	—	35	40	51	56	55
Stop illegal immigrants	—	—	—	—	—	51
Immigrant guest-worker program	—	—	—	—	—	17

Sources: *Fact Sheet: The State of American Public Opinion on Immigration in Spring 2006: A Review of Major Surveys*, Pew Hispanic Center, May 17, 2006, p. 2; *Economy Now Seen through Partisan Prism: Emerging Priorities for '06*, Pew Research Center, January 24, 2006, p. 2.

What's happening now is that immigrants are showing up in many more communities all across the country than they have ever been in. So it's easy for people to look around and not just see them, but feel the impact they're having in the communities. And a lot of these are communities that are not accustomed to seeing immigrants in their schools, at the workplace, in their hospitals.[61]

While this growing and dispersed population appears to be having a political impact, the impact in the United States has been quite different than the parallel impact in France or Britain. There have clearly been negative reactions, where anti-immigrant and immigration-control proposals have been increased on the levels of states and communities. However, as we shall see in chapter 10, immigrants have also been accepted as political actors and voters and potential voters. As table 9.10 indicates, attitudes toward immigrants, though generally divided, are more positive where there are high concentrations of immigrants than where they are less numerous.

Finally, there are striking differences between the attitudes toward immigrants and immigration among mass publics and those of elite opinion leaders (defined as top executives, media leaders, religious leaders, political and administrative leaders and university faculty). Elite respondents are generally more favorable to immigration, and less inclined to see immigration as a salient issue than are mass respondents. In 2002, 60 percent of a mass sample saw immigration as a "critical threat," compared with 14 percent of opinion leaders; there was a similar gap between mass and elite samples who thought that reduction of illegal immigration should be a "very important" foreign policy goal for the United States: 70 vs. 22 percent. Other studies have found similar divergent gaps between mass and elite opinion, but generally not quite as large.[62]

Citizenship

During the period of immigration that ended in 1924, the impact of immigration on citizenship was substantial in several ways. Asian exclusion, after 1882, not only excluded the entry of Chinese and Japanese immigrants, but also excluded the naturalization of those already here.[63] Nevertheless, *jus solis* continued to apply (and was enforced by the Supreme Court), thus making all Asians born in the United States American citizens at birth.[64] Exclusion from naturalization, however, was limited to Asians, despite the growing political movement in favor of more general immigration restriction that began to emerge in the 1890s.

The most important impact of the "new" immigration was the first government attempt to link citizenship and naturalization policy with ideas about what it meant to be an American.[65] In the literature on the development of American identity there are two distinctive ideas. One is the "new race" idea, that Americans were/are an amalgam of European cultures, and yet the whole is distinctive and different from the parts. The other is the "modified Englishman" idea, that Anglo-Saxon culture has dominated the American ideal, that other European cultures (Catholic and German in particular) were far less welcome as part of the Anglo-Saxon melting pot, and that Asians, Native Americans and Blacks were excluded from the pot entirely.[66] Nevertheless, there is little doubt that at least until WWI, there was a widespread assumption among public and private leaders on every level that there was a pervasive cultural homogeneity in the United States, and that "[i]nterchangeability and assimilability were deemed necessary conditions for citizenship."[67]

On the eve of WWI, six states in which large numbers of immigrants were concentrated organized commissions and programs that combined investigations into the living conditions of immigrant populations with civic education programs. Attempts to harmonize these efforts were coordinated by the Committee for Immigrants in America, a private group sponsored by wealthy progressive donors. The committee finally gained the support of the Bureau of Education in Washington, within which was established the Division of Immigrant Education, the unique goal of which was to publicize the need for immigrant Americanization through education.

While there was no single model of Americanism, there were overlapping themes in the educational programs. They associated survival of the national community with the dominance of Anglo-Saxon culture, with the suppression of ethnic culture and identity, and with the development of certain values and habits. "To be a good American included adopting everything from the American way to clean your house and brush your teeth to the Protestant values of self-control and self-reliance."[68]

Federal support for the Americanization effort began to ebb after 1920, but numerous states continued what had become a crusade by passing legislation that ranged from requiring that English be the sole language of instruction in all public and private primary schools in 25 states, to requiring that non–English-speaking aliens attend English classes, to more draconian measures that were eventually declared unconstitutional.[69] After 1921–1922 Americanization programs were cut back, due to the pressures of economic contraction, but the ideals and values remained dominant until after WWII (see ch. 10).

By the time the 1965 legislation came into effect in 1968, the public philosophy that dominated considerations of public policy on citizenship had changed. However, by the 1990s, one reaction to growing immigration was the provision in the The Personal Responsibility and Work Opportunity Act of 1996 that denied most public assistance to the majority of legal residents for five years (or until they gained citizenship). While this provision did not alter citizenship requirements, it did modify the rights of legal residents, and therefore provided a strong incentive for them to seek naturalization. The number of naturalizations increased from less than half a million in 1995 to more than a million in 1996, and remained high for the entire decade that followed. With the exception of the 1996 legislation, the federal government generally took a permissive approach to molding citizenship. The states, however, were increasingly inclined to act in this area, where they were able (see ch. 10).

Integration and Incorporation

From the "Automatic Society" to "Americanization"

Although there are few legislative enactments at the federal level in the United States that can be termed integration policy, policies originally developed to deal with race relations, rather than immigrant integration, have been important in shaping the integration of immigrant communities since the 1960s.

Immigrant integration through most of the nineteenth century, like much else in the United States, was part of the process that Theodore Lowi has called the "automatic society". Assimilation would flow from the operation of social institutions, what John Higham has called

> ...a confident faith in the natural, easy melting of many peoples into one. When fearful of disruptive influences, the Americans sought to brake the incoming current or to inhibit its political power; otherwise they trusted in the ordinary processes of a free society.[70]

Indeed, the literature on the ideal of immigrant integration during the nineteenth century in the United States—whatever the contradictions in reality—seemed destined to play a role in America not unlike that of the French Republican model. It supported intermarriage (at least among whites), the hegemony of English cultural and political values together with English as a common language. The ideal gained increased institutional support at the local level, as education spread after the Civil War, even if ethnicity did in fact form a basis for initial settlements and political organization for collective advancement.[71]

The Americanization programs financed by the federal government, and the more coercive programs sometimes established by the states, seemed to be a challenge to the optimism of the automatic society, and gave form to a cultural definition for membership in the national community. Once these programs came to an end, however, or were declared unconstitutional by the courts (see above), they were not renewed.

What took their place was more evident in school curricula than in law. By the late 1930s, American textbook authors were writing about a different kind of America by emphasizing the contribution of immigrants to American life.[72] Nevertheless the hegemony of Anglo-Saxon cultural ideals remained. It was only during the period after WWII that

the cultural ideals of a unified America slowly gave way to the multicultural ideals portrayed as "the American model" in the French literature,
but the model of the melting pot endured in school textbooks and popular
culture well into 1960s.[73]

Multiculturalism

The change emerged through a process that began with ethnic organization, by the recognition of the legitimacy of a multiethnic America that
was portrayed by government propaganda during WWII, and that was
reinforced by the emergence of what Martin Kilson has called "Black
neo-ethnicity" in the 1960s (see chapter 10).[74] Indeed, the ideal of neo-
ethnicity, a Nation of Nations, began to emerge at the same time that
intermarriage among the children and grand-children of European immigrants was sharply on the rise, and when important indicators of ethnic
"memberships" were on the decline (organizational membership and language ability above all). Government programs in the 1960s that effectively "created" minorities "...by ascribing to them certain characteristics
that serve to justify their assignment to particular societal roles," represented an attempt to deal with a racial crisis, not immigration or assertions
of multiculturalism, but had unanticipated responses.[75] Within a decade,
the impact of "re-ethnicization" had effectively challenged the melting
pot understanding among policymaking elites, and the breakdown of this
understanding became evident in the way that the national community
was being portrayed.

This approach challenges the very notion of universal commonality,
and instead emphasizes the legitimacy of diversity. It is more about broad
acceptance than about the strength of community based on common
heritage. As Desmond King notes in an excellent review of the debate:

> Multiculturalists advocate equal respect for all cultures and ethnic
> identities in a political system. Politically, these multiple identities
> have been integrated into public policy in a way purported to respect
> the inherent value of each tradition and not to privilege any one tra-
> dition over another.

Indeed, because the path to citizenship has often been a collective experience of groups that have come from the same countries and regions to the
United States, one that has reinforced the ethnic experience, King points
out that, as historian Linda Kerber has written

> ...behind the emphasis on multiculturalism lurks the knowledge
> that not everything melted in the melting pot, that the experi-
> ence of difference has been deeply embedded in the legal paths to
> citizenship.[76]

But what has multiculturalism meant in practice for the process of immigrant integration? Although it is not wrong to argue that "the United States follows a more laissez-faire assimilationist strategy providing little government support to minority groups but relatively few barriers to those accommodating to market incentives and electoral norms," this statement probably underestimates the positive incentives for multiculturalism that are provided by public policy. From school curricula, to the multitude of holidays recognized in various ways at the local level (including the Parking Calendar of the City of New York); to various identity programs that have taken root at universities; to the provisions of the 1990 Immigration Act that supports "diversity visas" to ensure diversity of immigration, multicultural incentives have become part of the fabric of American public policy.

The role of the federal government in shaping a multicultural approach to immigration can be understood on several levels. At the most basic level, immigration law now favors and promotes diversity. The diversity visas, introduced in 1990, provided for the admission, on an annual basis, of 55,000 immigrants from "under-represented" countries. Entries from these countries are required to have high-school equivalency and/or work experience, but are then chosen by lottery. Thus, what began as an effort to relieve the backlog of applications from Ireland—the initiative had been taken by Senator Kennedy on behalf of his Irish constituents—ended as a mechanism for increasing the diversity of the population of the United States. Indeed, when the House-Senate conferees emerged with a final agreement on the 1990 legislation, they called their compromise agreement a victory for cultural diversity, "for family unity, and for job creation."[77] What makes this statement particularly striking is that, even as an afterthought, American political leaders were seeking to promote what European leaders either feared or sought to carefully manage: cultural diversity.

A second key federal program that has shaped the national approach to multiculturalism is the anti-discrimination effort initiated by the Civil Rights Act of 1964. Under rules developed by the Equal Opportunity Employment Commission in 1965, employers were required to file annual reports not only about the race of their employees, but about their sex and ethnicity as well. These rules not only included immigrant groups in their mission, but also provided the basis for proactive action by the EEOC that promoted the employment rights of diverse groups, including immigrants.[78] In addition, the Voting Rights Act of 1965 (extended for another 25 years in 2006), originally intended to support the voting rights of African-Americans, now also protects a wide variety of ethnic groups against discrimination.[79]

Finally, the approach to religious diversity at the national, state and local levels has both permitted and encouraged multiculturalism in the United States. The absence of state sponsorship in the United States does not mean that religious organizations are not accorded a privileged status.[80]

Under specific conditions, they are granted a special tax status that permits them to be exempt from both national and local taxes. Various forms of recognition are also implied when local governments recognize religious holidays as a reason for school absence and suspension of restrictions for parking cars.

Comparing Integration

The pattern of integration for Muslims in the United States provides an interesting case study. In a way that followed similar arrangements for Jews after WWII, schools and workplaces recognized Muslim dress codes, dietary restrictions and holidays, (the lead having been taken by African American adherents, beginning in the 1970s).[81] Although officially there are no public funds for the construction of mosques available under the American version of separation of church and state, in general, there were no problems using funds from foreign sources for their construction, as well as for the construction of schools.

There have also been documented instances of the use of local government power to help in the construction of mosques in Massachusetts and California. In Boston, the office of the mayor subsidized land acquisition for the construction of the mosque in West Roxbury.[82] In Fremont California, the mayor and planning board helped a Methodist congregation and a Muslim *masjid* overcome homeowner opposition to find houses of worship.[83] This relatively easy relationship declined after 2001, but the process has remained the same, following the pattern established for Catholics and Jews. Perhaps the most important change is that Muslim organizations have now increased their role in defending their civil rights, much as Catholics and Jews had done in earlier periods.[84]

Thus, a relatively laissez-faire policy on integration is nevertheless a policy that is shaped in a variety of ways by the states and by the federal authorities. It is also a policy that has been relatively successful in its own terms. Overall, unemployment among immigrant groups, while higher than for the population as a whole, is lower than among immigrant groups in Britain and especially France. (See table 1.3.) As in Britain, there is also a significant difference among immigrant groups. In 2003, the unemployment rate among immigrants originating in Asia (6.2%) was two points lower than for immigrants from Latin America and Mexico (8.3%), but almost 2 points higher than those from Europe (4.6%). These differences are related both to what immigrants bring with them, as well as to employment opportunities in the United States, but they are far less pronounced than differences among groups in Britain.

Educational attainment of immigrants is both encouraging and discouraging in the American case. Table 1.4 indicates an achievement rate at the university level that is as high as that of the native population (as in France and Britain), but at the lower end of the scale, a lack of achievement that is far higher than the native population; higher than Britain, but not as high as in France. Table 1.5 indicates that, as in Britain, education is a key to economic success. However, table 1.4 hides the gap among immigrant groups, and indicates a significant failure to move Latin American immigrants up the educational ladder. While immigrants from Asia and Europe have dropout rates that are about the same as the native population, and have attained degrees in higher education that are well above the national average, the same is not true for immigrants from Latin America. Half of them have "less than a high school diploma," and only 11.6 percent have gained a B.A. degree or better (compared with 50% of Asian immigrants and 27% of the native population).[85]

Finally, in terms of political representation, the United States has had by far the best record of immigrant groups represented at the national level (table 1.6). In addition, political representation at the state and local level in is far higher than that is indicated for Hispanics in this table. More than 80 percent of the Hispanic elected officials have been elected at the local and sublocal level (mostly school boards), and thus table 1.6 gives only a partial picture at best. Table 9.12 compares the number of Hispanic office-holders in 2005, with numbers in 1984, and indicates an overall increase of more than 50 percent. The largest overall increase was during the first decade, and the number peaked in 1994. The overall number has declined since then, mostly due to a decline in representation on school boards. Three states account for 78 percent of these elected officials: Texas, California and New Mexico (in that order), with the number growing in both Texas and (above all) California since 1994. In addition, we should note, that Hispanic officials also hold important offices at the local level. Alba and Foner have noted:

> In 2005, three of the mayors in the nation's top ten gateway central cities were Hispanic; in another three cities, the main challenger in the last mayoral election was Hispanic. This, by the way, includes the "mega-gateways," Los Angeles and New York: Los Angeles's recently-elected mayor, Antonio Villaraigosa is Mexican-American, and the main challenger in the recent New York City mayoral election was

Table 9.12   Hispanic elected office-holders in the United States, 1984–2005

	1984	*1994*	*2005*
Total[a]	3,063	5,459	4,853
State	119	199	266
County and Local	1,276	2,196	2,149

Note:

a Total includes those elected to school boards, as well as judgeships and law-enforcement posts.

Source: U.S. Bureau of the Census, *Statistical Abstract of the United States, 2007* (Washington, DC: USGPO, 2007), Table 404.

Fernando Ferrer, a second-generation Puerto Rican. In one major US city, Miami, one immigrant group, Cubans, has attained a degree of political influence that is unmatched, to our knowledge, among all the major cities in [Europe]—by the end of the twentieth century; for example, six of the thirteen Miami-Dade commissioners were Cuban Americans as was the mayor.[86]

Americans are broadly receptive to the presence of immigrants, generally more receptive than Europeans (see table 1.7). They see the influence of immigration as positive and immigrants as able to adapt. Perhaps most interesting in the post-9/11 world, compared with Europeans, they tend to see growing Islamic identity as a good thing. The multicultural world of America in the twenty-first century is far different from the world of Americanization of the early twentieth century.

CHAPTER TEN

Politics of Immigration in the United States

The politicization of immigration in the United States has always been different from that of France and Britain. In general, although there are clear similarities in the ways that immigration issues have been framed, the cross-national differences between the United States, on one hand, and France and Britain on the other, are striking. While both the United States and the two European countries have focused on immigration as an identity issue, the former did so most intensely during the period before 1930, while the latter framed the issue in this way during the period of post-WWII immigration.

To some extent, this can be explained by the importance of the structural dimension. The American federal system has been, and remains an important political element. Agenda formation, the political process, the politics of change, and electoral strategies have all been deeply influenced by the dynamics of the federal system, although the system itself has changed in important ways over time. Until the last quarter of the nineteenth century, the states were more important than the federal government in agenda formation, and in some aspects of policy development. Although the balance changed after 1876, federal initiatives and the federal framing of the immigration issues were influenced by regional considerations expressed through the Senate and regional coalitions.

During the early period, regional divisions tended to deeply divide political parties on immigration issues, but so did major interest groups. Thus the Republicans were divided between their pro-immigration business wing, and their pro-restrictionist identity wing; the Democrats were divided between their pro-immigration electoralist wing, and their restrictionist labor wing. New England Republicans and Western Democrats tended to be the most restrictionist.

However, none of these dividing lines were hard and fast, and they did change over time. Nevertheless, many of the issues around which the politics of immigration were organized in the nineteenth century continued to be important during the period after 1965. The difference in outcomes can be explained by the changing strength of the actors, their ability to reframe immigration issues within the political system, as well as changes in the system itself.

Framing the Issue

The framing of the political issue of immigration in the United States has been linked to a complex history of racism, but it is also related to economic and geographic expansion and growing labor market needs. In the early years of the Republic, the conflict was entirely about framing the issue. At the same time the federal government was framing policy in terms of population, and promulgating policies that were destined to attract immigration from Europe, many of the receiving states were influenced by the reactions to the results of these same policies, and framing policies in terms of identity. The overall impact of the relatively permissive Passenger Acts in 1819 (relative to the more restrictive British counterparts), of the land policy pursued by the federal government, and the relatively easy naturalization, was to maintain an open door to successive waves of immigrants from Europe. Although these policies had as their object some elements of immigration control, they more generally reflect the desire to attract, rather than restrict immigration. The incentives built into these policies would endure, and in some ways be reinforced, until after the Civil War.

Immigration and Population Policy

Federal authorities were never completely insulated from the concerns of the states, particularly those states that received the bulk of immigrants entering the country. Thus, the Passenger Acts reflected some of the immigration control concerns of the German community in Pennsylvania and Maryland, as well as the concerns of shipping companies. On the other hand, the legislation was clearly framed as a way of molding, rather than restricting immigration. At the federal level, the immigration issue was framed largely in terms of what Aristide Zolberg has called "a comprehensive population policy" that was meant to stimulate economic growth and expansion[1] (see ch. 8).

This framing was subtle in the sense that immigration was seen largely in terms of a much broader policy that included natives as well as immigrants. Thus the Homestead Act of 1862 did not distinguish between citizens and immigrants, and citizens moving West were routinely referred to as "immigrants". The act was widely publicized by American consulates in Europe, some of which hired full-time recruitment agents. At the same time, railroad agents and representatives of Western states and territories also actively recruited European settlers. The Civil War only intensified the view that labor recruitment was essential, and new legislation authorized the establishment of a Bureau of Immigration to coordinate the recruitment effort. (See ch. 9.)

At the same time, at the state level, a movement was growing that framed immigration in an entirely different way, in terms of a challenge to American identity. In fact, in the politicization of immigration at the state and local level during the 1840s, issues of immigration were framed in two ways that would endure until the present. On one hand, during the decade-long rise of the American ("Know-Nothing") Party, the party and their supporters focused entirely on questions of identity and religion (they were both anti-immigration and anti-Catholic). On the other hand, those who opposed them, particularly the Democrats, focused more intensely on immigrants as voters and political resources.[2] In New England, the emerging Republican Party was often allied with the Know Nothings (see below), but in the Midwest other Republicans were influenced by the support from immigrant populations.[3] If considerations of growth and expansion dominated the way that immigration issues were framed at the national level, under the pressure of the American Party, the issues were framed in identity terms in a large number of states.

At the end of the Civil War, there appeared to be a consensus among party elites at the national level that immigration policy would be framed in terms of the benefits for economic expansion and settlement. The Republican Party platform of 1864 proclaimed:

> Resolved, That foreign immigration, which in the past has added so much to the wealth, development of resources and increase of power to the nation, the asylum of the oppressed of all nations, should be fostered and encouraged by a liberal and just policy.[4]

What made this view of immigration, and this commitment, more significant is that this was a period of virtual one-party Republican government at the national level. Indeed,

> If the Whigs and Republicans were more sympathetic to xenophobic sentiment than were the Democrats, then this period of one-party rule might seem opportune for Republican nativists to win passage of restrictionist legislation. But no such initiatives were enacted.[5]

In fact, as we have seen, quite the opposite was true. It is not that immigration was not on the political agenda; it was, but framed in a way to encourage immigration. The national Republican Party still regarded immigration as a component of population policy, necessary for labor and the settlement of a still expanding country.

It soon became obvious, however, that the separation between the national perspective of immigration policy and the very different state and local perspective that had been developing for 25 years were on a collision course. By the 1860s, Democrats in California had begun to mobilize in favor of legislation on Chinese exclusion, and were far more effective than Eastern exclusionists had been before the war. The Burlingame

Treaty had had the enthusiastic support of the national Republican party, and Western Republicans in particular, who saw in the treaty not only benefits for trade, but also an expression of the multiracial ideals of the Reconstruction period.

Reframing the Issue: Race and Identity

For Western Democrats, however, the expansive immigration policies of the Reconstructionist Congress in Washington provided a wedge issue in California that enabled them to gain control of the government of the state. The same political party that had successfully checked the Know Nothings in the east by mobilizing new immigrant voters now took the leadership of the anti-immigrant identity movement in the west. After the Democrats gained control over the California state government in 1867, measures to discourage, and then drive out, Chinese immigrants multiplied both at the local and state levels.[6] The Democratic success, however, also undermined the position of the Western Republicans at the national level, and, for the first time, broke the alliance between Western Republicans and the national Republican Party on the framework for understanding immigration.

At the same time, the courts redefined the balance between the states and the national government on questions of immigration. First the lower courts, and then the Supreme Court, in the *Ah Fong* case,[7] asserted the supremacy of federal jurisdiction in this area, forcing groups and the states seeking Chinese exclusion to switch venues to the federal level.[8] Had these decisions not come into play, Chinese exclusion—passed in 1882— certainly would have been voted at the state level in the early 1870s.

The process that evolved at the national level effectively altered the framework within which immigration was understood, and policy developed, albeit as applied specifically to immigration from China. In 1868, Republicans in Washington had given strong support to the Burlingame Treaty, which extended to free immigrants from China the protections of American citizens. But this was when the Chinese were understood to be part of a larger plan to build trade relations with the American West, and as "...pouring out over our land millions of willing hands and stout hearts, adding millions to our prosperity."[9]

The key move in the shift to Chinese exclusion to the national level came the year after the court decisions in 1875, when the U.S. Congress established a Joint Special Committee to Investigate Chinese Immigration. After extensive hearings, its report in 1877 served to mobilize a broader coalition of support for the Chinese Exclusion Act, which finally passed five years later. Thus, Chinese exclusion first emerged as a Western regional issue, initiated by the Democrats, where the issue was framed in terms of identity and race. Democrats and eventually Republicans, focused on the Chinese as a way to mobilize voters, but the way they framed the issue endured. As the proponents of exclusion sought to build a broad coalition at the federal level, among representatives of states in which there were few if any Chinese laborers, the issue became increasingly racialized.[10] A decade later, New England Republicans—who had deeply opposed Chinese exclusion—would take the lead in opposing the new wave of immigration from Southern and Eastern Europe, using many of the same arguments that had been used by others against the Chinese. Therefore, although the results of the debate appeared to be limited to Chinese exclusion, in fact the more profound result was to alter the framework within which all questions of immigration would be considered.

The framing of Chinese exclusion as a racial issue gradually solidified a coalition among a broad range of Democrats, that enabled Democratic supporters to differentiate the Chinese from European immigrants.[11] However, Chinese exclusion soon became a model of identity-based, racist legislation that would later be used to exclude European populations who were also designated as undesirable, not because of labor market challenges or immoral behavior, but because they were regarded as unintegratable. Therefore the joint Congressional Report of 1877 marks a turning point, not only because it initiated a process of exclusion, but because it reframed the immigration issue in a way that it had not been framed before. It was the first of a series of reports on immigration over the next 100 years, supported by a large number of witnesses (130), by more than 1,200 pages of testimony, by facts, figures and a tone of neutrality.[12] In this report, as in subsequent reports, each of these investigations developed (or attempted to develop) a new frame of reference for understanding the problem of immigration.

Until the mid-1890s, the focus of discussion among political elites had been almost entirely on Chinese exclusion. The racial arguments that were developed for this campaign in California and then used in Washington, most unambiguously by the Democrats, were then broadly extended and given a scientific base by Republican restrictionists in the 1890s.

Discussions of immigration were refocused on the problem of the assimilation of Europeans, and on an effort to define the content of American citizenship, and both were tied to more highly focused scientific discussions of race based on eugenics, and on a new nationalism based on racial and religious type.

The impetus for the redefinition of the immigration issue in nationalist and racial terms came from congressional leaders and intellectuals. After Chinese exclusion in 1882, the first indication of a more general shift in thinking about the immigration question came with the emergence of a movement to impose literacy tests on new immigrants in the 1890s. The movement was organized and led by the Immigration Restriction League, founded by Boston intellectuals in 1892, and for which Senators William E. Chandler and Henry Cabot Lodge were the chief spokesmen. Chandler was the chairman of the Senate Immigration Committee, which had been established in 1889. Literacy tests, argued Chandler, were the most effective means of restricting the entry of certain races, alien to American nationality. "No one," he said in 1892, "has suggested a race distinction.

We are confronted by the fact, however, that the poorest immigrants do come from certain races."[13]

Nevertheless, other views of immigration restriction during this early period remained open, and even dominant outside of the immigration committees and their allies. Both presidential party platforms in 1892 contained planks that supported restriction in the following terms. The Republicans simply favored "...the enactment of more stringent laws and regulations for the restriction of criminal, pauper, and contract immigration." The Democrats were both more forceful and more circumspect:

> We heartily approve all legitimate efforts to prevent the United States from being used as a dumping ground for the known criminals and professional paupers of Europe, and we demand the rigid enforcement of the laws against Chinese immigration, or the importation of foreign workmen under contract, to degrade American labor and lessen its wages, but we condemn and denounce any and all attempts to restrict the immigration of the industrious and worthy of foreign lands.

The earlier discussions of exclusion and restriction of individuals had evolved into debates about exclusion and restriction of groups that either could not or should not be assimilated into the American national community, or that could be assimilated only with great difficulty. In December 1896, Congress sent to President Grover Cleveland the legislation that embodied an important break with the American tradition of relatively unrestricted immigration. What made the break important was not the imposition of a literacy test as such, but what Congress acknowledged this test had come to represent. The Senate committee report noted a new approach to immigration—

> The illiteracy test will affect almost entirely those races whose immigration to the United States has begun within recent times and which are most alien in language and origin to the people who founded the 13 colonies and have built up the United States—

even as it argued that the legislation was a continuation of former policy:

> ...it would tell most heavily against those classes of immigrants which now furnish paupers, diseased and criminal, excluded by existing law, and is therefore a continuance of the present policy of the United States which has met with general acceptance.

The Senate report includes a survey of governors (26 responded) in which they were asked whether immigration was desired, and, if so, from which races. The report notes that "...with two exceptions none of the excluded races, as shown by the letters of the governors of the different States, are desired in 26 States of the Union from which reports have been received." (Germans seemed to be the most popular "race" overall.)[14]

In President Cleveland's veto of the legislation, he too noted the sharp departure from previous approaches, and argued that "The time is quite within recent memory when the same thing was said of immigrants who, with their descendants, are now numbered among our best citizens." Reflecting the concerns of many business interests at the time, he wrote that the exclusion of illiterates would hardly protect this country against "...one of those unruly agitators who can not only read and write, but delight in arousing by inflammatory speech the illiterate and peacefully inclined to discontent."[15] Literacy legislation was finally approved on the eve of America's entry into WWI, after twice being vetoed by President Woodrow Wilson (see below), but by then the changed view of the new immigration was already far more advanced.

Henry Cabot Lodge, the most important congressional leader of the political movement in favor of immigration restriction before WWI, went to considerable effort to build his case with scientific support for racial differences. As early as 1891, Lodge published his own statistical analysis of what he called the "distribution of ability" among different racial strains in the American population. The results clearly demonstrated, he argued, the threat of "...a great and perilous change in the very fabric of our race."[16]

Lodge's thinking (and writing), in fact, was part of an ongoing dialogue that included at least one university president (Francis Walker of MIT), one of the leading sociologists of the day (Franklin Giddings, the first professor of sociology at Columbia University), and, ultimately, the president of the United States, Theodore Roosevelt. In a wide-ranging debate on the ability of the United States to absorb the new tide of immigrants, the focus was increasingly on race and racial superiority or inferiority. On both sides of the issue the definition of the immigrant problem was becoming racial.

Walker argued that the superior Anglo-Saxon racial strains were being overwhelmed by inferior European strains, in part because of declining native birthrates, while Giddings contended that we had nothing to worry about, since the superior Anglo-Saxon races would dominate here as they dominated there.[17] Roosevelt, while rejecting the case for restriction, concluded that we may have something to worry about, and he initiated a campaign for more children (and against birth control) to prevent "race suicide."

The President's campaign, in itself, greatly accelerated and popularized race thinking. After analyzing the reaction to the campaign in the popular press, the historian John Higham concludes that

> In the end, the whole discussion probably caused more race-thinking than reproduction. At least it brought to a wider audience the racial pessimism previously confined to a limited group of upper-class intellectuals.[18]

One indication of this pattern of dissemination of race thinking in the public policy debate is the changes that began to take place in American history textbooks about 1900. Earlier nineteenth century texts had focused on the Protestant religious identification of Americans, and many had been violently anti-Catholic. In the 1890s, however, when the public secondary school system became larger than the church-based private school system, texts became neutral on the question of religion, emphasizing the common citizenship of Americans, but not neutral about immigrants.

School systems in large cities were often charged with offering special services for immigrants, as well as with their "Americanization," often at the encouragement of the Americanization Division of the U.S. Bureau of Education.[19] This charge created additional pressures for defining the content of what an American was, and it was about 1900 that major textbooks began to develop a new distinction between "we Americans" and "the immigrants," and texts began to emphasize English ancestry as the basis of being American. In sometimes subtle ways, the new texts reflected much of the racial pessimism of the time. Immigrants were a problem and a strain on American institutions, "a constant menace to our free institutions." Some texts were more explicit about the problem of race (used interchangeably with nationality): "Great racial groups, especially such as speak foreign languages, or belong to races with which we do not readily intermarry, do add to the difficulty of solving certain social problems."[20]

What is startling about reading these notions of Americanism is that these texts were most often meant to orient and educate the very people who were written off as "inassimilable." The Mussy text cited above appeared the same year as the report of the Immigration Commission, which reported that 57.8 percent of the children in the schools of 37 of the country's largest cities were of foreign-born parentage. In New York, the percentage was 71.5, in Chicago, 67.3 and Boston 63.5.[21]

At the same time that the new race thinking was being integrated into school texts, it was being given increased legitimacy by scientific and pseudo-scientific writing. As imported from continental Europe and England, the eugenics movement converted genetic theory into a social program for manipulating heredity, and added a sense of urgency to the now widespread notions of the danger of racial death. For the eugenicists, immigration was a biological problem that could not be solved by manipulating the environment through Americanization. The movement, which included a number of important patrician intellectuals, exerted considerable influence over the ongoing dialogue on immigration.

William Riply, an economist from MIT, published an early work on *The Races of Europe*, which related physiological traits to geographical and social conditions. He ultimately built this work into a thesis on how the mixing of inferior and superior races can undermine the superiority of the latter through a biological "reversion to primitive type."[22] The most influential of the books that came out of this movement was probably Madison Grant's *The Passing of the Great Race*, published in 1916.[23] Grant, the chairman of the New York Zoological Society, who was a committed anti–Semite, focused on the danger of reversion to primitive type, and the need for racial pride for the very survival of what he presumed to demonstrate was the superior race.[24]

Within the intellectual and scientific community there was certainly no consensus about the race thinking being advanced in scientific terms by the eugenics movement. Leading anthropologists such as Franz Boas, for example, wrote in opposition to much of this work, and Higham argues that anthropology as a discipline remained distant from most of the concerns and conclusions of eugenics. Nevertheless, it seems clear that the racial categories advanced by eugenicists provided the core of the evolving debate that was then disseminated through the popular press. One study indicates that between 1910 and 1914, popular magazines published more articles on eugenics than on slums and living standards combined.[25] One clear indication of the growing integration of race thinking into public policy thinking was the change that took place in the categorization of immigrants at the turn of the century. Until 1899, the Bureau of Immigration published immigration statistics (from census reports) that were based only on country of birth. After that, classification was switched to crude categories of "race" or "people."

The congressional committees set the stage for a massive research and education effort. The Immigration Act of 1907 established the U.S. Immigration Commission, which was charged with making a full investigation of the problem of immigration in the United States and making legislative recommendations to Congress. The commission was dominated by the immigration committees themselves (six of the nine members), and, therefore its conclusions were determined by the commitments of its members. After four years, the commission produced 42 volumes of data, documents and studies, on the basis of which it adopted a moderate restrictionist position. The report also inevitably strengthened the case for additional restrictive legislation, and set the agenda for the great changes in immigration policy.

By the time the Immigration Commission issued its massive report in 1911, race thinking was far advanced, but the report itself both framed and solidified the political agenda. Thus, the introduction to the report elaborates both the scope of the inquiry, as well as a way of understanding the difference between the "old" and the "new" immigration. The old immigration came primarily from Northern and Western Europe. It was:

> ...largely a movement of settlers who came from the most progressive sections of Europe for the purpose of making for themselves homes in the New World.... They mingled freely with native Americans [as opposed to immigrants] and were quickly assimilated, although a large proportion of them, particularly in later years, belonged to non-English-speaking races.

By contrast, the new immigration came from Eastern and Southern Europe. It was:

> ...in large part temporary, from the less progressive and advanced countries of Europe in response to the call for industrial workers in the eastern and Middle Western states. They have...congregated together in sections apart from native Americans and the older immigrants to such an extent that assimilation has been slow as compared to that of the earlier non-English-speaking races.

Perhaps more important,

> The new immigration as a class is far less intelligent than the old....Racially they are for the most part essentially unlike the British, German, and other peoples who came during the period prior to 1880, and, generally speaking they are actuated in coming by different ideals, for the old immigration came to be a part of the country, while the new, in large measure, comes with the intention of profiting, in a pecuniary way...and then returning to the old country.[26]

Thus the old immigration was comprised of "races" that came for settlement, were generally more intelligent, engaged in independent farming, and were easily integrated. The new immigrants had come temporarily, for pecuniary reasons, and were generally less integrated and integratable.

While the framing of the problem is relatively moderate, the Commission's report is laced with references to "racial" differences, and contains a full volume entitled *Dictionary of Races or Peoples*, which synthesized much of the information, if not the conclusions and concerns, of the eugenicists. There is considerable emphasis on physical types and differences, linked to the acceptability of different racial groups.[27]

The recommendations of the commission reflect its framing of the problem. First, the recommendations focus on which kinds of potential immigrants should be excluded from entering the United States: "...the physically and morally unfit". In addition, the United States should exclude those "...who have no intention to become American citizens..."

> As far as possible the aliens excluded should also be those who, by reason of their personal qualities or habits, would least readily be assimilated or would make the least desirable citizens.

> The following methods of restricting immigration have been suggested:
> (a) The exclusion of those unable to read or write in some language.
> (b) The limitation of the number of each race arriving during a given period of years.
> (c) The exclusion of unskilled laborers unaccompanied by wives or families....[28]

By the time of WWI, the problem of immigration had been clearly framed in terms of race thinking, and in terms of stark differences between what was termed the "old" and the "new" immigration from Europe. The census began publishing statistics on the racial origins of immigrants in 1899, and these categories were elaborated and solidified by the reports of the Immigration Commission a decade later. Although grounds for exclusion in the report focused on literacy, the recommendations also set the stage for quotas based on "race," conceptualized as nationality–including physical types that derive from race—rather than citizenship or place of birth. This framing of the issues, moreover, had become well established among virtually all political actors, and became integrated into political thinking through the actions and writing of government agencies.

Racial concerns made it possible for Republican restrictionists—based almost entirely in New England—to distance themselves from the business orientation of their party at the turn of the century, and finally to link their political agenda to that of Southern Democrats, who, with some reluctance, accepted the racialization of the new immigration. This definition of the problem of immigration from Europe did not become widespread beyond Congress until the turn of the century, when patrician concerns about race, supported by new areas of scientific enquiry, gave form to growing popular nativism.

From Racial Exclusion to Multicultural Integration

After the end of WWII pressure began to mount for the revision of the immigration process of the United States, mostly fueled by the executive branch and foreign policy concerns. President Truman ignored congressional opposition, as early as 1945, and issued executive orders admitting European refugees, a practice that would be continued by other presidents, who used the special "parole powers" of the McCarran-Walter Act of 1952. During the year prior to the 1952 election, Truman took the lead in a campaign to reframe the issue of immigration.[29] Indeed, the real contest over the next decade would be the struggle over how to define the question of immigration. What began as a "foreign policy necessity" of the 1950s ended up as question embedded in the civil rights struggle of the 1960s.

The Truman administration's answer to the pre-WWI Dillingham Commission appeared in the report of the President's Commission on Immigration and Naturalization: *Whom Shall We Welcome*.[30] "I suggested that the Congress create a representative commission of outstanding Americans to make a study of the basic assumptions of our immigration policy, the quota system and all that goes into it, the effect of our immigration and nationality laws, and the ways in which they can be brought into line with our national ideals and our foreign policy," Truman argued in his statement that established the commission. "The congress did not act upon these suggestions.... I am, therefore, appointing this Commission in the belief that its recommendations will enable the next Congress to consider the subject promptly and intelligently." None of the members of the commission were from the congress, and all of them were sympathetic to reform of the existing system.[31]

Incorporated into the report was President Truman's long veto message of the McCarran–Walter revision of the Immigration and Nationality Act (passed by Congress over his veto before the summer of 1952). The President emphasized, in this long message, two key objectives that he had been attempting to achieve since entering office: the abolition of racial or national barriers to naturalization; and the abolition of the existing system of quotas. The first he linked to his civil rights message of 1948, just prior to the Democratic Convention, in which he had urged Congress to pass strong civil rights legislation; the second to foreign policy needs.

> I have long urged that racial or national barriers to naturalization be abolished. This was one of the recommendations in my civil rights message to the Congress on February 2, 1948.... The basis of this quota system was false and unworthy in 1924. It is even worse now. At the present time this quota system keeps out the very people we want to bring in.... Today we have entered into an alliance, the North Atlantic Treaty, with Italy, Greece, and Turkey against one of the most terrible threats mankind has ever faced.... But, through this bill we say to their people: you are less worthy to come to this country than Englishmen or Irishmen....[32]

The hearings of the commission took place during the height of the presidential race of 1952, and the report was issued after the election, but before the inauguration President Eisenhower. In its key conclusions, the commission used testimony and new scientific evidence that it had gathered to argue against the eugenicist basis of the Dillingham Commission report, and offered arguments on race that were as applicable to questions of civil rights in the United States as to policy on immigration and naturalization. The Commission argued (bold text in the original):

- **The United States is the only major English-speaking country in the world which has written discrimination into its national immigration laws.... The basic racist assumption of the national origins system is scientifically invalid.... In summary, it would appear that there was no reliable evident that the new immigrants were inferior to old immigrants in terms of personal qualities.**[33]
- **The national origins system is based on false assumptions, unsubstantiated by physical science, history, sociology, economics, or anthropology.** The Commission found substantial evidence to corroborate the Senate Judiciary Committee statement that many of the considerations which lay behind the passage of the national origins quota law have now become of little significance. **The Commission recommends, therefore, that since**

the basis of the national origins system is gone, the system itself should go.[34]

- **American immigration policies have frustrated and handicapped the aims and programs of American foreign policy throughout the period since 1924.** The interference is acute today. The contradictions are sharper now in part because the 1952 law is more restrictive than before. **The major factor, however, is the new circumstance of American leadership in the world rivalry between democratic freedom and Communist tyranny. The major disruptive influence in our immigration law is the racial and national discrimination caused by the national origins system.**[35]

What was most evident from the commission report was that the weight of the scientific community had shifted against the intellectual foundations of the quota system. Those who supported the system could do so on pragmatic or political grounds, but could no longer ground their arguments in widely accepted scientific research. In the committee report for the McCarran-Walter Act—which had supported the continuation of quota system—the Senate Judiciary Committee no longer relied on the scientific basis behind the original act: "Many of the considerations which lay behind the passage of the national origins quota law have now become of little significance...." Instead, the committee relied on pragmatic considerations: "...quotas thus established by law are definite and automatically resist the pressures of special groups," and on the unsupported argument that quotas admitted immigrants "...considered to be more readily assimilable because of the similarity of their cultural background to those of the principal components of our population."[36]

Thus, both the research and the hearings of the commission framed not only the emerging case for immigration reform, but also presented a snapshot of an emerging expert consensus:

> The research and testimony gathered by the commission captured a growing expert support for more universalistic admissions standards. It also helped recast public discourse on immigration, drawing attention to the benefits of expanding immigration opportunities.

Opponents to reform were often reduced to simply referring to supporters of the commission report as "...well-meaning but misguided 'liberals' and the demagogues who auction the interests of America for alleged minority bloc votes."[37]

Political resistance to reform was strong (see below), but because immigration reform was increasingly embedded in the issue of civil rights, support and opposition to reform was increasingly molded by the way that the issue was defined in the 1952 commission report. By the 1960s, 40 years after the quota legislation was passed, the definition of the problem of immigration that had framed this legislation had disappeared. Moreover, the issue became increasingly linked to a multicultural understanding of American society. We were a "nation of nations," argued President Kennedy (quoting Walt Whitman), in what became a famous essay published by B'nai Brith in 1958.[38]

This framing of the immigration issue became dominant by the mid-1960s, but not unchallenged. At the national level, Americanization as a cultural requirement for American citizenship was replaced by an advocacy of permissive multiculturalism. In 1972, Congress voted $15 million to fund an ethnic heritage program, and history curricula were altered to include African Americans, Native Americans, as well as a variety of ethnic groups. Nevertheless, advocates for cultural requirements remained vocal. Some, such as Samuel P. Huntington, who had previously dismissed Americanization cultural arguments in favour of a civic culture, now embraced them with fervor .[39] It is striking that, given the long history of racism in the United States, the issue of immigration did not become racialized once again after 1965, even when it became apparent that the primary result of the new legislation was a rising wave of non-white immigration. Three commission reports, the first in 1978, the second in1981, the third in 1997, did reflect growing concerns about the about the impact of immigration after 1965, and helped to frame the issues of immigration. Although they accepted the general framework set in 1965, as well as the core policies that emerged out of that framework, they also focused on other issues that remain the key concerns of immigration policy today.

The Select Commission on Immigration and Refugee Policy (SCIRP) was created by Congress in 1978, largely in reaction to the refugee crisis after the end of the war in Vietnam, and growing popular opposition to immigration during a period of economic stagflation. The SCIRP, whose commissioners were weighted heavily in favor of those sympathetic to an open policy (the Commission was chaired by Father Theodore Hesburgh, president of Notre Dame University and former chair of the Civil Rights Commission), were charged with making legislative recommendations to what was broadly perceived as an immigration crisis that was a result of the unanticipated consequences of the Hart–Cellar Act of 1965: legal immigration was far higher than had been anticipated; illegal immigration was also growing; far larger numbers of immigrants were arriving from areas of the world that were also not anticipated by the legislation; there was a sharp growth in the admission of refugees in the late 1970s; and opposition to all forms of immigration was growing in public opinion.[40]

In addition, in the 1970s Congress had failed to pass legislation on employer sanctions for employers who knowingly employed illegal aliens, and then rejected proposals by President Carter in 1977 on enforcement and amnesty. The congressional supporters of immigration hoped that the commission would issue a strong defense of legal immigration, while finding some compromise way of dealing with illegal immigration.[41] Indeed, that is more or less what the SCIRP produced.

The final commission report in 1981strongly defended an open policy of immigration both as "a positive force" for the United States, and as in the national interest. It made a strong case that the existing system of legal immigration should be maintained: that the slots for family unification should be increased, and that there should be an increase of immigrants with no family ties but with special skills. Recommendations about illegal immigration, however, were quite different.

On one hand, the commission agreed—on the basis of existing studies—that there appeared to be 3.5 to 5 million illegal immigrants in the country, less than half of whom were from Mexico; that these immigrants were attracted by employment opportunities, and that they earned above the minimum wage; that they tended to depress the wages of those on the lowest end of the wage scale; that, while they paid payroll taxes, they tended not to benefit from social services.[42] On the other hand, the commission took a strong stand on the consequences of permitting illegal immigration to continue. Illegal immigration had to be curbed, not because of its social or economic consequences, but because "illegality breeds illegality."[43]

- This illegal flow, encouraged by employers who provide jobs, has created an underclass of workers who fear apprehension and deportation. Undocumented/illegal migrants, at the mercy of unscrupulous employers and coyotes who smuggle them across the border, cannot or will not avail themselves of the protection of U.S. laws. Not only do they suffer, but so too does U.S. society.
- Most serious is the fact that illegality breeds illegality. The presence of a substantial number of undocumented/illegal aliens in the United States has resulted not only in a disregard for immigration law but in the breaking of minimum wage and occupational safety laws, and statutes against smuggling as well. As long as undocumented migration flouts U.S. immigration law, its most devastating impact may be the disregard it breeds for other U.S. laws.
- The select commission holds the view that the existence of a large undocumented/illegal migrant population should not be tolerated.... Society is harmed every time an undocumented alien is afraid to testify as a witness in a legal proceeding, to report an illness that may constitute a public health hazard or disclose a violation of U.S. labor laws.

Therefore, the commission recommended stronger controls at the border and enforcement at the workplace, as well as a program of legalization for illegal immigrants then present in the United States. However, stronger controls were seen as a precondition for legalization: "...that legalization begin when appropriate enforcement mechanisms have been instituted." Tichenor argues that, during the two decades that followed, supporters of immigration would attempt to maintain this "decoupling," while restrictionists would attempt to fuse the two. In general, the supporters were successful.[44] By the early 1980s, the understanding of the immigration issue was that there should be broad acceptance of legal immigration, combined with a commitment to dealing with illegal immigration in some way.

A decade later, a broad movement to stem the tide of illegal immigration began to take shape. It was propelled largely by a reaction to illegal immigration in California, and fueled by the failure of the Immigration and Control Act of 1986 (IRCA). Indeed, the act ultimately authorized the legalization of about 3 million people, without legislating effective employer sanctions or successfully halting the arrival of increased numbers of illegal immigrants.

In a somewhat different form, for a short time, the politics of immigration in the United States would reproduce the racialized pattern of Europe, and, indeed, its own heritage from the early part of the century. Many of the elements seemed to be in place: a resounding Republican victory in the congressional elections of 1994; a political reaction in California in 1994 (the success of Proposition 187, that limited access of even the children of illegal immigrants to schools, hospitals and welfare services), led by the suddenly restrictionist governor, Pete Wilson, provided the cutting edge. An upsurge of negative public opinion that followed the political initiative and the beginning of a movement that resembled the eugenics movement of the turn of the century indicated both popular and intellectual support. Dorothy Nelkin wrote at the time that

> The immigration discourse of the mid-1990s is assuming an ominous but familiar tone. We hear, for example, that "natural" laws support "territorial integrity," that certain groups are "genetically inferior," that immutable biological differences underlie social distinctions, and that immigration will weaken the American "gene pool" and result in "race suicide." Once again, arguments about race relations in America (The Bell Curve) have been linked to immigration (Brimelow, Rushton, and the statements issued by FAIR).[45]

The Commission on Immigration Reform (The Jordan Commission) had been established by the 1990 Immigration Act, and it issued reports in 1994, 1995 and (a final report) in 1997. Its agenda was, therefore, strongly molded by this reaction of the 1990s. In addition, the composition of the commission was quite different from the SCIRP. In addition to supporters of immigration, the commissioners included strong restrictionists, and its reports represented a much broader compromise than the report in 1981. Although it recommended the maintenance of the principles of the existing system, it also recommended more important changes than had been previously addressed: a reduction of legal immigration, strengthened employer sanctions, and a well-supported program of "Americanization."

The commission supported the fundamental principles of the existing system of immigration control as follows:

The Commission supports the basic framework of current policy—family unification, employment-based immigration, and refugee admissions. We considered alternative frameworks, particularly a point system, but rejected these approaches.... At the same time, the Commission is convinced that our current immigration system must undergo major reform to ensure that admission continue to serve our national interests. Hence, the Commission recommends a significant redefinition of priorities and a reallocation of existing numbers to fulfill more effectively the objectives of our immigration policy.[46]

In its consideration of alternative systems of control of admission, the Commission argued that it decided to support the existing system because it "... relies on the judgment of American families and employers within a framework that protects U.S. workers from unfair competition."[47]

Nevertheless, the system set both standards of selection and the limits of acceptance within each category, and the Commission recommended that these standards be altered first by gradually reducing overall immigration by a third, to 550,000. The largest reduction (both absolute and relative) would be in family unification, and this would be achieved by giving strong preference to spouses and minor children of U.S. citizens. Secondary priority would be given to parents of U.S. citizens, but only if they are fully supported by those who sponsor them; and then to spouses, minor children and dependent children of legal permanent residents. The big losers under these proposals would be the parents of U.S. citizens and the families of legal permanent residents. The presumption was that the states would also gain if claims by immigrants to state services could also be reduced.[48]

Many of the Commission's recommendations with regard to illegal aliens would seem quite familiar today. It recommended strengthened border controls based on "Operation Hold the Line," (see chapter 9) then in its early stages, but also the use of new technologies to enhance security at airport ports of entry. However, then as now, the core of the problem was worksite enforcement, and the report implied that there was no political will for tough requirements. While the Commission did recommend an increase of inspection staff, the emphasis was placed on the employer initiative and responsibility to verify the legality of the workers that they hire through the use of the Social Security Administration data base. This, combined with enforcement of existing penalties was regarded as "the most promising option for eliminating fraud and reducing discrimination, while protecting individual privacy."[49]

Finally, the Commission placed considerable emphasis on new programs of "Americanization" as a way toward a more robust system of integration: "The Commission reiterated its call for the Americanization of new immigrants that is the cultivation of a shared commitment to the American values of liberty, democracy and equal opportunity." Although the Commission did not recommend specific programs, it did call on governments at all levels of the federal system to provide leadership and resources to educate immigrants in the English language and "core civic values."[50]

The Jordan Commission's hearings and reports spanned the years of the strongest negative reaction to immigration. By the time that its final report came out in 1997, the reaction to the reaction had begun to emerge. As a result, the general support for continued immigration was affirmed by the Clinton administration, but the more controversial recommendations for reductions in legal immigration—proposals that amounted to a reversal of the trend of immigration policy since 1965—were never implemented. Its recommendations on illegal immigration, however, which echoed those of the SCIRP, are still part of the immigration debate in 2007.

Thus, efforts over the years since 1965 to recast how the immigration issue is framed have met with only limited success. All efforts to limit legal immigration, as well as the general framework of legal immigration have been unsuccessful, and efforts to closely tie illegal immigration to the legal frame have been particularly unsuccessful. The failure to check the flow of illegal immigrants to the United States—indeed the doubling of the stock of illegal immigrants since 1996—has become the focus of immigration politics. Indeed, this failure has raised serious issues about the intentions of immigration policy, or the contradiction between intentions and implementation that this failure reveals.

The Political Process

Two Models

Daniel Tichenor has argued that two kinds of politics have driven open and expansionary immigration policies in the United States over time:

> ...one rooted in immigrant enfranchisement and competitive dem-
> ocratic elections, the other in the insulation of elite decisionmakers
> from mass publics. The first kind of politics shaped pro-immigration
> politics in the United States for much of the nineteenth century. The
> second kind animated new refugee admissions and passage of the land-
> mark Hart-Celler Act in the postwar era. Pro-immigration policies of
> the contemporary period have been fueled by *both* kinds of expansive
> politics.[51]

However, parallel to the politics of expansion has always been the politics of restriction and exclusion. At the same time that pro-immigration politics generated expansionary policies in the nineteenth century, restrictionist politics attempted to both constrain these policies and change them. At the same time that restrictionists succeeded in closing the front gates in

1921, expansionists succeeded in keeping the back gates open, and then slowly opened the front gates through refugee admissions and the Hart-Celler Act in 1965. Since 1965, pro-immigration politics have dominated the political agenda, but restrictionists have had some success as well.

Some scholars have related the insulation of elite decision-makers from public opinion and electoral pressures to patterns of client politics that have supported pro-immigration policies, even in a more hostile environment of public opinion (see ch. 1). They have also argued that "conditions of high salience," such as those related to competitive democratic elections, tend to be related to more restrictive patterns of policy because of the importance of hostile public opinion in the electoral arena.[52]

In fact, we have found that insulated elites and client politics in the United States have both promoted restriction (1890–1924) and more expansionary immigration policies (Western Hemisphere immigration after 1924, and Hart-Celler in 1965). Conditions of high salience have also supported restriction: the Know Nothings, Chinese exclusion, restrictionism after WWI, and some more recent reactions to immigration from the Western Hemisphere. They have also promoted pro-immigration policies, however: support for open immigration in some localities in the nineteenth century, and, more broadly since 1965.

The difference in outcomes is in the way that the immigration issue has been framed, the kinds of voters that have been mobilized on each side, and the kinds of mass publics from which elite decision-makers seek insulation. Thus, where there are high concentrations of immigrants, competitive democratic elections can generate support for pro-immigration policies only if immigrants are voters or are seen to be potential voters. In this case, decision-makers need little insulation from these mass publics to support expansionary policies. On the other hand, in these same districts, if policy-makers see voters reacting to immigrants as a challenge to identity, then, only by insulation from these voters would they be able to support pro-immigration policies.

The restrictionist policies of 1890–1965 were generated by the relatively autonomous decision-makers of the immigration committees of the Congress, but were also supported by strong anti-immigration majorities in each house, themselves supported by mass publics that favored restriction. As the immigrants of the pre-1921 period became voting citizens, the restrictionist positions of policy-makers became increasingly less tenable in electoral terms. Immigrants who became voters in big cities in large states became an important component of the Roosevelt presidential coalition, far more important than they had been between the Civil War and WWII (see below). Their interests also became increasingly important in Congress—but not among the key congressional actors who controlled the committee system.

Thus, restrictionists were able to keep the front door mostly closed because they were insulated from changing public opinion by the congressional committee system. With the policy shift in 1965, expansionary policies were then supported by the political patterns described by Tichenor.

At the same time, however, restrictionist forces were also animated by competitive democratic elections; but restrictionist policy-makers, lacking an important congressional committee base, were relegated to periphery at the state level.

Structural changes in the American political system have been important, moreover, in changing the balance of forces between the two patterns. The first change has been the way that federalism has influenced each pattern. The second has been the evolving role of the presidency. The third has been the evolution of the structure and forces within the congress.

The Balance of Federalism: Open Immigration and Restriction of Immigrants

The open immigration policies that were dominant until the 1870s were the product of a national political system in which immigration was embedded in larger considerations of expansion. Little legislation was passed by Congress to expand immigration, but few limits were placed in the way of executive action the encouraged the successive waves of immigration that supported American growth and expansion, at least until 1882. At the same time the national government was more or less insulated from the restrictionist forces that were becoming increasingly important at the state level. If federalism permitted and protected many of the worst discriminatory practices against immigrants that were initiated at the state level, it also protected the national government from these same forces.

Thus, open immigration was less the consequence of the fact that the United States was "a country of immigration" with broad support for growing immigration, and more a result of the complex politics of immigration that permitted the federal government to act in an expansionary manner, despite widespread electoral opposition that grew during the decades prior to the Civil War. Support for restriction increased significantly as immigration grew in the 1840s, and electoral support for the American ("Know Nothing") Party spread during the decade prior to the Civil War.

The Know Nothings—the name is presumed to derive from the secrecy of the early party organization, and the response that its members gave when they were asked about their membership— first gained significant support in New England, and came close to making a national breakthrough in 1855–1856. Indeed, by most electoral measures (support, elected representatives and expansion), it should be noted as the first successful anti-immigrant party in the Western world. One local predecessor of the Know Nothings in New York City elected a mayor and entire Common Council in 1837. In subsequent stages of development it expanded to all of New York State and New Jersey, then to Boston and Charleston, SC. Finally, in the 1850s the American Party was formed as a national party.

The success of their appeal was phenomenal, and in the state legislative elections of 1854 the new party carried Massachusetts, Delaware, and, in alliance with the Whigs, Pennsylvania. In Massachusetts, the governor and all state officers were Know-Nothings, as was the state senate and all but two of 378 members of the state house of representatives. In the fall election, about seventy-five party members were elected to Congress, and in the next year, major state offices in Rhode Island, New Hampshire, and Connecticut were won by nativists.[53]

Indeed, the party nominee for the presidency (former president Millard Fillmore) polled almost 25 percent of the vote in 1856. At the height of their influence (1855–1863), the Know Nothings had national representation in 17 (out of 33) states. (See table 10.1.)

In 1855–1857, the American Party was the third largest party in the House of Representatives, and was dominant in New England. Every representative from Massachusetts, Connecticut and New Hampshire was elected from the American Party. In all, about half the AP representatives in the House were from the Northeastern states. The other half were primarily from the Border States. In coalition with the Opposition Party, the AP was a component of the majority, and held the speakership of the House of Representatives, although it did take a record two months, and 133 ballots, before a speaker could be elected by plurality.

The Speaker, Nathaniel Banks of Massachusetts, embodied both the success and failure of the anti-immigrant movement. He linked nativism to antislavery, but with antislavery more dominant. By the elections of 1856, the entire AP delegation from Massachusetts had moved to the Republican Party, including Banks, as had the rest of the AP representatives from the Northeast. The movement into the Republican Party, and the subsequent collapse of the Know Nothings as a party, did not, however, end the commitment to nativism of many of those who passed

Table 10.1 "Know Nothing" representation in the U.S. Congress, 1855–1859

	The U.S. Senate		
	1855	*1857*	*1859*
Democrats	39	41	38
Whigs/Republicans	22	20	26
American Party	1	5	2
Total	62	66	66
	The U.S. House of Representatives		
Democrats	83	132	83
Whigs/Republicans	100	90	116
American Party	51	14	5
Others	0	1	34
Total	234	237	238

Sources: Kenneth C. Martis, *The Historical Atlas of United States Congressional Districts* (New York: Macmillan, 1982); Kenneth C. Martis, *The Historical Atlas of Political Parties in the United States* (New York: Macmillan, 1989).

through the American Party in New England. Banks, "...gave full vent to his Nativist inclinations" when he became governor of Massachusetts in 1858,[54] and identity-based nativism in the Republican party reemerged in Congress after the Civil War.

Given this significant electoral breakthrough at the national level, why were there no legislative traces of the movement? After all, the Know Nothings had broken through many of the constraints of the federal system, and achieved both local and widespread national support. If they were somewhat short of control of the only popularly elected legislative body, they certainly held strong influence during the four years before the war broke out. One explanation is the division of territorial interests under the federal system. In 1856, the House Committee on Foreign Affairs approved legislation that would have prohibited the entry of paupers and convicts, and initiated a program of what became known as "Americanization". Probably because of the regional opposition of southern representatives who were protecting states' rights against the central government (many of these were elected with the American Party label), the legislation proposed relatively little federal immigration control.[55]

A further explanation for Know Nothing failure is that a diverse coalition of political forces opposed to federal legislation in this area remained intact. In the end, even this very limited legislation failed to pass the House. An effective veto was maintained by the same coalition that would continue to keep the gates open for a few more decades:

> ...business-minded immigrationist Northerners, be they Whigs or already Republicans; Republicans and surviving Democrats seeking to court immigrant constituents; and Southerners...whose paramount objective was to forestall federal encroachment in the sphere of states' rights.[56]

Like all veto coalitions, however, it was defined more by what it did not want than what it would support. Business wanted to maintain cheap labor; Southerners wanted to maintain states' rights; and only the relatively few urban Democrats and Republics that depended on immigrant and ethnic votes actually supported open immigration as such. Thus, the importance of electoral considerations for the support of open immigration, either before the Civil War or after, has probably been exaggerated, and was far less important than considerations of cheap labor or states' rights.

Before the Civil War, the Know Nothings used electoral considerations to great advantage in building up support in the Northeast. After the war, the Democrats in the West were equally successful by using opposition to the Chinese to gain control of California. In both cases, success at the state level was resisted at the national level. As Zolberg has pointed out, however, the inability of the Know Nothings to effectuate restriction at the nation level should not diminish their success in various states, indeed the very states where immigrants were concentrated. This is equally true for the Democrats in California.[57] The federal system that limited the actions of the national government to restrict immigration, also granted considerable power to these states to restrict and oppress immigrants.

Finally, the dynamics of the federal system favored veto rather than change. There was no institutional organizer of policy. No regional interest was sufficiently strong to dominate policy-formation at the national level, and no national leader, including the president, was capable of mobilizing a majority in the Congress for serious immigration control. Before the Civil War, there was no political party that had a secure majority, nor were major interests organized nationally. Thus the most important outcome of the vast electoral sweep of the Know Nothings (aside from provoking Irish voters to vote in New England)[58] was to reemphasize the federal balance: the weakness of national policymaking for imposing immigration controls, and the importance of the states in dealing with immigration.

A New Policymaking System

The courts then radically altered the federal balance. The court decisions of 1875–1876 (see ch. 8) forced restrictionists at the state level to act at the national level. The formula implied in the report of the House Foreign Affairs Committee in 1856 was no longer applicable twenty years later. The issue of immigration had shifted to the national level, primarily as a result of court decisions, but also under pressure from electoral politics in the West. The issue of Chinese exclusion dominated the politics of the state of California, and the close popular votes in favor of the Republicans in the presidential elections of 1876 and 1880 greatly magnified the electoral priority in favor of exclusion for the Western Republicans. Thus, the object of regional initiatives shifted to Washington, and California took the lead both in promoting Chinese exclusion at the national level, and in constructing and mobilizing the coalitions in the Senate and the House that finally ensured its passage.[59]

The process began with the appointment of a Joint Congressional Special Committee to Investigate Chinese Immigration during the presidential race of 1876. The committee report was submitted in February 1877 by Senator Sargent of California, who was also honorary vice president of the Anti-Coolie Union of San Francisco. The process ended after the presidential election of 1880, after Congress reversed the veto of President Chester Arthur of the Chinese Exclusion Act; Arthur had justified his veto in terms of foreign policy considerations, but finally signed revised legislation that was harsher than the original.

Once immigration policy was forced to the national level, the dynamics of the federal system demanded positive coalition-building to overcome the veto-points of the system. This would prove to be a difficult and lengthy process. Nevertheless, the passage of the Chinese Exclusion Act in 1882 demonstrated that, given the proper framing of the issue (and given sufficient time), majorities in favor of immigration restriction and exclusion could be mobilized at the national level, even if the president opposed such legislation. A decade after the passage of the Chinese exclusion act, the same New England Republicans that bitterly opposed Chinese exclusion would use a similar approach to mobilize congressional support for control and exclusion of European immigrants.

This process was given form, and strength, by new institutional arrangements, beginning in the 1890s, that both reflected and accelerated the changing terms of the debate. The key innovation was the establishment by both houses of the Congress of standing committees to consider immigration legislation. Both committees were quickly captured by restrictionist interests, became the key organizers of the debate on restrictive legislation within Congress, and provided sustained legislative leadership that had been lacking until then.

It was these committees, with strong connections to the Immigration Restriction League, that not only produced the literacy legislation of 1896, but that also produced the considerable documentation and expert evidence that changed the terms of the immigration debate. With the Republicans in control of the Senate for almost the entire period between 1880 and 1913, and then again from 1919 until the election of Franklin Roosevelt, the Senate Committee on Immigration tended to take the lead during the early period (until about 1907), often supported by the House committee after 1897, when Republicans began to dominate the House as well. After 1907, the House Committee, under the control of representatives from the South and Far West, became more forceful, and, indeed, more radical in their approach than the Senate Committee.

During the 25 years between the end of the Civil War and 1890, with the exception of Chinese exclusion, three general, but relatively inconsequential pieces of legislation were passed. After the establishment of the Congressional committees in 1889, hardly a year passed without consideration of major legislation on immigration at the national level. Moreover, majorities in favor of immigration restriction became easier to mobilize more frequently. Restrictive legislation was passed in 1891, again in 1893, and literacy legislation was passed in 1896—then vetoed— then reproposed in 1898, passed by the Senate, but rejected by the House of Representatives.[60] By the time that the Dillingham Commission was established in 1907, a clear bi-partisan majority had emerged in both houses of congress in favor of immigration restriction, certainly in favor of legislation on literacy tests, which had become the benchmark indicator of restrictionism.

During the last decade of the nineteenth century, the leadership in the effort to restrict immigration passed from the West to the Northeast, and from a focus on Asian immigrants to a focus on immigrants arriving from Southern and Eastern Europe. Among the strongest opponents to restriction were legislators from the South, as well as business-oriented Republicans. Southern states hoped to stimulate economic expansion by recruiting large numbers of European immigrants. This effort was similar to the efforts of

French policy-makers before and after WWII. Therefore, it is not surprising that most Southern legislators generally opposed restrictive legislation.

This did not prevent literacy test legislation from passing both houses by substantial margins in 1896, strongly supported by legislators in the Senate and the House from the Northeast, states with growing immigrant populations. When the legislation was vetoed by President Cleveland, the failure to override his veto was due both to Southern opposition, and to opposition from the business wing of the Republican Party in the Senate.[61]

Sixteen years later, the racial framing of the immigration issue began to reap results in the South, as southern legislators adopted the eugenicist approach to justify the rejection of the new immigration, and became strong supporters of restriction. At the same time, there was evidence in congressional voting patterns that revealed increased opposition to restriction among legislators in states in the Northeast with growing immigrant populations. In the Senate (still indirectly elected), restrictionist votes in the Northeastern states, as measured by the votes to overturn the president's veto of the literacy bill, were overwhelming. In the House, however, voting patterns changed dramatically. Although Southern representatives shifted sharply toward restriction, those from the Northeast moved in the opposition direction (see table 10.2).

In each case, the movement both created and responded to electoral pressure—different kinds of electoral pressure. In the Northeast the shift was a response to immigrant enfranchisement, and the growing local importance of the immigrant vote Even as 14 of the 16 senators in the Northeast strongly supported restriction in 1913, less than a third of the elected representatives supported restriction (compared with almost 2/3 16 years before). In the South, the shift was related to a reaction against immigrants (and immigration) influenced by a surge of the racist-related identity movement mobilized by populism. In the Senate, 21 of the 22 senators supported restriction, as did 85 percent of the representatives (compared with less than a third sixteen years before). Majorities in both houses supported restriction, but different majorities than those that supported restriction in the earlier period.

This polarization represented a growing division within the Democratic Party that went well beyond the question of immigration restriction, and that would endure until the 1970s.

> When urban ethnics started voting in large numbers in the 1920s, they turned increasingly to the Democratic Party. The rise of urban power in the Democratic Party threatened the once dominant rural forces [overwhelmingly in the South], and urban-rural tensions increased and divided the Democrats. The battles in the 1920s may have represented the final grasp for power by rural Democrats.[62]

In 1897, there were about as many representatives from the South as there were from the Northeast, but this balance began to change by 1913, and

Table 10.2 The changing restrictionist majority in the House of Representative (Votes in the House of Representatives to overturn the presidential veto of Immigration Bills of 1896 and 1912 (Literacy Bills); in favor of Immigration Restriction Bills of 1920 and 1924 in 11 Southern states, 8 states in the Northeast, and California)

	1897							
	Yes Restrict[a]	%	No	%	Abstain	%	Total	%
South	28	31%	22	24.4%	40	44.4%	90	100%
NE	60	65%	9	10%	24	26%	93	100%
CA	4	57.1%	1	14.3%	2	28.6%	7	100%
Total	195	54.9%	137	38.6%	123	34.6%	355	100%

	1913							
	Yes Restrict[a]	%	No	%	Abstain	%	Total	%
South	80	85%	8	8.5%	6	6.4%	94	100%
NE	32	32%	45	45%	23	23%	100	100%
CA	5	62.5%	2	25%	1	12.5%	8	100%
Total	213	56.2%	186	49%	52	13.7%	379	100%

Note:
a Yes is a vote in favor of immigration restriction.

Source: All results are from the Congressional Record of the United States, 1897 and 1913 (see below).

	1920							
	Yes: Restrict[a]	%	No	%	Abstain	%	Total	%
South	89	85.6%	1	1%	14	13.5%	104	100%
NE	32	31.4%	28	27.5%	42	41.2%	102	100%
CA	9	81.8%	0	0%	2	18.2%	11	100%
Total	296	68.7%	42	9.7%	93	21.6%	431	100%

	1924							
	Yes: Restrict[a]	%	No	%	Abstain	%	Total	%
South	96	92.3%	0	0%	8	7.7%	104	100%
NE	44	37.6%	56	47.9%	17	14.5 %	117	100%
CA	9	81.8%	0	0%	2	18.2%	11	100%
Total	323	74.8%	71	16.4%	38	8.8%	432	100%

Note:
a Yes is a vote in favor of immigration restriction.

Sources: Congressional Record of the United States, March 3, 1897, pp. 2946–2947; February 18, 1913, p. 3429; December 13, 1920, p 286; April 12, 1924, pp. 6257–6258.

would change even more after immigration restriction was passed in 1924. Nevertheless, the number of representative who resisted restriction for electoral reasons were a clear minority in the House of Representatives, but a growing force within the Democratic Party.

Until 1917, however, the dynamics of the federal system effectively prevented the enactment of restrictive legislation. Presidents since the administration of Rutherford B. Hayes (1877–1881), had been regularly vetoing restrictionist legislation, generally successfully. Vetoes were sometimes justified on the grounds of foreign policy (as with Chinese exclusion), but just as often on other grounds, particularly at the beginning of the twentieth century.

Increasingly, the dynamics of presidential politics worked against the efforts by congress time and time again. If senators from the Northeast were insulated from the electoral influence of their growing immigrant populations, presidents were not. Thus, Theodore Roosevelt had indicated support for the literacy legislation in his first annual message to Congress, and Woodrow Wilson seemed quite sympathetic to the eugenics perspective in a history text that he had written in 1902. Nevertheless, Roosevelt, Taft and Wilson either vetoed or refused to support literacy legislation, and, in their presidential campaigns sought the support of ethnic voters opposed to restriction.[63]

Moreover, presidential vetoes were supported by a House of Representatives that was centrally controlled by strong party interests—generally Republican. At least until 1910, Republican leadership—influenced by both ethnic lobbies and traditional Republican business interests—prevented literacy legislation from reaching the floor of the House. By 1910, (Republican) Speaker Cannon was opposed by both a growing caucus of Southern Democrats, as well as progressive Republicans. Progressive Republicans, armed with "scientific" evidence to support restrictionist measures, finally used Cannon's manipulations to block the literacy legislation as an excuse to ally with the Democrats to seize control of the House and alter the rules. The new rules, with their emphasis on seniority for committee chairs, redistributed power to committee chairs in other ways as well, and maximized the power of the Immigration Committee, now firmly in control of restrictionists from both parties.

The override of Wilson's final veto of the literacy test in 1917 indicated the beginning of the collapse of resistance to restriction, certainly within the Congress, but more importantly by the President. It had taken 20 years after the emergence of restrictionist majorities in both houses of Congress for the first substantial piece of restrictionist legislation to be passed. The coalition that supported restriction then consolidated after WWI, despite the continued development of electoral influence of ethnic voters, and the growth in the number of representatives and senators who were sensitive to this influence.

The System Changes: The Front Door and the Back Door

In time, a clear majority in favor of reform would emerge from this process, but, just as the veto points in the federal system frustrated the restrictionist majorities, reform majorities would be stymied by the institutionalized power of the restrictionists. Beginning with Franklin Roosevelt, presidents courted immigrant voters and their children once again, and favored reform of the quota system that had gone into effect just prior to Roosevelt's election. Indeed, the Roosevelt coalition, which served to realign the party balance in favor of the Democrats for thirty years, was built on the entry of immigrants and their children into the electorate, and their mobilization primarily by the Democrats.[64] Therefore, Congressional minorities favorable to immigration reform continued to grow, particularly among Democratic representatives from urban areas where new immigrant voters and their children were concentrated.

Their weight was important for the passage of displaced persons legislation in 1948 and 1950, but on immigration reform they were blocked by the restrictionist Southern bloc within their own party, who were allied with Democratic isolationists (such as McCarran of Nevada and Walter of Pennsylvania) and Northern Republican conservative restrictionists. The southerners exacted conservative opposition to civil rights legislation in return for *their* opposition to social reform (health care for example) and support for anticommunism. For two decades after the end of the war, this conservative coalition succeeded in outmaneuvering their opponents in congress.[65]

By maintaining control of the immigration subcommittees of both houses during the post-war period (in 1947, Congress replaced the Immigration and Naturalization Committees with subcommittees within the Judiciary committees of both houses), restrictionists were able to shape proposals on immigration reform, and often prevented them from ever reaching the floor of congress. While restrictionist interests were more or less safe in the hands of the parent committee in the Senate during the first two decades after the war, with Pat McCarran of Nevada and James Eastland of Mississippi in control for most of this period, the House became somewhat less secure when Emmanuel Celler became chair in 1949, but he was effectively countered by his Democratic colleague, Francis Walter, who chaired the Immigration sub-committee.

The immigration sub-committees continued to be controlled by supporters of restriction long after there were no majorities in congress to back them up. The restrictionist South would come to dominate the process through the relevant congressional committees. The Northeast and California had become increasingly favorable to reform, but the it was not until the 1960s that the conservative coalition could be overcome when Celler and Hart detached reform from anticommunism, and successfully linked it to civil rights.[66]

It is important to note that the political party affiliation of representatives was less relevant than their region for understanding support (as

well as shifting support) for restrictive or expansionary immigration policy, even if partisanship within regions did become important during
the cold war. In 1924 (the vote in favor of Johnson-Reed quota act), in
states with large immigrant populations, such as New York, New Jersey
and Massachusetts, a larger proportion of Republicans than Democrats
supported immigration restriction, but they were a still a minority of
Republican representatives. In California, all of the Democratic representatives supported restriction, and so did every Democratic representative
in the "solid" Democratic South.

The institutional actors in the political process remained the same after
1924, but their roles changed radically. Restrictionist committees now
became the powerful veto-points rather than the initiators of change. The
President's role now changed from resistance to leadership in favor of
reform; and major (ethnic) interest groups now became the advocates of
change. Even as the growing electoral weight of ethnic voters tended to
favor reform, the structural context favored the status quo. No reform legislation reached the floor of the Congress until after the end of WWII.

On the other hand, there were structural changes that did favor reform.
The most important of these was the growing power of the presidency,
and the ability of the president to effectuate change without legislation.
In addition, though less important, was the diminished insulation of the
Senate and senators (after the seventeenth amendment became operational
in stages after WWI). Senators from such states as Massachusetts, New
York and Pennsylvania could no long avoid electoral responsibility for
their votes in favor of immigration restriction.

After WWII, the policy framework set in place in 1924 endured. The
political process had changed substantially, however. A substantial majority
in each house of Congress still supported the principles of the quota system, but there were changes around the edges that cumulatively resulted
in important expansionary changes. The Displaced Persons Acts of 1948
and 1950 were conservative measures, that represented far less than what
the president wanted (he referred to the 1948 legislation as "a pattern of
discrimination and intolerance"). Nevertheless, 400,000 refugees entered
under this legislation. President Eisenhower fought hard for the Refugee
Relief Act of 1953 that granted 209,000 special visas (nonquota) to refugees from Europe.

The McCarran-Walter Act was (unsuccessfully) vetoed by President
Truman in 1952. Nevertheless, even this conservative legislation contained provisions that expanded immigration in small ways. It abolished
racial restrictions imposed on the naturalization of Asians immigrants, and
created a preference system within the national quotas. Under McCarran-
Walter, the president was given "parole powers" to admit individuals to
the United States in an emergency situation. President Eisenhower first
used these powers to admit over 30,000 Hungarian refugees in 1956. This
precedent would be used by future presidents to admit thousands more.

As we indicated in chapter 9, under both presidential and congressional actions even before the end of WWII, nonquota exemptions had been

increased first in response to the war and then to foreign policy requirements, and in response to pressures from agribusiness for more labor. In
addition, selected groups of refugees from Europe gained special entry into
the United States during the years after the war. As the rule changes accumulated after 1945, the number of nonquota entries increased dramatically.
Table 9.1 indicates that, even as quota entries from Europe increased during the 1950s, the proportion of nonquota entries increased even more.

The effectiveness of presidential leadership cannot be seen in broad immigration reform. It can be seen in the broadening exceptions to the quota
rules, however. As we noted in chapters 8 and 9, by 1963, quota entries
from Europe represented only a third of immigrant entries to the United
States. A relatively large proportion of nonquota entries were related to the
cold war, but this way of framing the questions of entry had its downside as
well. It also resulted in broader criteria for exclusion, and accentuated party
differences. We can see this in the vote in June 1952 to override the veto
of the McCarranWalter Act. The vote accentuated partisan differences on
this immigration legislation particularly in regions where they had been
narrowing—in New England and the West (California in particular). In
these key regions, where there were concentrations of ethnic voters, the
anticommunist/national security framing of the legislation polarized the
vote even more than in 1924. (See table 10.3.)

Although the accumulated exemptions resulted in increased nonquota
immigration from Central Europe, and Germany and Britain provided the
largest number of quota immigrants during the decade of the 1950s, the
number of nonquota immigrants from Mexico more than doubled. In 1963,
the census reports that 55,000 legal immigrants entered from Mexico, slightly
more than the number that entered from Canada, and twice the number from
either German or Britain.[67] Under the 1924 legislation, Mexican immigration was limited only by literacy. Aliens with a minimum residency of ten
years in the Western Hemisphere could enter the United States as nonquota

Table 10.3 Votes in the House of Representatives to override the veto of President Truman of the
McCarran-Walter Act in 11 Southern states, 8 states in the Northeast, and California in 1952

	Yes Restrict	%	No	%	Abstain	%	Total	%
South-Dem	84	79.2%	2	1.9%	20	18.9%	106	100%
Rep	—	—	—	—	—	—	—	—
NE-Dems	2	4.4%	41	91.1%	2	4.4%	45	100%
Rep	45	69.2%	13	20.0%	7	10.8%	65	100%
NE Total	47	42.7%	54	49.0%	9	8.2%	110	100%
CA-Dems	1	9.1%	9	81.8%	1	9.1%	11	100%
Rep	12	100%	0	0.0%	0	0.0%	12	100%
CA Total	13	56.5%	9	39.1%	1	4.3%	23	100%
Total	278	64.7%	112	26.0%	40	9.3%	430	100%

Source: Congressional Record of the United States, June 26, 1952, pp. 8225–8226.

immigrants—a provision meant to restrict the entry of Europeans through the "back door," but not Latin Americans (or Canadians).

In fact, immigration from the Western Hemisphere was linked to a political process that was quite different from the process that governed immigration from Europe (see ch. 9). This process was supported by many of the same legislators and committee chairs in the South and West who provided the core of opposition to reform of the quota system. Generally insulated from electoral reaction, this client process had the support of agribusiness and employers of low-skilled labor. In 1934, the AFL proposed legislation to establish a quota for Mexican immigrants, but the proposals were quickly rejected by the immigration committees. After the war, the AFL-CIO unsuccessfully opposed the Bracero Program, which continued for another 20 years, until 1964.[68] By the end of the century Mexico became the single largest source of immigrants to the United States. During the decade of the 1960s, 14 percent of immigrants came from Mexico. This increased to 14.3 percent the following decade, 22.8 percent during the decade of the 1980s, and 24.7 percent during the decade of the 1990s.[69] Of course the number of undocumented aliens from Mexico also increased (see ch. 9).

The role of the back-door system is also evident in the pattern of cycles of enforcement described in chapter 9. Each cycle usually begins, either because the president would like to create pressure for related legislation, (such as Eisenhower's "Operation Wetback" support for employer sanctions in 1954,) or in reaction to expanding local movements in opposition to immigration, (such as Clinton's reaction "Operation Hold the Line" to the Proposition 187 movement in California in 1993). It may also be an attempt to pressure Congress to pass relatively pro-immigrant legislation, such as the Bush enforcement cycle that began in 2006. As we have seen in chapter 9, each cycle generally ends with diminished enforcement, as the agribusiness lobby—with the support of state governments—either gains additional benefits (as in the Eisenhower cycle), or gains relief (as it seems is happening in the Bush cycle).

In fact, it may be more useful to understand these cycles as an attempt to expand the scope of politics (or what Schattschneider call "the scope of conflict")[70] beyond the control of the understandings of insulated client politics, or to challenge (or appear to challenge) the constraints imposed by the agribusiness "iron triangle". By "going public," Eisenhower supported stronger employer sanctions, Clinton put California agribusiness on notice, and Bush challenged the congressional wing of the agribusiness of the iron triangle to support his proposals for immigration reform.

Thus, although the Hart-Celler Act and subsequent legislation appeared to have ended the policy differences between the two systems, the differences in political process appear to remain important. What did break down after 1965 was the myth that immigration from Mexico and Latin America was what Daniel Tichenor called "the returnable labor force,"[71] and that immigration from other parts of the world was for settlement.

The New System

By 1965, as immigration reform was framed once again in terms of civil rights, majorities emerged in both houses that supported immigration policy reform. This emergence was aided considerably by the large Democratic sweep in the elections of 1964. The Democrats gained 36 seats; the gains were among party supporters of civil rights and social reform, and the losses were among the members of the conservative coalition. Nevertheless, the primary impediment to revision of the immigration system was opposition from the congressional committees that still controlled the legislation.

The key to the success of reform was presidential leadership. President Johnson made the Hart-Celler bill a priority, and backed his decision up with impressive skill. Increasingly, what held the reformers together was fundamental opposition to the racial and discriminatory basis of the quota system, and support for a new system that was more consistent with emerging values. Public opinion never favored legislation that would increase immigration, but it did increasingly favor proposals for civil rights legislation. It was the persistent linkage between the two by liberal Democrats that finally convinced President Johnson to place immigration reform high on his legislative agenda in 1964, and this priority was nailed down by the Democratic electoral sweep in November, 1964.

With tremendous energy, President Johnson applied pressure to the Southern chairman of the Senate Immigration sub-committee, James Eastland. Eastland agreed to hand over control of the sub-committee temporarily to Senator Ted Kennedy, who then put the legislation to a vote. Eastland then voted against the immigration proposal, which nevertheless passed. In the House, the leadership agreed to expand the membership of the sub-committee, to prevent the chair, Michael Feighan of Ohio, from bottling up the legislation. Feighan, reflecting on a tough 1964 primary fight in a district with a significant immigrant population, insisted in 1965 that he had supported reform for some time.[72] The final vote was overwhelmingly favorable in both houses. In the key regions of ethnic concentration, the Northeast, the vote in the House was unanimous; in California, three Republicans opposed the legislation, but a majority voted in support. (See table 10.4.)

Very quickly, immigration from Europe, and even Asia, became relatively uncontroversial, indeed unchallenged. One indication of this was that the politics of European and Asian immigration rapidly became client politics, where issues were settled in the context of a policy community, hardly challenged on the floor of congress. On the other hand, changes in immigration law after 1965 also responded to perceived electoral pressures. What Tichenor dubbed "reproductive mechanisms" of expansive admission policy gradually took hold.

As more immigrants were admitted after 1965, particularly after they gained citizenship and the right to vote, they became better organized and exploited their local political influence. While local influence was

Table 10.4   The isolation of the restrictionist minority (Vote in the House of Representatives in favor of/opposed to Hart–Celler in 1965 in 11 Southern states, 8 states in the Northeast, and California)

	1965							
	Yes	%	No: Restrict	%	Abstain	%	Total	%
South	26	27.4%	68	64.2%	12	11.3%	106	100%
NE	109	93.2%	0	0%	8	6.8 %	117	100%
CA	33	84.6%	3	7.7%	3	7.7%	39	100%
Total	318	73.6%	95	22%	19	4.4%	432	100%

Note: No is a vote in favor of restriction.

Source: Congressional Record of the United States, August 25, 1965, pp. 21820–21821.

limited before 1924, it became more widespread after 1965. For this reason, the importance of ethnic voting no longer depended on the strength of national political parties, or on the dynamics of presidential politics, as it did before 1924. Thus, while this pattern of influence applied mostly to presidential politics before 1924, it applied broadly to congressional politics as well after 1965. Moreover, while these dynamics applied to European immigration before 1924, after 1965 they applied increasingly to immigration from Latin America. (See below.)

The back door was hardly considered in the debates on the Hart–Celler bill. Nevertheless, the differences between the two sources of immigration were breaking down even before the legislation was passed. By the early 1960s, at more than 40,000, legal immigration from Mexico was the largest single source of immigration for settlement (and has remained so) to the United States, and the numbers grew by 400 percent by 2000.[73] Therefore, just as the "temporary" and "guest" workers from Turkey and North Africa in Europe decided to stay, the "returnable labor force" from Mexico made the same decision. What made President Bush's proposal for a new contract labor program less credible in 2006 than previous programs had been was this change in settlement patterns.

At the same time, as we have seen, given the attractions of the American labor market, the population of undocumented aliens also began to accelerate to its present levels. In fact, it now appears that the same political dynamics that have been reinforced by legal immigrant settlement, have also contributed to the growth of undocumented immigration. Businesses that profit from illegal immigration have been a powerful force for limiting cycles of enforcement, but support for enforcement is also limited by the rising electoral power of Mexican immigrants who are legally settled.

The Electoral Factor

The United States is quite different from either France or Britain both with regard to the political geography of immigration, and with regard to the relationship between political geography and policy outcomes. One aspect of this is quite familiar, the importance of immigrant populations for presidential politics. In 1990, only six states (California, New York, Florida, Texas, New Jersey, and Illinois, in that order) accounted for almost three-quarters of the foreign-born population in the United States, (with California and New York alone accounting for almost half). Politically, immigrant populations in these states gained considerable importance—or at least potential importance—during the following decade because of the importance of these states in presidential elections.

Moreover, in each of these states, congressional districts (CDs) with 10 percent or more of the populations born abroad accounted for half or more of the CDs by 2000. Thus, with two exceptions, every CD in California had a population born abroad greater than 10 percent, as did two-thirds of those in New York, and more than half in Texas. In each state, the local political dilemma was how do deal with the question of immigration and immigrants.

One option was presented in California in 1994, where a sustained effort was made to mobilize growing negative public opinion against undocumented immigrants. In an environment of high immigration pressure and rising local unemployment, Proposition 187—that would limit access of these immigrants and their families to state services—qualified for the 1994 ballot, supported by Republican Governor Pete Wilson (who had previously supported immigration from Mexico). Wilson was reelected and the initiative passed in a campaign that grew increasingly anti-immigrant in general as it wore on. During the same time-period, both Democratic senators from California introduced immigration control legislation in the U.S. Senate. During the next two years, President Clinton toughened the patrols along the Mexican border, supported legislation that restricted the rights of legal aliens, and established the Commission on Immigration Reform, the Jordan Commission, which quickly recommended a reduction in annual immigration limits. Finally, Pat Buchanan became the most prominent political leader in favor of immigration restriction after his Republican primary victory in the New Hampshire presidential primary in 1996. Thus the California conflagration spread quickly to national politics.

A second option, however, was presented in other states with high immigrant concentration, an electoral option that saw immigrants as a political resource, and that gave priority to the mobilization of potential immigrant voters. The politics of immigration in both France and Britain was built around the mobilization of sentiment against immigrants. However, the other impact of immigration is the potential of citizenship, its impact on the distribution of votes among political parties, and the speed with which this impact is felt.

We have noted that Kristi Andersen demonstrates that the party realignment that took place in the United States between 1928 and 1936 was essentially related to a new electorate of immigrants and their children voting for the first time in large cities in the United States, rather than voters switching from the Republican to the Democratic Party. More recently, in areas of high immigration, where immigrants are voters or are perceived as voters or potential voters, the electoral pressure has increasingly moved political elites toward a more favorable position on immigration. This dynamic appears to have taken hold in the United States, first in localities like New York and California, and more recently at the national level.[74]

A decade after Proposition 187, it was clear that the impact in California was to mobilize new immigrant voters by the Democratic Party. Republican Pete Wilson lost his second race for governor, and Orange County, long a conservative Republican bastion, became increasingly competitive, thanks to the incorporation of Latin American immigrants and their children into the electorate.[75]

It is in this context that the president decided to court the Latino and prospective Latino vote. Existing studies show that Latinos (with the exception of Cubans) are strongly Democratic in orientation, and become more so with increasing education and tenure in the United States. Nevertheless, as Republican governor of Texas, President George W. Bush had some success in attracting Latino voters, and the president seemed to feel that not to make this effort would be to surrender the electoral future to the Democrats. Indeed, this gamble had some payoff in the 2004 presidential election.[76]

At least some of this shift in orientation can be attributed to the different kind of political geography of immigration in the United States as compared to Europe. Although concentrations of immigrant populations are limited to certain areas of the country, these areas are also far more widespread than in Europe. (See table 10.5.) More than a third of the states (35%)[77] and more than a third of the congressional districts (35%) in 2000 had immigrant populations of 10 percent or more. This distribution of CDs with a high proportion of immigrants is far greater than in France or Britain (about twice as great), and provides a reasonable measure of the potential electoral gains and the dangers of ignoring this population.

Although these gains can be particularly important for the Democrats, since two-thirds of these congressional districts (CDs) have Democratic

Table 10.5 U.S. Congressional Districts 10 percent + born outside of the United States (2000) after congressional elections of 1998

	New York/CA	%	Remainder of United States	%	Total Number
Republican CDs (50%+ 1998)	21	38.2%	34	61.8%	55
Democratic CDs (50%+ 1998)	48	50%	48	50%	96
Total	69	45.7%	82	54.3%	151(34.7% of CDs)

Note: CDs= 435.

Source: U.S. Bureau of the Census, *Congressional District Data Book.*

representation, their importance is also quite real for the Republicans who represent the other third. With this number of CDs at stake, neither party can afford to ignore the electoral potential of immigrant populations. Thus, compared to France and Britain, the electoral stakes are far more important in the United States. While the mobilization of immigrant citizens and ethnic voters has become central to American party competition at the national level, it has been marginal and episodic in France and Britain.

Therefore, the electoral stakes in the United States of such questions as illegal immigration and border control can be high. However, when such issues become politically salient, the electoral consequences can be both the mobilization of an anti-immigration electorate, as well as an immigrant electorate favorable to more open immigration policies, as the struggle over Proposition 187 demonstrates. In 2006 and 2007, the Bush administration attempted to balance these consequences, by offering immigration legislation that would appear to be favorable to immigrant interests, while the Department of Homeland Security initiated a cycle of enforcement.

The early primary campaign for the presidency also demonstrated the challenge of electoral consequences. On one hand, Republican candidates in particular have taken a harsh stand on illegal immigration, in an attempt to play to the Republican-Right electorate that may determine their fate in the early primaries. On the other hand, numerous Republican strategists have warned about the price they will have to ultimately pay in the general election:

> Michael Gerson, a former speech-writer for President Bush wrote... that the electoral math made it shortsighted for the Republicans to use immigration as a "weapon." "At least five swing states that Bush carried in 2004 are rich in Hispanic voters—Arizona, New Mexico, Nevada, Colorado and Florida," he said... A substantial shift of Hispanic voters toward the Democrats in these states could make the national political map unwinnable for Republicans.[78]

The Role of the States

Related to the national process of policy formation, policy development at the state level remains important. When the federal government has found it difficult to act on questions of illegal immigration, both because the stakes are so high, and because the veto points are so numerous, state governments have been increasingly acting either exclude or protect these same illegal immigrants.

On one hand, there is evidence that restrictive legislation as the state level has diminished in importance, and has been limited by the courts. Over the last two decades the six states with the highest concentrations of immigrant populations have generally reduced the citizenship requirements for dozens of occupations, many of which had been imposed since the nineteenth century. Other requirements have been poorly enforced.

> Our data show that the number and range of citizenship requirements have declined dramatically. These changes are largely in response to federal court rulings and the legal opinions of state attorneys general that anticipate court oversight.[79]

Many states have acted as a result of limits imposed by judicial decisions in these areas. However, in other areas where the law continues to impose limits on the political activities of immigrants, states have broadly interpreted the limits of such laws.

The states have also remained important initiators of policy. In 1921–1922 the vast majority of the states had implemented laws dealing with Americanization.[80] Initiatives appear to have diminished after that. In 2006–2007, however, there was a major increase of state initiatives, largely in reaction to the failure of congressional action. The National Conference of State Legislatures reported that 1404 proposals dealing with immigration had been considered by August 2007, more than twice the number in 2006, and 170 laws had been passed in 41 states. Some states have passed legislation that would ease the passage to citizenship of legal residents; while others have sought to constrain and define those who could help and advise immigrants in the process of naturalization.

In 2006 California voted to provide free naturalization services, and Vermont required courts to advise defendants that they could they could be denied citizenship or be deported if they pled guilty to a criminal offense. Kansas, Maine, and Tennessee, on the other hand, voted to allow only immigration lawyers who have passed the bar to give legal advice to immigrants; notary-publics in particular (more available in immigrant communities) are prohibited from giving such advice.[81] Indeed, this is part of a more general pattern of state activism in various aspects of policymaking that affects immigrants.

Twenty-six states have enacted laws that have dealt with questions of identity cards and licenses of various kinds. Many of the new laws were meant to strengthen requirements for drivers licenses and require valid identity papers for state services. However, there was evidence of a growing rebellion among the states in opposition to the federal Real ID Act. As of this writing, Maine, Georgia, Montana, New Mexico, Washington, Wyoming, and Vermont have either passed or are considering actions that would resist the requirements for a federally standardized driver's license that would be used to confirm identity. Opposition seems to reflect both resistance to what would amount to a national ID card, as well as the considerable expense of such cards for the states.[82]

As in the past, state initiatives have been coordinated through intergovernmental networks, and are an integral part of the policymaking process.[83] They are an intergovernmental lobby for promoting federal legislation, but also for changing and resisting it. State legislatures, are often far more sensitive to the costs of immigration than the federal government, in part because they are required to bear the costs imposed by federal law. This is particularly true in the area in which the states play the most critical role—in shaping the settlement and incorporation of immigrants.

Conclusion

The politics of immigration in the United States has changed dramatically during the past century. Framed in terms of population policy by the federal government until after the Civil War, immigration policy remained open and relatively expansive until state reactions against Chinese immigration forced a change of course at the national level that eventually had an impact on European immigration as well. The politics of identity dominated the policy process until after WWII.

The growing electoral importance of the great wave of immigrants of the early twentieth century first became evident in the 1930s. The weight of this electorate, in turn, gradually forced not only a change of immigration policy, but also altered the process through which policy was developed. The tension between an identity frame and an electoral frame gave way to a domination of the latter—but not entirely. It is primarily in this way that we can understand why immigration from Europe at the beginning of the twentieth century provoked policies of exclusion, while immigration from Asia and Latin America at the end of century did not alter the expansionist system put into place in 1965.

What changed most was both the framing of the immigration question and the policy process in congress. The presidency had always been more favorable to open and expansionist immigration policies for two reasons: first because presidents were more aware of and sensitive to the implications for foreign relations; second because, since the end of the nineteenth century, big states with large urban areas had been at the core of the president's electoral constituency. It was only when the relative power of the presidency and the executive increased, however, that the president could be the focal point for leadership in policy formation, and not simply a veto-point.

CHAPTER ELEVEN

Conclusion

Western Europe and the United States have both become "countries" of immigration during the past 30 years. With no end in sight, moreover, these trends are likely to continue into the foreseeable future. So, the question is not whether immigration will continue, but how that immigration will be controlled. For France and Britain, the result has been the longest sustained wave of immigration in their history, and Britain has now become a country of net immigration for the first time in its modern history. The wave of immigration since 1965 has reinforced and given new meaning to the idea of the United States as a country of immigrants.

However, as we have seen, the broad policy objectives of France, Britain, and the United States have been quite different during the past 40 years. French policy was to reduce immigration to more or less "zero"; British policy was to reduce sharply the number of immigrants entering the United Kingdom from New Commonwealth countries in Asia and the Caribbean. By contrast, American policy was to permit, even promote, immigration based on criteria of family unification, labor needs, and diversity. In fact, each of these policy objectives more or less failed. Immigration into France has continued at levels lower than before 1973, but at levels far higher than policy would indicate. Immigration into Britain has gradually increased, in general, and from New Commonwealth countries in particular. Policy in the United States has supported and promoted high levels of immigration, but record numbers of undocumented immigrants have either entered or remained in the country.

Is Immigration Out of Control?

Yet the preceding analysis does not support the conclusion that immigration is "out of control," (in the European cases) or that immigration policy is ineffective (in the American case). I have argued in various ways throughout this volume that, regardless of the broad, stated policy objectives of governments, the actual policies on immigration in place reflect the complexities of the democratic political process, complexities that are hardly new, and that do not necessarily reflect diminished state sovereignty or loss of control.

By far, the largest single category of immigrants entering France and the United States each year is admitted under some form of family unification (see table 1.1C). For France, these entries are a result of court decisions, but are shaped by public policy. For the United States, family unification is a result of public policy. Recently, French governments have referred to this category of immigration as "immigration subie," suffered immigration that is not chosen by policy decisions. However, this is not entirely plausible for two reasons: first, governments have had considerable discretion in how they apply the court mandates, discretion that has been written into legislation over the past 20 years; second, it is useful to compare the French result with that of Britain. In Britain, the relatively high level of labor compared to family immigration, appears to be a result of policy decisions made by the Blair government, which encouraged labor immigration, but also imposed stringent rules for family unification. In addition, it is useful to keep in mind that "embedded liberalism" represented by court decisions is not new, and is part of the democratic process.

In the American case, the "out of control" southern border is a result of a two-tiered immigration policy that has existed since the implementation of the Johnson-Reed Act in the 1930s.[1] Only after 1965 were the same criteria applied to the Western Hemisphere as were applied to the rest of the world. Until then, as we have seen, the labor requirements of agribusiness were tied to easy access of migration across the southern border. Business resistance to the imposition of serious controls of movement from Mexico after 1965 resulted in politically motivated cycles of enforcement that have continued into the twenty-first century. However, the number of resident undocumented immigrants has grown dramatically since the 1980s, as workers attracted by the open labor market in the United States have decided to stay, and have become an integral part of regional economies.

In short, illegal immigration is not out of control; enforcement, however, is caught in the political tension between a well-established, open process of providing labor for agribusiness, and widespread public opinion that has been periodically mobilized against the presence of undocumented residents.[2] In fact, the political process of cycles of enforcement analyzed in chapter 9 implies not a failure of policy, but a contradiction of policies in different arenas, that sometimes come into conflict. If family immigrants are frequently referred to as "suffered" in France and Britain, in the United States it is the labor immigrants from south of the border—both legal and illegal—that are often referred to in the same way, except of course by those who seek to employ them.

Are Policies Converging?

In a broad sense, immigration policies in Europe and the United States appear to be converging in practice. A relatively large number of immigrants continue to arrive each year, particularly those that come to join their families. Increasingly, however, France, Britain, and the United States have given preference to skilled immigrants, who are capable of filling needs in the labor market, and who are generally regarded as presenting the fewest potential social problems.

Convergence is also evident in other aspects of policy as well, integration policy in particular. Indeed, for the first time, France, Britain, and the United States seem to be developing explicit integration policies that combine civic integration programs with enforced policies on anti-discrimination.[3] The Dutch program for civic integration, initiated in 1998, has now become a model for the rest of Europe. In France, a much-reduced version of civic education was initiated by the Socialists in 1998, and beefed up as a voluntary program by the Right in 2003. By 2006, demonstration of "Republican integration" was made obligatory for a long-term residence visa; and then, in one of the first moves of the Sarkozy presidency, the process was shifted abroad for applicants for family unification.

The process in Britain was more complicated, in part because of the commitment to multiculturalism that began in the 1960s. Beginning in 2001 (even before the attacks in the United States), policy began to change. In the aftermath of urban riots in the summer, and then the attacks in the United States in September, government reports indicate the beginning of a reassertion of policies of civic integration to support shared British values. The attacks in London in 2005 accelerated a process that had begun four years before. Although the actual policy requirements in place by 2007 were not as coercive as those in France or the Netherlands, they were moving in the same direction.[4]

At the same time, as I noted in chapter 1, programs on anti-discrimination, modeled on the British program which was strongly influenced by the program in the United States, have become widespread in Europe since the two directives of the European Council in 2000.[5] National differences remain, of course, particularly between the coordinated state programs for civic integration now being initiated in Europe, and the far more modest efforts in the United States that focus on requirements for the citizenship examination initiated in the 1950s. Also striking is the difference between the multicultural programs in Britain and the United States, most evident in the education system, and the relative lack of such programs in France.

On the other hand, we have seen in chapters 1, 3, and 6 that integration policies have led to sometimes puzzling and unexpected results. Employment and education outcomes for British immigrants have been quite good. These results are probably related to strong anti-discrimination institutions, and may be helped by multicultural programs in education. The same outcomes in France are comparatively poor, and France is only beginning to struggle with questions of discrimination and programs of "positive discrimination" to promote better access for young people from immigrant families. Political representation is roughly similar for

France and Britain at the local level, but sharply different at the national level, where the more porous American system has generally succeeded in providing better access than either Britain or France. By most measures, it appears clear that France has also consistently had a worse record than Britain in political representation. These differences are generally accounted for by scholars by relatively strong resistance by French political parties of the Left, compared to their British counterparts, to naming minority-group candidates in areas in which the left is entrenched. (We will come back to this question further on.)

By contrast, survey data on Muslim immigrants, generally considered the most difficult to integrate by European policy-makers, show clearly that French Muslims are, by far, the most integrative in their orientation, and show the least conflict between their Muslim and national identities. In addition, they are the most positively oriented toward "national customs," and are the most accepting of Christians and Jews in their societies. In Klausen's study of Muslim elites, the French sample had the lowest "neo-orthodox" response of any of the European groups she studied. Compared with their French counterparts, the responses of British Muslim elites indicate a strong sense of isolation from British norms that makes the British sample different from every other country studied by Klausen.

Therefore the French results are important because value integration appears to be emerging despite significant failures in education and employment. Reports on the French suburban riots of 2005—cited in chapter 3—are hardly encouraging, but they reflect both the failures and the successes of French integration efforts. Failures of access to education and employment are strongly related to the alienation expressed by young people from immigrant families. Such failures are more reminiscent of the class gap of the twentieth century, than of the ethnoreligious gap often cited in popular accounts. Compared to their British counterparts, angry young rioters are demanding access, not isolation, and access in terms that very much resemble existing French norms. Islam played no evident role in the riots, and even such a hot-button issue as the "head-scarf affair" in 2004 did not serve as a rallying point for ethnic conflict. Thus, although real policy differences within Europe, and between Europe and the United States, have narrowed considerably in recent years, outcomes have varied considerably.

Why Are Patterns of Politics Different?

The forces that are driving the politics of immigration remain quite different in the countries that we have analyzed in this volume. Although policies have changed in each country over time, the dynamics of politics have changed very little. It is in this context that we return to the question of how it is possible to promulgate policies on immigration when public opinion consistently, but to varying degrees, opposes the entry of immigrants.

In France and Britain policies have been driven by very different dynamics of party politics. In the United States, Daniel Tichenor provides one answer to the question that I posed above. He argues that through the nineteenth century, and then again more recently, the openness of American immigration policy has been driven by electoral dynamics, the core of which has been the perceived electoral importance of immigrant voters (see ch. 10). This "self reinforcing mechanism" broke down during the progressive era, but reemerged after 1965.[6] In the nineteenth century, these electoral dynamics were part of a set of "reproductive mechanisms" that reinforced one another in a path dependent process.[7]

> Like earlier European groups, southern and eastern Europeans arrived in large numbers, easily acquired voting rights, were defended by powerful ethnic and business interests, and were courted by major party leaders.[8]

However, Tichenor argues, the Progressive reforms of the early twentieth century generally undermined the power of political party leadership in both houses of Congress, and such reforms as "direct democracy" and reliance on experts for the formulation of public policy tended to undermine the role and power of political parties on the state and national levels. The weakening, then, of party control eroded the strongest political supports for an open immigration policy. Tichenor's analysis raises important questions for comparative analysis, questions that have implications for both Britain and France, and that merit exploration.

In the British case, and to a lesser extent in the French case, a similar set of conditions has not created a similar dynamic or a similar reproductive mechanism—generally quite the opposite. In Britain, New Commonwealth immigrants arrived in large numbers, easily acquired voting rights, and were courted by some Labour MPs (see table 7.1). At the very same time, however, the Labour Party and the Conservative Party proceeded to pass a series of laws that increasingly restricted entry to these very same immigrants (see ch. 5). Finally, the presence of a significant and growing number of ethnic voters appears not to have created a dynamic for more open policy.

Part of the difference of impact is probably institutional, the lack of a directly elected executive. As we have seen in chapter 10, ethic/immigrant voters in the United States have been important in key states for presidential races since the nineteenth century. In the British case, the influence of these voters can be contained more easily in relatively small constituencies. In addition, as we have seen, immigrant/ethnic voters are concentrated in fewer constituencies than they are in the United States, and tend to weigh less heavily in major party decisions on immigration policy.

Also, the British case demonstrates that political parties can and do use the presence of immigrant/ethnic voters to frame the immigration issue in different ways. Thus, while Labour MPs who represent constituencies with large numbers of ethnic voters have tended to support relatively open immigration policies, Conservative MPs from similar constituencies have framed the issue of immigration in terms of national identity, and have supported highly restrictive policies (ch. 7). In addition, party strategies, even when they are informed by electoral considerations, are not necessarily driven by them. The decision of both British parties to converge and compromise on the issue of immigration, and neutralize their extremes, has generally served to minimize the influence of immigrant groups.

In the French case, neither the Left nor the Right has been much responsive to the potential of an immigrant vote. The sensitivity to immigrant voters from other parts of Europe before WWII, particularly by the Communist Party, has not been matched by electoral sensitivity to new ethnic voters from the countries of North Africa among parties of the Left. The availability of this electorate has been somewhat delayed by French citizenship law (immigrants to Britain are eligible to vote with the establishment of residency), and their concentration in relatively few constituencies makes them less important than comparable voters in the United States. Nevertheless, increasingly, they are capable of providing marginal votes in presidential elections.

However, pressure from the National Front since the early 1980s has driven the politics of immigration in a way that has minimized considerations of ethnic voting. In part because the National Front has mobilized significant electoral support and has challenged the Left in constituencies historically dominated by the Left, the Socialist, and the Communist Parties have refrained from committing to more open policies of immigration, despite indications that their supporters in constituencies where there are concentrations of immigrants would favor such policies (see table 4.2 and ch. 4).

There are other factors that contribute to the weakness of the reinforcing dynamic of electoral mobilization, in particular the weak organization of immigrant groups, and the ability of political parties to ignore their interests even at the local level. As we have seen in chapter 4, the Socialist party has frequently resisted naming minority candidates both at the local and national levels in order to maintain in place established local elites and the balance of power within the party. Even in comparison with the British Labour Party (see ch. 7), the French Socialist Party has been less disposed to see immigrant voters as a political resource, because decisions on candidates are made beyond the neighborhood level, and are often dictated by national priorities. Note Garbaye's conclusion that the relative success of the town of Roubaix in electing an unusually high percentage of minority candidates can be attributed to party *weakness*, and the countervailing strength of community organizations capable of challenging the local party.[9] For these reasons, relatively strong political parties in

Britain and France have chosen to frame the immigration issue in identity terms, and have tended to emphasize restriction rather than openness in immigration policy.

. In the United States, on the other hand, the tendency by national political parties to view ethnic/immigrant voters as a political resource grew after 1965. This occurred even though most of the conditions of party weakness cited by Tichenor changed only modestly after the post-Watergate Congressional reforms.[10] This tendency, with some lapses, has supported relatively open immigration policy through good and bad economic times since 1965. Moreover, in the United States, the electoral balance has tended to tip toward sensitivity toward immigrant interests, in part because they are more difficult to ignore. Ethnic/immigrant populations tend to be concentrated in states that are important in presidential races, and there are concentrations of these populations in more than a third of congressional districts.

Politics and Policy

Thus, the political dynamics that are driving immigration policymaking in each country are different in ways that do not appear to change easily, although each case demonstrates how they do change. However, if we consider these very different political processes, how can we account for the degree of policy convergence that seems to have evolved in recent years, and that has resulted in: the high levels of immigration, particularly family unification, decisions by each country to favor entry of highly skilled immigrants, and the development of policies on integration that focus on a combination of civic integration tempered by anti-discrimination programs?

Recent policy on civic integration in Europe has been shaped in part by the influence of the extreme right, as in the case of France. In its most benign form, it represents the institutionalization of a process that had previously been assumed by the education system, and by civil society. In its more aggressive forms, such as the French legislation in 2007, and the Dutch program initiated in 1994, it is also an attempt to discourage some people from entering. It has also been shaped by events and fears, as in the case of Britain. On the other hand, the development of anti-discrimination programs are a result of EU directives that have been heavily influenced by British programs of long-standing, which in turn were influenced by American programs established shortly before. At least some of these programs are also a result of what Virginie Guiraudon has called "policy by stealthy," insulated policymaking, disconnected from electoral politics.[11] In some sense, these programs are the result of policy "puzzling" (see ch. 1) rather than electoral politics, although some aspects of civic integration programs are meant to appease voters concerned about identity issues.

The convergence of entry policies are another matter, and returns us to the question that I posed above. With the exception of the United States, most other countries have been obliged to recognize entry for family unification because of court decisions; what has varied has been the constraints and conditions that have been imposed on those otherwise eligible to enter in this way, typified by the French legislation that was passed in 2007. On the other hand, the entry of highly qualified workers, either temporarily or for settlement, has generally been decided administratively, by decision-makers who are relatively insulated from the political process. The use of a process of policymaking by stealth in Europe for the expansion of entry, or even for the development of more positive aspects of civic-integration policy reflects the political realities of identity politics.

In general, this same problem of the relatively greater importance of identity politics in Europe helps us to understand the broader differences in patterns of policy between the United States and Europe. American immigration legislation specifies the criteria and requirements for entry into the United States. Similar legislation in France and Britain specifies restrictions on entry. While American legislation establishes ceilings that imply a positive approach to entry, legislation in France has never specified numbers, and similar legislation in Britain has done so only occasionally (e.g., the 1962 Act). The United States has attempted to shape entry through legislation since 1965. British and French policy-makers, on the other hand, have used legislative acts to shape restrictive patterns, without focusing on the kinds of immigrants they would like to have enter.

Because legal immigration has continued, but there are few explicit legislative criteria against which immigration results can be measured in Europe, voters often have the impression that immigration is out of control. By comparison, American voters have generally accepted high levels of legal immigration each year, levels that are more or less consistent with legislative ceilings. On the other hand illegal entry across the southern border has been far more controversial. Agribusiness has welcomed these immigrants, often with the stealthy cooperation of the federal government and state authorities (see ch. 9). Other undocumented immigrants in the United States have arrived quite legally, and either have not left when they were required to leave, or are awaiting documentation. They too are an integral part of the workforce, accepted and employed by a broad range of Americans. Nevertheless, voters are left with the impression that immigration is out of control.

In both cases, this study shows that the political consequences are substantial. In Europe these impressions feed the electorate of the extreme right. In the United States, the political reaction has crushed all efforts at immigration reform, has nurtured the politics of the exteme right, and has tended to blur the distinction between legal and illegal immigrants. Although there are always unanticipated consequences, as well as differences between the goals of public policy and the eventual outcomes, the gaps in these cases are built into the policies themselves. European policy-makers have been reluctant to formalize in legislative texts (and therefore in published parliamentary debates) the need for immigration that is evident in continuing immigration flows. American policy-makers have been reluctant to modify a two-tiered system that has served a broad range of business interests (as well as untold numbers of households and gardens), and that many believed worked as well as could be hoped for, except at those times when immigration became a high-salience issue. Although the political "crisis" of immigration is quite different on either side of the Atlantic, it emerges from a similar dynamic: the reluctance of governments to acknowledge the policies that they are pursuing.

NOTES

One   Introduction

1. On this discussion, see Aristide Zolberg, "Matters of State: Theorizing Immigration Policy," in Noah M.J. Pickus, Ed., *Becoming American, America Becoming* (New York: Russell Sage Foundation, 1999).
2. Ibid.
3. James Hollifield, *Immigrants, Markets and States: The Political Economy of Postwar Europe* (Cambridge, MA: Harvard University Press, 1994).
4. See John Torpey, *The Invention of the Passport* (London: Cambridge University Press, 2000).
5. See Didier Bigo and Elspeth Guild, *Controlling Frontiers: Free Movement into and within Europe* (Burlington, VT: Ashgate, 2005), pp. 55–57.
6. Christian Joppke, *Challenge to the Nation-State: Immigration in Western Europe and the United States* (Oxford: Oxford University Press, 1998), Ch. 2.
7. Gary Freeman, "The Decline of Sovereignty? Politics and Immigration Restriction in Liberal States" in ibid., pp. 101–104.
8. Saskia Sassen, "The De Facto Transnationalizing of Immigration Policy," in ibid., p. 68.
9. Ray Kozlowski, "European Union Migration Regimes, Established and Emergent," in ibid., Ch. 5.
10. See Terri Givens and Adam Luedke, "The Politics of European Union Immigration Policy: Institutions, Salience and Harmonization," *The Policy Studies Journal*, Vol. 32, No. 1, 2004, pp. 145–165.
11. Moisés Naim, "Borderline: It's Not about Maps," *Washington Post*, May 28, 2006.
12. See Zolberg, "Matters of State."
13. Virginie Guiraudon and Gallya Lahav, "The State Sovereignty Debate Revisited: The Case of Immigration Control," *Comparative Political Studies*, Vol. 33, No. 2, 2000, pp. 163–195.
14. It is useful to note that free movement of people was not legally established in the United States until 1941, when the U.S. Supreme Court overturned a California depression-era law that made it a misdemeanor to bring into California, "any indigent person who is not a resident of the State, knowing him to be an indigent person." In *Edwards v. California* (314 U.S. 160 /1941), the Court unanimously overturned the law.
15. See Bigo and Guild, *Controlling Frontiers*, esp. pp. 59–91.
16. The data on the United States is from Rey Koslowski, "Toward Virtual Borders: Expanding European Border Control Policy Initiatives and Technology Implementation," Unpublished paper, May 2005, p. 7. The estimates for the United Kingdom are of officers from Customs, Special Branch, ports police, and immigration, working on British border controls, reported by BBC news on March 29, 2005 on their Web site. The data from France are from the Ministry of the Interior, "Rapport d'activité de la DCPAF 2003," p. 9.
17. Wayne Cornelius and Marc Rosenblum summarize public opinion evidence as follows: "...general public responses to immigration...are characterized throughout the industrialized world by opposition to existing immigration levels and negative feelings about the most recent cohort of migrants." See "Immigration and Politics," *Annual Review of Political Science*, 2005, p. 104.

18. See *Eurobarometer* No. 30, 1988. Gallya Lahav, "Ideological and Party Constraints on Immigration Attitudes," *Journal of Common Market Studies*, Vol. 35, No. 3, 1997, pp. 393–395, analyzes this data, and compares it with her own data on Euro deputies.

19. See L. Quillian's analysis of the EU member-states, based on *Eurobarometer* No. 30, 1988, in "Prejudice as a Response to Perceived Group Threat: Population Composition and Anti-immigrant and Racial Prejudice in Europe," *American Sociological Review*, Vol. 60, No. 4, 1995, pp. 586–611.

20. Joel Fetzer, *Public Attitudes toward Immigration in the United States, France and Germany* (New York: Cambridge University Press, 2000). Also see Gallya Lahav, *Immigration and Politics in the New Europe* (Cambridge: Cambridge University Press, 2004), Ch. 1.

21. P.M. Sniderman, L. Hagendoorn, and M. Prior, "Predisposing Factors and Situational Triggers: Exclusionary Reactions to Immigrant Minorities," *American Political Science Review*, Vol. 98, No. 1, 2004, pp. 35–49.

22. See Jason Kehrberg, "Public Opinion on Immigration in Western Europe," *Comparative European Politics*, Vol. 5, No. 3, 2007, pp. 264–281. Also see John Sides and Jack Citron, "European Opinion about Immigration: The Role of Identities, Interests and Information," *British Journal of Political Science*, Vol. 37, No. 3, July 2007, pp. 477–504.

23. Gary Freeman, "Modes of Immigration Politics in Liberal Democracies," *International Migration Review*, Vol. 29, 1995, pp. 881–902.

24. Jeannette Money, *Fences and Neighbors: The Political Geography of Immigration Control* (Ithaca, NY: Cornell University Press, 1999), Ch. 1.

25. Lahav, "Ideological and Party Constraints," p. 394. The exceptions may be related to the weight of right-wing representation in the delegations of these countries, pp. 388–390.

26. Michèle Lamont, *The Dignity of Working Men: Morality and the Boundaries of Race, Class, and Immigration* (Cambridge, MA: Harvard University Press, 2000), pp. 212–213.

27. Riva Kastoryano, *Negotiating Identities: States and Immigrants in France and Germany* (Princeton: Princeton University Press, 2002).

28. See Rogers Brubaker's impressive study of this question, *Citizenship and Nationhood in France and Germany* (Cambridge, MA: Harvard University Press, 1992); for the United States, see Aristide Zolberg, *A Nation by Design* (Cambridge: Cambridge University Press, 2006), Ch. 4.

29. See Yasemin Nuhoglu Soysal, *Limits of Citizenship: Migrants and Postnational Membership in Europe* (Chicago: University of Chicago Press, 1994).

30. Miram Feldblum, *Reconstructing Citizenship: The Politics of Nationality Reform and Immigration in Contemporary France* (Albany, NY: SUNY Press, 1999), Ch. 1.

31. Peter Schuck, "The Reevaluation of American Citizenship," in Joppke, *Challenge to the Nation-State*, Ch. 6, p. 223

32. See the introduction and Ch. 7 by Miriam Feldblum , "Reconfiguring Citizenship in Western Europe," in ibid.

33. A useful summary of the right to return is contained in http://en.wikipedia.org/wiki/Right_of_return#Other.

34. See Andrew Geddes, *Immigration and European Integration* (Manchester: Manchester University Press, 2000), Ch. 7.

35. This is Soysal's argument in *Limits of Citizenship*.

36. See Martin A. Schain, "Minorities and Immigrant Incorporation in France," in Christian Joppke and Steven Lukes, *Multicultural Questions* (Oxford: Oxford University Press, 1999).

37. See Lawrence H. Fuchs, *The American Kaleidoscope: Race, Ethnicity and the Civic Culture* (Middletown, CT: Wesleyan University Press, 1990) Ch. 1; and Amy Bridges, *A City in the Republic: Antebellum New York and the Origins of Machine Politics* (Ithaca, NY: Cornell University Press, 1987), Chs. 3–5.

38. See John F. McClymer, "The Federal Government and the Americanization Movement, 1915–1924," *Prologue: The Journal of the National Archives*, Vol. 10, Spring 1978, pp. 22–41, cited in Noah Pickus, "'Human Nature Cannot Be Changed Overnight:' Re-assessing the Americanization Movement of the 1920s," delivered at the 1993 Annual Meeting of the Southwestern Political Science Association, New Orleans, Louisiana, March 17–20, 1993, p. 13.

39. Martin Kilson, "Blacks and Neo-ethnicity in America," in Nathan Glazer and Daniel P. Moynihan, Eds., *Ethnicity: Theory and Experience* (Cambridge, MA: Harvard University Press, 1975), Ch. 8.

40. Ira Katznelson, *Black Men, White Cities: Race, Politics, and Migration in the United States, 1900–30 and Britain, 1948–68* (London, New York: Published for the Institute of Race Relations by Oxford University Press, 1973), pp. 125–126.

41. Randall Hansen, *Citizenship and Immigration in Post-War Britain* (Oxford: Oxford University Press: 2000), p. 128 and Ch. 6.

42. See Erik Bleich, *Race Politics in Britain and France: Ideas and Policymaking since the 1960s* (New York: Cambridge University Press, 2003), pp. 84–85; and Money, *Fences and Neighbors*, p. 100.

43. Patrick Weil and John Crowley, "Integration in Theory and Practice: A Comparison of France and Britain," in Martin Baldwin-Edwards and Martin A. Schain, Eds., *The Politics of Immigration in Western Europe* (London: Cass, 1994), p. 118.

44. Theodore Lowi, *The End of Liberalism* (New York: W.W. Norton, 1969), Ch. 1.

45. Gerard Noiriel, in *Le creuset français* (Paris: Ed, du Seuil, 1988), pp. 189–245, gives a good summary of the principles of integration. A reaffirmation of this approach can be found in the Rapport de la Commission de la nationalité (Marcel Long), *Etre français aujourd'hui et demain* (Paris: Union Générale d'Editions, 1988), pp. 82–105.

46. Marco Martiniello, *Sortir des ghettos culturels* (Paris: Presses de SciencesPo, 1997), pp. 58–63.

47. Dominique Schnapper, "Immigration and the Crisis of National Identity," *West European Politics*, Vol. 17, No. 2, April 1994, pp. 133–134. Another way that the difference between France and the United States has been portrayed is that "...the French promote the ethnicization of majorities, and Americans that of minorities." See Sophie Body-Gendrot, "Models of Immigrant Integration in France and the U.S.: Signs of Convergence?" in M.P. Smith and I. Feagin, Eds., *The Bubbling Cauldron* (Minneapolis: University of Minnesota Press, 1995).

48. Riva Kastoryano, *Negotiating Identities* (Princeton: Princeton University Press, 2002).

49. See Christian Joppke, "Transformation of Immigrant Integration: Civic Integration and Antidiscrimination in the Netherlands, France and Germany," *World Politics*, Vol. 59, No. 2, January 2007, p. 243.

50. Council Directive 2000/43/EC, June 29, 2000; and Council Directive 2000/78/EC, November 27, 2000.

51. Council of the European Union, Justice and Home Affairs, Press Release, 2618th Council Meeting, November 19, 2004, pp. 19–24.

52. Jytte Klausen, *The Islamic Challenge: Politics and Religion in Western Europe* (Oxford: Oxford University Press, 2005), p. 87.

53. See in particular, Samuel Huntington, "Political Development or Political Decay," *World Politics,* April 1965, pp. 405–411; and Marvin Rogers, "The Politics of Malay Villagers," *Comparative Politics*, Vol. 7, No. 2, January 1975, pp. 205–225.

54. See Sidney Verba and Norman Nie, *Participation in America: Politics, Democracy and Social Equality* (New York: Harper & Row, 1972); Lester W. Milbrath, *Political Participation* (Chicago: Rand McNally, 1965); Philip Converse and Georges Dupeux, "Politicization of the Electorate in France and the United States," *Public Opinion Quarterly*, Vol. 26, No. 1, Spring 1962. pp. 1–23.

55. Philippe Schmitter, "Three Neofunctional Hypotheses about International Integration," *International Organization*, Vol. 23, No. 1, 1969, pp. 161–166.

56. Hugh Heclo, *Modern Social Politics in Britain and Sweden* (New Haven: Yale University Press, 1974), p. 305.

57. See Jack Knight, *Institutions and Social Conflict* (Cambridge: Cambridge University Press, 1992) and John Kingdon, *Agendas, Alternatives and Public Policies* (New York: Harper Collins, 1995).

58. Terri Givens and Adam Luedke, "European Immigration Policies in Comparative Perspective: Issue Salience, Partisanship and Immigrant Rights," *Comparative European Politics*, Vol. 3, No. 1, April 2005, pp. 6–7; also see: Gary Freeman, "Winners and Losers: Politics and the Costs and Benefits of Migration," in Antony M. Messina, Ed., *West European Immigration and Immigrant Policy in the New Century* (Westport, CT: Praeger, 2002), pp. 76–96.

59. E.E. Schattschneider, *The Semisovereign People* (New York: Holt, Rinehart and Winston, 1960), Ch. 2.

60. Erik Bleich, *Race Politics in Britain and France: Ideas and Policymaking since the 1960s* (New York: Cambridge University Press, 2003), pp. 172–174.

61. Steven Krasner, "Sovereignty: An Institutional Perspective," *Comparative Political Studies*, Vol. 21, No. 1, 1988, pp. 71–72.

62. See Peter Hall, "Policy Paradigms, Social Learning and the State: The Case of Economic Policymaking in Britain," *Comparative Politics*, Vol. 25, No. 3, April 1993, pp. 275–296.

63. In particular, see Kingdon, *Agendas, Alternatives and Public Policies*.

64. In part, this helps us understand why trade unions have often supported immigration restriction. However, this has not been universally true. Leah Haus explores why unions have sometimes (and increasingly) supported more open immigration policies in France and the United States in *Unions, Immigration and Internationalization: New Challenges and Changing Coalitions in The United States and France* (New York: Palgrave Macmillan, 2002).

65. See Freeman, "Modes of Immigration Politics in Liberal Democracies," pp. 881–902. Christian Joppke, *Immigration and the Nation-State* (Oxford: Oxford University Press, 1999), introduction, p. 18.

66. The concept of arenas of power was first developed by E.E. Schnattschneider, in *The Semi-sovereign People*. Theodore Lowi, then applied it more extensively in *The End of Liberalism*, Ch. 1.

67. See Hall, "Policy Paradigms" and Peter Hall, *Governing the Economy* (Oxford: Oxford University Press, 1986).

68. The one notable exception is the comparative study of policy change in the France and United States by Jeffrey Togman: *The Ramparts of Nations: Institutions and Immigration Policies in France and the United States* (Westport, CT: Praeger, 2002). Also, see Hansen, *Citizenship and Immigration in Post-war Britain*, pp. 6–7.

69. In fact, this is the core argument of Freeman, in "Modes of Immigration Politics in Liberal Democracies," and Money, in *Fences and Neighbors*, Ch. 1.

70. Money, *Fences and Neighbors*, p. 62.

71. Richard Alba and Nancy Foner, "Entering the Precincts of Power: Do National Differences Matter for Immigrant-Minority Political Representation?" Unpublished paper, February 2006, p. 8. Also see: Richard Alba and Victor Nee, *Remaking the American Mainstream* (Cambridge, MA: Harvard University Press, 2003).

72. See Alba and Foner, "Entering the Precincts of Power." Also see Stephen Erie, *Rainbow's End: Irish-Americans and the Dilemma of Urban Machine Politics, 1840–1985* (Berkeley: University of California Press, 1988) and Roger Waldinger, *Still the Promised City? African-Americans and New Immigrants in Postindustrial New York* (Cambridge, MA: Harvard University Press, 1996).

73. This is the point made by Patrick Weil in his commission report to the prime minister in August 1997. Patrick Weil, *Mission d'étude des les legislations de la nationalité et de l'immigration* (Paris: la Documentation Française, 1997), pp. 24–27.

74. In a detailed report, *Le Monde* has reviewed the parts of the program of the National Front that have been put into effect by governments of the Right and the Left. See *Le Monde*, "Le Pen dans le texte...des autres," December 27, 2005, p. 3.

75. This is the argument developed by Givens and Leudtke, "The Politics of European Union Immigration Policy," pp. 158–160.

76. Andrew Geddes is particularly good at analyzing some of these trends in *The Politics of Migration and Immigration in Europe* (London: Sage, 2003), pp. 50–51.

77. Desmond King, *Making Americans: Immigration, Race and the Origins of the Diverse Democracy* (Cambridge, MA: Harvard University Press, 2000), p. 242.

78. Daniel J. Tichenor, *Dividing the Lines: The Politics of Immigration Control in America* (Princeton: Princeton University Press, 2002), p. 179.

79. See ibid., pp. 211–216; and David Reimers, *Still the Golden Door: The Third World Comes to America* (New York: Columbia University Press, 1985), pp. 71–72.

Two   Development of French Immigration Policy

1. For a further elaboration of this section, see Martin A. Schain, "Politics in France," in Gabriel A. Almond, G. Bingham Powell, Jr., Russell J. Dalton, and Kaare Strøm, Eds., *Comparative Politics Today, A World View*, 9th edition (New York: Pearson Longman, 2008).

2. For an elaboration of what this means, see John T.S. Keeler and Martin A. Schain, *Chirac's Challenge: Liberalization, Europeanization, and Malaise in France* (New York: St. Martin's Press, 1996), Ch. 2.

3. See Alec Stone, *The Birth of Judicial Politics in France* (New York: Oxford University Press, 1992).

4. See Alec Stone Sweet, *The Judicial Construction of Europe* (Oxford: Oxford University Press, 2004).

5. Patrick Weil has argued that France has been a country of immigration since the thirteenth century. Indeed, until the middle of the nineteenth century, there was no discussion of a "problem" of immigration. See Patrick Weil, *La France et ses étrangers* (Paris: Gallimard, 1991), pp. 26–27.

6. Gérard Noiriel, *Le Creuset Francais* (Paris: Editions du Seuil, 1988), p. 89.

7. Vincent Viet, *La France immigrée: Construction d'une politique 1914–1997* (Paris: Fayard, 1998), p. 27.

8. Gary S. Cross, *Immigrant Workers in Industrial France: The Making of a New Laboring Class* (Philadelphia, PA: Temple University Press, 1983), pp. 13–15.

9. Catherine Wihtol de Wenden, *Les Immigrés et la politique* (Paris: Presses de la FNSP, 1988), p. 54.

10. The best estimates of immigrant employment in the 1980s can be found in Jeanne Singer-Kérel, *La Population active étrangère au recensement de 1982* (Paris: FNSP, Service d'étude de l'activité économique, 1985).

11. Weil, *La France et ses étrangers*, p. 32.

12. Cross, *Immigrant Workers in Industrial France*, p. 194. However, the number of decrees on quotas increased over time, and varied considerably by government. Weil, *La France et ses étrangers*, p. 33.

13. Cross, *Immigrant Workers in Industrial France*, p. 213.

14. The best account of limits imposed by both regulations and practice is Mary Dewhurst Lewis, *The Boundaries of the Republic: Migrant Rights and the Limits of Universalism in France, 1918–1940* (Stanford: Stanford University Press, 2007).

15. Cross, *Immigrant Workers in Industrial France*, Ch. 8.

16. Maxim Silverman, *Deconstructing the Nation: Immigration, Racism and Citizenship in Modern France* (London: Routeledge, 1992), Ch. 4.

17. Noiriel, *Le creuset français*, p. 171. His source is George Mauco, *Mémoire sur l'assimilation des étrangers in France,* (Paris: Institut international de coopération intellectuelle, 1937).

18. The organization of immigration in the 1920s is described by Noiriel in *Le Creuset français*, pp. 306–312, and Cross, *Immigrant Workers in Industrial France*, pp. 52–63.

19. Emmanuel Todd, *La Nouvelle France* (Paris: Seuil, 1988), p. 232.

20. Weil, *La France et ses étrangers*, pp. 88–90. Weil notes, however, that ethnic and racial criteria—together with a quota system modeled after the system then in force in the United States—were seriously considered, and advocated by Alfred Sauvy and Robert Debré (p. 80).

21. Ibid., p. 93.

22. Ibid., pp. 95–100.

23. Jeannette Money, *Fences and Neighbors: The Political Geography of Immigration Control* (Ithaca, NY: Cornell University Press, 1999), pp. 109–110. The legislation was an amendment to the Labor Code, that made it illegal for to employ workers who lacked "a permit to do salaried work in France," a category that applied only to Algerians and Francophone Africans.

24. The 1999 census indicates that this proportion was close to the national average, but also that the absolute number of immigrant children in primary schools was declining, compared with the early 1990s. See OECD/SOMPI, *Trends in International Migration 2001*, p. 166

25. There were some other restrictions as well, such as a limit of one-third on the proportion of trade union administrators. See Patrick Ireland, *The Policy Challenge of Ethnic Diversity*, pp. 76–77.

26. *Journal Officiel de l'Assemblé Nationale*, June 16, 1975, p. 4241. In fact, Dijoud's reforms were part of a larger package that included increased spending for Housing, special classes for immigrants in primary and secondary schools, and special scholarships for universities. See Douglas Ashford, *Politics and Policy in France, Living with Uncertainty* (Philadelphia, PA: Temple University Press, 1982), p. 280.

27. The decision of the Conseil d'Etat was on December 8, 1978 (G.I.S.T.I., C.F.D.T., et C.G.T.-Rec. Lebon p. 493), on an action brought by a rights group and two trade union organizations.

28. Weil, *La France et ses étrangers*, pp. 166–167. It is interesting to note that Weil's argument that Algerians constituted a special target is based on quasi- private communications among high civil servants, rather than on public documents. See Viet, *La France immigrée*, p. 387, fn. 2.

These communications, however, have been made available in a special archive established at the Fondation Nationale des Sciences Politiques.

29. Article in *Le Monde*, June 15, 1979, reprinted in Weil, *La France et ses étrangers*, p. 197.
30. Viet, *La France immigrée*, p. 409.
31. Money, *Fences and Neighbors*, p. 116.
32. The second law, passed in 1994, prohibited the regularization of illegal status through marriage, gave significant power to mayors to annul what they believed to be marriages of convenience, and denied welfare benefits to undocumented immigrants, except for emergency health care and (compulsory) schooling.
33. The constitution was officially amended on November 19, 1993. The procedure was necessitated by the decision of the Constitutional Council of August 13, 1993 (confirmed by the Council of State a month later), which had declared eight articles of the immigration legislation of July 13 unconstitutional. Many of the provisions of the new immigration legislation, including those that deal with family unification, stricter rules regarding marriage, the deportation of undocumented aliens, and new judicial procedures would not have been possible without this amendment.
34. See Andrew Geddes, *The Politics of Migration and Immigration in Europe* (London: Sage, 2003), pp. 64–65.
35. The basis for this approach is contained in the report by Patrick Weil, *Mission d'étude des législations de la nationalité et de l'immigration* (Paris: La Documentation Française, 1997). See pp. 47–48. Also see the commentary in *Le Monde*, July 31, 1997, p. 6.
36. See the discussion of this in *Le Monde*, November 30, 1997, p. 6.
37. See the reports in *Le Monde*, December 16, 18, 19. The law was finally passed in May, 1998.
38. *Le Monde*, November 24, 2003.
39. *Le Monde*, March 4, 2003.
40. See, for example, the report of the French Economic and Social Council of October 29, 2003, reported in *Le Monde*, November 8, 2003, which calls for 10,000 more skilled immigrants per year.
41. See *Le Monde*, August 29, October 21, and November 9, 2007.
42. For the details on the new law, see *Le Monde*, October 23, 2007.
43. See *Le Monde*, September 12 2007: "Hortefeux Mobilise des préfets sur les expulsions d'étrangers."
44. Virginie Guiraudon, "The EU 'Garbage Can': Accounting for Policy Developments in the Immigration Domain," Paper presented at the 2001 Conference of the European Community Studies Association, Madison WI, May 29–June 1, 2001, p. 7.
45. Dietmar Herz, "European Immigration and Asylum Policy: Scope and Limits of Intergovernmental Europeanization," Paper presented at 8th EUSA Conference, March 27–29, 2003, Nashville, TN, p. 13.
46. See Andrew Geddes, "Thin Europeanisation: The Social Rights of Migrants in an Integrating Europe," in Michael Bommes and Andrew Geddes, Eds., *Immigration and Welfare: Challenging the Borders of the Welfare State* (London: Routeledge, 2000).
47. See, for example, the failed trial balloon floated by Alain Juppé in October 1999, *Le Monde*, October 1, 1999.
48. See "Communication from the Commission to the Council and the European Parliament on a Community Immigration Policy," November 22, 2000, COM (2000) 757 final.
49. Final Report of Working Group X (Freedom, Security and Justice), CONV 426/02, December 2, 2002, p. 5.
50. Hugh Williamson, "EU Six Consider Introduction of 'Integration Contracts' for Immigrants," *The Financial Times*, March 24, 2006.
51. Cross, *Immigrant Workers in Industrial France,* p. 6.
52. Paul Leroy-Beaulieu, "La question des étrangers en France au point de vue économique," *Journal de droit international privée* (1988), p. 175, cited in Cross, *Immigrant Workers in Industrial France*, p, 8.
53. In 1920, for example, legislation that outlawed abortion was passed, along with severe limitations on access to birth control. Nevertheless, the birth and fertility rates remained stagnant between the wars.
54. See Rogers Brubaker, *Citizenship and Nationhood in France and Germany* (Cambridge, MA: Harvard University Press, 1992), pp. 1–2, 6–8.

Three   Understanding French Immigration Policy

1. Gary S. Cross, *Immigrant Workers in Industrial France: The Making of a New Laboring Class* (Philadelphia, MA: Temple University Press, 1983), p. 195.
2. Vincent Viet, *La France immigrée: Construction d'une politique 1914–1997* (Paris: Fayard, 1998), p. 161.
3. The term was coined by Aristide Zolberg, to identify U.S. controls by consulates, put in place. See Aristide Zolberg, *A Nation by Design: Immigration Policy in the Fashioning of America* (New York and Cambridge, MA: Russell Sage Foundation and Harvard University Press, 2006), pp. 264–267.
4. Patrick Weil made these estimates in *La France et ses Etrangers* (Paris: Calman-Lévy, 1991), Annex VII
5. See François Héran, "Cinq idées reçu sur l'immigration," *Population et Sociétés*, No. 397, January 2004.
6. See Conseil d'Etat, 8 décembre 1978—G.I.S.T.I., C.F.D.T. et C.G.T.—Rec. Lebon, p. 493.
7. OECD, *Trends in International Migration* (Washington, DC: SOMEPI, 2003), p. 193.
8. OECD, *International Migration Outlook* (Washington, DC: SOMEPI, 2006), p. 238. The latest INSEE figures are reported in Catherine Borel, *Enquêtes annuelles de recensement 2004 et 2005*, INSEE Première, No. 1098, August 2006. The reported increase in percentages are for "immigrés," that is people born abroad, some of whom are French citizens; as opposed to "étrangers," who are resident in France, but not French citizens, and may have been born in France, of parents themselves born abroad.
9. All of these figures are from the Office Français de Protection des Réfugiés et des Apatrides (OPFRA).
10. Reported in *Le Monde*, December 22, 2006, p. 22.
11. See Catherine Wihtol de Wenden, "The French Response to the Asylum Seeker Influx, 1980–93," *Annals of the American Academy of Political and Social Science*, Vol. 534, July 1994, p. 86.
12. See Georges Tapinos, "Immigration et marché du travail," *l'Observateur OCDE*, December 1999.
13. The French estimate was given by the minister of the interior in an interview in the *Figaro*, May 11, 2005; the British figures were quoted by Professor John Salt in *The Sunday Times* as estimates that he did for the Home Office, on April 17, 2005; and the American figure was cited by Thomas Freedman in the *International Herald Tribune* on April 6, 2006. In each case, the government has argued that there has been an increase; in the U.S. case, this is double the numbers cited by Tapinos in 1999. In general, the comparison among France, Britain, and the United States—if not the exact figures—is confirmed in a massive report by the French Senate in April 2006. The report also deals with the complex problem of estimating the population of "irregular immigrants," which includes both those who entered the country legally, and whose situation evolved into illegality (the majority), as well as those who entered the country illegally (a relatively small number). See *Rapport de la commission d'enquête sur l'immigration clandestine, créé en vertu d'une résolution adoptée par le Sénat le 27 octobre 2005* (2 volumes). In particular, see the testimony of François Héran in Volume II, and cited on p. 47 of Volume I. He also cites the United State as one of the countries where the informal labor market is most important. The data cited by the report (Vol. I, p. 47), indicates that no country in Europe has a lower rate of irregular immigration than France.
14. See the testimony of François Héron, in Volume II of the Senate Report.
15. Reported in Le Monde, November 10, 2007, p. 19. Also see the book by the Socialist senator, Louis Mermaz, *Les Géôles de la République* (Paris: Stock, 2001).
16. "Rapport de la commission d'enquête sur l'immigration calndestine," Sénat, 2005–2006, p. 83.
17. See *Le Monde*, November 16, 2000 and March 17, 2003.
18. See the comments by Cimade in *Le Monde*, May 2, 2003, that the vast majority of expulsions that place within the first week, and that the percentage of expulsions (of those detained) has remained generally constant—45–53%—through the vicissitudes in the law over a ten-year period.
19. See Cour des Comptes, *L'Acceuil des immigrants et l'integration des populations issues de l'immigration*, rapport au president de la republique suivi des réponses des administrations et des organismes intéressés, novembre, 2004, p. 433.

20. The announcement was made on the Web site of the National Police on January 18, 2006.

21. Ministry of the Interior, "Rapport d'activité de la DCPAF 2003," p. 9.

22. Ministry of the Interior, "Rapport d'activité de la DCPAF 2000," p. 9.

23. Joel Fetzer, *Public Attitudes toward Immigration in the United States, France and Germany* (New York: Cambridge University Press, 2000), pp. 56–57.

24. Michèle Lamont, *The Dignity of Working Men: Morality and the Boundaries of Race, Class, and Immigration* (Cambridge, MA: Harvard University Press, 2000), pp. 212–213.

25. This data is also cited by Erik Bleich, in his article "Antiracism with Races," *French Politics, Culture and Society*, Vol. 18, No. 3, Fall 2000, p. 52, in which he focuses on the problem of legislative attempts to deal with racism, while applying the concept only to immigrants and foreigners. Indeed, it is clear from the article that the concept is applied almost solely to those from Africa and the Caribbean.

26. On the other hand, in 1997 a question worded in a somewhat different way, evoked a more optimistic response. In Table 3.8, respondents were asked to compare North Africans with other immigrant groups in terms of whether in terms of whether they could integrate easily, with difficulty or not at all. In 1997 respondents were simply asked if they thought that North Africans would "…become French like the others." In this case, the index of integration was far more positive: +26.3. See CEVIPOF/Sofres survey of voters, May 26, 1997.

27. Yvan Gastaut, *L'immigration et l'opinion en France sous la Ve République* (Paris: Éditions du Seuil, 2000), pp. 116–117.

28. This story is told very well in Miriam Feldblum, *Reconstructing Citizenship: The Politics of Nationality Reform and Immigration in Contemporary France* (Albany, NY: SUNY Press, 1999).

29. M. Long, *Être français Aujourd'hui et Demain:* Rapport de la Commission de la Nationalité présenté par M. Marceau Long au Premier Ministre, vols. 1 and 2, (Paris: La Documentation Française, 1988), p. 85.

30. There is a rich literature on the evolution of this debate. See Sarah Wayland, "Mobilizing to Defend Nationality Law in France," *New Community*, Vol. 20, No. 1, October 1993, pp. 93–111.

31. Feldblum, *Reconstructing Citizenship*, p. 151.

32. Patrick Weil, *Mission d'étude des legislations de la nationalité et de l'immigration* (Paris: la documentation française,1997), p. 26.

33. See OECD, *Trends in International Migration* (Washington, DC: SOMEPI, 2003), p. 194.

34. Dominique Schnapper, *La France de l'intégration* (Paris: Editions Gallimard, 1991), pp. 81–104. Also see Dominique Schnapper, "Immigration and the Crisis of National Identity," *West European Politics*, Vol. 17, No. 2, April 1994, pp. 133–135.

35. Schnapper, *La France d'intégration*, p. 91.

36. Loïc Wacquant, "Banlieues françaises et ghetto noir américain: de L'amalgame à la comparaison," *French Politics and Society*, Vol. 10, No. 4, 1992, pp. 81–104.

37. National origin, for example, has played a relatively unimportant role in identifying important political leaders. Thus, former prime minister Edouard Balladur was born in Turkey, while his predecessor, Pierre Bérégovoy though born in France, is from a family that immigrated from Yugoslavia. On the other hand, there are some exceptions. The fact that Léon Blum and Pierre Mendès-France were of Jewish origin was an important element of how they were evaluated in political life.

38. Schnapper, "Immigration and the Crisis of National Identity," pp. 133–134. Another way that the difference between France and the United States has been portrayed is that "…the French promote the ethnicization of majorities, and Americans that of minorities." See Sophie Body-Gendrot, "Models of Immigrant Integration in France and the U.S.: Signs of Convergence?" in M.P. Smith and I. Feagin, Eds., *The Bubbling Cauldron* (Minneapolis: University of Minnesota Press, 1995).

39. Catherine Wihtol de Wenden, *Les Immigrés et la politique* (Paris: Presses de la FNSP, 1988), p. 50.

40. I have looked at the relationship between immigrant mobilization and the rise and decline of the PCF in "The Decline of French Communism: Party Construction and Party Decline," in Anthony Daley, Ed., *The Mitterrand Era: Policy Alternatives and Political Mobilization in France* (New York: New York University Press, 1996).

41. Martin A. Schain, "Immigrants and Politics in France," in John Ambler, Ed., *The French Socialist Experiment* (Philadelphia, PA: ISHI Press, 1985).

42. R.D. Grillo, *Ideologies and Institutions in Urban France* (London: Cambridge University Press, 1985), pp. 125–127. The initiative taken by the prefect of the Rhone to block immigrants

from public housing is also referred to by Jacques Barou, *Processus de segregation et ethnicisation de l'espace*, final report to DPM, October 1994, p. 24.

43. Schain, "Immigration and Politics in France, pp. 176–181.

44. Alex Hargreaves, *Immigration, "Race" and Ethnicity in Contemporary France* (London: Routledge, 1995), p. 198.

45. There is an excellent summary of this period in Patrick Ireland, *The Policy Challenge of Ethnic Diversity* (Cambridge, MA: Harvard University Press, 1994), Ch. 2.

46. Cited by Miriam Feldblum, "Paradoxes of Ethnic Politics: The Case of Franco-Maghrebis in France," *Ethnic and Racial Studies*, Vol. 16, No. 1, January 1993, p. 57. This article contains an important and insightful analysis of the evolution of the association movement among immigrant groups.

47. See Sophie Body-Gendrot, *Ville et Violence: l'irruption de nouvaux acteurs* (Paris: PUF, 1993), Chs. 5 and 6; and Adil Jazouli, *Les années banlieues* (Paris: Seuil, 1992).

48. *Le Point*, August 28, 1993, quoted in John A. McKesson, "Concepts and Realities in a Multiethnic France," *French Politics and Society* Vol. 12, No. 1, Winter, 1994, p. 30.

49. Many of these programs are described by Michel Caron in "Immigration, intégration et solidarité," *Regards sur l'actualité*, No. 166, December, 1990.

50. See Jacqueline Costa-Lascoux, *De l'immigré au citoyen* (Paris: La Documentation Française, 1989), pp. 93–95.

51. F. Lorcerie, "Les ZEP 1990–1993 pour mémoire," *Migrants-formation*, No. 97, June 1994.

52. See Jacqueline Costa-Lascoux, *De l'immigré au citoyen* (Paris: La Documentation Française, 1989), pp. 93–94.

53. The legislation that authorizes the prohibition against the collection of ethnic data is the *Loi No. 78–17 du 6 janvier 1978 relative à l'informatique, aux fichiers et aux libertés*. However, this law was modified in 2004, and the National Commission on Computers and Liberty list seven criteria that could be used to measure "diversity." See http://www.cnil.fr/index.php?id=1844. Last accessed June 7, 2008.

54. The Law of November 16, 2001 goes well beyond the minimum requirements of the Race Directive, banning discrimination in salaries and promotion, as well as hiring and firing. See Christian Joppke, "Transformation of Immigrant Integration: Civic Integration and Antidiscrimination in the Netherlands, France and Germany," *World Politics*, Vol. 59, No. 2, January 2007, p. 261.

55. See the extensive article in *Le Monde* on May 4, 2006.

56. The 1995 *Appel à projets* states clearly (p. 3) that "The FAS is a partner in urban public policy: also, local projects must be related to the logic of territorial integration."

57. See Jonathan Laurence and Justin Vaise, *Integrating Islam: Political and Religious Challenges in Contemporary France* (Washington, DC: Brookings Institution Press, 2006).

58. See Hargreaves, *Immigration, "Race" and Ethnicity*, pp. 206–208.

59. Quoted by Jonathan Laurence, in "Managing Transnational Islam: Muslims and the State in Western Europe," Paper prepared for the workshop on *Comparative Immigration Policies after 9/11* at the Ford Institute, University of Pittsburgh, on September 9 and 10, 2005, p. 6.

60. Only 22% report going to a mosque at least once a month (compared with 18% of a general French survey). See the groundbreaking study by Sylvain Brouard and Vincent Tiberj, *Français Comme les Autres? Enquête sur les citoyens d'origine maghrébine, africaine et turque* (Paris: Presses de Sciences-Po, 2005), pp. 23, 27–28. This does not mean that Muslims are not religious in a less conventional sense. Higher percentages (43%) report praying daily outside of a mosque, and mosque attendance is slightly higher among younger subsamples.

61. "L'Islam en France et les réactions aux attentats du 11 septembre 2001, Résultats détaillés," IFOP, September 2001.

62. See Michèle Tribalat, *Faire France* (Paris: Découverte, 1995), p. 108. Also see the remainder of Ch. 4.

63. On this question, see Miriam Feldblum, *Reconstructing Citizenship: The Politics of Nationality and Immigration Reform in Contemporary France* (Albany, NY: SUNY Press, 1999), esp. pp. 135–145).

64. Commission de reflexion sur l'application du principe de laïcité dans la République, *Rapport au Président de la République*, décembre 12, 2003, p. 61.

65. Patrick Weil, "Lifting the Veil," *French Politics, Culture and Society*, Vol. 22, No. 3, Fall 2004, pp. 142–149.

66. The surveys are reported in an article in the *Economist*, February 5, 2004.

67. The Ministry of the Interior claimed that 138,000 people had voluntarily agreed to this CAI by April 2006. While 72% enrolled in civics training course, only 25% enrolled in language training. It is also useful to point out that, in this contractual arrangement, the French state also agrees to protect immigrant rights, and to act against discriminatory practices. The form of the contract—which can be found on the Web site of the Ministry of the Interior—indicates rights and duties on both sides. See *Le Monde*, April 25, 2006.

68. See *Le Monde*, July 3, 2006.

69. *Le Monde*, November 25, 2007.

70. INSEE, *Enquête emploi de 2005*.

71. See Brouard and Tiberj, *Français Comme les Autres?* pp. 33, 47–51.

72. They are, for example, the only Muslim group in Europe in which a majority believe the attacks of September 11, 2001 were carried out by Arabs. Pew Research Center, *The Great Divide: How Westerners and Muslims View Each Other* (Washington, DC: Pew Global Attitude Project, June 2006), p. 4.

73. See Mark Kesselman and Joel Kreiger, *European Politics in Transition*, 5th edition (New York: Houghton Mifflin Co., 2006), introduction; George Lichtheim, *The New Europe, Today and Tomorrow*, 2nd edition (New York: Praeger, 1963), Ch. 5; Seymour Martin Lipset, *Political Man: The Social Basis of Politics* (New York: Doubleday, 1960), Ch. 2.

74. See *Le Monde*, December 29, 2005.

75. See, for example, the televised speech by President Chirac, *Le Monde*, November 16, 2005; and the analysis in *Le Monde* on November 15, 2005. Also, see the study by Dominique Meurs, Ariane Paihé and Patrick Simon, "Mobilité intergénérationalle et persistance des inégalités" (INED, Document de travail, no. 130, 2005). Also see the report in *Le Figaro*, May 19, 2006 on participants in the riots.

76. On this, see the excellent analysis by Virginie Guiraudon, "Different Nation, Same Neighborhood: The Challenges of Immigrant Policy," in Pepper D. Culpepper, Peter Hall, and Bruno Palier, Eds., *Changing France: The Politics that Market Make* (Basingstoke, UK: Palgrave Macmillan, 2006), pp. 129–149. Also, see Stéphane Beau and Michel Pauloux, *Violences urbaines, violence sociale: Genèse des nouvelles classes dangereuse* (Paris: Fayard, 2003); and Sophie Body-Gendrot and Catherine Wihtol de Wenden, *Sortir des banlieues: Pour en finir avec la tyrannie des territories* (Paris: Autrement-Frontières, 2007).

Four Politics of Immigration in France

1. Gérard Noiriel, *Le Creuset Français* (Paris: Éditions du Seuil, 1988), pp. 83–84.

2. Ibid., p. 95.

3. Ibid., pp. 84–90.

4. Mauco is cited by Patrick Weil, *La France et ses Etrangers* (Paris: Calman-Lévy, 1991), pp. 44–46. The key table from the report is in Annex III of Weil's book. Mauco, however, went well beyond cultural racism during the war, when he gave intellectual support to Vichy's anti-Semitic policies. See pp. 47–53.

5. See ibid., pp. 63–75.

6. Alexis Spire, *Etrangers à la carte: l'administration de l'immigration en France (1945–1975)* (Paris: Grasset, 2005), p. 13.

7. Correntin Calvez, "Le Problème de travailleurs étrangers," *Journal Officiel de la Republique Française, Avis et Rapports du Conseil Economique et Social*, March 27, 1969, p. 315. Also see Calvez, *Politique de l'immigration*, CES, *Avis adopté par le Conseil Economique et Social au cours de sa séance du 26 fevrier 1969 sur Le Problème des Travailleurs Étrangers*.

8. Africans were still a *minority* of all resident immigrants in France in 1990. See INSEE, *Les étrangers in France: portrait social* (Paris: INSEE, 1994).

9. Martin A. Schain, "Immigrants and Politics in France," in John Ambler, Ed., *The French Socialist Experiment* (Philadelphia, PA: ISHI Press, 1985).

10. Letter from the OHLM at St. Denis, November 28, 1980.

11. Letter from OHLM of Nanterre, September 20, 1980.

12. R.D. Grillo, *Ideologies and Institutions in Urban France* (London: Cambridge University Press, 1985), pp. 125–127.

13. Gary Freeman, "Immigrant Labour and Racial Conflict: The Role of the State," in Philip E. Ogden and Paul E. White, Eds., *Migrants in Modern France: Population Mobility in the Later 19th and 20th Centuries* (London: Unwin Hyman, 1989), p. 169.

14. Interview with Sarkozy in *Le Monde*, April 28, 2006, p. 9.

15. Nevertheless, between 1924 and 1930, only 35 percent of the titres de séjour were delivered by SGI, Weil, *La France et ses étrangers*, p. 32

16. Vincent Viet, *La France immigrée: Construction d'une politique 1914–1997* (Paris: Fayard, 1998), pp. 39–40.

17. Gary S. Cross, *Immigrant Workers in Industrial France: The Making of a New Laboring Class* (Philadelphia, PA: Temple University Press, 1983), p. 217.

18. Gérard Noiriel, "Communisme et immigration, éléments pour une recherche," *Communisme*, Nos. 15–16, 1987, p. 95.

19. Cited in Cross, *Immigrant Workers in Industrial France*, pp. 147–148.

20. Catherine Wihtol de Wenden, *Les Immigrés et la politique* (Paris: Presses de la FNSP, 1988), p. 50.

21. See Jacques Girault, "L'Implantation du parti communiste français dans l'entre-deux-guerres quelques jalons," in Jacques Girault, *Sur l'implantation du parti communiste français dans l'entre-deux-guerres* (Paris: Éditions Sociales, 1977), p. 51.

22. I have looked at the relationship between immigrant mobilization and the rise and decline of the PCF in "The Decline of French Communism: Party Construction and Party Decline," in Anthony Daley, Ed., *The Mitterrand Era: Policy Alternatives and Political Mobilization in France* (New York: New York University Press, 1996).

23. Gérard Noiriel, *Longwy: immigrés et prolétaires 1880–1980* (Paris: P.U.F., 1984), p. 387. See pp. 371–391 for some challenging ideas on the decline of communism in the region.

24. Spire, *Etrangers à la carte*, p. 13.

25. Alec Hargreaves, *Immigration, "Race" and Ethnicity in Contemporary France* (London: Routledge, 1995), pp. 178–179. The Labor-market argument is also cited by Mark Miller, *Foreign Workers in Europe: An Emerging Political Force* (New York: Praeger, 1981), p. xx, and by Andrew Geddes, *The Politics of Migration and Immigration in Europe* (London: Sage, 2003), p. 53.

26. Weil, *La France et ses étrangers*, pp. 95–100.

27. Jeannette Money, *Fences and Neighbors: The Political Geography of Immigration Control* (Ithaca, NY: Cornell University Press, 1999), pp. 109–110. The legislation was an amendment to the Labor Code, that made it illegal for to employ workers who lacked "a permit to do salaried work in France," a category that applied only to Algerians and Francophone Africans.

28. For a full account of this episode, see Jeffrey Togman, *The Ramparts of Nations* (Westport, CT: Praeger, 2002), pp. 106–107; and for the complex sociopolitical crisis that these circulars set off, see Viet, *La France immigrée*, pp. 318–322.

29. See Christiane Chambeau, "Le Pen dans le texte…des autres," *Le Monde*, December 27, 2005, p. 3. This long analysis focuses on the period since 2002. However, a similar case can be made for policy over a much longer period of time.

30. *Le Monde*, February 11 and December 7, 1989; See Judith Vichniac, "French Socialists and Droit à la différence," *French Politics and Society* Vol. 9, No. 1, Winter 1991, pp. 40–57.

31. This process is analyzed in an excellent article in *Le Monde* on December 16, 1997.

32. See Andrew Geddes, *The Politics of Migration and Immigration in Europe* (London: Sage, 2003), p. 55.

33. The initiatives of the government and the opposition are reported in *Le Monde*, April 3 and 4, 1990.

34. The Méhaignerie law. See Geddes, *The Politics of Migration and Immigration in Europe*, pp. 63–65.

35. *Le Monde*, April 3, 1990, p. 12.

36. See *Le Monde*, September 20, 1994.

37. *Le Monde*, April 27, 1995. On these questions, see James G, Shields, "Le Pen and the Progression of the Far Right in France," *French Politics and Society*, Vol. 3, No. 2, Spring 1995, pp. 34–35.

38. These and other early moves by the government are documented in *The European*, July 21–27, 1995.

39. Implementation of the Schengen Accords was formally delayed until the end of the year, a procedure that was permitted under the accords. See *Le Monde*, July 18, 1995. Implementation was then further delayed, with the French government citing as its reason the inability of the Benelux states to control the movement of drugs across their frontiers, and has now been only partially implemented. *Le Monde*, March 26, 1996.

40. Ibid.; See also *The European*, July 28–August 3, 1995.
41. *Le Monde*, April 17 and 19, 1996.
42. *Le Monde*, April 19, 1996.
43. *Le Monde*, October 1, 1999.
44. See *Le Monde*, June 23, 2005.
45. Patrick Weil, in an interview in *Le Monde*, July 10, 2007.
46. Interview with Sarkozy in *Le Monde*, April 28, 2006, p. 9.
47. *Le Monde* June 2, 1981. I have analyzed these programs in "Immigrants and Politics in France."
48. An analysis of the various kinds of associations that have emerged since 1981 can be found in Catherine Wihtol de Wenden, "Les associations "beur" et immigrés, leurs leaders, leurs stratégies," in *Regards sur l'actualité* No. 178, February, 1992.
49. See Martin A. Schain, "Ordinary Politics: Immigrants, Direct Action and the Political Process in France," *French Politics and Society*, No. 2–3, Spring–Summer 1994, pp. 65–84.
50. Jacques Barou, *Processus de segregation et ethnicisation de l'espace*, final report to DPM, October 1994, p. 24.
51. Miriam Feldblum, "Paradoxes of Ethnic Politics: the Case of Franco-Maghrebis in France," *Ethnic and Racial Studies*, Vol. 16, No. 1, January 1993, p. 57. This article contains an important and insightful analysis of the evolution of the association movement among immigrant groups. p. 59. For an extended analysis of the emergence of ethnicity in France, see Jocelyne Cesari, *Etre musulman en France* (Paris: Kathala-Iremam, 1994).
52. *Le Monde*, May 9, 2006.
53. Cesari, *Etre musulman in France*, pp. 250–251.
54. Money, *Fences and Neighbors*, pp. 135–155.
55. See Schain, "Immigrants and Politics in France."
56. See Schain, "The Politics of Immigration in France, Britain and the United States," in Craig A. Parsens and Timothy M. Smeeding, Eds., *Immigration and the Transformation of Europe* (Cambridge: Cambridge University Press, 2006).
57. See the analysis of the decision to suspend immigration in Jeffrey Togman, *The Ramparts of Nations*, Ch. 6.
58. Paul Dijoud, "La politique de l'immigration," *Droit Social*, No. 5, May 1976, cited in Viet, *La France immigrée*, pp. 364–365.
59. *Le Monde*, October 1 and October 7, 1999.
60. Speech before the National Assembly, *Journal Officiel*, July 3, 2003.
61. *Le Monde*, June 9, 2005. Indeed, surveys in 2004 indicated a sharp drop in the priority of the immigration issue, both among voters on the Right and on the Left, and among voters for the National Front. See, for example, CSA, "Les élections régionales: explication de vote et perspectives politiques," March 22, 2004, pp. 5–6.
62. See his proposals in the *Nouvel Observateur*, May 11, 2005.
63. One of Sarkozy's objectives was also to set an "objective," in fact a projected ceiling, for immigration each year. However, this was not placed in the bill that was presented in 2006 because of constitutional restrictions elaborated in a decision by the Constitutional Council in 2003. For complicated reasons, this provision would have necessitated a much long legislative procedure, one that was not compatible with Sarkozy's political objective of quick passage. See *Le Monde*, May 4, 2006.
64. *Le Monde*, June 9, 2005.
65. *Le Monde*, July 4, 2005.
66. *Le Monde*, May 9 and June 30, 2005, as well as the long analytic article on February 21, 2006. Also see the book by Jack Lang and Hervé le Bras, *l'Immigration Positive* (Paris: Odile Jacob, 2006).
67. By June 2006, he dropped the voting proposition. The law of 1905 transferred all houses of worship that then existed to the control of the state. In effect, this now means that most churches and many synagogues are subsidized by the state, but that mosques are not.
68. *Le Monde*, October 25, 2005. The legislation, passed in July, stipulates that applications after ten years can be made to the ministry of the interior on a case by case basis.
69. An article in Le Monde—entitled "M. Sarkozy: les communautés, c'est moi"—focused on these efforts, not only among the various Muslim communities, but among Jews as well. See *Le Monde*, March 8, 2006.

70. The turning point—argues Pierre Martin—was the European elections of 1984, the first break-through of the National Front. See Pierre Martin, *Comprendre les evolutions électorales: la théorie des réalignements revisitée* (Paris: Presses de Sciences Po, 2000), Part 3. Martin's analysis is supported by Nonna Mayer's work, where she argues that "...la présence de populations étrangères exerce un effet spécifique sur le vote FN, indépendant des charactéristiques sociales et culturelles de l'électeur." See *Ces français qui votent Le Pen* (Paris: Flammarion 1999), pp. 258–259.

71. Richard Alba and Nancy Foner, "Entering the Precincts of Power: Do National Differences Matter for Immigrant-Minority Political Representation?" Unpublished paper, February 2006.

72. Romaine Garbaye, "Ethnic Minority Local Councillors in French and British Cities: Social Determinants and Political Opportunity Structures," in Rinus Penninx, Karen Kraal, Marco Martiniello, and Steven Vertovec Eds., *Citizenship in European Cities* (London: Ashgate, 2004), pp. 47–48.

73. Vincent Geisser and Schérazade Kelfaoui, "Marseille 2001, la communauté réinventé par des politiques," *Migrations/Société,* September/October 2001, pp. 55–77 and Romain Garbaye, *Getting into Local Power: The Politics of Ethnic Minorities in British and French Cities* (Oxford: Blackwell, 2005), p. 32. The pattern was repeated in the run-up for the 2007 legislative elections. The party set aside 42 (out of 555) for "minority candidates," but 22 of these would be filled by another party of the Left coalition. It is unclear how many of the 42 or 20 can or will be won by the left. See *Liberation,* June 15, 2006.

74. See *Le Monde,* December 29, 2005. The surge was due in large part to a process of automatic registration that was provided by legislation passed in 1997.

75 Some sense of resistance to government actions can been seen in the refusal of 8 mayors of the Left to help the ministry of the interior pursue undocumented immigrants in 2007. See *Le Monde,* September 13, 2007.

76. I have presented this argument in "The Decline of French Communism: Party Construction and Party Decline," in Anthony Daley, Ed., *The Mitterrand Era: Policy Alternatives and Political Mobilization in France* (New York: New York University Press, 1996).

77. See Cour des Comptes, "L'Accueil des immigrants et l'intégration des populations issues de l'immigration," Rapport au Président de la République, November 2004, pp. 159–161; 425–430.

Five   Development of British Immigration Policy

1. See Richard Rose, "Politics in England," in Gabriel A. Almond, Russell J. Daloton, G. Bingham Powell, Jr., Kaare Strøm, Eds., *Comparative Politics Today: A World View,* updated 8th edition (New York: Pearson-Longman, 2006), pp. 157–204.

2. See Richard Rose, *The Territorial Dimension in Government: Understanding the United Kingdom* (Chatham, NJ: Chatham House, 1982), p. 14.

3. The British Empire slowly evolved into the Commonwealth, a process that began with the gradual independence of "old" Commonwealth countries of Canada, Australia, and New Zealand before WWII, and continued with the independence of the "new" Commonwealth countries of India and Pakistan after the war. By the end of the twentieth century the loose association of the Commonwealth ties of 53 independent countries had replaced those of the Empire. See W.D. McIntyre, *A Guide to the Contemporary Commonwealth* (London: Palgrave, 2001).

4. See Paul Foot, *Immigration and Race in British Politics* (Baltimore, MD: Penguin, 1965), p. 80. These figures are from the 1949 report of the Royal Commission on Population. Massy, 1989

5. See Mary J. Hickman, *Religion, Class and Identity: The State, the Catholic Church and the Education of the Irish in Britain* (Brookfield, VT: Avebury, 1995), pp. 205–212.

6. This argument is supported by a number of studies cited below, but especially by the classic book by Ian R.G. Spencer, *British Immigration Policy since 1939: The Making of Multi-racial Britain* (London: Routledge, 1997).

7. Paul Gordon, *Policing Immigration: Britain's Internal Controls* (London: Pluto Press, 1985), pp. 5–13.

8. Spencer, *British Immigration Policy since 1939,* p. 8.

9. See ibid., pp. 21–33.

10. See the account by Colin Holmes, *John Bull's Island: Immigration and British Society, 1871–1971* (London: Macmillan Education, 1988), pp. 82–85.

11. Spencer, *British Immigration Policy since 1939*, p, 106. On the riots, also see Holmes, *John Bull's Island*, pp. 107–112.

12. See U.S. Bureau of the Census, *Historical Statistics of the United States*, Part 1 (Washington, DC: USGPO, 1975), p. 117.

13. These first estimates of national origins were based on work of Quota Board, a commission established under the Johnson-Reed Act of 1924. Although these are highly controversial estimates, they give us some indication of the continuing importance of immigration from the United Kingdom to the United States throughout the nineteenth century. Between the Civil War and 1890, only immigration from Germany rivaled that from Great Britain, and British immigration was—on average—about the same as immigration from Ireland (then part of the United Kingdom). See *Historical Statistics*, p. 106. For national origins, see Desmond King, *Making Americans: Immigration, Race, and the Origins of the Diverse Democracy* (Cambridge, MA: Harvard University Press, 2000), pp. 208–209.

14. Joe Hicks and Grahame Allen, *A Century of Change: Trends in UK Statistics since 1900*, Research Paper 99/111, Social and General Statistics Section, House of Commons Library, December 21, 1999.

15. In fact, this power was rarely used. An Immigration Appeal Board was also established in every port, with the right to appeal. By 1919, the right to appeal was abandoned. See Ian Macdonald and Nicholas J. Blake, *Macdonald's Immigration Law and Practice in the United Kingdom*, 3rd edition (London: Butterworths, 1991), pp. 8–9.

16. Gordon, *Policing Immigration*, p. 9.

17. The Aliens Restrictions Acts of 1914 and 1919 did not repeat the exemption of refugees from restriction stipulated by the Aliens Act of 1905. As a result, jurisprudence has indicated that only the Home Secretary and not the courts can rule on refugee status. See Macdonald and Blake, *Macdonald's Immigration Law*, pp. 302–303.

18. Foot, *Immigration*, pp. 110–114.

19. The best analysis of the 1948 legislation that I have seen is Randall Hansen, *Citizenship and Immigration in Post-war Britain* (London: Oxford University Press, 2000), pp. 37–61.

20. Christian Joppke, *Immigration and the Nation-State: The United States, Germany and Great Britain* (London: Oxford University Press, 1999), p. 106.

21. Hansen, *Citizenship and Immigration*, pp. 109–110

22. Macdonald and Blake, *Macdonald's Immigration Law*, p. 11.

23. Ibid., p. 496.

24. Gordon, *Policing Immigration*, pp. 15–16.

25. Ibid., pp. 16–17.

26. This is the point made by Macdonald and Blake in *Macdonald's Immigration Law*, p. 11. A variation of the Natal formula was first applied in South Africa in 1897. See pp. 13–15.

27. Hansen, *Citizenship and Immigration*, pp. 170–174.

28. On the "husband war," see Joppke, *Immigration and the Nation-State*, pp. 114–128.

29. This eligibility has not been changed, and is available at the Web site of the UK Electoral Commission: www.electoralcommission.org.uk.

30. Macdonald and Blake, *Macdonald's Immigration Law*, p. 108.

31. Ibid., p. 117.

32. Ibid., p. 109–111, 117–118.

33. See Hansen, *Citizenship and Immigration*, pp. 213–214.

34. Citation for German *jus sanguinis*.

35. See *Migration Information Source*, June 16, 2004, pp. 3–4, and OECD, *Trends in International Migration: SOPEMI 2003 Edition* (Paris: OECD, 2004), pp. 288–289.

36. Joppke tells this story in great detail. See *Immigration and the Nation-State*, pp. 122–127. The 1988 legislation also made it easier for EU residents in the United Kingdom to bring in their immediate family without having to go through the admissions procedures required of immigrants from the Commonwealth, or even of British citizens.

37. Hansen, *Citizenship and Immigration*, pp. 218–219.

38. See Geddes, *The Politics of Migration and Immigration in Europe*, p. 43.

39. "Why the British Government's Plan for Controlling Immigration is a Bad Idea," *The Economist*, February 10, 2005.

40. "Out with the New," *The Economist*, December 9, 2004.

41. See the report of the MORI survey in the *Financial Times*, February 23, 2005.

42. "Howard's Way," *The Economist*, January 27, 2005.

43. See Janet Dobson, Khalid Koser, Gail Mclaughlan, and John Salt, "International Migration and the United Kingdom: Recent Patters and Trends," Final report to the Home Office, December 2001, RDS Occasional Paper No. 75, Table 4.1, p. 39.

Six   Understanding British Immigration Policy

1. One of the best accounts of this "incident" is in Christian Joppke, *Immigration and the Nation-State: The United States, Germany and Great Britain* (Oxford: Oxford University Press, 1999), pp. 105–106.

2. Ibid.

3. See ibid., p. 106.

4. It is not easy to make these comparisons. For example, France does not regularly publish statistics on outflows. Estimates, that about 25% of those who entered after 1990, then left, are generally support by figures published by the French Ministry of Foreign Affairs of French citizens living abroad. (See below).

5. See OECD, *SOPEMI Trends in International Migration, 2004* (Washington, DC: OECD, 2005), p. 284.

6. Ministry of Foreign Affairs, DFAE, "Evolution de la Population Française établie hors de la France, 1995–2004," Table 1.

7. OECD, SOPEMI *Trends in International Migration 2004*, p. 284.

8. BBC News (http://news.bbc.co.uk/go/pr/fr/-/1/hi/uk_politics/4389761.stm), March 29, 2005.

9. Nicola Gilpin, Matthew Henty, Sara Lemos, Jonathan Portes, and Chris Bullen, "The Impact of Free Movement of Workers from Central and Eastern Europe on the UK Labour Market" (UK Department for Work and Pensions, Working Paper 29).

10. OECD, *SOPEMI Trends in International Migration, 2004* (Washington, DC: OECD, 2005), p. 286. These figures also include those who left the country voluntarily after enforcement action was initiated.

11. These figures were quoted by Professor John Salt in *The Sunday Times,* as estimates that he did for the Home Office, on April 17, 2005.

12. The French were more serious about enforcement from 1982 on. See Mark J. Miller, "Employer Sanctions in France: From the Campaign against Illegal Aliens Employment to the Campaign against Illegal Work," *United States Commission on Immigration Reform* (Washington, DC: USGPO, 1995). See esp. Table 9. The British figures come from the Home Office: Illegal Working Taskforce, "Regulatory Impact Assessment for Immigration, Asylum and Nationality Bill," June 22, 2005, p. 3.

13. This literature is summarized by Jeannette Money, *Fences and Neighbors: The Political Geography of Immigration Control* (Ithaca, NY: Cornell University Press), pp. 71–86.

14. Rita Simon and James P. Lynch, "A Comparative Assessment of Public Opinion toward Immigrants and Immigration Policies," *International Migration Review*, Vol. 32, No. 2, Summer 1999, pp. 45–46.

15. Marilyn Hoskin and Roy Fitzgerald, "Public Acceptance of Racial and Ethnic Minorities: A Comparative Analysis," in Anthony Messina, Luis Fraga, Laurie Rhodebeck, and Frederick Wright, Eds., *Ethnic and Racial Minorities in Advanced Industrial Democracies* (Westport, CT: Greenwood Press, 1992), pp. 63–64.

16. Anthony M. Messina, *Race and Party Competition in Britain* (New York: Oxford University Press, 1989), p. 11.

17. See the account of this now famous interview in Randall Hansen, *Citizenship and Immigration in Post-war Britain* (Oxford: Oxford University Press: 2000), pp. 210–211.

18. *Eurobarometre* No. 62, December 2004, Q. 33.

19. "Immigration: Out with the New," *The Economist*, December 9, 2004.

20. See OECD, *SOPEMI Trends in International Migration, 2004* (Washington, DC: OECD, 2005), p. 284.

21. "Out with the New," *The Economist*, December 9, 2004.

22. Gordon Brown keynote address, the Fabian New Year Conference 2006—"Who Do We Want To Be? The Future of Britishness"—held at Imperial College, London on Saturday January 14, 2006.

23. Patrick Weil, "Access to Citizenship: A Comparison of 25 Nationality Laws," Canada Metropolis, no date, p. 3.

24. Hansen, *Citizenship and Immigration*, p. 128 and Ch. 6.

25. See Erik Bleich, *Race Politics in Britain and France: Ideas and Policymaking since the 1960s* (New York: Cambridge University Press, 2003), pp. 84–85.

26. See Money, *Fences and Neighbors*, p. 100.

27. Patrick Weil and John Crowley, "Integration in Theory and Practice: A Comparison of France and Britain," in Martin Baldwin-Edwards and Martin A. Schain, Eds., *The Politics of Immigration in Western Europe* (London: Cass, 1994), p. 118.

28. Quoted in Michael Benton, *Promoting Racial Harmony* (Cambridge: Cambridge University Press, 1985), p. 71.

29. Lord Swann, *Education for All: The Report of the Committee of Inquiry into the Education Children from Ethnic Minority Groups* (London: Cmnd 9453, HMSO, 1985).

30. Shane Brighton, "British Muslims, Multiculturalism and UK Foreign Policy: 'Integration' and 'Cohesion' in and beyond the State," *International Affairs*, Vol. 83, No. 1, January 2007, p. 5.

31. Tariq Modood, "Multiculturalism, Ethnicity and Integration: Contemporary Challenges," Paper presented at the Leverhulme Programme on Migration and Citizenship conference, "Ethnicity, Mobility and Society," University of Bristol, March 2006, p. 2, http://www.bristol.ac.uk/sociology/leverhulme/conference/conferencepapers/modood.pdf, cited by Brighton, "British Muslims, Multiculturalism and UK Foreign Policy," p. 6.

32. See Erik Bleich, *Race Politics in Britain and France: Ideas and Policymaking since the 1960s*, p. 104.

33. *New York Times*, March 3, 2005. This was consistent with earlier court decisions. In *Mandla v. Dowell* (1983), the court ruled that a headmaster was in violation of the 1976 Racial Discrimination Act for forbidding turban as violation of dress code. See Joppke, *Immigration and the Nation-State*, p. 235.

34. Robert Miles, "The Riots of 1958: Notes on the Ideological Construction of 'Race Relations' as a Political Issue in Britain," *Immigrants and Minorities*, Vol. 3, No. 3, 1984, pp. 262–264.

35. Bleich, *Race Politics in Britain and France*, p. 45.

36. Hansard, 711: 927, cited by Bleich, *Race Politics in Britain and France*.

37. Home Office, *Community Cohesion: A Report of the Independent Review Team chaired by Ted Cantle* (London: Stationery Office, 2001).

38. Cited in Brighton, "British Muslims, Multiculturalism and UK Foreign Policy," p. 10.

39. Christian Joppke, "The Retreat of Multiculturalism in the Liberal State: Theory and Policy," *British Journal of Sociology*, Vol. 55, No. 2, 2004, p. 253.

40. Brighton, "British Muslims, Multiculturalism and UK Foreign Policy."

41. See *International Herald Tribune*, January 10, 2006.

42. The report by the Historical Association, entitled Teaching Emotive and Controversial History 3–19 (April, 2007), is reported by BBC News on April 2, 2007: http://news.bbc.co.uk/2/hi/uk_news/education/

43. BBC News, January 25, 2007.

44. Trevor Phillips, "Multiculturalism's Legacy," *The Guardian*, May 28, 2004.

45. See "One Man's Ghetto," *The Economist*, September 22, 2005.

46. For more information about these initiatives, see the Web sites of the UK Foreign and Commonwealth Office, http://www.fco.gov.uk, and the department of Communities and Local Government, http://www.communities.gov.uk. Communities and Local Government was established in May 2006; one of its policy remits is to build community cohesion and tackle extremism.

47. The Mosques and Imams National Advisory Board led by Lord Ahmed, a Muslim member of the House of Lords, has yet to deliver a report on this subject that was commissioned in 2006.

48. These proposals have not been endorsed by the Muslim Council of Britain. See Jane Perlez, "Britain Aims to Isolate Muslim Extremists, Official Says," *New York Times*, April 6, 2007.

49. Jane Perlez, "New Civics Class Asks, What Would Mohammad Do?" *New York Times*, August 21, 2007.

50. Hugh Williamson, "EU Six Consider Introduction of 'Integration Contracts' for Immigrants," *The Financial Times*, March 24, 2006.

51. Bleich, *Race Politics in Britain and France*.

52. See the data in the *International Herald Tribune*, March 21, 2006, p. 2.

53. UK National Statistics: http://www.statistics.gov.uk/cci, unemployment rates for 2004.

54. Richard Alba and Nancy Foner, 2006, "Entering the Precincts of Power: Do National Differences Matter for Immigrant Minority Political Representation?" Unpublished paper, February 2006, Table 1.
55. See the results of the Pew *Global Attitudes Project*, July 6, 2006. Of the respondents 45% of British Muslim respondents are "very worried about" the decline of religion, compared with 21% in France.
56. Brighton, "British Muslims, Multiculturalism and UK Foreign Policy."

Seven   Politics of Immigration in Britain

1. Paul Foot, *Immigration and Race in British Politics* (Baltimore, MD: Penguin, 1965), pp. 88–93.
2. See Randall Hansen, *Citizenship and Immigration in Post-war Britain* (London: Oxford University Press, 2000), pp. 49–50.
3. Christain Joppke, *Immigration and the Nation-State: The United States, Germany and Great Britain* (Oxford: Oxford University Press, 1999), pp. 196–107.
4. Jeannette Money, *Fences and Neighbors: The Political Geography of Immigration Control* (Ithaca, NY: Cornell University Press, 1998), pp. 73–75 and 84–86. Electoral incentives seem much more plausible as an explanation for Labor behavior after 1962. See pp. 86–89.
5. Until the enforcement of the 1962 legislation, "...no official statistics were kept on entry or departure of citizens of the UK and Colonies, nor of citizens of the Commonwealth to the UK." The only official statistics that were kept until 1991 were those of entry and departure by ship, by country of departure and destination. The census, however, did record country of birth, and—by 1971—parents' country of birth. In addition, the Home Office kept unofficial statistics on race. Table 2 is based on census results. See Ceri Peach, Alisdair Rogers, Judith Chance and Patricia Daley, "Immigration and Ethnicity," in A.H. Halsey with Josephine Webb, Eds., *Twentieth Century British Social Trends* (New York: St. Martin's Press, 2000), pp. 139–140.
6. Peach, Rogers, Chance, and Daley in Halsey and Webb, *Twentieth Century British Social Trends*, p. 139.
7. Crossman, *Diaries of a Cabinet Minister*, p. 299, quoted in Hansen, *Citizenship and Immigration*, p. 151.
8. Home Secretary's memorandum, quoted in Hansen, *Citizenship and Immigration*, p. 161.
9. Hansen tells this story in some detail in ibid., pp. 197–201.
10. Ian Macdonald and Nicholas J. Blake, *Macdonald's Immigration Law and Practice in the United Kingdom,* 3rd edition (London: Butterworth's, 1991), pp. 1–2.
11. Foot, *Immigration and Race in British Politics*, pp. 88–92.
12. Ibid., p. 93.
13. Ibid., p. 99.
14. Much of this story is told in Colin Holmes, *John Bull's Island: Immigration and British Society, 1871–1971* (London: Macmillan Education, 1988), pp. 146–148.
15. Ibid., pp. 146–147.
16. Cited in Foot, *Immigration and Race in British Politics,* p. 107.
17. Macdonald and Blake, *Macdonald's Immigration Law*, pp. 9–10.
18. Money, *Fences and Neighbors*, p. 80.
19. See Duncan Gallie, "The Labour Force," in A.H. Halsey and Josephine Webb, Eds., *Twentieth Century British Social Trends* (New York: St. Martin's Press, 2000), pp. 313–315.
20. Hansen, *Citizenship and Migration*, p. 91.
21. Ibid., p. 84.
22. See Money, *Fences and Neighbors,* p. 76.
23. Hansen, *Citizenship and Migration*, p. 85.
24. See ibid., pp. 197–201.
25. It was also a clear reference to a speech by Enoch Powell, which is often referred to as the "rivers of blood" speech. See *New York Times*, February 1, 1978, and Enoch Powell, *Reflections of a Statesman: Writings and Speeches of Enoch Powell* (London, Bellow, 1991), p. 373.
26. See the account of this now famous interview in Hansen, *Citizenship and Immigration*, pp. 210–211.
27. "Playing the Race Card," *The Economist*, May 10, 2001.
28. "A New, Improved Race Card," *The Economist*, April 7, 2005.

29. See Joppke, *Immigration and the Nation-State*, pp. 117–118. Nevertheless, there have been checks from both the UK and European courts. See Macdonald and Blake, *Macdonald's Immigration Law*, p. 243–245.

30. See Kathleen Paul, *Whitewashing Britain: Race and Citizenship in the Postwar Era* (Ithaca, NY: Cornell University Press, 1997), Ian R.G. Spenser, *British Immigration Policy since 1939: The Making of Multi-Racial Britain* (London: Routledge, 1997), Robert Miles and Annie Phizacklea, *White Man's Country: Racism in British Politics* (London: Pluto Press, 1984), especially Ch. 1, and B. Carter, C. Harris, and S Joshi, "The 1951–55 Conservative Government and the Racialization of Black Immigration," *Immigrants and Minorities*, Vol. 6, No. 3, 1987, pp. 335–347. Much of this literature is summarized in Hansen, *Citizenship and*, pp. 10–16.

31. See Hansen, *Citizenship and Migration*, p. 14.

32. Money, *Fences and Neighbors*, p. 85. Frasure, on the other hand, using a somewhat different measure, gives the clear advantage to Labour during this same period. (See table 7.1).

33. David Butler and Donald Stokes, *Political Change in Britain*, 2nd edition (New York: St. Martin's Press, 1976), pp. 207–212.

34. Cited in Anthony Messina, *Race and Party Competition in Britain* (Oxford: Oxford University Press, 1989), pp. 34–36.

35. In 1975, the Community Relations Commission published a report that argued that minorities had played a key role in the 1974 Labour victory, although Ivor Crewe has demonstrated that the report exaggerated the importance of the minority vote. See Erik Bleich, *Race Politics in Britain and France: Ideas and Policymaking since the 1960s* (New York: Cambridge University Press, 2003), p. 92, fn 7.

36. Money, *Fences and Neighbors*, p. 79.

37. Ibid., p. 85; Anthony Frasure, "Constituency Racial Composition and the Attitudes of British MPs," *Comparative Politics*, January 1971, p. 206.

38. These estimates are from Alba and Foner, and are based on census data. "Ethnic minorities" include first and subsequent generations. Richard Alba and Nancy Foner, "Entering the Precincts of Power: Do National Differences Matter for Immigrant_Minority Political Representation?" Unpublished paper, February 2006, Table 1.

39. Vincent Geisser and Schérazade Kelfaoui, "Marseille 2001, la communauté réinventé par des politiques," *Migrations/Société*, September/October 2001, pp. 55–77 and Romain Garbaye, *Getting into Local Power: The Politics of Ethnic Minorities in British and French Cities* (Oxford: Blackwell, 2005), p. 32.

40. See Bleich, *Race Politics in Britain and*, pp. 92–93.

41. Some recent surveys have indicated that the tendency of immigrant voters to vote for the left has declined among the second generation born in France. See Syvain Brouard and Vincent Tiberj, *Français comme les autres?* (Paris: Presses de Sciences-Po, 2005), p. 56.

42. Messina, *Race and Party Competition in Britain*, pp. 109–125 and Ch. 6.

43. See Bleich, *Race Politics in Britain and France*, pp. 91–92.

Eight   Development of U.S. Immigration Policy

1. Austin Ranny, "Politics in the United States," in Gabriel A. Almond, Russell Dalton, C. Bingham Powell, Jr., and Kaare Strøm, Eds., *Comparative Politics Today: A World View*, updated 8th edition (New York: Pearson-Longman, 2006).

2. Cohesion indices are regularly reported by *Congressional Quarterly*. See Ranny, "Politics in the United States," pp. 764–766.

3. See David Mahew, *Divided We Govern* (New Haven, CT: Yale University Press, 1991).

4. Samuel H. Beer, "Federalism, Nationalism and Democracy in America," *American Political Science Review*, Vol. 72, No. 1, 1978, pp. 17–19.

5. U.S. House of Representatives, Committee on the Judiciary, *Immigration and Nationality Act*, 9th edition (Washington, DC: UGPO, 1992), p. 551.

6. Ibid.

7. Indeed, this is the assumption of most literature on U.S. immigration. See, for example, Danial J. Tichenor, *Dividing Lines: The Politics of Immigration Control in America* (Princeton: Princeton University Press, 2002), p. 2; Desmond King, *Making Americans: Immigration, Race and the Origins*

of the Diverse Democracy (Cambridge, MA: Harvard University Press, 2000), Ch. 3. Cheryl Shanks, *Immigration and the Politics of American Sovereignty, 1890–1990* (Ann Arbor: University of Michigan Press, 2004), Ch. 3.

8. See Aristide Zolberg, *A Nation by Design: Immigration Policy in the Fashioning of the United States* (Cambridge, MA: Harvard University Press, 2006), Chs. 1 and 4.

9. Ibid., Ch. 4.

10. Aristide Zolberg, "Rethinking the Last 200 Years of US Immigration Policy," Migration Information Source (Washington, DC: *Migration Policy Institute*, June, 2006), p. 1.

11. Tichenor, *Dividing Lines*, pp. 58–59.

12. The two defining decisions were *Mayor of New York v. Milne*, 36 U.S. (11 Pet) 102 in 1837, which clearly established the right of states to regulate by through head-taxes and bonds; this decision was effectively reversed in the *Passenger Cases* in 1848, but states made minor adjustments, and continued to regulate as best they could. See Tichenor, *Dividing Lines*, p. 58.

13. In re *Ah Fong*, Fed. Cas. No. 102, 3 Sawy., 144. Reported in *Digest of Immigration Decisions* (Washington, DC: USGPO, 1911), Senate Documents, Vol. 21, 61st Congress, 3rd Session, 1910–1911, p. 151.

14. *Henderson et al. v. Mayor of New York et al.* and *Commissioners of Immigration v. North German Lloyd*, 92 U.S. 259 (1875); *Chy Lung v. Freeman*, 92 U.S. 275 (1875).

15. Both the Supreme Court decision and the attempts to pass national legislation as a result are documented in the report of the Immigration Commission in 1911. See ibid., pp. 24–35.

16. John Higham, *Strangers in the Land: Patterns of American Nativism 1860–1925* (New York: Atheneum, 1969), pp. 44–45. Higham argues that this was the last time that reformers played a significant role in the making of immigration policy.

17. Tichenor, *Dividing Lines*, pp. 108–109.

18. Ibid., p. 109.

19. *Chae Chan Ping v. United States*, 130 U.S. 581 (1889), cited in Tichenor, *Dividing Lines*, p. 109.

20. See Lucy Salyer, "Captives of Law: Judicial Enforcement of the Chinese Exclusion Laws: 1891–1905," *The Journal of American History*, Vol. 76, No. 1 (June, 1989), pp. 91–117 presents an account of the Chinese petitioners in the California courts. My thanks to Professor Martin Shapiro for this reference.

21. Prior to this, some 5,000 state courts were responsible for the process, and there was no federal supervision. On the eve of elections, urban political machines had been easily able to secure citizenship papers in return for votes. Higham, *Strangers in the Land*, p. 118.

22. See Committee of the Judiciary, House of Representatives, *Immigration and Nationality Act*, 9th edition (Washington, DC: USGPO, 1992), p. 554. The act was not promulgated until after the war, when it proved to be a relatively ineffective instrument for limiting immigration from Southern and Eastern Europe, in part because literacy had increased since the legislation was first proposed 30 years earlier. See Higham, *Strangers in the Land*, p. 308.

23. Tichenor, *Dividing Lines*, pp. 152–153.

24. For a good account of the passage of the 1921 legislation, see Higham, *Strangers in the Land*, pp. 310–311.

25. Committee of the Judiciary, House of Representatives, *Immigration and Nationality Act*, 9th edition, p. 555.

26. Desmond King, *Making Americans: Immigration, Race, and the Origins of the Diverse Democracy* (Cambridge, MA: Harvard University Press, 2000), pp. 206–213.

27. Ibid., p. 208.

28. See Robert Divine, *American Immigration Policy, 1924–1952* (New Haven, CT: Yale University Press, 1957), p. 104.

29. Tichenor, *Dividing Lines*, pp. 173–175.

30. Ibid., pp. 187–188.

31. Ibid., p. 189.

32. The Asian provisions were originally proposed by Congressman Walter Judd in 1948, and ultimately included in the McCarran-Walter Bill. Because of this incorporation, the bill was supported by the Japanese-American Citizens League. See David M. Reimers, *Still the Golden Door: The Third World Comes to America* (New York: Columbia University Press, 1985), pp. 16–21.

33. Committee of the Judiciary, House of Representatives, *Immigration and Nationality Act*, p. 557. The act also excluded homosexuals, epileptics, and the mentally retarded.

34. Philip B. Perlman et al., *Whom Shall We Welcome: Report of the President's Commission on Immigration and Naturalization* (Washington, DC: USGPO, 1953).
35. Quoted from a 1965 congressional report in King, *Making Americans*, p. 243.
36. Elizabeth Harper, *Immigration Laws of the United States*, 3rd edition (Indianapolis: Bobbs Merrill, 1975), p. 38.
37. Tichenor, *Dividing Lines*, p. 218.
38. Reimers, *Still the Golden Door*, pp. 235–237.
39. Reported in Tichenor, *Dividing Lines*, p. 251.
40. Committee of the Judiciary, House of Representatives, *Immigration and Nationality Act*, p. 560
41. Tichenor, *Dividing Lines*, pp. 262–263.
42. Ibid. pp. 264–265.
43. Philip L. Martin, "Good Intentions Gone Awry: IRCA and U.S. Agriculture, " *Annals of the American Academy of Political and Social Science*, Vol. 534, Strategies for Immigration Control: An International Comparison, July 1994, pp. 44–57.
44. Jennifer Van Hook, Frank D. Bean, and Jeffrey Passel, *Unauthorized Migrants Living in the United States: A Mid-decade Portrait*. Migration Information Source, (Washington, DC: *Migration Policy Institute*, September 1, 2005).
45. See release of the president's speech on May 15, 2006: http://www.whitehouse.gov/news/releases/2006/05/20060515_7.html.
46. *New York Times*, December 17, 2005.
47. *Washington Post*, May 26, 2006.
48. *Washington Post*, April 12, 2006.
49. See Peter Brownell, "Declining Enforcement of Employer Sanctions," Migration Information Source (Washington, DC: *Migration Policy Institute*, 2005.).

Nine   Understanding U.S. Immigration Policy

1. Some of the most frequent references to the early perception of the United States as a country of immigration are from J. Hector St. John Crevecoeur, an eighteenth-century French immigrant to the United States:

> I think he was a Frenchman and a sailor on board an English man of war. Being discontented, he had stripped himself and swam ashore; where finding clothes and friends, he settled afterwards at Maraneck, in the county of Chester, in the province of New York: he married and left a good farm to each of his sons.... Where is then the industrious European who ought to despair? After a foreigner from any part of Europe is arrived, and become a citizen; let him devoutly listen to the voice of our great parent, which says to him, Welcome to my shores, distressed European; bless the hour in which thou didst see my verdant fields my fair navigable rivers, and my green mountains!

> Letters from an American farmer, by J. Hector St. John Crevecoeur, reprinted from the original ed., New York, Fox, Duffield, 1904, p. 90.

2. Aristide Zolberg devotes an entire chapter to what he calls "Tocqueville's Footnote," a footnote in a later edition *Democracy in America* in which Tocqueville questions the future of the American system in the light of the arrival of European immigrants who bring "the greatest vices" to the shores of the United States. Indeed, Zolberg notes that Tocqueville did not think of the United States as a country of multicultural immigrants, but "...as a thoroughly formed 'Anglo-American' people, whose political culture was founded on a collective character molded in the course of many generations of shared co-existence." Aristide Zolberg, *A Nation by Design: Immigration Policy in the Fashioning of America* (New York and Cambridge, MA: Russell Sage Foundation and Harvard University Press, 2006), pp. 125–127. The perception of immigrants as a danger to democracy and democratic values were also expressed by Hannah Arendt, at a time when multicultural values were becoming more accepted.

3. Aristide Zolberg, "Rethinking the Last 200 Years of US Immigration Policy," Migration Information Source (Washington, DC: *Migration Policy Institute*, June, 2006), p. 1.

4. The comment was in the decision on federal supremacy in interstate commerce, in *Gibbons v. Ogden* (1824), See Zolberg, *Nation by Design*, Ch. 4.

5. Zolberg, "Rethinking," p. 2.

6. Zolberg, *Nation by Design*, Ch. 4.
7. Daniel J. Tichenor, *Dividing Lines: The Politics of Immigration Control in America*, p. 66.
8. Ibid., pp. 93–94.
9. These figures are from Tichenor, *Dividing Lines*, p. 188. David Reimers gives a much higher figure of 700,000, see David Reimers, *Still the Golden Door: The Third World Comes to America* (New York: Columbia University Press, 1985), p. x.
10. Immigration from Canada was seen as generally benign, although the immigration of French-Canadians to work in factories in New England was sometimes posed in the same terms as migration from Mexico ("the Mexicans of the Northeast") See Zolberg, *Nation by Design*, p. 256.
11. Ibid., pp. 264–267. In fact, Zolberg first applies the term to the Passenger Acts (pp. 110–112). John Torpey notes that the use of U.S. consulates was initiated to police "return certificates" or rights of entry for Chinese were legally in the United States before the Chinese Exclusion Act in 1882, and who maintained a right to travel abroad and return to the United States if they had the proper certificate, as well as for Chinese scholars and merchants to who the exclusion did not apply. See John Torpey, *Invention of the Passport: Surveillance, Citizenship and the State* (Cambridge: Cambridge University Press, 2000), p. 99.
12. Zolberg, *Nation by Design*, p. 266.
13. Tichenor, *Dividing Lines*, p. 174.
14. Ibid., p. 202.
15. Reimers, *Still the Golden Door*, pp. 94–97.
16. The annual lottery is open to citizens of a very large number of countries, since generally no more than 15 countries send more than 50,000 immigrants to the United States each year. In fact, the lottery provides for limited entry of the relatively unskilled and relatively uneducated. It is widely advertized in eligible countries. Just over 40% of the entries are generally reserved for European countries.
17. These figures are cited in ch. 3. The French estimate was given by the minister of the interior in an interview in the *Figaro*, May 11, 2005; the British figures were quoted by Professor John Salt in *The Sunday Times* as estimates that he did for the Home Office, on April 17, 2005; and the American figure was cited by Thomas Freedman in *the International Herald Tribune* on April 6, 2006. In each case, the government has argued that there has been an increase; in the U.S. case, this is double the numbers cited by Tapinos in 1999. In general, the comparison among France, Britain, and the United States—if not the exact figures—is confirmed in a massive report by the French Senate in April 2006. See *Rapport de la commission d'enquête sur l'immigration clandestine, créé en vertu d'une résolution adoptée par le Sénat le 27 octobre 2005* (2 volumes).
18. See Jeffery Passel, "Size and Characteristics of the Unauthorized Migrant Population in the U.S." (Washington, DC: Pew Hispanic Center, 2006).
19. Zolberg, *Nation by Design*, p. 267.
20. Tichenor, *Dividing Lines: The Politics of Immigration Control in America*, pp. 172–173.
21. *Annual Report of the Immigration and Naturalization Service, 1955* (Washington, DC: USGPO, 1956), pp. 15–16.
22. Reimers, *Still the Golden Door*, p. 57.
23. These figures are taken from the INS statistics.
24. These are people who have been apprehended at the Mexican border, and have agreed to leave. They are then escorted to the border. However, these numbers represent "events," rather than individuals, and include large numbers of recidivists who often cross several times within a short period of time. See Department of Homeland Security, Office of Immigration Statistics, *2005 Yearbook of Immigration Statistics*, p. 4.
25. In fact, the decision to focus enforcement on the border itself, rather than work-site enforcement, was based on a report that had been commissioned in September 1991, often referred to as the "Sandia Report." Sandia National Laboratories, through INS, was asked to do a "systematic analysis of the security along the United States/Mexico Border between the ports of entry and to recommend measures by which control of the border could be improved." In January 1993, Sandia issued its report entitled *Systematic Analysis of the Southwest Border*, and the major recommendations of the report was implemented in 1994.
26. See David Dixon and Julia Gelatt, "Immigration and Enforcement Spending since IRCA," Background paper prepared for the Independent Task Force on Immigration and America's Future, September, 2005, Table 2, cited in Debra Walter Meyers, "From Horseback to High-Tech: U.S.

Border Enforcement," Migration Information Source (Washington, DC: *Migration Policy Iinstitute*, February, 2006), p. 8.

27. *Washington Post*, May 16, 2006.

28. Passel, "Size and Characteristics," p. 2.

29. Rey Koslowski, "Toward Virtual Borders: Expanding European Border Control Policy Initiatives and Technology Implementation," Unpublished paper, May 2005, p. 8.

30. Peter Andreas, *Border Games: Policing the US-Mexican Divide* (Ithaca, NY: Cornell University Press, 2000).

31. See *Rapport de la commission d'enquête sur l'immigration clandestine, créé en vertu d'une résolution adoptée par le Sénat le 27 octobre 2005* (2 volumes). In particular, see the testimony of François Héran in Volume II, and cited on p. 47 of Volume I. He also cites the United State as one of the countries where the informal labor market is most important. The data cited by the report (Vol. I, p. 47), indicates that no country in Europe has a lower rate of irregular immigration than France.

32. Wayne Cornelius, "Evaluating Enhanced US Border Enforcement," Migration Information Source (Washington, DC: *Migration Policy Institute*, 2004), p. 1.

33. Peter Brownell, "The Declining Enforcement of Employer Sanctions," Migration Information Source (Washington, DC: *Migration Policy Institute*, 2005), pp. 3–5.

34. Spencer Hsu and Kari Lydersen, "Illegal Hiring Is Rarely Penalized," *Washington Post*, June 19, 2006.

35. Julia Preston, "US Puts Onus on Employers of Immigrants," *New York Times*, July 31, 2006.

36. *New York Times*, December 18, 2006.

37. *New York Times*, April 5, 2007.

38. *New York Times*, December 24, 2006, March 22 and March 30, 2007.

39. *New York Times*, December 18, 2006, March 22, 2007.

40. Julia Preston, "Government Set for a Crackdown on Illegal Hiring," *New York Times*, August 8, 2007

41. See the report by Julia Preston, "270 Illegal Immigrants Sent to Prison in Federal Push," in the *New York Times* on May 24, 2008, as well as the *New York Times* editorial on June 3, 2008.

42. Hsu and Lydersen, "Illegal Hiring."

43. Julia Preston, "Farmers Call Crackdown on Illegal Workers Unfair," *New York Times*, August 11, 2007.

44. Hsu and Lydersen, "Illegal Hiring."

45. Under the H-2/H2A program, which require farmers to demonstrate that American labor is not available, and to provide housing.

46. Edouardo Porter, "Attack on Illegal Immigration Wilts on America's Farms," *International Herald Tribune*, March 23, 2006.

47. See Lawrence Downes, "After and Anti Immigrant Flare-Up, Texas Gets Back to Business," *New York Times*, April 2, 2007.

48. See Julia Preston, "In Increments, Senate Revisits Immigrant Bill," *New York Times*, August 3, 2007.

49. See Eric Lipton, "Rebellion Growing as States Challenge a Federal Law to Standardize Driver's Licenses," New York Times, September 29, 2006; Robert Pear, "Lacking Papers, Citizens Are Cut from Medicaid," *New York Times*, March 12, 2007. Reports of the National Conference of State Legislatures: *2006 Enacted State Legislation Related to Immigrants and Immigration*, October 2006; *2007 Enacted State Legislation Related to Immigrants and Immigration*, August 2007.

50. Passel, "Size and Characteristics."

51. Amanda Levinson, "Why Countries Continue to Consider Regularization," Migration Information Source, (Washington, DC: *Migration Policy Institute*, September 2005), pp. 2–3.

52. Ibid.

53. See BBC News on Line: http://news.bbc.co.uk/ June 12, 2006: "An Immigration Amnesty is ruled out"; June 14, 2006: Dominic Casciani, "An Illegal Immigration Amnesty?"

54. BBC News on Line: http://news.bbc.co.uk/ May 10, 2006: "Ten Years to Deport All Illegals"; Casciani, "An Illegal Immigration Amnesty?"

55. Cornelius, "Evaluating Enhanced US Border Enforcement," p. 2; D. S. Massey, J. Durand, and N.J. Malone, *Beyond Smoke and Mirrors: Mexican Immigration in an Era of Economic Integration* (New York: Russell Sage Foundation, 2002).

56. These estimates are mostly from a University of Houston Center for Immigration research project, supplemented by figures from the Border Patrol. See Karl Eschbach, Jacqueline Hagan, and Nestor Rodríguez "Deaths during Undocumented Migration: Trends and Policy Implications in the New Era of Homeland Security," Presented at the *26th Annual National Legal Conference on Immigration and Refugee Policy*, Washington, DC, April 2003.

57. These tables are based on data from Gallup, primarily because Gallup provides us with a time-series on the same questions. We should note that the approval ratings from these surveys are relatively low. A New York Times/CBS poll in 2006 found that 22% of respondents favored increasing immigration, and a Quinnipiac survey found that 24%favored increase. A Pew survey at the same time (February/May 2006) found 17% in favor of an increase, but only 40 percent in favor of a decrease. See *Fact Sheet: The State of American Public Opinion on Immigration in Spring 2006: A Review of Major Surveys*, Pew Hispanic Center, May 17, 2006.

58. Gallup Organization Polls on Immigration.

59. Rita J. Simon and Susan H. Alexander, *The Ambivalent Welcome: Print Media, Public Opinion and Immigration* (Westport, CT: Praeger, 1993), p. 46.

60. See the results of the U.S. Bureau of the Census, American Community Survey 2005, Table GCT0501, "Percentage of People Who Are Foreign-Born."

61. Audrey Singer, immigration fellow at the Brookings Institution, in Rick Lyman, "New Data show Immigrants' Growth and Reach," *New York Times*, August 15, 2006.

62. This data is from Roy Beck and Steven A. Camarota, "Elite vs. Public Opinion: An Examination of Divergent Views on Immigration," Center for Immigration Studies, December, 2002. Also see Gallya Lahav, *Immigration and Politics in the New Europe: Reinventing Borders* (Cambridge, U.K.: Cambridge University Press, 2004), ch. 3.

63. The Naturalization Act of 1790 specifically stated that naturalization was limited to "free white persons." Although the legislation intended to restrict the naturalization of those brought to the United States as slaves, legislation passed in 1870 then included persons of "African nativity and…descent" among those who are eligible for nationalization. With the passage of the Chinese Exclusion Act in 1882, the racial provisions of the amended 1790 legislation were applied principally to Asians, an application that was upheld by the Supreme Court. For court decisions, see *The Constitution of the United States of America: Analysis and Interpretation* (Washington, DC: USGPO, 1982), pp. 296–298.

64. See John Torpey, *Invention of the Passport: Surveillance, Citizenship and the State*, pp. 97–101.

65. Higham elaborates these new laws in *Strangers in the Land*, pp. 140–142.

66. This literature is summed up by Desmond King in *Making Americans: Immigration, Race and the Origins of the Diverse Democracy* (Cambridge, MA: Harvard University Press, 2000), pp. 14–19.

67. Ibid, p. 18.

68. See Noah Pickus, "'Human Nature Cannot Be Changed Overnight:' Re-assessing the Americanization Movement of the 1920s," delivered at the 1993 Annual Meeting of the Southwestern Political Science Association, New Orleans, LA, March 17–20, 1993, pp. 24–26.

69. Higham elaborates these new laws in *Strangers in the Land*, p. 260.

70. Theodore Lowi, *The End of Liberalism* (New York: W.W. Norton, 1969), Ch. 1. Higham, *Strangers in the Land: Patterns of American Nativism 1860–1925* (Forge Village, MA: Atheneum, 1963), p. 234.

71. See, Lawrence H. Fuchs *The American Kaleidoscope: Race, Ethnicity and the Civic Culture* (Hanover, NH: Wesleyan University Press, 1990), Ch. 1; and Amy Bridges, *A City in the Republic: Antebellum New York and the Origins of Machine Politics* (Ithaca, NY: Cornell University Press, 1987), Chs. 3–5.

72. Frances Fitzgerald, *America Revised: History Schoolbooks in the Twentieth Century* (New York: Little Brown, 1979), pp. 79–83.

73. Which is exactly the point that Salins makes in *Assimilation American Style*

74. Martin Kilson, "Blacks and Neo-ethnicity in America," in Nathan Glazer and Daniel P. Moynihan, Eds., *Ethnicity: Theory and Experience* (Cambridge: Harvard University Press, 1975), Ch. 8. Nathan Glazer referred to African-Americans as the "storm troops" of multiculturalism, because of their ejection from the melting pot from the very beginning. Nathan Glazer, *We Are All Multiculturalists Now* (Cambridge, MA: Harvard University Press, 1997), p. 95

75. The quote is meant to apply to France, not the United States, but is cross-referenced to Nathan Glazer, "Ethnic Groups in America: From National Culture to Ideology, in Monroe Berger, Theodore Abel, and Charles H. Page, Eds., *Freedom and Control in Modern Society* (New York: Van Nostrand,

1954), pp. 158–173. See Patrick Ireland, *The Policy Challenge of Ethnic Diversity* (Cambridge, MA: Harvard University Press, 1994), pp. 10–11.

76. King, *Making Americans*, pp. 266–267; Linda K. Kerber, "The Meaning of Citizenship, *Journal of American History*, Vol., 84, 1977, pp. 833–854.

77. Tichenor, *Dividing Lines*, p. 274.

78. Alfred Blumrosen and Alexander B. Blumrosen, "The Collection of Race/Sex/Ethnic Origin Statistics in France to Identify and Combat Employment Discrimination: Lessons from the US Experience," *French American Foundation Roundtable Conference on Measuring Discrimination*, November 13, 2006, p. 4.

79. Neil A. Lewis, "Court Upholds Key Provision of the Voting Rights Act," The New York Times, May 31, 2008.

80. For a look at the privileges afforded to religious organizations in the United States, see the *New York Times* series, "Religion-Based Tax Breaks: Housing to Paychecks to Books," (October 11, 2006) and "Religion Trumps Regulation as Legal Exemptions Grow" (October 8, 2006), as well as other pieces in a special series about religion.

81. Aristide Zolberg, "The Democratic Management of Cultural Differences: Building Inclusive Societies in Westerns Europe and North America," in *Human Development Report* (New York: United Nations Development Programme, 2004), pp. 17, 51.

82. Charles A. Radin and Yvonne Abraham, "Aide's Role in Mosque Deal Eyed," *Boston Globe*, March 4, 2006. The reports in the *Boston Globe* indicate that this local subsidy was quite controversial, and was both opposed and supported when it was revealed in early 2006.

83. Diana Eck, *A New Religious America: How a Christian Country Has Become the World's Most Religiously Diverse Nation* (San Francisco, CA: Harper, 2002), p. 348.

84. Zolberg, "Democratic Management of Cultural Differences," p. 52; Elaine C. Hagopian, *Civil Rights in Peril: The Targeting of Arabs and Muslims* (London: Pluto Press, 2004), pp. 9–71; Neil MacFarquhar, "Fears of Inquiry Dampen Giving by U.S. Muslims," *New York Times*, October 30, 2006.

85. U.S. Bureau of the Census and U.S. Congress, Congressional Budget Office, *A Description of the Immigrant Population, November 2004*, Table 12.

86. Richard Alba and Nancy Foner, "Entering the Precincts of Power: Do National Differences Matter for Immigrant-Minority Political Representation?" Unpublished paper, February 2006, p. 12.

Ten   Politics of Immigration in the United States

1. See Aristide Zolberg, *A Nation by Design: Immigration Policy in the Fashioning of the United States* (Cambridge, MA: Harvard University Press, 2006), Chs. 1and 4 and pp. 110–120.

2. Lawrence H. Fuchs, *The American Kaleidoscope: Race, Ethnicity and the Civic Culture* (Hanover, NH: Wesleyan University Press, 1990), p. 41–42.

3. Daniel J. Tichenor, *Dividing Lines: The Politics of Immigration Control in America* (Princeton: Princeton University Press, 2002), pp. 60–66.

4. John Woolley and Gerhard Peters, The American Presidency Project [online]. Santa Barbara, CA: University of California (hosted), Gerhard Peters (database). Available from http://www.presidency.ucsb.edu/ws/?pid=29621, last accessed June 7, 2008.

5. Tichenor, *Dividing Lines*, p. 65.

6. See Gwendolyn Mink, *Old Labor and New Immigrants in American Political Development: Union, Party and State, 1975–1920* (Ithaca, NY: Cornell University Press, 1986), Ch. 3, for an historical account of the development of the anti-Chinese movement.

7. Ah Fong, Fed. Cas. No. 102, 3 Sawy, 144, Senate Documents, 1911, 151. The other key decisions in this shift were: *Henderson et al. v. Mayor of New York et al.* and *Commissioners of Immigration v. North German Lloyd*, 92 U.S. 259 (1875); *Chy Lung v. Freeman*, 92 U.S. 275 (1875).

8. The key case was the *Henderson* case, that involved a challenge by shippers to right of New York (and Louisiana) to impose head taxes on arriving immigrants. The decision of the court effectively reversed a decision rendered in *City of New York v. Miln*; 2 Paine 429; 8 Peters 120 (1834); 11 Peters 102 (1837), which concluded that the regulation of immigration was police-power (rather than regulation of international commerce) that rightfully belonged to the states. See Zolberg, *A Nation by Design* pp. 142 and 189–190.

9. From a speech at the Republican National Convention of 1868, cited in Tichenor, *Dividing Lines*, p. 93.

10. Patrick Fisher and Shane Fisher, "Congressional Passage of the Chinese Exclusion Act of 1882," *Immigrants and Minorities*, Vol. 20, No. 2, 2001, pp. 58–74.

11. Tichenor, *Dividing Lines*, Ch. 4, and Fisher and Fisher, "Congressional Passage of the Chinese Exclusion Act."

12. See the introduction to the Report of the *Joint Special Committee to Investigate Chinese Immigration*, 44th Congress, 2nd Session, Senate Report No. 689, February 27, 1877 (Washington, DC: USGPO, 1877).

13. Ibid., p. 101.

14. Senate Report No. 290, 44th Congress, 1st Session, cited by *Reports of the Immigration Commission*, 1911, pp. 47–48.

15. Ibid., p. 48.

16. Henry Cabot Lodge, "The Distribution of Ability in the United States," *Century Magazine*, Vol. 42, 1891, cited by Higham, *Strangers in the Land*, p. 142.

17. Giddings was the author of an important sociology text, *Principles of Sociology*, first published in 1896. The text devoted relatively little space to questions of race, but where it did, it reflected the author's somewhat ambivalent social Darwinism that emphasized the survival and dominance of "superior" white races. See Carl N. Degler, *In Search of Human Nature: The Decline and Revival of Darwinism in American Social Thought* (New York: Oxford University Press, 1991), pp. 17–18.

18. Higham, *Strangers in the Land*, p. 148.

19. The results were not always very successful. See Lawrence Cremin, *The Transformation of the School* (New York: Vintage, 1964), pp. 72–73.

20. The quote is from David Saville Mussey's *American History* (1911), and is quoted in Frances FitzGerald's review of history textbooks, *America Revisited* (New York: Vintage, 1979), pp. 78–79.

21. U.S. Immigration Commission, *Abstract of the Report on the Children of Immigrants in Schools* (Washington, DC: USGPO, 1911), pp. 18–19.

22. William Z. Riply, *The Races of Europe* (New York, Appleton, 1923).

23. Madison Grant, *The Passing of the Great Race* (New York: Scribner's sons, 1916).

24. See the summary of Grant's ideas in Higham, *Strangers in the Land*, pp. 155–157.

25. The President's Research Committee on Social Trends, *Recent Social Trends in the United States* (Washington, DC: USGPO, 1933), p. 428.

26. U.S. Immigration Commission, Vol. 1, *Brief Statement of the Investigations of the Immigration Commission, with Conclusions and Recommendations and Views of the Minority* (Washington, DC, 1911), pp. 13–14.

27. Reports of the Immigration Commission, *Dictionary of Races or Peoples* (Washington, DC, 1911), p. 74.

28. U.S. Immigration Commission, Vol. 1, *Brief Statement of the Investigations of the Immigration Commission*, pp. 45–48.

29. Tichenor, *Dividing Lines*, p. 197.

30. Philip B. Perlman et al., *Whom Shall We Welcome: Report of the President's Commission on Immigration and Naturalization* (Washington, DC: USGPO, 1953).

31. Ibid., p. 272–273.

32. "Message from the President of the United States," Ibid., pp. 276–278.

33. Ibid., pp. 88–96; Also see pp. 91–95 for a point by point refutation of the assumptions behind the Dillingham Commission reports. (Emphasis in bold is in the report.)

34. Ibid., p. 97.

35. Ibid., p. 52.

36. Ibid., p. 89.

37. Tichenor, *Dividing Lines*, p. 199.

38. The phrase is a title of an essay written by John F. Kennedy in 1957, and published by the Anti-Defamation League in 1958. It was published commercially 1964 (New York: Harper and Row, 1964). Kennedy's remarks echoed the main lines of *The President's Commission on Immigration and Naturalization* (Washington, DC: USGPO, 1953), introduction.

39. King, *Making Americans*, pp. 32, 266–276. Title V of the Education Act of 1972. The movement of public support for multiculturalism was severely criticized by the 1990s. See in particular, Peter Salins' approving account of the success of Americanization policies in *Assimilation American Style* (New York: HarperCollins, 1997), Part III; and Arthur M. Schlessinger, Jr.,

The Disuniting of America: Reflections on a Multicultural Society (New York: W.W. Norton, 1991 and 1998); and Samuel P. Huntington, *Who Are We: The Challenges to American's National Identity* (New York: Simon and Schuster, 2004). See Huntington's previous position in his text first published in 1981, *American Politics: The Promise of Disharmony* (Cambridge, MA: Belknap Press, 1981). My thanks to Christopher Mitchell for referring me to this book, as well as Huntington's argument for a cultural basis for American citizenship.

40. The sense of crisis is summarized by Philip L. Martin in "Select Commission Suggests Changes in Immigration Policy—A Review Essay," *Monthly Labor Review*, February 1982, pp. 31–32; and Vernon M. Briggs, Jr., "Report of the Select Commission on Immigration and Refugee Policy: A Critique," *Texas Business Review*, January–February 1982, pp. 11–12.

41. Tichenor, *Dividing Lines*, p. 239.

42. All of these positions are controversial. See Martin, "Select Commission," p. 36.

43. See the summary of SCIRP conclusions and proposals in *New York Times*, February 28, 1981, Section B, p. 5.

44. Tichenor, *Dividing Lines*, p. 251.

45. Dorothy Nelkin and Mark Michaels, "Biological Categories and Border Controls: The Revival of Eugenics in Anti-immigration Rhetoric," *International Journal of Sociology and Social Policy*, Vol. 18, No. 5/6, 1998, p. 33. Also, see Richard Herrnstein and Charles Murray, *The Bell Curve* (New York: Free Press, 1994); Seymour W. Itzkoff, *The Decline of Intelligence in America* (Westport, CT: Praeger, 1994); Philippe Rushton, *Race, Evolution and Behavior* (New Brunswick, NJ: Transaction Press, 1994).

46. United States Commission on Immigration Reform (USCIR), *Report to Congress, U.S. Immigration Policy: Restoring Credibility* (Washington, DC: USGPO, 1994), p. 3.

47. USCIR, *Report to Congress, Legal Immigration: Setting Priorities* (Washington, DC: USGPO, 1995), p. 1.

48. Ibid., pp. 13–16.

49. USCIR, *Restoring Credibility*, p. 13.

50. USCIR, *Report to Congress, Becoming an American: Immigration and Immigrant Policy* (Washington, DC: USGPO, 1997), pp. 26 and 29.

51. Tichenor, *Dividing Lines*, p. 246.

52. See chapter 1, and Terri Givens and Adam Luedke, "European Immigration Policies in Comparative Perspective: Issue Salience, Partisanship and Immigrant Rights," *Comparative European Politics*, Vol. 3, No. 1, April 2005, pp. 6–7; also see Gary Freeman, "Winners and Losers: Politics and the Costs and Benefits of Migration," in Antony M. Messina, Ed., *West European Immigration and Immigrant Policy in the New Century* (Westport, CT: Praeger, 2002), pp. 76–96.

53. Lawrence H. Fuchs, *The American Kaleidoscope: Race, Ethnicity and the Civic Culture* (Hanover, NH: Wesleyan University Press, 1990), p. 41. In fact, I have found no evidence of 75 American Party members of the House of Representatives. However, the elections of 1854 and 1856 were marked by shifting party allegiances. The largest single party in the House in 1857 was the "Opposition Party," most whom had become Republicans by 1856, and some of whom may have been identifies as Know Nothings. The estimates vary for the House—between 43 and 62 (although Fuchs' estimates are even higher). Fuchs writes that 8 Senators and 104 members of the House of Representatives campaigned on the Know Nothing platform were elected (see note 3, above). Part of the problem is that some American Party representatives appear to have run on both the American and the Republican tickets. See Tichenor, *Dividing Lines*, p. 62 The Historical Statistics of the United States reports 43– see U.S. Department of Commerce Bureau of the Census, *Historical Statistics of the United States* (Washington, DC: USGPO, 1975), Part 2, p. 1083.

54. Zolberg, *A Nation by Design*, p. 528, note 139.

55. Ibid., pp. 162–163.

56. Ibid., p. 164.

57. Ibid., p. 165.

58. Fuchs, *The American Kaleidoscope*, pp. 42–48.

59. Tichenor, *Dividing Lines*, pp. 102–106.

60. *Reports of the Immigration Commission, Immigration legislation: Federal Immigration Legislation*, Vol 40, 61st Congress, 3rd Session, Senate. Doc. 758.

61. See Henry Pratt Fairchild, "The Literacy Test and Its Making," *The Quarterly Journal of Economics*, Vol. 31, No. 3, 1917, pp. 453–454.

62. Charles W. Eagles, "Congressional Voting in the 1920s: A Test of Urban-Rural Conflict," *The Journal of American History*, Vol. 76, No. 2, September 1989, 533–534.

63. Tichenor, *Dividing Lines*, pp. 132–138; Zolberg, *A Nation by Design*, pp. 221–223.

64. Kristi Andersen, *The Creation of a Democratic Majority: 1928–1936* (Chicago: University of Chicago Press, 1979), pp. 31–32, 40–42, 89–93.

65. Tichenor, *Dividing Lines*, pp. 188–196.

66. This had been attempted in 1952 by Hubert Humphrey, Herbert Lehman, and James Roosevelt, but their proposal was effectively squashed by Chairman McCarran in the Senate, and by the chair of the Immigration Sub-committee in the House, Francis Walter.

67. Bureau of the Census, *Historical Statistics of the United States* (Washington, DC: UGPO, 1975), pp. 105 and 107.

68. On the agribusiness "iron triangle," see Kitty Calavita, *Inside the State* (New York: Routledge, 1992).

69. Department of Homeland Security, Office of Immigration Statistics, *2003 Yearbook of Immigration Statistics* (September 2004), Table 5.

70. E.E. Schattschneider, *The Semisovereign People* (New York: Holt, Rinehart and Winston, 1960), Chapter 2.

71. Tichenor, *Dividing Lines*, p. 172.

72. Ibid., pp. 211–216; and David M. Reimers, *Still the Golden Door: The Third World Comes to America* (New York: Columbia University Press, 1985), pp. 71–72.

73. Bureau of the Census, *Historical Statistics of the United States*, p. 107.

74. This analysis relies on Roger Waldinger and Mehdi Bozorgmehr, "From Ellis Island to LAX," Department of Sociology, UCLA. August 1993.

75. Two of the six congressional districts that are all or in part in Orange County, CA are solidly Democratic, with 60% or more of the vote in 2000, 2002, and 2006 (CDs 39 and 47).

76. See James G. Gimpel and Karen Kaufman, "Impossible Dream or Distant Reality? Republican Efforts to Attract Latino Voters," *Center for Immigration Studies Reports*, August 2001.

77. Bureau of the Census, 2005 *American Community Survey; Congressional District Data Book* (Washington DC: UGPO, 2005).

78. Michael Luo, "Walking a Tightrope on Immigration," *New York Times*, November 18, 2007.

79. Luis F.B. Plascencia, Gary Freeman, and Mark Selzer, "The Decline of Barriers to Immigrant Economic and Political Rights in the American States: 1977–2001," *International Migration Review*, Vol. 37, No. 1, Spring 2003, p. 7.

80. Desmond King, *Making Americans: Immigration, Race and the Origins of the Diverse Democracy* (Cambridge, MA: Harvard University Press, 2000), p. 114.

81. See National Conference of State Legislatures, *2006 Enacted State Legislation Related to Immigrants and Immigration* (Washington, DC: USGPO, 2006).

82. Ibid., and Eric Lipton, "Rebellion Growing as States Challenge a Federal Law to Standardize Driver's Licenses," *New York Times*, September 29, 2006.

83. Samuel Beer, "Federalism, Nationalism and Democracy in America," *The American Political Science Review*, Vol. 72, No. 1, 1978, pp. 17–18.

Eleven   Conclusion

1. See Daniel J. Tichenor, *Dividing Lines: The Politics of Immigration Control in America* (Princeton: Princeton University Press, 2002), Ch. 6.

2. Employment of immigrants in agribusiness is far less important in France and Britain, where illegal immigrants tend to be concentrated in cities and tend to work in services and small industry. See OECD, *International Migration Outlook, 2006* (Washington DC: 2006), p. 57.

3. See Christian Joppke, "Transformation of Immigrant Integration: Civic Integration and Antidiscrimination in the Netherlands, France and Germany," *World Politics*, Vol. 59, January 2007, No. 2, p. 243.

4. Shane Brighton, "British Muslims, Multiculturalism and UK Foreign Policy: 'Integration' and 'Cohesion' in and beyond the State," *International Affairs*, Vol. 83, No. 1, January 2007, pp. 1–17.

5. Council Directive 2000/43/EC, June 29, 2000; and Council Directive 2000/78/EC, November 27, 2000.

6. Tichenor, *Dividing Lines*, pp. 148–149 and 245–246.

7. See Paul Pierson, "Increasing Returns, Path Dependence, and the Study of Politics," *American Political Science Review*, Vol. 94, No. 2, June 2000, pp. 251–267.

8. Tichenor, *Dividing Lines*, p. 148.

9. Romain Garbaye, *Getting into Local Power: The Politics of Ethnic Minorities in British and French Cities* (Oxford: Blackwell, 2005), p. 32.

10. Austin Ranny, "Politics in the United States," in Gabriel A. Almond, Russell Dalton, C. Bingham Powell, Jr., and Kaare Strøm, Eds., *Comparative Politics Today: A World View*, updated 8th edition (New York: Pearson-Longman, 2006).

11. Virginie Guiraudon, "Different Nation, Same Nationhood: The Challenges of Immigration Policy," in Pepper D. Culpepper, Peter A. Hall, and Bruno Palier, Eds., *Changing France: The Politics That Markets Make* (Basingstoke, UK: Palgrave Macmillan, 2006), pp. 137–140.

BIBLIOGRAPHY

Alba, Richard and Nancy Foner, "Entering the Precincts of Power: Do National Differences Matter for Immigrant Minority Political Representation?" Unpublished paper, February 2006.

Alba, Richard and Victor Nee, *Remaking the American Mainstream* (Cambridge, MA: Harvard University Press, 2003).

Andersen, Kristi, *The Creation of a Democratic Majority: 1928–1936* (Chicago: University of Chicago Press, 1979).

Andreas, Peter, *Border Games: Policing the US-Mexican Divide* (Ithaca, NY: Cornell University Press, 2000).

Annual Report of the Immigration and Naturalization Service, 1955 (Washington, DC: USGPO, 1956), pp. 15–16.

Ashford, Douglas, *Politics and Policy in France, Living with Uncertainty* (Philadelphia, PA: Temple University Press, 1982).

Baldwin-Edwards, Martin and Martin A. Schain, Eds., *The Politics of Immigration in Western Europe* (London: Cass, 1994).

Barou, Jacques, *Processus de segregation et ethnicisation de l'espace*, Final report to DPM, October, 1994.

Beau, Stéphane and Michel Pauloux, *Violences urbaines, violence sociale: Genèse des nouvelles classes dangereuse* (Paris: Fayard, 2003).

Beck, Roy and Steven A. Camarota, "Elite vs. Public Opinion: An Examination of Divergent Views on Immigration," Center for Immigration Studies, December 2002.

Beer, Samuel, "Federalism, Nationalism and Democracy in America," *The American Political Science Review,* Vol. 72, No. 1, 1978, pp. 9–21.

Benton, Michael, *Promoting Racial Harmony* (Cambridge: Cambridge University Press, 1985).

Bigo, Didier and Elspeth Guild, *Controlling Frontiers: Free Movement into and within Europe* (Hampshire, UK: Ashgate, 2005).

Bleich, Erik, "Antiracism with Races," *French Politics, Culture and Society,* Vol. 18, No. 3, Fall 2000, pp. 4–74.

———, *Race Politics in Britain and France: Ideas and Policymaking since the 1960s* (New York: Cambridge University Press, 2003).

Blumrosen, Alfred and Alexander B. Blumrosen, "The Collection of Race/Sex/Ethnic Origin Statistics in France to Identify and Combat Employment Discrimination: Lessons from the US Experience," *French American Foundation Roundtable Conference on Measuring Discrimination,* November 13, 2006.

Body-Gendrot, Sophie, "Models of Immigrant Integration in France and the U.S.: Signs of Convergence?" in M.P. Smith and I. Feagin, Eds., *The Bubbling Cauldron* (Minneapolis: University of Minnesota Press, 1995).

———, *Ville et Violence: l'irruption de nouvaux acteurs* (Paris: PUF, 1993).

Body-Gendrot, Sophie and Catherine de Wenden, *Sortir des banlieues: Pour en finir avec la tyrannie des territories* (Paris: Autrement-Frontières, 2007).

Borel, Catherine, *Enquêtes annuelles de recensement 2004 et 2005*, INSEE Première, No. 1098, August 2006.

Bridges, Amy, *A City in the Republic: Antebellum New York and and the Origins of Machine Politics* (Ithaca, NY: Cornell University Press, 1987).

Briggs, Jr., Vernon M., "Report of the Select Commission on Immigration and Refugee Policy: A Critique," *Texas Business Review*, January–February 1982, pp. 11–12.

Brighton, Shane, "British Muslims, Multiculturalism and UK Foreign Policy:'Integration' and 'Cohesion' in and beyond the State," *International Affairs*, Vol. 83, No. 1, January 2007, pp. 1–17.

Brouard, Sylvain and Vincent Tiberj, *Français Comme les Autres? Enquête sur les citoyens d'origine maghrébine, africaine et turque* (Paris: Presses de Sciences-Po, 2005).

Brownell, Peter, "The Declining Enforcement of Employer Sanctions," Migration Information Source (Washington, DC, *Migration Policy Institute*, 2005), pp. 3–5.

Brubaker, Rogers, *Citizenship and Nationhood in France and Germany* (Cambridge, MA: Harvard University Press, 1992).

Butler, David and Donald Stokes, *Political Change in Britain*, 2nd edition (New York: St. Martin's Press, 1976).

Calavita, Kitty, *Inside the State* (New York: Routledge, 1992).

Calvez, Correntin, "Le Problème de travailleurs étrangers," *Journal Officiel de la Republique Française, Avis et Rapports du Conseil Economique et Social*, March 27, 1969.

Caron, Michel, "Immigration, intégration et solidarité," *Regards sur l'actualité*, No. 166, December 1990.

Carter, B., C. Harris, and S. Joshi, "The 1951–55 Conservative Government and the Racialization of Black Immigration," *Immigrants and Minorities*, Vol. 6, No. 3, 1987, pp. 335–347.

Cesari, Jocelyne, *Etre musulman en France* (Paris: Kathala-Iremam, 1994).

Commission de reflexion sur l'application du principe de laïcité dans la République, *Rapport au President de la République*, December 12, 2003.

Converse Philip, and Georges Dupeux, "Politicization of the Electorate in France and the United States," *Public Opinion Quarterly*, Vol. 26, No. 1, Spring 1962, pp. 1–23.

Cornelius, Wayne, "Evaluating Enhanced US Border Enforcement," Migration Information Source (Washington, DC: *Migration Policy Institute*, 2004).

Cornelius Wayne, and Marc Rosenblum, "Immigration and Politics," *Annual Review of Political Science*, 2005, p. 104.

Costa-Lascoux, Jacqueline, *De l'immigré au citoyen* (Paris: La Documentation Française, 1989).

Council of Ministers of the European Union, Council Directive 2000/43/EC, June 29, 2000.

———, Council Directive 2000/78/EC, November 27, 2000.

Cour des Comptes, *L'Acceuil de immigrants et l'integration des populations issues de l'immigration*, rapport au president de la republique suivi des réponses des administrations et des organismes intéressés, November 2004.

Cremin, Lawrence, *The Transformation of the School* (New York: Vintage, 1964).

Cross, Gary S., *Immigrant Workers in Industrial France: The Making of a New Laboring Class* (Philadelphia, PA: Temple University Press, 1983), pp. 13–15.

Degler, Carl N., *In Search of Human Nature: The Decline and Revival of Darwinism in American Social Thought* (New York: Oxford University Press, 1991).

Dewhurst Lewis, Mary, *The Boundaries of the Republic: Migrant Rights and the Limits of Universalism in France, 1918–1940* (Stanford: Stanford University Press, 2007).

Dijoud, Paul, "La politique de l'immigration," *Droit Social*, No. 5, May 1976.

Divine, Robert, *American Immigration Policy, 1924–1952* (New Haven, CT: Yale University Press, 1957).

Dixon, David and Julia Gelatt, "Immigration and Enforcement Spending since IRCA," Background paper prepared for the Independent Task Force on Immigration and America's Future, September, 2005, Table 2, cited in Debra Walter Meyers, "From Horseback to High-Tech: U.S. Border Enforcement," Migration Information Source (Washington, DC: *Migration Policy Institute*, February, 2006).

Dobson, Janet, Khalid Koser, Gail Mclaughlan, and John Salt, "International Migration and the United Kingdom: Recent Patters and Trends," Final report to the Home Office, December 2001, RDS Occasional Paper No. 75, Table 4.1, p. 39.

Meurs, Dominique, Ariane Paihé, and Patrick Simon, "Mobilité intergénérationalle et persistance des inégalités," INED, Document de travail, No. 130, 2005.

Eagles, Charles W., "Congressional Voting in the 1920s: A Test of Urban-Rural Conflict," *The Journal of American History*, Vol. 76, No. 2, September 1989, 533–534.

Eck, Diana, *A New Religious America: How a Christian Country Has Become the World's Most Religiously Diverse Nation* (San Francisco, CA: Harper, 2002).

Erie, Stephen, *Rainbow's End: Irish-Americans and the Dilemma of Urban Machine Politics, 1840–1985* (Berkeley: University of California Press, 1988).

Eschbach, Karl, Jacqueline Hagan, and Nestor Rodríguez "Deaths during Undocumented Migration: Trends and Policy Implications in the New Era of Homeland Security," Presented at the *26th Annual National Legal Conference on Immigration and Refugee Policy*, Washington, DC, April 2003.

Feldblum, Miriam "Paradoxes of Ethnic Politics: The Case of Franco-Maghrebis in France," *Ethnic and Racial Studies*, Vol. 16, No. 1, January 1993, pp. 52–74.

———, *Reconstructing Citizenship: The Politics of Nationality Reform and Immigration in Contemporary France* (Albany, NY: SUNY Press, 1999).

Fetzer, Joel, *Public Attitudes toward Immigration in the United States, France and Germany* (New York: Cambridge University Press, 2000).

Fisher, Patrick and Shane Fisher, "Congressional Passage of the Chinese Exclusion Act of 1882," *Immigrants and Minorities*, Vol. 20, No. 2, 2001, pp. 58–74.

Fitzgerald, Frances, *America Revised: History Schoolbooks in the Twentieth Century* (New York: Little Brown, 1979).

Foot, Paul, *Immigration and Race in British Politics* (Baltimore, MD: Penguin, 1965).

Frasure, Anthony, "Constituency Racial Composition and the Attitudes of British MPs," *Comparative Politics*, Vol 3, No. 2, January 1971, pp. 201–210.

Freeman, Gary, "Immigrant Labour and Racial Conflict: The Role of the State," in Philip E. Ogden and Paul E. White, Eds., *Migrants in Modern France: Population Mobility in the Later 19th and 20th Centuries* (London: Unwin Hyman, 1989).

———, "Modes of Immigration Politics in Liberal Democracies," *International Migration Review*, Vol. 29, No. 2, 1995, pp. 881–902.

———, "Winners and Losers: Politics and the Costs and Benefits of Migration," in Antony M. Messina, Ed., *West European Immigration and Immigrant Policy in the New Century* (Westport, CT: Praeger, 2002).

French Senate, *Rapport de la commission d'enquête sur l'immigration clandestine, créé en vertu d'une résolution adoptée par le Sénat le 27 octobre 2005* (2 volumes) (Paris: Journal Officiel, 2005).

Fuchs, Lawrence H. *The American Kaleidoscope: Race, Ethnicity and the Civic Culture* (Middletown, CT: Wesleyan University Press, 1990).

Gallie, Duncan, "The Labour Force," in A.H. Halsey and Josephine Webb, Eds., *Twentieth Century British Social Trends* (New York: St. Martin's Press, 2000), pp. 313–315.

Garbaye, Romain, *Getting Into Local Power: The Politics of Ethnic Minorities in British and French Cities* (Oxford: Blackwell, 2005).

———, "Ethnic Minority Local Councillors in French and British Cities: Social Determinants and Political Opportunity Structures," in Rinus Pennix, Karen Kraal, Marco Martiniello, and Steven Vertovec Eds., *Citizenship in European Cities* (London: Ashgate, 2004).

Gastaut, Yvan, *L'immigration et l'opinion en France sous la Ve République* (Paris: Éditions du Seuil, 2000).

Geddes, Andrew, *Immigration and European Integration* (Manchester: Manchester University Press, 2000).

———, The *Politics of Migration and Immigration in Europe* (London: Sage, 2003).

———, "Thin Europeanisation: The Social Rights of Migrants in an Integrating Europe," in Michael Bommes and Andrew Geddes, Eds., *Immigration and Welfare: Challenging the Borders of the Welfare State* (London: Routledge, 2000).

Geisser, Vincent and Schérazade Kelfaoui, "Marseille 2001, la communauté réinventé par des politiques," *Migrations Société*, No. 77, September/October 2001.

Gimpel, James G. and Karen Kaufman, "Impossible Dream or Distant Reality? Republican Efforts to Attract Latino Voters," *Center for Immigration Studies Reports*, August 2001.

Givens, Terri and Adam Luedke, "European Immigration Policies in Comparative Perspective: Issue Salience, Partisanship and Immigrant Rights," *Comparative European Politics*, Vol. 3, No. 1, April 2005, pp. 1–22.

———, "The Politics of European Union Immigration Policy: Institutions, Salience and Harmonization," *The Policy Studies Journal*, Vol. 32, No. 1, 2004, pp. 145–166.

Glazer, Nathan, "Ethnic Groups in America, From National Culture to Ideology," in Monroe Berger, Theodore Abel and Charles H. Page, Eds., *Freedom and Control in Modern Society* (New York: Van Nostrand, 1954).

Glazer, Nathan, *We Are All Multiculturalists Now* (Cambridge, MA: Harvard University Press, 1997).

Gordon, Paul, *Policing Immigration: Britain's Internal Controls* (London: Pluto Press, 1985).

Grant, Madison, *The Passing of the Great Race* (New York: Scribner's sons, 1916).

Grillo, R.D., *Ideologies and Institutions in Urban France* (London: Cambridge University Press, 1985).

Guiraudon, Virginie, "Different Nation, Same Neighborhood: The Challenges of Immigrant Policy," in Pepper D. Culpepper, Peter Hall, and Bruno Palier, Eds., *Changing France: The Politics that Market Make* (Basingstoke, UK: Palgrave Macmillan, 2006).

———, "The EU 'Garbage Can': Accounting for Policy Developments in the Immigration Domain," Paper presented at the 2001 Conference of the European Community Studies Association, Madison WI, May 29–June 1, 2001, p. 7.

Guiraudon, Virginie and Gallya Lahav, "The State Sovereignty Debate Revisited: The Case of Immigration Control," *Comparative Political Studies*, Vol. 33, No. 2, 2000, pp. 163–195.

Hagopian, Elaine C., *Civil Rights in Peril: The Targeting of Arabs and Muslims.* (London: Pluto Press 2004).

Hall, Peter, *Governing the Economy* (Oxford: Oxford University Press, 1986).

———, "Policy Paradigms, Social Learning and the State: The Case of Economic Policymaking in Britain," *Comparative Politics*, Vol. 25, No. 3, April 1993, pp. 275–296.

Hansen, Randall, *Citizenship and Immigration in Post-war Britain* (Oxford: Oxford University Press 2000).

Hargreaves, Alec, *Immigration, "Race" and Ethnicity in Contemporary France* (London: Routledge, 1995).

Harper, Elizabeth, *Immigration Laws of the United States*, 3rd edition (Indianapolis: Bobbs Merrill, 1975).

Haus, Leah, *Unions, Immigration and Internationalization: New Challenges and Changing Coalitions in the United States and France* (New York: Palgrave Macmillan, 2002).

Heclo, Hugh, *Modern Social Politics in Britain and Sweden* (New Haven, CT: Yale University Press, 1974)

Héran, François, "Cinq idées reçu sur l'immigration," *Population et Sociétés*, No. 397, January 2004.

Herrnstein, Richard and Charles Murray, *The Bell Curve* (New York: Free Press, 1994).

Herz, Dietmar, "European Immigration and Asylum Policy: Scope and Limits of Intergovernmental Europeanization," Paper presented at 8th EUSA Conference, March 27–29, 2003, Nashville, TN, p. 13.

Hickman, Mary J., *Religion, Class and Identity: The State, the Catholic Church and the Education of the Irish in Britain* (Brookfield: Avebury, 1995).

Hicks, Joe and Grahame Allen, *A Century of Change: Trends in UK Statistics since 1900*, Research Paper 99/111, Social and General Statistics Section, House of Commons Library, December 21, 1999.

Higham, John, *Strangers in the Land: Patterns of American Nativism 1860–1925* (New York: Atheneum 1969).

The Historical Association, "Teaching Emotive and Controversial History," April, 2007, reported by BBC News on April 2, 2007: http://news.bbc.co.uk/2/hi/uk_news/education/6294643.stm.

Hollifield, James, *Immigrants, Markets and States: The Political Economy of Postwar Europe* (Cambridge, MA Harvard University Press, 1994).

Holmes, Colin, *John Bull's Island: Immigration and British Society, 1871–1971* (London: Macmillan Education, 1988).

Home Office, *Community Cohesion: A Report of the Independent Review Team Chaired by Ted Cantle* (London: Stationery Office, 2001).

Hoskin, Marilyn and Roy Fitzgerald, "Public Acceptance of Racial and Ethnic Minorities: A Comparative Analysis," in Anthony Messina, Luis Fraga, Laurie Rhodebeck, and Frederick Wright, Eds., *Ethnic and Racial Minorities in Advanced Industrial Democracies* (Westport, CT: Greenwood Press, 1992).

Huntington, Samuel P., "Political Development or Political Decay," *World Politics*, Vol. 17, No. 3, April 1965, pp. 386–430.

———, *American Politics: The Promise of Disharmony* (Cambridge, MA: Belknap Press, 1981).

———, *Who Are We: The Challenges to American's National Identity* (New York: Simon and Schuster 2004).

IFOP, "L'Islam en France et les réactions aux attentats du 11 septembre 2001, Résultats détaillés," IFOP September, 2001.

INSEE, *Les étrangers in France: portrait social* (Paris: INSEE, 1994).

Ireland, Patrick, *The Policy Challenge of Ethnic Diversity* (Cambridge, MA: Harvard University Press 1994).

Itzkoff, Seymour W., *The Decline of Intelligence in America* (Westport, CT: Praeger, 1994).

Jazouli, Adil, *Les années banlieues* (Paris: Seuil, 1992).

Joppke, Christian, *Challenge to the Nation-State: Immigration in Western Europe and the United States* (Oxford: Oxford University Press 1998).

———, *Immigration and the Nation-State: The United States, Germany and Great Britain* (Oxford: Oxford University Press, 1999).

———, "The Retreat of Multiculturalism in the Liberal State: Theory and Policy," *British Journal of Sociology*, Vol. 55, No. 2, 2004, p. 253.

———, "Transformation of Immigrant Integration: Civic Integration and Antidiscrimination in the Netherlands, France and Germany," *World Politics*, Vol. 59, No. 2, January 2007, pp. 243–275.

Kastoryano, Riva, *Negotiating Identities: States and Immigrants in France and Germany* (Princeton: Princeton University Press, 2002).

Katznelson, Ira, *Black Men, White Cities; Race, Politics, and Migration in the United States, 1900–30 and Britain, 1948–68* (London, New York: Published for the Institute of Race Relations by Oxford University Press, 1973).

Keeler, John T.S. and Martin A. Schain, *Chirac's Challenge: Liberalization, Europeanization, and Malaise in France* (New York: St. Martin's Press, 1996).

Kehrberg, Jason, "Public Opinion on Immigration in Western Europe," *Comparative European Politics*, Vol. 5, No. 3, 2007, pp. 264–282.

Kesselman, Mark and Joel Kreiger, *European Politics in Transition*, 5th edition (New York: Houghton Mifflin Co., 2006).

Kilson, Martin, "Blacks and Neo-ethnicity in America," in Nathan Glazer and Daniel P. Moynihan, Eds., *Ethnicity: Theory and Experience* (Cambridge, MA: Harvard University Press, 1975).

King, Desmond, *Making Americans: Immigration, Race, and the Origins of the Diverse Democracy* (Cambridge, MA: Harvard, 2000).

Kingdon, John, *Agendas, Alternatives and Public Policies* (New York: HarperCollins, 1995).

Klausen, Jytte, *The Islamic Challenge: Politics and Religion in Western Europe* (Oxford: Oxford University Press, 2005).

Knight, Jack, *Institutions and Social Conflict* (Cambridge: Cambridge University Press, 1992).

Krasner, Steven, "Sovereignty: An Institutional Perspective," *Comparative Political Studies*, Vol. 21, No. 1, 1988, pp. 71–72.

Lahav, Gallya, "Ideological and Party Constraints on Immigration Attitudes," *Journal of Common Market Studies*, Vol. 35, No. 3, 1997, pp. 377–406.

———, *Immigration and Politics in the New Europe* (Cambridge: Cambridge University Press, 2004).

Lamont, Michèle, *The Dignity of Working Men: Morality and the Boundaries of Race, Class, and Immigration* (Cambridge, MA: Harvard University Press, 2000).

Lang, Jack and Hervé le Bras, *l'Immigration Positive* (Paris: Odile Jacob, 2006).

Laurence, Jonathan, "Managing Transnational Islam: Muslims and the State in Western Europe," Paper prepared for the workshop on *Comparative Immigration Policies after 9/11* at the Ford Institute, University of Pittsburgh, September 9 and 10, 2005.

Laurence, Jonathan and Justin Vaise, *Integrating Islam: Political and Religious Challenges in Contemporary France* (Washington, DC: Brookings Institution Press, 2006).

Levinson, Amanda, "Why Countries Continue to Consider Regularization," Migration Information Source (Washington, DC: *Migration Policy Institute*, September, 2005).

Lichtheim, George, *The New Europe, Today and Tomorrow*, 2nd edition (New York: Praeger, 1963).

Long, Marcel, *Être français Aujourd'hui et Demain:* Rapport de la Commission de la Nationalité présenté par M. Marceau Long au Premier Ministre, vols. 1 and 2 (Paris: La Documentation Française, 1988).

Lorcerie, F., "Les ZEP 1990–1993 pour mémoire," *Migrants Formation*, No. 97, June 1994.

Lowi, Theodore, *The End of Liberalism* (New York: W.W. Norton, 1969).

Macdonald, Ian and Nicholas J. Blake, *Macdonald's Immigration Law and Practice in the United Kingdom*, 3rd edition (London: Butterworth's, 1991).

Mahew, David, *Divided We Govern* (New Haven, CT: Yale University Press, 1991).

Martin, Philip L., "Good Intentions Gone Awry: IRCA and U.S. Agriculture," *Annals of the American Academy of Political and Social Science*, Vol. 534, Strategies for Immigration Control: An International Comparison, July 1994, pp. 44–57.

Martin, Philip L., "Select Commission Suggests Changed in Immigration Policy—A Review Essay," *Monthly Labor Review,* Vol. 105, No. 2, February 1982, pp. 31–38.

Martin, Pierre, *Comprendre les evolutions électorales: la théorie des réalignements revisitée* (Paris: Presses de Sciences Po, 2000).

Martin Lipset, Seymour, *Political Man: The Social Basis of Politics* (New York: Doubleday, 1960).

Martiniello, Marco, *Sortir des ghettos culturels* (Paris: Presses de SciencesPo, 1997).

Massey, D.S., J. Durand, and N.J. Malone, *Beyond Smoke and Mirrors: Mexican Immigration in an Era of Economic Integration.* (New York: Russell Sage Foundation, 2002).

Mauco, George, *Mémoire sur l'assimilation des étrangers in France* (Paris: Institut international de coopération intellectuelle, 1937).

Mayer, Nonna, *Ces français qui votent Le Pen* (Paris: Flammarion 1999), pp. 258–259.

McClymer, John F., "The Federal Government and the Americanization Movement, 1915–1924," *Prologue: the Journal of the National Archives,* Vol. 10, Spring 1978, pp. 22–41.

McKesson, John A., "Concepts and Realities in a Multiethnic France," *French Politics and Society,* Vol. 12, No. 1, Winter 1994, pp. 16–39.

Mermaz, Louis, *Les Géôles de la République* (Paris: Stock, 2001).

Messina, Anthony M., *Race and Party Competition in Britain* (New York: Oxford University Press, 1989).

Milbrath, Lester, *Political Participation* (Chicago: Rand McNally, 1965).

Miles, Robert, "The Riots of 1958: Notes on the Ideological Construction of 'Race Relations' as a Political Issue in Britain," *Immigrants and Minorities,* Vol. 3, No. 3, 1984, pp. 262–264.

Miles, Robert and Annie Phizacklea, *White Man's Country: Racism in British Politics* (London: Pluto Press, 1984).

Miller, Mark J., *Foreign Workers in Europe: An Emerging Political Force* (New York: Praeger, 1981).

Miller, Mark J., "Employer Sanctions in France: From the Campaign against Illegal Aliens Employment to the Campaign against Illegal Work," *United States Commission on Immigration Reform* (Washington, DC: USGPO, 1995).

Mink, Gwendolyn, *Old Labor and New Immigrants in American Political Development: Union, Party and State, 1975–1920* (Ithaca, NY: Cornell University Press, 1986).

Modood, Tariq, "Multiculturalism, Ethnicity and Integration: Contemporary Challenges," Paper presented at the Leverhulme Programme on Migration and Citizenship Conference, 'Ethnicity, Mobility and Society', University of Bristol, March 2006: http://www.bristol.ac.uk/sociology/leverhulme/conference/conferencepapers/.

Money, Jeannette, *Fences and Neighbors: The Political Geography of Immigration Control* (Ithaca, NY: Cornell University Press, 1999).

Naim, Moisés, "Borderline: It's Not about Maps," *Washington Post,* May 28, 2006.

The National Conference of State Legislatures, Immigrant Policy Project, *2006 Enacted State Legislation Related to Immigrants and Immigration* (Washington DC: NCSL, October 2006).

———. *2007 Enacted State Legislation Related to Immigrants and Immigration* (Washington, DC: NCSL, August 2007).

Nelkin, Dorothy and Mark Michaels, "Biological Categories and Border Controls: The Revival of Eugenics in Anti-immigration Rhetoric," *International Journal of Sociology and Social Policy,* Vol. 18, Nos. 5/6, 1998, pp. 35–63.

Noiriel, Gérard, "Communisme et immigration, éléments pour une recherche," *Communisme,* Nos. 15–16, 1987, pp. 90–96.

———, *Le Creuset Francais* (Paris: Editions du Seuil, 1988).

———, *Longwy: Immigrés et prolétaires 1880–1980* (Paris: PUF, 1984).

OECD, *International Migration Outlook* (Washington, DC: SOMEPI, 2006).

———, *Trends in International Migration* (Washington, DC: SOMEPI, 2003).

Passel, Jeffery, "Size and Characteristics of the Unauthorized Migrant Population in the US" (Washington, DC: Pew Hispanic Center, 2006).

Paul, Kathleen, *Whitewashing Britain: Race and Citizenship in the Postwar Era* (Ithaca, NY: Cornell University Press, 1997).

Peach, Ceri, Alisdair Rogers, Judith Chance, and Patricia Daley, "Immigration and Ethnicity," in A.H. Halsey with Josephine Webb, Eds., *Twentieth Century British Social Trends* (New York: St. Martin's Press, 2000), pp. 139–140.

Pew Hispanic Center, *Fact Sheet: The State of American Public Opinion on Immigration in Spring 2006: A Review of Major Surveys* (Washington, DC: Pew Hispanic Center, May 17, 2006).

Pew Research Center, *The Great Divide: How Westerners and Muslims View Each Other* (Washington, DC: Pew Global Attitude Project, June 2006).

Pierson, Paul, "Increasing Returns, Path Dependence, and the Study of Politics," *American Political Science Review,* Vol. 94, No. 2, June 2000, pp. 251–267.

Plascencia, Luis F.B., Gary Freeman, and Mark Selzer, "The Decline of Barriers to Immigrant Economic and Political Rights in the American States: 1977–2001," *International Migration Review,* Vol. 37, No. 1, Spring 2003, p. 7.

Powell, Enoch, *Reflections of a Statesman: Writings and Speeches of Enoch Powell* (London, Bellow, 1991).

Pratt Fairchild, Henry, "The Literacy Test and Its Making," *The Quarterly Journal of Economics,* Vol. 31, No. 3, 1917, pp. 453–454.

Perlman , Philip B. et. al., *Whom Shall We Welcome: Report of the President's Commission on Immigration and Naturalization* (Washington, DC: USGPO, 1953.

The President's Research Committee on Social Trends, *Recent Social Trends in the United States* (Washington, DC: USGPO, 1933).

Quillian, L., "Prejudice as a Response to Perceived Group Threat: Population Composition and Anti-immigrant and Racial Prejudice in Europe," *American Sociological Review,* Vol. 60, No. 4, 1995, pp. 586–611.

Spencer, Ian R.G., *British Immigration Policy Since 1939: The Making of Multi-racial Britain* (London: Routledge, 1997).

Ranny, Austin, "Politics in the United States," in Gabriel A. Almond, Russell Dalton, C. Bingham Powell, Jr., and Kaare Strøm, Eds., *Comparative Politics Today: A World View,* updated 8th edition (New York: Pearson-Longman, 2006).

Reimers, David, *Still the Golden Door: The Third World Comes to America* (New York: Columbia University Press, 1985).

Reports of the Immigration Commission, *Dictionary of Races or Peoples* (Washington, DC, 1911).

———, *Immigration Legislation: Federal Immigration Legislation,* Vol. 40, 61st Congress, 3rd Session, Senate. Doc. 758.

Report of the *Joint Special Committee to Investigate Chinese Immigration,* 44th Congress, 2nd Session, Senate Report No. 689, February 27, 1877 (Washington, DC: USGPO, 1877).

Rose, Richard, "Politics in England," in Gabriel A. Almond, Russell J. Daloton, G. Bingham Powell, Jr., and Kaare Strøm, Eds., *Comparative Politics Today: A World View,* updated 8th edition (New York: Pearson-Longman, 2006).

———, *The Territorial Dimension in Government: Understanding the United Kingdom* (Chatham, NJ: Chatham House, 1982),

Riply, William Z., *The Races of Europe* (New York, Appleton, 1923).

Rushton, Philippe, *Race, Evolution and Behavior* (New Brunswick, NJ: Transaction Press, 1994).

Salins, Peter, *Assimilation American Style* (New York: HarperCollins, 1997).

Salyer, Lucy, "Captives of Law: Judicial Enforcement of the Chinese Exclusion Laws: 1891–1905," *The Journal of American History,* Vol. 76, No.1, June 1989, pp. 91–117.

Schain, Martin A., "The Decline of French Communism: Party Construction and Party Decline," in Anthony Daley, Ed., *The Mitterrand Era: Policy Alternatives and Political Mobilization in France* (New York: New York University Press, 1996).

———, "Immigrants and Politics in France," in John Ambler, Ed., *The French Socialist Experiment* (Philadelphia, PA: ISHI Press, 1985).

———, "Ordinary Politics: Immigrants, Direct Action and the Political Process in France," *French Politics and Society,* Nos. 2–3, Spring–Summer, 1994.

———, "Politics in France," in Gabriel A. Almond, G. Bingham Powell, Jr., Russell J. Dalton and Kaare Strøm, Eds., *Comparative Politics Today, A World View,* 9th edition (New York: Pearson Longman, 2008).

———, "The Politics of Immigration in France, Britain and the United States," in Craig A. Parsens and Timothy M. Smeeding, Eds., *Immigration and the Transformation of Europe* (Cambridge: Cambridge University Press, 2006).

Schattschneider, E.E., *The Semisovereign People* (New York: Holt, Rinehart and Winston, 1960).

Schlessinger, Jr., Arthur M., *The Disuniting of America: Reflections on a Multicultural Society* (New York: W.W. Norton, 1991 and 1998).

Schmitter, Philippe, "Three Neofunctional Hypotheses About International Integration," *International Organization*, Vol. 23, No. 1, 1969, pp. 161–166.

Schnapper, Dominique, "Immigration and the Crisis of National Identity," *West European Politics*, Vol. 17, No. 2, April 1994, pp. 133–134.

Shanks, Cheryl, *Immigration and the Politics of American Sovereignty, 1890–1990* (Ann Arbor: University of Michigan Press, 2004).

Sides, John, and Jack Citron, "European Opinion About Immigration: The Role of Identities, Interests and Information," *British Journal of Political Science*, Vol. 37, No. 3, July 2007, pp. 477–504.

Silverman, Maxim, *Deconstructing the Nation: Immigration, Racism and Citizenship in Modern France* (London: Routledge, 1992).

Simon, Rita J. and James P. Lynch, "A Comparative Assessment of Public Opinion toward Immigrants and Immigration Policies," *International Migration Review*, Vol. 32, No. 2, Summer 1999, p. 45–46.

Simon, Rita J. and Susan H. Alexander, *The Ambivalent Welcome: Print Media, Public Opinion and Immigration* (Westport: Praeger, 1993).

Singer-Kérel, Jeanne, *La Population active étrangère au recensement de 1982* (Paris: FNSP, Service d'étude de l'activité économique, 1985).

Soysal, Yasemin, *Limits of Citizenship: Migrants and Postnational Membership in Europe* (Chicago: University of Chicago Press, 1994).

Sniderman, P. M., L. Hagendoorn, and M. Prior, "Predisposing Factors and Situational Triggers: Exclusionary Reactions to Immigrant Minorities," *American Political Science Review*, Vol. 98, No. 1, 2004, pp. 35–49.

Spire, Alexis, *Etrangers à la carte: l'administration de l'immigration en France (1945–1975)* (Paris: Grasset, 2005).

Stone, Alec, *The Birth of Judicial Politics in France* (New York: Oxford University Press, 1992).

Sweet, Alec Stone, *The Judicial Construction of Europe* (Oxford: Oxford University Press, 2004).

Lord Swann, *Education for All: The Report of the Committee of Inquiry into the Education Children from Ethnic Minority Groups* (London: Cmnd 9453, HMSO, 1985).

Tapinos, Georges, "Immigration et marché du travail," *l'Observateur OCDE*, December 1999.

Tichenor, Daniel J., *Dividing Lines: The Politics of Immigration Control in America* (Princeton: Princeton University Press, 2002).

Todd, Emmanuel, *La Nouvelle France* (Paris: Seuil, 1988).

Togman, Jeffrey, *The Ramparts of Nations: Institutions and Immigration Policies in France and the United States* (Westport, CT: Praeger, 2002).

Torpey, John, *Invention of the Passport: Surveillance, Citizenship and the State* (Cambridge: Cambridge University Press, 2000).

Tribalat, Michèle, *Faire France* (Paris: Découverte, 1995).

U.S. Bureau of Census, 2005 *American Community Survey; Congressional District Data Book*.

U.S. Bureau of the Census and U.S. Congress, Congressional Budget Office, *A Description of the Immigrant Population, November 2004*.

U.S. Commission on Immigration Reform, *Report to Congress, Becoming an American: Immigration and Immigrant Policy* (Washington, DC: USGPO, 1997).

———, *Report to Congress, Legal Immigration: Setting Priorities* (Washington, DC: USGPO, 1995).

———, *Report to Congress, U.S. Immigration Policy: Restoring Credibility* (Washington, DC: USGPO, 1994).

U.S. Committee of the Judiciary, House of Representatives, *Immigration and Nationality Act* (Washington, DC: USGPO, 1953).

———, *Immigration and Nationality Act*, 9th edition (Washington, DC: USGPO, 1992).

U.S. Department of Commerce, U.S. Bureau of the Census, *Historical Statistics of the United States* (Washington, DC: USGPO, 1975), Part 2.

U.S. Department of Homeland Security, Office of Immigration Statistics, *2003 Yearbook of Immigration Statistics* (Washington, DC: USGPO, 2004).

———, *2005 Yearbook of Immigration Statistics* (Washington, DC: USGPO, 2006).

U.S. Immigration Commission, *Abstract of the Report on the Children of Immigrants in Schools* (Washington, DC: USGPO, 1911).

————,Volume 1, *Brief Statement of the Investigations of the Immigration Commission, with Conclusions and Recommendations and Views of the Minority* (Washington, DC: USGPO, 1911).

Van Hook, Jennifer, Frank D. Bean, and Jeffrey Passel, *Unauthorized Migrants Living in the United States: A Mid-decade Portrait.* Migration Information Source (Washington, DC: *Migration Policy Institute*, September 1, 2005).

Verba, Sidney and Norman Nie, *Participation in America: Politics, Democracy and Social Equality* (New York: Harper & Row, 1972).

Vichniac, Judith, "French Socialists and *Droit à la différence,*" *French Politics and Society,* Vol. 9, No. 1, Winter 1991, pp. 40–57.

Viet, Vincent, *La France immigrée: Construction d'une politique 1914–1997* (Paris: Fayard, 1998).

Wacquant, Loïc, "Banlieues françaises et ghetto noir américain: De L'amalgame à la comparaison," *French Politics and Society,* Vol. 10, No. 4, 1992, pp. 81–104.

Waldinger, Roger, *Still the Promised City? African_Americans and New Immigrants in Postindustrial New York* (Cambridge, MA: Harvard University Press, 1996).

Waldinger, Roger and Mehdi Bozorgmehr, "From Ellis Island to LAX," Department of Sociology, UCLA. August 1993.

Wayland, Sarah, "Mobilizing to Defend Nationality Law in France," *New Community,* Vol. 20, No. 1, October 1993, pp. 93–111.

Weil, Patrick, *La France et ses étrangers* (Paris: Gallimard, 1991).

————, "Lifting the Veil," *French Politics, Culture and Society,* Vol. 22, No.3, Fall, 2004, pp. 142–149.

————, *Mission d'étude des les legislations de la nationalité et de l'immigration* (Paris: la Documentation Française, 1997).

Weil, Patrick and John Crowley, "Integration in Theory and Practice: A Comparison of France and Britain," in Martin Baldwin-Edwards and Martin A. Schain, Eds., *The Politics of Immigration in Western Europe* (London: Cass, 1994).

Wihtol de Wenden, Catherine, "The French Response to the Asylum Seeker Influx, 1980–93," *Annals of the American Academy of Political and Social Science,* Vol. 534, July 1994, pp. 81–90.

————, "Les associations 'beur' et immigrés, leurs leaders, leurs stratégies," *Regards sur l'actualité,* No. 178, February, 1992.

————, *Les Immigrés et la politique* (Paris: Presses de la FNSP, 1988).

Zolberg, Aristide, "The Democratic Management of Cultural Differences: Building Inclusive Societies in Westerns Europe and North America," Human Development Report (United Nations Development Progam, 2004).

————, "Matters of State: Theorizing Immigration Policy," in Noah M.J. Pickus, Ed., *Becoming American, America Becoming* (New York: Russell Sage Foundation, 1999).

————, *A Nation by Design: Immigration Policy in the Fashioning of the United States* (Cambridge, MA: Harvard University Press, 2006).

————, "Rethinking the Last 200 Years of US Immigration Policy," *Migration Information Source* (Washington, DC: *Migration Policy Institute,* June 2006).

INDEX

LaVergne, TN USA
01 December 2009
165522LV00001B/7/P